Technologies for Intuition

The publisher and the University of California Press Foundation gratefully acknowledge the generous support of the Barbara S. Isgur Endowment Fund in Public Affairs.

Technologies for Intuition

Cold War Circles and Telepathic Rays

ALAINA LEMON

University of California Press

University of California Press, one of the most distinguished university presses in the United States, enriches lives around the world by advancing scholarship in the humanities, social sciences, and natural sciences. Its activities are supported by the UC Press Foundation and by philanthropic contributions from individuals and institutions. For more information, visit www.ucpress.edu.

University of California Press
Oakland, California

Library of Congress Cataloging-in-Publication Data

Names: Lemon, Alaina, 1965- author.
Title: Technologies for intuition : Cold War circles and telegraphic rays / Alaina Lemon.
Description: Oakland, California : University of California Press, [2018] | Includes bibliographical references and index.
Identifiers: LCCN 2017026641 (print) | LCCN 2017030515 (ebook) | ISBN 9780520967458 (ebook) | ISBN 9780520294271 (cloth : alk. paper) | ISBN 9780520294288 (pbk. : alk. paper)
Subjects: LCSH: Telepathy. | Paranoia—Political aspects. | Cold War—Influence.
Classification: LCC BF1171 (ebook) | LCC BF1171 .L38 2018 (print) | DDC 33.8—dc23
LC record available at https://lccn.loc.gov/2017026641

Manufactured in the United States of America

27 26 25 24 23 22 21 20 19 18
10 9 8 7 6 5 4 3 2 1

Contents

Illustrations

Prologue: Cold War, Contact, and Ethnography

CIRCLES AND RAYS

In August 1991 I stood in the vestibule of one of the most remote stations of the Moscow metro listening to people excitedly convey the events of the day. I was returning from the center streets, where the tanks had rolled in that morning. The conservative contingent had staged a coup, and their first act had been to limit communications, cut off contacts: I had managed to send a telegram home from the Central Telegraph building near Red Square before it shuttered its doors. Television was jammed, but they had missed another important channel: the metro. Public transit infrastructure was itself an active circuit for other media, from flyers to good old face-to-face talk with strangers (Lemon 2000b). Phone calls were barely getting through, but the Moscow metro, built in a circle cut by radials, was running underneath the capital's rings of roads. Meanwhile, Americans were taking the credit for keeping up flows of communication for the resistance, who soon prevailed, as Western nongovernmental organizations (NGOs) sent faxes on their upgraded lines, embassy satellite dishes amplifying waves abroad. No one paid much attention to the ways a socialist-built infrastructure like the metro carried messages along with people—and people as messages, their very numbers swelling to tell a story.

Fast forward. One hundred years after the Russian Revolution and more than fifty since the McCarthy era, we see more clearly that Americans, too, work to cut off what they label excess communication when we worry about foreign influence and contact. Yet we continue to pay little attention to the material and mundane ways *in which* people are already distanced, even severed from channels along which they might get in touch. Moreover, instead of following particular transnational circuits (the money, the oil, the real estate) to see which circuits are clear and which are blocked, to whom, and to acknowledge the specific channels that we have dug, we continue to behave as if the main thing to worry about is the diffuse hypnotic power of foreign memes over the minds of the masses or about whether politicians are vulnerable to attack by vague manipulations or even telepathic rays.

This book is an attempt to theorize channels and contacts in social, political, historical, and semiotic terms. It is also an attempt to deflate anxiety about mental influence, be the threat imagined to emanate from televisions or psychic spies. The material and social forces for and against communications, across state borders and within them, can be difficult to see, and less visible to some than to others. So let us begin with what can be easily seen, with spectacle, even with fantasy, with one of the late Soviet era's best-known science fiction films, *Solaris* (dir. Tarkovsky, 1972).

The film depicts telepathic emanations less as rays and more like expanding circles of swirling biomatter and energy. The planet Solaris exudes a mental force, a "noospheric" sheath of consciousness (see Vernadsky 1926). Solaris reads the minds of the cosmonauts in her orbit, to materialize their most troubled memories, the people they have lost. The readings are limited: corporeal copies live and breathe—but manifest their *mourners'* guilt, missing the originals' perspectives; one cosmonaut's wife lacks a back zipper on her dress because he had never noticed it. The cosmonauts think the planet tortures them while they fail to intuit much about either the planet or each other. The American remake of *Solaris* settles deeply into a Freudian meditation on hidden psyches; the Soviet version unsettles the human psyche as a player in galactic communications. The Soviet ending frames an evocative detail: one cosmonaut has brought a small houseplant from Earth; just when the humans abandon the exploration, a long shot shows the plant facing out to Solaris from a window in the space station. In the next scenes Solaris morphs, becoming earthlike; gaseous masses congeal into green forest and blue ocean. Some viewers interpret these last scenes as occurring within the protagonist's broken mind; others see real planetary changes imperfectly catalyzed by human memories of home. But what if it is the *plant* who finally establishes a channel with a planetary mind?

Cold War fictions of all genres famously worry about influence over the very conditions for and forms of contact. Much science fiction of the era ends more happily than *Solaris*: someone cracks a code, the army finally telephones a linguistic anthropologist just in time to prevent nuclear catastrophe over a misunderstanding. The aliens mean no harm. Such tales warn of the limitations of individual intuitions, like nervous reflexes that lead us to misread attempts to make contact, misreadings that threaten to scatter the world with ash.

The little houseplant in *Solaris* presents a suggestive contrast. Even before science fiction emerged as a late Imperial genre, social circles, fields of friendship, practices of kinship, and institutional circuits chained across state borders. Those who recognize the long centuries of such relations tend shoots that sprout and thrive across borders, but that look like untidy weeds to the paranoid perspective. Xenophobia erases efforts to make contacts that, from a limited, purified perspective, seem inconsequential, ignoring most everyday contacts while magnifying the winks and handshakes of the powerful, mistaking circles for rays.

Throughout the nineteenth century, paranoia about mental influence oscillated with hopes for spiritual health *through* empathic and psychic union. As trains and telegraph wires spanned imperial territories, performances and experiments blended occult and scientific genres, to make and break such contacts via mesmerism, hypnosis, spirit communication, and telepathy. The twentieth-century Cold War intensified this dynamic, militarizing fears while energizing speculation about the nature of contact: children in the United States and in the USSR grew up with tales and films encouraging us both to dread and to long for contact with other sentient beings, be they cosmic, animal, or human others.[1]

This book tracks worries and hopes about communication and its channels when they are conceived in relation to movements of *thought* across borders—bodily, social, architectural, geopolitical—borders that themselves serve, even covertly, as semiotic material, as media, or as channels. Along the way we see how ideologies about communicative contact and channels reinforce social segregations as much as they forge connections. Likewise, we see that it takes effort to make or break contact, to sustain or distort communication channels.

These efforts are guided not by linguistic grammars, but by bundles of social habits, structures, and discursive practices that people speak of through categories such as *propriety* or *intuition* ("One doesn't speak with such people, we just know they lie"). Such clusters were generated historically, neither flowing only top down nor bubbling out of bare interaction. The clusters can be difficult to track because historical encounters unfold where spaces and channels are already divided — and where common sense has long depicted communication *as if* it could be explained by grammatical or binary logics. The twentieth century was saturated by images graphing communication as a line between two points, a speaker/hearer dyad echoing dualisms so common to social thought: concept/sign, word/thought, spirit/matter, agency/structure, and so forth. Even thinkers in the nineteenth century, however, saw alternatives. Theosophical tracts on thoughts and chan-

FIGURE P.1. *The Music of Gounud* a plate from a book of theosophy by C.W. Leadbetter and Annie Besant, *Thought Forms* (1908).

nels, for example, jostled with scientific research to paint thought not as *mediated by* forms and matter, but *as* matter taking form.

Fred Meyers coined the term *telepathy* when he founded the Society for Psychical Research in England in 1882 to describe transmission of thought-feeling from a distance, without known form of mediation. *The Music of Gounod*, printed in Annie Besant and G. W. Leadbetter's 1901 book *Thought Forms*, depicts moving thought-feelings a bit differently: not as a line of communication between beings, transmission without discernible wires, but as clouds of smoky matter that, once piped up the church organ and through the roof, extrudes and dissipates, perhaps to float on by itself as form, even without receivers, detached from thinkers. Another illustration depicts "Vague Pure Affection" as a coral pink cloud that "frequently surrounds a gently purring cat" (1901, 41), a thought-form not aimed in meaningful rays at anyone in particular.

Theosophical images of thought forms traveled, captivating artists Vasily Kandinsky and Hilma af Klint,[2] each credited separately with creating the first abstract painting (af Klint in 1906, Kandinsky in 1911). Artistic abstraction is often defined (for nonspecialists) merely as nonrepresentational; Kandinsky and af Klint sought in addition to make contact through art with other planes of reality, to conduct energies among planes through channels formed not only by the material mediation of shape and color, of paper and paint, but also via the motion of the artist's hand: moving matter leaving traces for intuition. Such art, Kandinsky hoped, might live its own life, reaching from the canvas; extruding energy generated by changes in tempo or direction beyond the moment of painting; vibrating within the soul of the attentive viewer; and creating "inner resonance," as he wrote in *The Spiritual in Art* ([1911] 1946). Art is the imprint of thought as moving matter spirit (see also Carlson 2000).

In *Point and Line to Plane* ([1926] 1979), Kandinsky defined the line not from a bird's-eye, seemingly objective perspective from which to chart a distance between two points, but at the concrete, specific spot where the painter touches brush to surface: the line is a visceral "track made by the moving point." That moving point is the result of a historical contact, a specific, singular confrontation "through encounter between implement and material surface" ([1926] 1979, 542). Kandinsky came to these ideas through his experience of synesthesia, while working to convey how he felt color as sound, lines as movement, and drawn shapes as reactions to changes in balance and gravity, like a projected proprioception. Observations of his own sensory events, touching hand to paper through brush while *making* art, led him to write and paint against Euclidean geometry. A line will move straight*ly*, he argued, *only* when contact is not subject to additional forces that torque and curve any part of some concrete assemblage of pen, hand, paper, or mind. For the theosophical artist, every singular point begins its own center, emanating thought-forms potentially in all directions, as ripples mark water, or globes of light appear around streetlamps in rain or fog: forces that counter representing contact through a straight line. Kandinsky's trope, in other words, counters imaginations of telepathic rays. The ray, if abstracted from those forces its depiction must overcome, erases all but one cross-section of broadcasts that otherwise extend in many directions at once. The telepathic ray is but an illusion, an abstracted radius; it only *seems* to be formed by aiming from one point to another.

V. N. Voloshinov, by no means a theosophist, writing in Moscow in the 1920s about trajectories of quotation, observed that no word arrives from mouth to ear without refracting, shifting direction and meaning as it is torqued by social contexts and material forces (Voloshinov [1929] 1986). I derive much from Russian and American thinkers such as Voloshinov, who were pragmatically attentive to the historical specificity of signs as we make them, as we recognize emissions or movements *as* signs, as we repeat their direction faithfully or purposely distort them.

Kandinsky's *Point and Line* echoes early American pragmatists: we know that theosophists discussed pragmatic philosophy in their reading circles, and that pragmatists such as William James and C. S. Peirce interested themselves in theosophy—and also in the methods of telepathic research. These circuits of discussion ran contemporary with Peirce's insights about indexical meaning: while symbolic meaning is grounded to rule sets, logics, or conventions, such as semantic paradigms or dictionary definitions, indexical meaning is grounded by contact to specific spaces in specific moments. Peirce's famous example is smoke rising to index a fire ([1897] 1932). To some, his example might resemble the drawing of thought-form floating up from a church organ, but Peirce, who after all devised the double-blind method while investigating the protocols of the new telepathy science, was less interested in the nature or color or texture of indexical smoke, and more interested in how an indexical sign connects to its context for production, and all in relation to any mind that would perceive smoke as such a sign.

I have always found it odd to parse conversations among theosophists and pragmatic philosophers through affinities alone: as a linguistic and historical anthropologist attentive to social hierarchies, I look also to trajectories and material channels that afford such circuits. Kandinsky, for example, was born in Moscow in 1866, raised in Odessa, educated in Moscow, and moved in

1896, after a career in ethnography and law, to art school in Munich, after which he lived in Moscow, Berlin, and Paris; his biography sketches a spiral across the borders of empires. The theosophical thought-forms that inspired him were likewise drawn by people of means who crossed many borders, reinforcing imperial-era circuits among Russian, British, American, and Turkish territories. Elena Blavatsky embodied those channels in her migrations, from her birth in Ekaterinaslav in 1831; to her marriage in Erevan around 1848; and then on trips to Istanbul, London, Ceylon, the Rockies, and back to the Caucasus for a good five years. She then moved on to Odessa, finally settling more or less in New York City, with oscillations between London and Bombay (Washington 1993). Her theosophical writings not only referenced imperial spaces and hierarchies by describing, for example, subject people's mastery of occult energies and channels, but also indexed them. Blavatsky's biographers marvel at her travels but rarely pause to study the specifics of her launch from elite aristocratic (she was a Dolgorukhov!), bureaucratic, mercantile, and artistic circles. This background made her travels possible, paying for her passage by train and ship and helping her channel her thoughts in print across great distances. Few biographers consider her aristocratic upbringing or the fact that her father was a high-ranking military officer who moved frequently across the southern and eastern parts of the Russian Empire. Theosophists in the United States still marvel at Blavatsky's erudition in the philosophy and history of religions, at all the knowledge she acquired without having attended school—without noting that few aristocratic children in the Russian Empire attended schools, as their families maintained impressive libraries and hired tutors.

Theosophy itself skirted discussion of social hierarchy even as it posited a universal hierarchy of cosmic evolution, a future infused by the peacemaking, healing capacities of mental and energetic communion. All the while, it anchored sensitive capacities to connect to theories of race and evolution. Thought-forms were visible only to those with the evolved, artistic sensibility to perceive radiating color-sound vibrations. Moreover, a crude, unrefined person can only emanate rough, ugly thought-forms: "Selfish Greed" is sloppy, all mud-green tentacles, like "people gathered in front of a shop window" (Besant and Leadbetter 1901, 56–57). "Intellectual Aspiration," by contrast, sends out a thrusting ray of yellow, depicting a "much advanced development of the part of the thinker" (72). Kandinsky's abstract modernist sat in the apex of society, as in the glassy tip of a pyramid or moving pencil, making contact with a new plane: only the genius artist could see ahead.

The ideal of the evolved, telepathic, empathic genius has risen historically across human conflicts and hierarchies, the events of wars, imperial extensions, colonial extractions, and rationalizing governments. So also has the anti-ideal, in images of failed contacts and of excesses of mental manipulation. All the while, specific institutions have fervently worked to open doors to perception that systematize intuitions about contact, even while keeping their channels narrow.

COLD WAR OPTICS

My friend is driving on the wooded road from the dacha belonging to a psychologist and television celebrity, a man who tested telepathy claims in Soviet labs in the 1960s, leaving me free to ponder our tea with him. He had enlightened us, reaching inside his jacket for a Nokia phone to punctuate the claim, about how competition between our governments to harness telepathic energies paralleled lines of technological espionage in the race to perfect cell phones. The birch forest that grows so thick and green just outside Moscow seems an unsuitable setting to belabor our respective states' claims to have invented this or that communication technology. My friend breaks the silence to remark upon something else. She is struck by our host's stories about a 1960s experiment in which subjects were to read colors or numbers via skin vision, or *dermooptika* (dermo-optics): "How embarrassing! For science, they make you sit on colored paper with your naked bottom." Her words prompted me, as they often do, to ponder our diverging perspectives: while I have been primed to fix on technological rivalry, educated into nationalist, paranoid narratives that oppose Russia to America, my friend was exercising a finer sensibility to both broader and more specific concerns, demonstrating empathy while gesturing toward hierarchy and sacrifice in divisions of laboratory labor. Poor Roza Kuleshova, shivering blindfolded while scientists measured her pulse.

Until my friend spoke, I had given little thought to any indignities that might have occurred in the telepathy lab. This chord runs through the fictions and spectacles of both superpowers; stories about shame and social awkwardness when true thoughts are exposed resonate with Kuleshova's nakedeness. Such discomforts escalate exponentially in fears that an enemy might access the mind, steal the keys to drive the will—historically, they intensified where state projects intersected, looped into Cold War circuits, for we share more of institutional histories and networks of expertise than we admit.

Throughout the Cold War and afterward, in Russia and the United States alike, films, books, and news reports on telepathy experiments have projected fantasies and warnings about ways to sense over distance and communicate through barriers. At best, humanity unites to discover ever more sleek technologies to open channels through space and time, while we evolve hitherto hidden capacities for intuition, to see into the future or into the minds even of aliens. These dreams, in the pastels of collective effervescence, contrast with the nightmare shades of mass manipulation and mental bondage, in parallel with the ways that, for example, Americans debate the mental influence of Russian propaganda or fake news while they also produce videos of dolphins communicating and films about linguists cracking alien code.

The paranoid perspective all too easily dominates. Fear of mental influence, of mind control as a subtype of enslavement, has ranked high among justifications for building walls, segregating people, limiting currencies, jamming radio signals, and deporting populations. Cold War states fed paranoia in two ways. First, both superpowers cast the enemies alternately as manufacturers of ideological robots or as slaves to suspicion and superstition. Second, both did in fact launch massive efforts to use technology (including psychopharmaceutical technologies) to affect opinions, proclivities, and habits. From television advertising to boot camp, in elementary schools and elections, people witnessed naked attempts to influence motives and actions.

Why so much effort to educate a paranoid perspective? Both superpowers claimed to oppose oppressive states. After World War II both pressed for dismantling colonial orders that had produced slavery, resource extraction, and white nationalism—yet both the United States and the USSR continued to build upon colonial institutions and imperial infrastructures. For instance, both extended prison and military systems in ways that appropriated free labor and fed proxy wars. Both states, to sustain these contradictions without losing credibility, veiled or denied their similarities and connections, even in spaces of cooperation or intersection.[3] In paranoia, we together shaped a militarized, carceral world.

In the United States, critics and comics mocked fear of enemy influence, exhorting us to fear instead our own failures to understand, as in *Dr. Strangelove* (1964), in which U.S. leaders mistakenly attack the Soviets, believing they have poisoned American waters. The year before *Dr. Strangelove* was released, the U.S. Air Force released educational videos addressing such concerns (Air Force Audio Visual Service,1963). The film demonstrates checks and balances along a chain of communication contacts through channels of telephone, radio, and then finally gesture. The U.S. president picks up a special phone to reach Strategic Air Command (SAC); his command, as a radio signal, is verified by two fighter planes; and then SAC relays the command down to individual missile silos. In each silo two men sit at matching consoles, equipped with matching keys. The pair confirms receipt of the command, each nodding to the other, holding eye contact as they turn their keys in synchrony to launch the missile. Just as a beautiful system of government is checked and balanced to prevent tyranny, all will be well with the system mediating nuclear commands; no contacts will break, no circuits misfire, because the agents confirming that the authorized contact has occurred are duplicated at each point. Of course this reassured few, and people searched elsewhere for the promise to survive planetary destruction, reviving New Age movements, writing science fiction in which humanity evolves skills for intuition and empathy. Meanwhile, the so-called Iron Curtain did not just divide and block communication and movement; it also motivated attempts to communicate, generated "excess" communications, and shaped longings for more contact.

Soviets and Americans faced those barriers differently, and we produced and performed knowledge of the other differently. As an ethnographer and American citizen, I have had ample opportunity to incite talk about superpower competition, and it has always struck me that random taxi drivers in Moscow ask me more informed questions about the United States than anyone I know in America, no matter how brilliant, has ever asked me about Russia or the USSR, except other specialists. In the Urals countryside, on trains crossing the Volga and the Kama, I have spent days and nights talking to people—people who identify as Russian, Romani, Chuvash, or Armenian (often some mix, as all may live as Russian citizens). My path has led me to speak with scientists and linguists, actors and bankers, designers and shop clerks, beading artists and metalworkers. All have commanded more detail about U.S. history and literature than the other way around, asking specific questions about state taxes, politicians, roads, breakfast cereals, and race politics in the United States. Back home, conversely, old classmates and even colleagues suggest that there is something awry in my interest in learning anything about Russia at all. My Russian visitors in the United States have rarely been greeted by the detailed comparative discussions I have met with in Moscow, Tver', and Perm'. In Russia, print news, television, and radio produce a better baseline of knowledge about events beyond the borders than is usual in the United States; for example, one program on the independent radio channel Echo of Moscow devotes an hour each week to exploring unusual legal cases in America. Mainstream papers give full citations in daily reviews of the American press. Post-Soviets of several generations, in both city and country, even those having no contact with foreigners, sing songs by the Beatles, Stevie Wonder, Beyoncé. How many U.S. citizens know a single poem by Pushkin or would even recognize a song by psychedelic folk-rock band AuktsYon? Perhaps if American paranoia flourishes over blind spots, Russian versions adhere almost affectionately to details.

Patterns of migration explain some of the difference; many Russians published their American impressions to circulate back home (via *tamizdat*), and contacts did not completely wither with immigration even during the deepest frosts. It was Russian friends who taught me how the U.S. federal highway infrastructure works in tandem with trucking hospitality plazas and weigh stations; they have an émigré friend who drives a freight truck across the continent, and I do not. In the real world, where some Russians become better Americans than I can be, paranoia is a means to erase such inconvenient impurities—it can even transform the immigrant's or tourist's very affection for things American into a reason to reject all things Russian.

ROMANCING OPACITY

When I first began to plan pursuing ethnography in the USSR, around 1987, a graduate adviser warned me, "No one will ever trust you over there." This was even before the world order changed in 1989. Political regime changes from Eastern Europe to South Africa, monetary reforms and educational overhauls after the fall of socialist states drew attention to new crises of representation and reanimated older ones: "Is this a counterfeit ruble?" "Can we trust our Swedish colleague?" "Does she really love me, or want a visa to Canada?" The stakes for interpretation within Russia shifted for a good while, from fearing enemies of the state to fearing enemies in the markets. Russians in the 1990s warned me to avoid merchants, to avoid Roma; women cautioned against *alfonsy*, men looking for sugar mommas. People debated: Were Russians the *samyj iskrennij narod* ("most sincere people"), or the most ironic, or the most suspicious?

Still no one, not one of these people, nor any of those about whom they warned me, ever let me down, cheated me, robbed me, or took advantage of me. Some gave *me* advice, rides, repairs, birthday parties—an engagement party!—meals, shawls, books, jewelry, candy, cards, embraces, opinions, stories . . . and time. I tried to reciprocate. Did they give to cultivate an American spy or a connection overseas? It has been thirty years, and by now it is clear that I have no good information and not a lot of money—and people still spend time with me. Moreover, I have too often seen too many of these people treat even strangers with careful responsibility, if not cheer, orienting to an ethic of mutual aid—one that some complain has vanished since the demise of the USSR, but that (to my American sensitivity to preserving individuality and refusing aid) seems vital and alive. Where markets blossomed in Russia, they did so without the objectivist strains of extreme individualism that dominate among American financial elites (thanks to another Russian émigré, Ayn

Rand, who made more ripples in Chicago and New York than in St. Petersburg and Moscow). After three decades of fieldwork and study, I reject assertions that mistrust and illusion structure the ways people in Russia actually relate, any more than they do in other places I have lived. Instead, people there begin, probe, and nurture relationships even against proliferations of narratives driven by paranoid logic, filling them out over time.

Mistrust is not the motor for this book. It is but one approach to contact, one that sparks and recharges not within the space of a single state but across them, and that is embedded among specific technologies for intuition, sets of skills, procedures, networks and institutions for interpreting others. In Moscow in early 1992 the mother of one friend, a talented tailor, gave me a photocopy of a "very useful book," a recent translation of Dale Carnegie's *How to Make Friends and Influence People.* As I read it for the first time, I recalled that the giver was already assiduously following its precepts; for example, she began every turn at talking by addressing her interlocutor by name, a practice to which I developed an aversion after reading about its purpose and function according to Carnegie. A decade later, a different friend in Moscow, a writer, voiced a position closer to mine, asking whether people in the United States read Carnegie's "lessons in hypocrisy" as avidly as did people in Russia. I told her that, while many know of Carnegie, I know few who quote the text—but we seem to have already absorbed many of its principles.[4] A decade later in Moscow, living experts such as Paul Ekman were in vogue, teaching not how to make friends, but how to discern false friends. He has become popular both there and elsewhere through translations of his books and a fictional television series based on his work (*Lie to Me,* 2009–2011).

It turns out that Ekman started visiting psychologist colleagues in St. Petersburg, Russia, in the 1970s, giving lectures on how to read facial micro-expressions in order to spot lies. Ekman may owe a great deal to his Russian interlocutors. Self-help authors publishing in Russia weave references to Ekman and other Anglophone writers, such as Allan Pease, into handbooks on how to read motivation and detect lies, how to see past words or through gestures in specific kinds of social interactions: courting, marketing, healing, studying, voting. As the Soviet system wound down, although streams of advice offered to help people interpret each other in new local circumstances, they did not burble up from local springs alone.

Beginning around 1990, advertising exponentially increased from places such as AIP-Tsentr in St. Petersburg, offering training by authors of books such as *Basic Instinct: The Psychology of Intimate Relations* (Vagin and Glushchaj 2002). By the twenty-first century Moscow enterprises offered courses, such as *Genij obshchenija* (The Genius of Communication), that promised to teach "the lie detector technique" and "scanning the inner state of your partner." One also could take Methods of Evoking Sympathy or The Art of Bluffing. A. P. Egides, author of books such as *Labyrinths of Communication, or How to Learn to Tune in with People* (2002), ran a school in Moscow called The Little Prince, offering psychological training on topics such as "how to deport yourself in conflicts" and "how to distinguish among people." The Moscow continuing education offices of CitiKlass (www.cityclass.ru) offered the course *Tekhnika Uspeshnykh Peregovorov* [Techniques of Successful Negotiations], which included dramatic role-playing to learn, among other things, "how to correctly crack the secrets of gestures," "how to read faces," and "the peculiarities of conducting negotiations with representatives of various nations and peoples." These texts mystified communication and projected shifty types of persons even as they offered secret decoder rings.

In many languages in many countries, journalists and filmmakers, parliaments and diplomats saturate media with reports and depictions of betrayals, failures of trust, and tests of authenticity—and also with reports of techniques, designed by professionals and experts, to distinguish good contacts from bad, to judge communications as transparent or opaque. Moreover, in contradiction to the many famous claims about exceptional Russian obfuscation and mystery, people in Russia have just as frequently as anyone else rallied to the value of transparent clarity. When Russian Decembrists renounced monarchy in 1825, they also championed plain speaking, rejecting the Francophone registers of the Russian aristocratic courts.[5] Early Soviets called back to those Decembrist aesthetics when they removed extra alphabet letters, trimming the "Language of Lenin" down to spare, modular forms thought best to manifest both clarity and modernity to foster new thought and action.[6]

By the 1960s, intellectuals vexed by Soviet versions of rationalism had turned toward opacity and ambiguity.[7] Soft focus translucence marked films beloved by the intelligentsia, such as Tarkovsky's 1979 *Stalker*. Based on a science fiction novel by the Strugatsky brothers, the story unfolds in The Zone, a space polluted and warped by an extraterrestrial visitation. The authorities have fenced it off from all but the most daring poachers of alien technological artifacts. Adventurers hire these Stalkers to seek a room where, it is said, one's secret wishes are divined and fulfilled.

Filmed several years before *Blade Runner* (1982) depicted a half-decayed, half-shiny-chrome future Los Angeles, *Stalker*'s marshy, wet, and rusted industrial landscape projected late Soviet perceptions of ecological ruin, the corroded metal and crumbled concrete that increasingly threaded through day-to-day life, but were still largely absent from film or television (as they were then in mainstream U.S. productions). However, the worst dangers of The Zone were not its earthly ruins but its cracks in space-time, which zig across the landscape, shifting location unexpectedly. Matter that contacts such a crack is consumed: your arm is sheared right off, hair just singed if you are lucky (a possibility that is clearer in the book). The Stalker finds safe paths by testing all that seems most transparent; his simple technology for intuition is to appropriate the metal lug nuts discarded by the aliens. He throws one; silence means that way is fatal, while the sound of metal hitting ground indicates open passage. Inside The Zone one can never move along a straight path, for space there is just like time, each step as opaque as tomorrow; upon finding the enchanted space, the adventurers discover that they cannot read even their own desires.[8] Only the Stalker accepts the knowledge that seemingly transparent paths nonetheless require extra senses—even just to listen, not only to look—before moving on.

Some argue that the thematic and formal opacity in the film signal elitism (see Faraday 2000,164–67). Tarkovsky was certainly steeped in 1960s elite intellectual Soviet debates about sincerity and opacity,[9] and in his autobiography he expresses disdain for Eisenstein-style film montage as too fast, too limiting of interpretation, too obvious (1986, 21). It was better, he thought, to leave some things unsaid, out of respect for viewers' intellectual and emotional intelligence.

As these brief examples suggest, by the time of *glasnost'* in the late 1980s, the Soviet Union had passed through several cycles wherein claims to clear, transparent, open communication alternated with romantic or postmodern rejections of its possibility. Soon afterward, however, many responded to 1990s advertising and electoral campaigns as harbingers of mystifying reenchantment, political dramaturgy as thaumaturgy. Victor Pelevin hit this note in 1996 with the hilarious blockbuster *Generation P*, a novel depicting a world flooded by PR and commercials for foreign cigarettes and soda. The protagonist is a translator of Uzbek and Kirghiz poetry who finds his profession suddenly erased; "the new era had no use for him" (Pelevin 1999, 5). He takes a gig for a new advertising firm, conjuring jingles during Castaneda-inspired, Ouija-board sessions with the spirit of Che Guevara that marry hallucinogens to structural linguistics. He never does find clarity, ascending instead a vertical maze of occult esoterica to couple with an ancient masked goddess.

Anthropologists, historians, and literary scholars of Russia have creatively analyzed all these themes, devoting special attention to the virtuosity and humanity, for many, of the unsaid and the half-said in Soviet times (Boym 1994; Pesmen 2000; Oushakine 2000) and the social play of ambiguity and irony (Yurchak 2005; see also Lipovetsky 2010; Nadkarni 2007), complicating images of the USSR as a place where poets and tricksters only perished, as if all free thinkers were whisked away merely for hinting at a double meaning. As Yurchak stresses, by the time of late socialism, many people easily went about their lives, neither chafing against government slogans nor animating them with soul, but standing indifferent to them—or having fun with them, repurposing Lenin's words in bricolage that sometimes (not always) provided subversive means to "signify on" official signs (Gates 1988), but that more significantly also marked out fields of social allegiance.[10]

One Moscow friend gives me an example from her teen years, around 1983, of righteous uses of opacity. After a demonstration against Soviet military force in Afghanistan, she had been taken in for a *beseda* (a "chat," a euphemism for "interrogation"). She recalls feeling, "internally compelled to answer all the questions honestly," until she realized, after comparing notes with friends, that one should refuse to answer at all, if not for one's own sake, then for that of others in custody.[11] The morality of deliberate opacity subverts dominant strands of European, Christian, Bolshevik, and modernist incitements to speak, to speak sincerely—and to speak as an individual;[12] in her case, speaking truth to power would betray others. Such truthful speaking can be a cynical act, insincerely aimed. To refuse transparency along one channel—in sincere words to these people in this place— affirms other ongoing channels. For many people, and not only in Russia, this is how the "sense of trust" emerges over time, not through individually sincere expressions of referential fact. To eschew semantic transparency was less a manifestation of what has been called "a culture of dissimulation"[13] and more a socially alert tactic that left room for others to navigate discursive situations otherwise out of their control. For those in such situations, American-style outrage when communication shifts, to work differently within bureaucratic corridors than outside them seems silly.[14] The American NGOs that came in the late 1990s to teach Russians communication skills in lessons bundling transparency with capitalism and democracy quickly came to seem not only meddling, but naïve (see also Larson 2013; Cohen 2015a).

Many foreign consultants entered Russian spaces in the 1990s with little in the way of language or historical training, unaware of the debt that global scholarship on communication owes, in fact, to robust theories developed both in Russia and by Russian-speaking émigrés. Like Pelevin's hero, many urban Russians had earned degrees in philology and read semiotic and literary theory (Vladimir Propp, Roman Jakobson, Mikhail Bakhtin, Yuri Lotman) and structural and post-structural theories of language in French (Ferdinand de Saussure, Jacques Derrida) and other languages. My own training in linguistic anthropology engages much of the same scholarship, and I often randomly encountered people who enjoyed speaking about concrete situations of communication in ways amenable to it (asking who addresses whom, in what social relation, for whose interests, and to which ends?) We shared ground to frame discussions about whether "democracy" always aligns with "transparency," or whether "sincerity" (as a matter of referential truth calibrated to an individual speaking voice), is really the deepest, or best, measure of morality or for true communication, and whether it is not best to refuse the squeamishness that categories like sincerity can call into being.[15]

MANY RAYS, MANY RUSSIAS

Pelevin's hero survives the dissolution of Soviet hierarchies of expertise. The order of labor by which a translator could eat by poetry alone ends, so he aims his semiotic energies elsewhere, taking precarious contracts to craft advertising jingles and political slogans. I conceived of fieldwork for this book in 1997, a summer when my friends in Russia and I were reading and laughing at *Generation P*. We had all seen other friends juggle, and some struggled themselves to recombine older techniques for interpretation, to transvalue them for credible use across formerly disparate social circles and institutional structures (Kelly, 2012)—actors teaching their craft to businessmen or to politicians, if they were lucky, tending bar or hauling cargo to market if they were not.

Their crossings motivate this book's attention to competing rays of semiotic effort, launched from diverse points: theater schools, university courses, self-help courses, television programs, scientific demonstrations, bureaucratic encounters, film sets, and prison barracks. Through them I track filaments of longing and worry about making and breaking contact, the possibilities for and obstacles to communicative intuition. The book follows modes of tuning and testing channels that escape original fields of activity, and we see techniques to project feeling through theatrical prosceniums intertwine with those developed in lab tests of long-distance thought transfer. We see playwrights do ethnography, literary scholars interview psychics on talk shows, psychologists read Constantine Stanislavsky, and actors study Ekman.

This book moves from starting point to end point not along a single, straight line, but by working through series of circles of expertise and circuits for influence. I begin inside a theatrical academy in Moscow and end on a film set in the Urals, both points at which the nature of contact is under scrutiny and given shape.

Neither my America nor my Russia is the same as yours. Since 1988 I have lived in Russia for approximately five years and in Eastern Europe for a year and a half. Both durable structures and sudden contingencies opened and closed my paths, some affording me unusual perspectives on encounters across multiple national and social borders. For one thing, long-term research and contact with Romani communities in Russia and Eastern Europe forced me to attend to the rise of right-wing nationalism and to ways American and British encouragement of local nationalism to counter socialism was not innocent in that rise. I learned to heed colleagues from both Russia and the other formerly socialist states, who knew that while histories of socialism in their countries were linked, they were diverse, never in lockstep. Indeed, people like Roma experienced post-socialist reforms in Russia very differently than those who faced reforms in the Czech Republic or Hungary, because different socialist-era legal systems and labor practices had built differing social and legal environments for Roma to act upon.

Although I started my fieldwork during the very last days of state socialism, it is not the end of socialism that motivates this book, but a broader and more persistent set of concerns about how categories of intuition are shaped by understandings of communication that in turn have been torqued through both material channels and politically charged ideologies that either allow or constrain contacts. In the early 1990s I spent much time on film shoots and at stage rehearsals, where Russian directors told Roma to "turn up the emotional volume" in order to "be more real, more Gypsy" so that they would "touch" the audience. (Roma would rarely communicate their distaste for these directives in the moment, saving bitter complaints and arch hilarity for later, "among ourselves.") I met a few Russians who claimed to know everything that matters about Gypsies by intuition, triggered by tiny sense data, a "look in the eye" that told them that "Gypsies are criminals." Similar profiling judgments flourish in the United States; whence such confidence in intuitions about certain others? These processes have as much to do with regulations of contacts and channels as they do with stereotypes, and they have long histories.

I reach then for a historical theorization of the ways people check, maintain, or break contact, semiotic acts also known as *phatic*. Such acts manifest not only in words but also in cleared throats and pauses, in the ways people move or juxtapose media materials or arrange bodies in various kinds of situations, for example, on the stage, at passport control, and in the kitchen.

People *learn* to communicate with others within particular situations. Moreover, they do so as they also learn how situations contrast. To claim to discern a criminal mind by the luster of an eye will rest on some scaffolding—such as the socialized recognition of policing as a mobile and invasive discursive situation, one that can be imposed over others, with its own interpretive experts. Attention itself is socially weighted as we learn each situation, taught how and where to aim our eyes and ears (at the teacher) or urged not to stare or not to eavesdrop (on the bus). Attention centers the directives embedded in moral judgments about proper channels and contacts: "Why do you even watch that show?" "Talking to those people is a waste of time." "Look at the blackboard, not at your friends." We learn about social distinctions every time we witness another being invited to look, or when bodies angle to shoulder us out of a conversation. These discursive divisions of labor are also sensory, even when they go unremarked. They shape social possibilities unless we purposely—and at cost—override pressure to stay inside our circles.

My specialization in Russian studies and anthropology was incomprehensible, even unethical, to some of the people who grew up on my street; a few prickled aggressively at the idea that I would study "that communist language," would actually make contact with those people. Paranoia about espionage, however, is only one among many material and social conditions that hold knowledge of other countries out of reach in the United States. Never mind Russia; New York City was a fantasy place to most of us kids in Nebraska. Few people traveled even across state lines; tickets cost money, even on Greyhound, and where would one crash if one did not have kin? It still shocks me how few academics and professionals know about these limits on many, perhaps most, Americans' possibilities for travel.

I would not have come to study Russian or travel to Moscow if not for luck, hitting upon a channel opened by the generation before. The post–World War II G.I. Bill allowed my adoptive father to enroll in college and then graduate school after his military service during the Korean War. The army had taught him Russian and sent him to Alaska to monitor radio transmissions. After obtaining his graduate degree, he copublished the first English translations of the Russian formalist literary critics, most notably Shklovsky's theory of art as estrangement. Raised during the Great Depression of the 1930s in a union town on the edge of St. Louis, he feared socialism; as a kid working after school while other college-bound kids studied, I did not. We argued fiercely about the means to economic and social justice, and perhaps that conflict inspired me to study Russian and to go see for myself.

There was another condition that situated my perceptions of Russia: our house, while stocked with novels, was draughty and our clothes were secondhand (cultural capital does not transform into economic capital when one academic salary supports two families of children). Accounts of Moscow that compared it implicitly with, say, suburban Massachusetts (not even with Manhattan) made no sense to me at all; I have yet to find comparisons that presuppose readers who live in a Florida trailer park, as some of my relatives do. Americans without means—many of us—rarely travel by air, much less abroad, much less to Russia, and rarely for more than a few weeks, young scholars on fellowships and young journalists being among the exceptions. On my first trip to Russia, a study tour in 1988, my observations never synced with those of most of my tripmates, children of lawyers and doctors and ambassadors. Beyond our relatively successful little nuclear pod, our adult kin work as infantry soldiers, sailors, assembly line workers, paramedics, meat cutters, harvest laborers, seamstresses, cashiers, mortuary workers, construction workers, one pool shark, and one painter. When I first visited Russia, my points of reference for gauging living conditions included our house, a tiny, grim Manhattan dorm room with speedy little roaches, decrepit student rentals with sagging porches in Madison and Chicago, a trailer set on concrete blocks in the northern Alabama mountains, and occasional glimpses of the domestic paradises in which a few beloved schoolmates lived, where I learned about concepts like "cable television," and "finished basement." Skills and chores learned from maternal kin helped me more in Russia than did academic hints: my girl cousin showed me how to weave beads; my aunt spent sweaty days canning. Boy cousins showed us how to track deer and to play chess, a game learned in the army. Our grandparents taught everybody to sing harmony.

While many Americans on that trip reported bleak impressions of a grey, crumbling Russia—how much better is our country, they would agree on the tour bus—my impressions never lined up with theirs. First encounters with Soviet objects stirred sentiments not of American superiority, but of comfort and delight in discovery, admiration for humans who had differently imagined techniques and tools for living and made them accessible to more of us. When I first stepped onto a Soviet train from Helsinki to Leningrad in 1988, the cars smelled of wood paneling and hot steel wheels. A huge electric kettle was built in at the front of the car—a samovar always ready to dispense hot water: convenience. Next to the samovars, a chart labeled all parts of the machine, indicating how it worked and how it might be repaired, inviting us to learn and to act if need be: genius. Russia offered luxuries new to me, in things I was allowed to touch: porcelain tea sets and Czech cut-glass chandeliers (and also imitation plastic ones, which I thought just as cool). Real butter at every meal, carved into shells. Flowers, fresh flowers, people always buying and carrying flowers. The giant, lush house plants in the lobby of the Leningrad youth hostel, late afternoon summer sun streaming between rubber plant leaves, a disco up in the mezzanine playing Michael Jackson, the sound bending around towering palms and ferns.

These early tourist impressions were later tempered in village buildings with no indoor plumbing (with outhouses like those of my country relatives), and during the hardest days of the early 1990s by searches for food in grocery stores or for supplies in hospitals, where a lack of cotton, gloves, and antiseptics meant taking care of people at home instead (as we had done for my mother in the 1970s, when the hospital would not nurse her after an operation). I was not blind to the rough state of mailboxes in the high-rise entryways. However, I have come to prickle when I hear contrasts between some specific Russian bit of trouble and an American ideal of plenty, or a dream of luxury, color, and variety that many of us did not live. Compare Urals plumbing to Michigan water pipes, if you will, but look not only at contrasts, or even similarities, but also for connections. To avoid standing upon the sands of covert comparison to American ideals, as if they exemplify a neutral standard, this book keeps contrasts and comparisons specific, and when I do incorporate American places and patterns, it is in ways that attempt symmetry and acknowledge influence.

FIELDWORK

This books draws from several decades of ethnographic and archival research in Russia from 1988, the year before the Berlin Wall fell and three years before the USSR would deconstruct itself, through 2017, one hundred years after the Russian Revolution. I write at a time when Americans are acutely unsure about how to interpret anyone, how to intuit the intentions of their own leaders, not to mention those of other states. This moment would be different had government encouraged Americans to learn multiple languages; perhaps we would be more brave about tuning in to foreign channels and attempting our own translations. Outside academe, the very fact that I study Russian is an anomaly, either exotic or suspect. All this in mind, Throughout the book, whenever possible, I provide the time and place of observations from my fieldnotes; in some cases, doing so would violate standard ethnographic ethical practice, and so I deliberately leave time and place unstated.

In 1988, after six years of formal Russian study, I spent a summer in Leningrad. In 1990 and 1991, my several monthlong trips included family home stays and research affiliations to survey the archives. In August 1991 I began my first long, two-year sojourn in Moscow; I arrived in time to witness the attempted coup that catalyzed the dismantling of the USSR. I visited many times throughout the 1990s and carried out another long-term field project in 2002–2003 and 2005 at the Russian State Theatrical Academy, living with students in the dorm, documenting interactions in classrooms and rehearsals, as well as backstage and in the hallways.[16] I keep in touch with that cohort and with a few other cohorts, and return about once a year. Over the decades, I have lived in Moscow, Tver', Perm', and Kungur and have visited other cities and villages. I have lived with Roma and with other Russians, in cities and in villages, with friends and with families of friends, in cottages and dachas, and in apartments and dormitories.

Over time I accumulated many observations by accident, for example, by translating pro bono for a British lawyer observing a court trial or wandering around Moscow talking to strangers during the 1991 coup attempt. Ethnographers study encounters among beings who are not made to sit naked in a lab—and while we might influence, we cannot control, what will happen in any situation. Some people try, and it is our job to understand how, not to try to control situations ourselves. To capture variation across such situations, this book thus draws from events that reached beyond the bounds of research sites or moments of interviewing.

There are nevertheless ethical reasons that anthropologists endeavor, in writing and in note taking, to separate "research" from "life" and to report only on the former. For such reasons, I have waited many years to write about certain encounters that did not at the time fall under the umbrella of research. I still take care to write in ways that do not identify anyone. For similar reasons, I draw from films, radio, and books. For one thing, because such media are not produced *for* me, they offer coordinates from which to triangulate examples that are more ethnographic, situations in which I was present and possibly affected what might have been said or done. For another thing, such media also offer surrogate examples, to shield actual people from censure or embarrassment while demonstrating the ubiquity of certain themes. In addition, many of my interlocutors' livelihoods involve creating and curating photos, plays, films, or radio broadcasts, which makes it all the more important that I show Anglophone readers a few landmarks in the Russian mediascape that serve as common points for their work, as well as for the play of laughter and debate.

The fact is, however, that I came to know many people in spaces where being an anthropologist, or even a being foreigner, was subsumed under other, joint work. My friends include people with whom I spent hours on a song chorus, guitar riff, or recording level or on deciding a camera angle or a costume choice. I spent time with people seeking perfection of this karate technique or that roller derby rule or this beading skill. Some of us collaborated on stage plays, translations, films, musical concerts, and recordings. In 1992, between research grants, I helped proof the English edition of a telephone directory. On film sets (one on which Romani consultants were

working, one in a Urals prison), I played tiny roles as an extra actor. In Perm'
I collaborated on an anthology of Russian rock to benefit a children's oncol-
ogy center. In Moscow I acted and directed for an expat theatrical ensemble.
Throughout, when not "doing fieldwork"—when not out at 4:00 A.M. at a
wedding table, taping an interview, or writing up notes—I might be arguing
with a musician about phrasing, running a sound check in a blues club, buying a fish for New Year's, or weeding around cucumbers. Such joint projects
make it difficult to ignore interests and relationships that research parameters can otherwise eclipse.

Over time both research and other collaborations can transcend original
contexts and points of contact; after an interview, the interviewee and I might
set out to undo a bureaucratic knot. Meeting someone in the metro for afternoon tea might involve a detour for an hour to stand in line to get on a waiting
list for a sofa (that was in Soviet times—now it might mean a detour to compare new appliances). A ride from the train station could include turning down
a side road to stop by the dentist or to drop off a little gift (or by 2014 to visit
a new cat café). Such detours brought me to witness interactional struggles for
attention and solutions to awkward requests as they arose, especially ways to
make or avoid contact that interviews alone never can (Briggs 1986).

American military and soft power have framed many encounters overseas. I attribute some of people's willingness to collaborate with me to my
American passport, my access to dollars during a period of extreme ruble
devaluation, and their own early optimism about changes promised by
Western business and markets, but friends also recognize that I try to avoid
measuring by American ideals. Three decades of birthdays and New Year's
eves, weddings, and funerals—with fireworks, herring, and vodka—and the
relaxing labors of preparing ordinary dinners and companionable walks on
errands have turned some of us into friends. As we become friends, we try
to smooth channels: I decode the American "service smile"; they socialize
me to serve politely at table. When we are together, we sometimes amplify
each other's familiar channels, so no one is homesick: in Moscow we saw
Alice Cooper; near Detroit we turned up the volume for AukstYon.

Some places in Moscow are set up to cater to tourists' preferences or to
seek foreign influence. The Russian State Theatrical Academy, even as an
elite institution that accepts foreign students, is not one of them. There, I
was accorded no authority to define encounters or determine the manner of
my own participation. For example, I had planned to participate in acting
lessons, to compare them to prior years of such experience, and stood ready
with the class on September 1—but the master instructor walked over, took
me by the elbow, and led me to sit in a chair by his side. I wanted to flout

that bodily directive,[17] but consider: these students had passed through several rounds of intense auditions, so who was I to poach on their instruction time? I was sometimes recruited to act or sing "as an American" in a few short projects, and I folded easily into classes like stage combat and vocals, in which students received collective rather than individual attention, and in which previous training in choral singing and martial arts gave me specific skills to contribute. With room to jump across the sprung wooden floor, to practice flips and kicks, we worked in small groups as teachers moved around us. My leaping shoulder rolls received the same range of critique as theirs, my favorite being a dry, "*Ochen'* ne plokho" ("*Very* not bad"). As a result, I have full notebooks on acting classes and less on paper about stage combat. But my handstands are pretty good.

To define a field site or even a topic, scholars draw lines between selves and others, but some lines dissolve as social involvement stretches over time. We cannot put the entire world inside a lab or on a stage. Over the course of what anthropologists call events of *participant observation*, obligations arise and play out into friendships, rivalries, and other kinds of bonds. Even gifts change functions over time; what might originate in hopes for help surviving or material return can transform into promises to reunite, evoking different feelings than they once did; expectations of a return gift matter less than looking forward to coming together again. Memories of past aid or cheer attach fiercely to some gifted objects, and collecting gifts to give becomes part of the pleasure in planning a visit. Theories that emphasize the socially strategic functions of the gift may require revision to account for exchanges over periods longer than most rounds of fieldwork.

For example, from a longer perspective, we see that some gifts involve more than a single, dyadic axis of giver-receiver. One spring day in Michigan a box arrived at my house containing an Indiana Jones mask. Was this sent to harass me, perhaps by a disgruntled student of anthropology? I am not even an archaeologist, so, offended, I punched the thing before remembering that Moscow friends had ordered a toy online for their son. I forwarded it with a letter making fun of my forgetful reaction. A month later in Moscow, a small boy jumped out from behind the front door wearing this rubber face, after which for a good hour none of us could walk from laughing. Now he is taller than we are. And now we more often say "we." We have hosted each other many times, a month here, two weeks there, have traveled together in other lands. The sense of being a foreign guest recedes not only when we channel gifts, but also whenever we arrange a table together to welcome still other guests, to my house or theirs. We have even mediated each others' social networks: I introduced friends who later created a godparent relationship. Other friends introduced me to someone who ended up married to an in-law of mine in Nebraska. Such bonds and intimacies are not unique; similar stories enfold many scholars of Russia not born there, and some marry there. In the twenty-first century, bilingual families line up at the gates for flights to Moscow from Detroit, Atlanta, or New York. While our politicians and media work to define us as opponents, our communications continue through many types of relationships and collaborations. We are shaken each time our states sharpen conflict, but we do not let go.

The facts of such crossings and exchanges, however, do not often lead to depictions that include them as conditions for knowledge. Many beautiful, detailed representations of Russian life made both by Americans (diplomats, journalists, tourists, and scholars) and by émigrés to the United States mark out their topic by excluding such connections. When possible, This book aims to show how contacts influence research; for example, it was a Russian friend's who urged me to study the reality show *Battle of the Psychics*. I could choose to absorb her questions, such as: "*Battle* always tests psychics in a tragic situation, but is there anything funny about being a psychic?"[18] "Can psychics marry each other?" Doing so would negate the opportunity to compare and contrast perspectives. Instead I try, where I can, puzzle through ways we converge and diverge. The result, I hope, is a book that incorporates layers of conditions for contact into discussion of intuitions about contact. To convey and theorize these layers, the book chapters each shift screens and spaces in order to light up spirals of contrast-making, following Gregory Bateson's (1936) insights about this reflexive process of differentiation, which he called shizmogenic.

ETHNOGRAPHY AS CONTACT

This book posits two additional, historically emergent, material and social conditions of the field. First, divisions of labor, even artistic and semiotic labors, are carved out not only within institutions but also across them—and across the territories that claim to encircle them. Second, while communication runs along habitual paths, channels, conduits, and infrastructures that enable contact, communicative engagements can hop such structures, sometimes violating familiar ways to conceptualize communication. To capture both possibilities, this book juxtaposes situations, genres, and venues that are usually analyzed as if they were separate, not just to set telepaths alongside film directors or to compare auditions to prison walls, but to be alert to moments when people jump lanes.

Comparing conditions for contact can be revealing. Making ethnographic contact during early fieldwork in Russia went more slowly than it did later, for instance, at one of the central sites this book draws upon, the Russian State Theatrical Academy. I conducted that fieldwork in the early to mid-1990s with Roma who were going through the regime changes alongside everyone else. I started in places such as the Moscow Romani Theater, where weekly rehearsals were just public enough that people might decide to ignore me or not, to invite me home or not, to introduce me to others or not. Those rehearsals were sporadic, however. The Theatrical Academy was quite a different site; it demanded full, daily immersion (only years later did students command chunks of time and space for home-style hospitality). We all spent all our waking hours there, from 9:00 A.M. to nearly midnight. Conversations begun in the courtyard continued on the metro and into the dormitory. Students both extolled these conditions and, especially in the first year, mourned being cut off from other relations for quite a long period, longer than any boot camp.

This mourning of lost contacts, by the way, made it into the stage work that built cohort collectives. Each fall at midterm, students in many Russian schools stage a *kapustnik* ("cabbage festival"), a satirical variety show. Village collectives stage them as amateur talent parties; urban working theaters stage them as internal festivities. At the academy, cohorts introduce themselves to each other with *kapustnik* skits that parody theatrical education; the second-year directing cohort sent up the concept of "internal dialogue" with an actor confused by his own voice booming over the loud speakers, commenting absurdly on his every encounter with stage props: "There is that chair, again." Our younger cohort crafted a sketch with cameos by all of us non-native Russian speakers, singing in Arabic, Korean, French, Ukrainian, Daghestani, and English while an actor standing to the side pretended to translate. My snippet of "Downhome Blues" was translated into a Russian verse about the free kasha offered free at the academy until 11:00 A.M., while a Kuwaiti student's round in Arabic on the Ud became a verse about sleeping four hours a night and missing home.

Officially, the academy prefers to stress its function as a node for new contacts, bringing people into communication from far-flung places. Funded by the Ministry of Culture, this elite school is tasked with nurturing a national theatrical tradition and competes with the Moscow Art Theater (MKhAT) for international fame: to learn here, with students of students of Stanislavsky or of Vsevolod Meyerhold, is to drink at the fount of modern stagecraft. For more than a century, people have come from all over the world, to observe or to enroll for weeks, months, or years. I was easily admitted as an observer; the road had already been paved by a century of institutional procedures for including and recruiting observers from other places.

Students were not always so ready to animate such channels or maintain all foreign contacts; while I was there, an entire delegation of American drama students who spoke no Russian joined our cohort for two weeks in the spring. A few students complained later that they had crowded the rooms and slowed them all down, to which the instructors chided, "They are not 'ballast'! No! How do you think we pay for these light bulbs!" Still, American cultural and social capital earned a lower exchange rate at the academy than it did in other contexts. Contra allegations of Russian inferiority complexes after state socialism ended, at the academy, American know-how was of limited interest. For example, any tenuously imagined connection between me and say, Hollywood, was trumped by teachers' contacts in the Moscow theater world. No academic or foreigner could compete with the gazes of these directors. On the contrary, they absorbed my camera into their rehearsals, appropriating not only its recording functions, but also its capacity to quickly key shifts in contexts, to stage frames within frames: "Ready? Action!"

Ethnography presupposes presence or proximity, the possibility for making contact not only through technologies like camera or telephone, but also through long-term mediations of the body: the technologies of voice, hand, and eye. Many of my interlocutors at the academy shared this definition of ethnography and valued the observational power of prolonged contact. In the summer of 2001, a visit I made to the office for foreign students secured for me a meeting with the chancellor, to whom I explained that I wanted to observe directing courses and student life in order to write ethnography. She looked at my university card, took a long drag from her cigarette, and through the smoke pronounced knowingly, "Ahhh! Yes! Ethnography! Then you will stay in the dormitory with the students, so that you learn how they live!"

To observe, to listen, to attend to, to take in—these acts can perform contact. In theatrical work or filmmaking, too, to observe is not to distance oneself from others, but to involve oneself in collaborations that demand organization via reflection—to provide mirrors. I was never the only observer, foreign or internal; observation was a central activity offstage and on, learning to observe and to mirror others being among the earliest lessons. The teachers taught in teams, two or three at a time: a master, his or her assistant, and sometimes an intern. To watch and listen as an ethnographer among the instructors and students not onstage was just a minor variation in the social field; my notes roused little notice when all the interns and assistants took them, as did students. Looking over people's shoulders, I would see the same phrases copied into quad-rule, vinyl-covered notebooks as captured dialogue between teachers and students or in streams of teachers' discourses. The academy archives volumes of notes, transcripts, and fictional dialogues like those published by Stanislavsky, depicting a version of himself and an imaginary student. To carry out rehearsal ethnography has long been a phase in the curriculum. In 1936 visiting American director Norris Houghton wrote that when observing rehearsals at the Vakhtangov Theater he "used regularly to meet a boy and girl from GITIS [abbreviation for the Soviet-era name for the Academy, Gosudarstvennij Institut Teatral'nogo Iskusstva, or The State Institute for Theater Arts] who were watching rehearsals, and at the rehearsals of Enemies at the Moscow Art Theater, two young men from the Institute were present, like myself, to study the director's methods (1936, 48).

All this did not make all research methods easy or appropriate. Teachers cheerfully allowed me into classes, and when I asked permission to photograph or record, would exclaim, "Radi boga! Chto ty sprosish'!" ("For God's sake! Why even ask!"), but at day's end they would apologetically run to rehearsals at other theaters; overextended, they had little time or incentive to sit down with a foreign scholar. Dyadic channels, such as those afforded by interview situations, were difficult to set up. The head instructor might agree to an interview, but by the end of rehearsal would sigh from exhaustion and avoid eye contact, collecting his things, while students would mediate, "He likes you! He had a hard life; he hates to talk about himself." During previous fieldwork I had avoided the interview genre when it seemed it would be an imposition in families or spaces where people rarely practice the tête-à-tête. The point of ethnography of communication is to comprehend relations and patterns across a range of situations, not only those created by an interviewer. At the academy, while many had experience with the genre, and while people frequently staged dyadic interactions (romantic scenes, showdowns with landlords), it was nevertheless difficult to get anyone to sit one-on-one. For one thing, to the vexation of those in their first year, the schedule saturated every moment from nine in the morning until midnight, leaving little time to participate in smaller conversations, much less an interview: we began talking, someone suddenly notified us of a turn with the vocal teacher, someone walked by having finally found that red gauze, or someone wanted me to film a scene. Conversations always broke off when a teacher entered the room for the first time of the day, as we stood to greet him or her.

There were also differences in the ease of making contact. Despite my age and academic rank in the United States, I made enduring connections only with students. During acting lessons, critique sessions, or talks by important visitors, directors like Zakharov, Heifetz, or Fomenko, I sat with students on the floor. When students demonstrated their work, we mixed in behind the instructors on benches or chairs—although students sometimes rushed to free a seat for me, or even fetch a chair, as they might for an instructor, suggesting that my identification with them was partial. During breaks between classes, I stayed with the students as they practiced in the homeroom or paced in the corridors, memorizing poems, making tea, or experimenting with makeup. We tried to peer behind the weekly paper schedule filled in by hand and pasted over the glass walls of the directing department office, where instructors met to evaluate students' work before returning with critical notes. We could watch them talk, but never hear them behind the glass. But sometimes, in noticing that we shared a space cut from contact, we might start a new circle or send out a fresh ray.

Introduction

TECHNOLOGIES FOR INTUITION

It is deep December in the center of Moscow. A dozen acting and directing students in sweatpants or tights sprawl across a wooden floor in a studio at the top of the central building of the Russian Academy for the Theatrical Arts. The central campus occupies a block on a quiet, tree-lined street that curves off a central artery to the Kremlin, across from stately prerevolutionary neighbors, an embassy, an elementary school, and a theater. That morning students had cleaned the herringbone parquet with thin lengths of grey muslin, but now it is afternoon and dusty again. Facing the dozen at work sit senior and junior instructors, interns and apprentices, this author, and the other half of the class; many of us take notes in quadrille journals. Some sit on the floor, back to the wall, legs curled, or on the wide ledges of double-paned windows that reach from hip toward the ceiling, laced by frost.

We have just finished a morning of stage movement (*tsenicheskoe dvizhenie*), in which we carried each other on our backs, loping in a circle (a eurythmic drill attributed to Émile Dalcroze), and then practiced falling backward in chairs. The students now face a deceptively simple task: merely to establish "contact." For months they have progressed through techniques to establish communication with partners—*partnerstvo*—working multiple sensory channels through contact improvisation and mirroring drills, playing physical and verbal games to build collective tableaux and narratives, games familiar from the playground and culled from psychology books, games like Mafia, Ant Wars, Freeze, Die, and Come to Life. Today a new game is taking place: one student waits in the corridor while those remaining in the room agree on a simple command. "Close the *fortochka*," they decide. Even with the cold out on the street, someone has opened a *fortochka*—a little window

FIGURE 1.1.   Opening the *fortochka* may seem like wasting steam heat, but it also saves on the electricity and maintenance for localized thermostat systems—and moreover allows fresh air to circulate high across a room without creating a draft, balancing values of efficiency with those of comfort and health.

within a window, set high in the top frame. Central Moscow buildings are snug, well-warmed by hot water flowing to radiators through pipes in the walls supplied by larger pipes that run under and over city streets. The water temperature is set by region, not building: one opens a *fortochka* when a room becomes too warm. People are always opening or closing the *fortochka*, asking each other whether they ought to open or close this little point where outside and inside make contact, even in winter.

"Think that exact phrase," an instructor advises them. "Think: 'Close the *fortochka*'." The classmate returns from the corridor, and we quietly watch him stand still, head tilted, trying to intuit our collective wish. He regards the other students watching him, then the instructor who watches us watching him. He expounds advice, techniques for becoming more receptive to wordless contact: "Relax, listen . . . then take an action . . . listen to your body, even the silliest little thing . . . take that first impression." He tells the others to "concentrate with the chosen words. Relax, so there is no muscle tension. No analysis, no fighting within yourself." All efforts fail; the window stays open. They try again with a new command and a different classmate . . . and succeed! On the third attempt, they fail again. No matter, reassures the instructor; learning to balance principles of relaxation *and* concentration, this is hard work, a lifetime's work, this work of making a channel, opening up, making contact. They will labor at this for some part of every single day, for five years, running through an arsenal of what I call technologies for intuition.

Technologies for intuition are sets of techniques and tools designed to catch and to act on those signs, tells, information streams, vibes, and so forth that sentient beings emit without meaning to, or that we try not to express. These techniques include familiar mundane skills of interactional attention, the kind a schoolteacher might use to assess who is engaged and who is bored, that a waiter might use to decide when to approach a table. They might include specialized psychological skills, such as reading shifts among facial micro-expressions, or occult means to sense vibrations in the ether.

In some social settings, to discuss another's expressions (not to mention one's fleeting micro-expressions) or to point out lack of attention is considered awkward or rude, but these acting teachers insist on it—the profession demands undoing earlier social training in speech etiquette to develop active sensitivity for all those stray signs that spool out alongside more explicit words or acts.

At this point I want to define my usage of *channel* to refer to real or imagined conduits that afford communicative contact. They combine material media, persons, and structures. A channel can ride a single material medium or link multiple media: a phone call to a secretary, who sends a memo. Conversely, a medium like television can carry more than one channel along a single transmission, usually perceived as interference. Channels might also be thought of as constituted by materials and structures that together afford the very possibility for contact or communication without themselves being taken up as the main media for messages (although they can also be interpreted as messages, as can their blockages: a closed window, a roadblock, a first-class airplane cabin).

On another morning, the instructor has students face each other in parallel lines. Those in one line silently select targets from the other, and then "without words or external signs, only in your mind" call their targets, whose task is to intuit who is paying attention to them. Everyone concentrates; this time, most guess correctly. The teacher asks: "How can you explain this?" They call out words and phrases like "*Tjanet!*" ([She/he/it] pulls), "*Glaza!*" (The eyes!), or "A whole sum of minute things." The teacher recollects learning the same drill under Maria Osipovna Knebel', stage director and student of Stanislavsky (and main rival to Mikhail Kedrov, more often in the United States considered Stanislavsky's heir because he headed the Moscow Art Theater), who had learned it under Mikhail Chekhov (Stanislavsky's most theosophical student, who left the USSR in 1928). In her autobiography, Knebel' reminisces about early 1960s student reactions, posing the same questions as did her former student in 2003:[1]

> How did the students guess, surprising those who saw this exercise for the first time? Telepathy? No. Each student did it differently . . . One got it because his selector behaved too casually, another seemed suspicious, another did not meet his eyes, another caught the shadow of a quickly hidden smile. They noticed the subtle, barely discernible. And if sometimes they did not guess, still the process of attention was all the same creatively sharpened, and after the exercise evoked, for most,

thoughts and examples of lively observational skills and sensitivity. And is not sensitivity, the ability to penetrate that which lies on the surface, the obligatory quality of a director? (1967, 546)

Actors trained by Knebel' and her colleagues yielded captivating performances: quirky, clever, and still beloved by fans. Brilliant ensemble work is marked by exchanges of glances and gestures even among the extras in Soviet-era comedies like *Carnival Nights* (1968) and tragedies like *King Lear* (1971).

INFORMATION WARS: FROM *DRACULA* TO RUSSOPHOBIA

Around 1961, both superpowers invested in developing the sensitive "ability to penetrate," increased funding for telepathy research. Sources on both sides credit a specific moment when French journalists reported that a research team aboard an American submarine, the USS *Nautilus*, had successfully received mental images from a remote location in Virginia while under ice and water. The *Nautilus* was the world's first nuclear-powered submarine and the first sub to reach the North Pole wholly submerged—a deep sea counter to the first cosmic satellite launched by the USSR in 1957. In *Military Psychotronics: The Science of Enchantment*, Popov writes: "[A]s the "beep-beep" of Sputnik-1 rang over the world like a bell, leading American scientists decided it was time to move in all directions . . . in this way, the quests to conquer the planets and win human minds reached out their hands to each other" (2006, 2). Some call the press reports about the *Nautilus* a hoax, old school fake news that spun out spirals of mirrored rumors. All the same, the press reports attending to ongoing lab work increased, as did internal government reports suggesting that telepathic phenomena had military potential (see declassified and unclassified reports for the DIA, such as those prepared by the Air Force Systems Command in 1978 or by the Army Medical Intelligence and Information Agency in 1972). In 1973 a report prepared by the RAND corporation asserted that the superpowers had devoted equal resources to extrasensory perception (ESP) and paranormal research, commenting that "if these phenomena do exist," the "Soviets would be ahead" (Van Dyke and Juncosa 1973).

Why the Pentagon and the Kremlin cultivated paranormal science as a militarized technology for intuition is a question well masticated in the popular literature and film. The usual answer is to emphasize intelligence or military ends, strategic and paranoid motivations. Such motives are clearly part of the story. All the same, to focus only on such ends and motives can distract us not only from other motives, but also from the myriad and unintended outcomes of those experiments and discourses about them. To understand decades later how people deployed the techniques and the media spun around Cold War era events and institutions (and even rumors) requires that we cast our gaze more broadly, and farther back.

Cold War paranoia appears to some to have begun only after World War II. However, the outlines of that anxious discourse, and in particular the appeal to tropes of mind control, go back to the nineteenth century, to British suspicions of sabotaged imperial communication and enemy intelligence. Literary historian Jill Galvan reads Bram Stoker's *Dracula* as its contemporaneous readers might have, through the filters of reports of British conflicts in India and with Russia in Asia during the so-called Great Game. Regarding Britain's Indian holdings, "The most sensational rumor to this effect was that the Indians had sent messages to each other by way of native telepathic abilities, sometimes known as the 'Hindu Secret Mail,'" an occult channel for spreading mutiny (Galvan 2015, 446). Galvan argues that Stoker played on fears about Britain's imperial conflicts, from stories of both Indian rebel communications and Russian military intelligence: Dracula, exerting mesmeric power across great distances, collects intelligence on his prey better than any military spies. British Russophobia, Galvan notes, had already intensified after the Crimean War (1853–1856), increasing throughout the competing empires' struggles to control pieces of Central Asia. Reports of events there built "collective memory of a vigorous conflict between Eastern and Western realms of information" and "extreme investment in information and in depicting warring orders of information" (Galvan 2015, 449).

In *Dracula*, the narrative of British victory over the Orient is vexed in still another way, as the book emphasizes the Occident's practical informational weaknesses relative to the mysterious other, weaknesses improbable and unnerving for a nation aspiring to champion modernity (Galvan 2015, 458). *Dracula*, written during the decade after Frederic W. H. Myers coined the term *telepathy* in 1882,[2] parallels efforts of the Society for Psychical Research in England to catalog "native systems of communication that outpaced Western devices," perhaps, as Luckhurst notes, as "a mechanism of projection where anxieties about the fragility of colonial rule and scanty communication conjured occult doubles that mysteriously exceed European structures" (2002, 157–58). The British Society for Psychical Research involved itself with reports from all over the empire and beyond; one of its first acts, in 1884, was to send a member to India to investigate some of Elena Blavatsky's psychic claims.

By the time of the Russian Revolution, the ground was well prepared for continuing accounts of Soviet Russia that obsessed about deciphering the

Russian mind: *The Mind and Face of Bolshevism: An Examination of Cultural Life in Soviet Russia* (Fülöp-Miller, Flint, and Tait 1929); *New Minds, New Men? The Emergence of the Soviet Citizen* (Woody 1932); *Mind and Spirit in the Land of Soviets* (Lyons 1947); *The Soviet Mind: Russian Culture under Communism* (Berlin and Hardy [1949] [2004]); *The Country of the Blind: The Soviet System of Mind Control* (Counts and Perlmutter 1949); *The Mind of Modern Russia; Historical and Political Thought of Russia's Great Age* (Kohn 1955); *The Revolt of the Mind: A Case History of Intellectual Resistance behind the Iron Curtain* (Aczél and Méray 1959); *The Russian Mind* (Hingley 1978); and *The Russian Mind since Stalin's Death* (Glazov 1985).

These titles do not describe brain activity so much as they signal a need to figure out the aims of the state, a need for intelligence, often by triangulating the words of intellectuals and artists for their relation to the state. The reference to the Russian mind signals worries about what might befall those who fail to read it. On October 1, 1939, Winston Churchill famously remarked over radio: "I cannot forecast to you the action of Russia. It is a riddle, wrapped in a mystery, inside an enigma." Churchill's words still ring like an incantation, even though he went on, in fact, to predict what the USSR would soon do (perceive German expansion as aggressive). The cliché that Russia poses *special* and inscrutable puzzles lives on.

During the Cold War American scholars approached the hermeneutic puzzle allegedly posed by Russians by projecting it inward, into Soviet and Russian national character. Right after World War II, the Rand Corporation commissioned anthropologist Margaret Mead and others to conduct a study that led to a collection of essays, *Soviet Attitudes Toward Authority* (1951). The authors interviewed Soviets who had immigrated during and just after the war and argued that Soviet social life was shaped by the ways Soviet people were uniquely paranoid about deceptive enemies within, paranoid that "every individual maintains the capacity for complete betrayal of all those values to which he has hitherto shown devoted allegiance" (197).[3]

Mead and her colleagues named fear of internal enemies as alien to "the Western mind" (an odd claim, given that they had just lived through McCarthy's purges). While they acknowledged that the refugees entered interview situations conducted by officials and scholars representing the state that was granting asylum after a devastating war, they did not reflect on how such conditions primed identification of paranoia. Anthropological thinking about interview methods and contexts prompts me to consider how such research conditions resembled discursive genres such as interrogation, thus priming themes like betrayal.[4] This is not to deny the existence of discourses of betrayal in the USSR; as discussed previously, historians have amply illuminated forms of Soviet unmasking and *samokritika* ("self-criticism") in show trials, at work, in schools, and in diaries. What I do deny is the radical alterity of a "Soviet mind." I mistrust claims of a specifically Soviet "culture of dissimulation" (Shlapentokh 1984; Sinyavsky 1991) and ask whether such claims are not themselves products of circuits *for* suspicion, channels charged by their functions and closures during imperial and then Cold War conflicts, because those functions and closures, their points of contact, extended beyond the borders of either state.

Paranoia and attention to others' paranoia are both precipitates of conditions such as diplomacy and war (but see also Ngai 2005). Conditions shape demands for particular kinds of truth as useful intelligence; interview situations in service to aims of diplomacy or war strictly manage the channels for contact and structures for communicating.[5] In 1998 the head of the Russian Academy for Theatrical Arts declared, in an official pamphlet describing the departments and admissions, that theater aims to make holes in the "defensive structures" of the audience (GITIS 1998); perhaps such aggressive metaphors for theatrical communication reverberate with previous painful encounters across political rifts.

GEOPOLITICAL PARANOIA AND INTUITION

During the years when Knebel' ran telepathy drills for Soviet acting students, Americans were firing up related enchantments with intuition. The nineteenth-century movements of spiritualism and theosophy, the allied genres of gothic and science fiction, had moved into the mainstream by the 1960s. Themes of mind reading and mental control proliferated in American and British television series and films (*The Prisoner, Doctor Who, Star Trek*), as through New Age philosophy and popular publications on ESP experiments. Skeptics, too, redoubled public demonstrations to debunk ESP; belief in telepathy became a symptom of mental illness, as in the figure of the schizophrenic who receives FBI broadcasts by brain wave or claims psychic contact with aliens.[6]

In 1972 a report prepared for the U.S. Defense Intelligence Agency by the Army Medical Intelligence and Information Agency enumerated the practical military applications of extrasensory powers in ways that echoed Knebel's words on developing sensitivity and attention within technologies for intuition: "In view of [animals'] perceptive processes, it has been difficult to differentiate between those sensory processes which are merely sharpened or highly honed, and those that are extra or super-normal. Certain military advantages would come from the application and control of these perceptive processes. For example, such application and control could be used in the detection and identification of animate objects or humans through brainwave interactions, mass hypnosis or mind control through long-distance telepathy, thermal receptors, and sensitivity to changes in magnetic electrical gravitational fields" (Army Medical Intelligence and Information Agency 1972, 26). Distant acting academies and military researchers converged to suggest that matters like intuition may not emerge naturally, that structures of governance or education can improve intuition, even to make contact in new ways via "thermal receptors." In all their work about and on intuition, they could not but also effect changes across commonsense and theoretical models of communication.

American-style Cold War technologies for intuition engaged paranoia early on, later exemplified by anxiety about Madison Avenue subliminal barrages and musical messages embedded backward on vinyl, but originally over the wiles of foreign communists. The enemy seemed to spread propaganda through ever less detectable channels: How could we shut them out or even detect their invasive touch and influence? Looking back to 1962 from 2002, television critic Lee Siegel (2004) proposed "reading" the classic film *The Manchurian Candidate* (1962) as John Frankenheimer's arch commentary on Cold War paranoia that linked media to mind control. In the opening scenes, North Korean communists inject American war prisoners with psychopharmaceuticals to program them with classically Freudian associations to mechanical cues: this playing card will remind you of your mother and trigger an urge to kill. Siegel, with an eye to the director's other works critical of American-style propaganda, reads the film as subtly mocking those who during the McCarthy purges of the late 1940s rabidly accused Hollywood actors and directors of allowing ideological infiltration. They had demonized not only commie ideas—the semantic *contents* of mental influence—but also the diabolical *means* for making contact to implant ideas, techniques that were powerful because they came without words, seemingly hidden. A corrupted Hollywood would implant impulses in audiences through acting techniques, recruiting with a stage kiss:

> In the original movie, there was something suspiciously familiar about the way the Commies manipulated American minds by playing on their buried emotions. Somewhere in the depths of Manchuria, we see Soviet and Chinese spymasters implanting new memories and associations

into their [American] captives' subconscious. The film's central assassin is driven to murder by exposure to a queen-of-diamonds, which is intended to remind him of his powerful, threatening mother. The Communists in *The Manchurian Candidate* have developed a diabolical method of mind control based on memory's emotional power. It is an ingenious method. It is a highly effective method. It is, in fact, the Method. The Method style of acting, that is. Developed in Moscow by Konstantin Stanislavsky in the early 20th century, the "System," as it was first known, was composed of several principles. Chief among them was relying on "emotional memory" to play a role. . . . If the character is feeling shame, the actor might recall a humiliation in her own past that occurred in high school. . . . The Method soon became the most influential acting technique in the country. . . . At the white hot zenith of the Cold War, when Russian missiles were being aimed at American cities, tens of millions of impressionable American adolescents were learning how to walk, talk, smile, court and kiss from American actors who had been trained by left-wing, socially adversarial disseminators of the acting ideas formulated by a Russian theoretician who had had Lenin's esteem and Stalin's twisted admiration. (Siegel 2004, 17)

Siegel was onto something: the belief that acting could influence through wordless, bodily technique—*the way* a hand turns a playing card, *the way* eyes meet before a kiss. Like theories of ideology on the left, from Adorno through Bourdieu, Cold War paranoia about mind control and influence sought the forces of inculcation right here, in what comes and goes without saying.

The Manchurian Candidate foregrounded anxiety that channels not usually suspected of mediation—playing cards, gestures—might bear suspect content. Theatrical and film genres themselves could stir more such worry than could even socialist pamphlets. Even while the latter directly challenged the system in words, they rarely attracted large groups in public to read them aloud. In the theater, by contrast, all those implicit hints about "how to walk, talk, smile, and court" reached large, flesh-and-blood audiences gathered together, a visceral crowd exposed not only to foreign ideas *about* society, but also to moves that might rearrange social means for making connections.[7]

Social restructuring was, after all, the aim of avant-garde and conceptualist art and performance; its makers believed that rearrangements of forms and media, from color to architecture, could bring people into contact not only as audiences, but also as interlocutors and as actors themselves. Of course one man's fantasy of the people discovering their agency is to another the nightmare of the masses, especially when they are mesmerized by demagoguery. Jean-Jacques Rousseau, Theodor Adorno, Hannah Arendt,

Sigmund Freud, Bertolt Brecht, Georg Lukács, Jacques Rancière—all have warned of and lauded the theatrical for its effects on thought and social action.[8] Siegel suggests that McCarthy-era politicians mobilized similar logics to other ends: to rationalize blacklisting even actors, as avatars of mental penetration from Moscow.[9] Meanwhile, politicians manipulated xenophobic anxiety around unwitting contact with the Soviet in ways that fed fears of "mixing" classes or races.

CIRCLES IN CIRCLES

Scholarship on nineteenth-century European or American interest in the occult and the paranormal typically reaches beyond state borders to ask how such fascinations articulated worries about and hopes for new infrastructures and media for travel, exchange, information, and communication: the trains, steamships, and telegraphs that conquered and connected colonies. Newly mechanized means of crossing great distances along rails and wires or over the air posed new problems and possibilities. If *Dracula* expressed paranoia about military intelligence and colonial governance from the perspective of one empire's center, spiritualists and theosophists joined international movements, the struggles for abolition, suffrage, and colonial independence. Scientists and artists reforged eighteenth- and nineteenth-century formations of mesmerism and hypnosis in the crucible of industrial and colonial extractions of labor and shaped a "modern occult" of telepathy and clairvoyance just when the first European nation-states were carving their borders.

Despite scholarship recognizing movement, it is rare for discussion of the Russian paranormal to cross borders. Other Russian and Soviet topics, like film and theater, have long received transnational treatment. The traces are easier to discern: the products and their makers and performers traveled, and so left tracks, allowing scholars to follow editing techniques from Sergei Eisenstein to Alfred Hitchcock, to see where MGM producers studied the Soviet avant-garde (Eagle 1992). To be fair, transnational approaches to almost any other Soviet or Russian phenomena are rare.[10]

Anglophone media typically depict "Russian fascination" with the occult as homegrown. British journalist Marc Bennetts wonders "where Russia's eternal passion for the paranormal and the occult will take it?" (2012, 8). Decades earlier, researchers for the U.S. Department of Defense (DoD) similarly summarized intelligence on Eastern bloc paranormal research. Even while allowing that "investigation of paranormal mental phenomena generally began during the latter part of the 1800s in various countries," and even after crediting imperial scientific luminaries Dmitry Mendeleyev and Naum Kotik for studying "thought transmission" in order to "separate natural phenomena from mysticism," the DoD researchers nevertheless fell back on asserting that "the Soviet public in general has always appeared open to mystical type phenomena, an openness that was somewhat officially acknowledged by Czar Nicholas II and his family's association with the highly controversial Rasputin" (Air Force Systems Command 1978, 11).

Reference to Rasputin and the imperial family finds its way again and again into documentaries, articles, and books anchoring mysticism to the Russian soul and soil, imposing the myth of the nation-state over a world whose powers were constituted in imperial circuits. Consider the circular knots of imperial kinship, the aristocratic matches that linked European capitals while bringing rulers to rule in places far from where they were raised. The last tsar, Nicholas, was first cousin to Britain's King George V and to three other European monarchs (Christian X of Denmark, Constantine I of Greece, and Haakon VII of Norway). The tsarina was born Alix of Hesse and by Rhine, in Darmstadt, then part of the German Empire. A granddaughter of Queen Victoria of Britain, she was already related to her husband as a second cousin (both were great-grandchildren of Princess Wilhelmina of Baden). Alix came to Russia at age twenty-two and was given the name Alexandra Feodorovna upon being received into the Russian Orthodox Church, but unlike Catherine the Great, she never learned much Russian. The last tsarina kept close company with the monk Rasputin, having brought interest in spiritualism with her.

American scholars and journalists may be adept at linking local American problems to distant causes (e.g., the loss of jobs to foreign industries, loss of votes to foreign meddling), but we are less motivated to see such links elsewhere, asking "Why are Russians given to mysticism?" without registering the extent to which "Russian mysticism" is also the product of diplomacy and conflict, and neglecting all the skeptics in Russia who have influenced our own skeptics. We will get further if we also ask: How did we learn to pose such questions in terms of inherent dispositions or national traits rather than historical entanglements? Who asks them, how, and to what ends?

Points of foreign connection are more apparent in Russian-language sources than in texts created by the DoD. Here is an example: in a Russian documentary titled *Telepatija* (*Teorija Neverojatnosti*, October 23, 2006; dir. Baxrusheva), a female engineer recounts her career path to becoming a leading paranormal expert during Soviet times. In the 1960s she had worked at the Institute for the Study of Information Transfer in Moscow, where she did not herself work in one of the telepathy labs, "but got a whiff of them in the *kurilki.*" The Soviet "smoking corner" nested divisions of public and private—stairwells near a *fortuchka,* balconies, little nooks for conversation which, like talk around the kitchen table, some treated as if outside the system even as the system built those spaces for contact in the first place (see also Humphrey 2005). In this case, the smoking corner for telepathy tales was tucked within an institution itself sustained in order to communicate about communication.

Many institutions like this one extend across borders, and for scholars to trace lines through them, instead of within state boundaries, loosens the hold of exceptional claims. This book juxtaposes and connects moments of encounter that cross specifically Russian (or Soviet) and U.S. borders. It attempts to do so concretely and symmetrically—without assuming either position as neutral or standard (Latour 1993; Chakrabarty 1995)—while also suggesting how a history of implicit comparisons has led us astray.

Rather than staging closed, site-based comparisons, the chapters juxtapose and connect among places, encounters, and texts through a filament running across their terrains, through problems of *contact.* This book thus aims to serve as an analysis of the historical grounds and categories for contact and failures of contact, whereby mediations, be they through words and gestures, broadcast and print, or even by telepathy ray, are recognized as more or less material, more or less subsumed into both contact and its obstacles.

BATTLE OF THE PSYCHICS

One fascinating site for seeing these issues brought into explicit discussion is the Russian-language *Bitva Ekstrasensov,* or *Battle of the Psychics,* a reality show first developed in Sweden and the United Kingdom, then picked up in Israel, Ukraine, Bulgaria, Mongolia, the United States, and other places.[11] An entire book could compare the variants. The formula adapts the form's magic shows and demonstrations of occult debunking going back a long time. In the 1970s *The Amazing Kreskin!* was broadcast from Canada, inviting guests to discuss the paranormal or demonstrate their skills. In 1972 Kreskin invited the authors of *Psychic Discoveries Behind the Iron Curtain* to discuss famous Soviet telepaths such as Wolf Messing and footage they had brought back demonstrating telekinesis, and to banter about how they had been "banned in Russia"—because sections of the book were read on the air by Radio Liberty, the American organization broadcasting to the Soviet bloc since World War II.

The U.S. version of *Battle, America's Psychic Challenge,* lasted only half a season in 2007 (the Russian was past its seventeenth season by 2017). We cannot credit its cancellation to American sophistication regarding the occult; U.S. media are saturated with supernatural plots, talk shows with mediums, and ghost-seeking reality shows (Bastien 2010). On the contrary, cheery confidence in magical forces suffused *America's Psychic Challenge*: the game host, the voice-over, and even the musical sound track all introduced each scene with breathy, hushed expectation. By contrast, the Russian *Battle of the Psychics,* ranked number one for several years running, poses tests of extrasensory detection and telepathic contact after which experts debate, evaluate performances, and eliminate losers. Dramatic conflict sets wishful psychics against each other and their skeptics. In the American version, neither the host, the narrators, nor any formal elements indicate the slightest note of skeptical challenge. As Lamont (2013, 228) notes, psychics commonly blame their failures on interference from a hostile or skeptical audience, and the American show's producers made sure nothing like this disrupted the action. Bright, optimistic affect ruled tone and tempo, even when the host had to tell a contestant that she had earned only 12 of 25 points. In *America's Psychic Challenge,* all participants were perfectly groomed and styled, always smiling, never tired, never worn out. And there was no discussion of how or why contestants failed, no accusations of faking or psychic weakness; points alone were added to calculate success, without additional review.

The Russian version, in contrast, frames each scene with questioning rigor. A few times per episode, a narrating voice stresses that "this is just an experiment," that viewers are free to judge—"decide yourselves"—whether the phenomena on display are real. Multiple frames jostle, cuing the viewer to recognize frames within frames, as layers of experts talk about how the psychics make telepathic contact or communicate with another dimension. This editing strategy attracts engagement—as comments testify on fan websites devoted to judging how the judges do their judging. Viewers watch skeptics and experts set up double-blinds and controls, watch the crew position multiple cameras. In one episode, before the psychics search for a plastic bomb hidden in an empty stadium, the crew times a search dog and a platoon of soldiers—the dog finds it quickly, and the platoon needs a bit more time, but only one of the psychics comes close.

We watch people whom the producers have hired to be observed while observing: a psychologist who claims to have worked in military ESP labs in the 1960s and three young magicians, brothers "who sniff out any tricks," because their very "profession it is to fool the public." All of these differently skeptical experts trail behind each psychic, checking procedures, adjusting boxes and blindfolds, asking questions, and setting limits as the host reminds viewers that the tests are modeled after laboratory science, to follow protocols for randomization and double-blind. These experts also monitor video screens (sometimes alongside participating civilians), commenting throughout: "She is feeling the rails, she's just using deduction"; "He's studying her eyes for a reaction." In this way, even apparent successes become failures as the experts deconstruct *how* the deeds are done: "too much talk," "using too many senses."

The expert panel format is familiar to the genre everywhere, as well as to telepathy shows on variety stages in the Soviet and Russian imperial eras. We might compare them to U.S. shows like *Project Runway*, for its public shaming, or *MythBusters* for its debunkings (see also Hanks 2016). This makes the American version something of an outlier, as it does not even attempt to stage controls—the contrast also undermines any claims that Americans are less prone than Russians to magical thinking. Although back in the 1970s Johnny Carson brought professional magician James Randi onstage to unmask Uri Geller, and magicians like Penn and Teller make entertainment of debunking others on stage, in the twenty-first century such skeptical shows are at least equaled in America by shows that amplify the mystical without question. They achieve this amplification by technical means and collective efforts to focus perception of contacts and communication. Mentalist John Edwards, for example, performs for audiences who do not see the panorama of facial expressions from which Edwards, observing from the stage, can choose (and for broadcast, the cameras avoid capturing this view). His viewers lack access to a range of minute details that performers from the stage can see to select among (better to choose more mobile faces for easier readings).

As a number of anthropologists have argued, spirals of skepticism themselves enchant magic, the occult, and the paranormal.[12] Indeed, the number of contestants who complain in interviews, blogs, or biographies that others cheat seems only to have increased viewership. One of the show's experts even recounted how, during the first season, a contestant arranged to take her turn at a test last, to gain time to glean information from the crew. Another former contestant countered similar judgments against him, claiming in a number of forums that the show's editors manipulated video cuts to make the contestants look like charlatans. To trick people into believing that someone else has tried to trick them seems indeed to incite involvement, to have further developed into a rewarding spiral upon which to capitalize.

COLD WAR CONTACTS

Technologies to intuit "the shadow of a quickly hidden smile" compete across specific tangles of institutional relations and geopolitical interests, in conflict even as they connect. Relations of conflicted connection—and connection across conflict—are difficult to articulate even under the best of conditions. For decades anthropologists and historians have tried to follow social networks and circuits for ideas and techniques across geopolitical borders, through boardrooms and shipping lanes, mapping points where goods and bodies, words and images, government structures and corporate franchises touch ground across borders.[13] Despite their work, relations across borders are rendered subversive and unpatriotic—or invisible, incoherent to the story of a nation. To account for affiliations across borders that involve people or things tagged as belonging to a geopolitical opponent is even more problematic.[14]

Barriers and broadcast points built or maintained during the Cold War retained force even after walls came down. Some barriers transcend any particular conflict: State Department rules forbid diplomatic staff to fraternize with locals and refuse security clearance to people who maintain too many foreign contacts. Such practices aim to regulate borders by delimiting not just spaces, but also channels for communication, constraining certain kinds of contact in ways that affect the imagination of possible social bonds, that project the purposes of communication or imagine its futility. As Vincent Rafael has argued regarding communication during military conflicts, "war bears some relationship to the movement of translation that leads not to the privileging of meaning but to the emergence of the untranslatable . . . translation in a time of war intensifies the experience of untranslatability" (2007, 8; see also Galison 2012).

All the same, even at the height of the Cold War, science fiction writers fashioned characters who breached Cold War walls—and *not* to manipulate minds or wills, but to share discoveries, usually discoveries to do precisely with breaches in conventional barriers to communication or to travel. Soviet science fiction writers especially sowed texts with footnotes to foreign publications, sending scientist protagonists to conferences in New York or Tokyo.[15] Science fiction heroes sought contact beyond the bounds of planet—never mind the the bounds of nation. In real life, Soviets aspired to this future in ways that fewer Americans cottoned to; the USSR educated not only the most literate population, but among the most multilingual, who read and listened to media in more languages than did most Americans.

In regard to telepathy science alone, Soviets commanded more detail about experiments conducted in the West than was true the other way around (Ostrander and Schroeder 1970, 9). Late Soviet newspapers followed the labs of Dr. Rhine at Duke University and the exploits of Dutch psychic detective Gerard Croiset. Soviet citizens understood paranormal science much as they did film, literature, and theater: as simultaneously cosmopolitan and homegrown.

With this in mind, consider the insights of communications scholar John Peters, who has masterfully argued that European anxieties about communicative contact took shape as new media confronted people with new problems, which we projected onto more familiar ways to communicate: "[L]ost letters, wrong numbers, dubious signals from the dead, downed wires and missed deliveries have since come to describe the vexations of face-to-face converse as well. Communication as a person-to-person activity became thinkable only in the shadow of mediated communication. Mass communication came first" (1999, 6). Peters rightly suggests that dreams for perfect communitas came into being mainly when means and materials for communicating multiplied: "The history of thinking about our mutual ties, as well as the history of modes for connections, from writing to the development of electrical media, shows that the quest for consummation with others is motivated by the experience of blockage and breakdown" (268).

Communicative infelicities and broken contacts *are* ubiquitous. For this book, the next question to ask is: Whose experiences of breakdown, of downed wires or radio static, do we have in mind? Experiences differ less because of inherent qualities in either people or in media and more because states and localities differently organize relations among media, differently politicize genres and situations for communication, and differently rank and separate those who can broadcast, publish, and stand at the microphone from those whose access to channels is more limited. Channels for speaking, writing, and acting are historically configured not only by the material affordances of media, but also through divisions of labor and authority, separations in time and space. The sound of static only *partly* defines an experience of failed radio contact. A person trying to tune a shortwave radio in mid-twentieth-century Perm' encountered disturbance differently than did the person in Omaha. The static may have sounded different through jamming, for one thing. Moreover, ideologies *about* media in each place, similar in some ways, differed (Gershon 2010). They differed increasingly—or claimed to—by mirroring and reversing relations imagined on the other side of the so-called Iron Curtain, the cold war a spectacular display of what Gregory Bateson (1936) called *symmetrical schismogenesis*:

the process of differentiation through competitive and dyadic mirroring (in his case, to exaggerate the differences among genders).

Certainly local experiences and events also determine access to media and affect ideologies about them. World War II, for example, destroyed Soviet infrastructure and communications in ways that most Americans cannot imagine. The sheer number of dead compounded a loss akin to that of post–Civil War America, under devastation of which spiritualism found a welcome among those who were missing kin. A twenty-first-century Russian documentary titled *Telepatija* opens with such loss, with specific mortalities from that war, not vague superpower paranoia, including a woman recounting her mother's intuition that her father had not been killed at the front, as a telegram had informed the family. Years later the state released the records—indeed, her father had died not during the war, but in a prison camp in 1947.

So rather than assuming a generalized historicism under which to explain modern worries about contact, this book both contrasts and connects specific events, texts, situations, and institutions, following them across state borders when that is where they point. From archives and ethnography it tracks how, for example, accusations of radio jamming or book burning paralleled expressions of longing for romantic communion and fantasies for telepathic connection or interstellar contact. In the end, neither U.S. nor post-Soviet anxieties and dreams about communication and contact can be understood purely in local terms, in relation only to local ideologies or media ecologies. Anxieties about communicative intuition, about one's own capacities to read through what we are taught are barriers of radical alterity, run up and down scales: worries about courtship (American men puzzling over e-mails from Siberian brides) morph into myths of diplomacy (Can the president divine the mind of a counterpart?). In the laboratory, on the stage, in broadcasts to outer space, and "in the heart,"[16] people draw from other situations and scales, from story and from experience, in efforts to make and break channels to communicate—or even to intuit more subtle rays of contact, as thought, as feeling, as impulse.

Several anthropologists have argued that inclinations to imagine the thoughts of others are not universal—that some peoples simply regard the minds of others as opaque. Others counter that to avoid claims about others' thoughts need not indicate belief that they are unknowable. Linguistic anthropologist Niko Besnier (1992), building on Schieffelin (1990), argued that where he did fieldwork, people avoided bald conjectures about others' inner states—but they also devised covert ways, through prosody, tempo, and volume, to shade quotations of others' words in ways that conveyed opinions about motives or goals. Others have since agreed that people may well wonder what someone else is thinking, yet refrain from speculating out loud,[17] in deference to ethical and hierarchical sensibilities about good and appropriate ways to speak and to be silent.

Imperatives to read or to avoid reading others' minds divide along with other communicative and emotional labors: *some* people are charged to represent the thoughts or emotions or motives of certain others, exhorted to aspire to do so; others are not. Some face consequences for misreading the boss's wishes; others do not. Talk about others' minds emerges in historical, social, and geopolitical conditions that figure such talk as dangerous and strange, or as important and coherent.

Anthropologists have long attended to the ways people take interest in others' perspectives, minds, and judgments. Nancy Munn, in *The Fame of Gawa* (1986) theorized chains of labors through which Gawans invested in being well-thought-of as a collective, in trying to shape others' future memories and return words and actions. It troubled people that despite all their labor, they might yet be unsure about others' present and future judgments, whether they would value and remember the luster of gifts or heartiness of meals. Similar uncertainty plays out in American advertising and election campaigns—similar but not the same, for the creative ad maker works in a world in which fame and accumulation and hierarchy connect differently than they did in 1970s Gawa.

Feminist, postcolonial, and race-critical scholarship is useful here. Histories of race and class inequalities and violence set material infrastructure and social conditions for the situational politics that hinder or encourage speaking at all, let alone speaking about others' communications or thoughts. Scholars such as Henry Louis Gates, for example, theorize how people "signify on" others' unstated purposes or assumptions indirectly, through verbal style, prosody, and other means (see Morgan 2002), and link this indirectness to histories of slavery. Scholars of gender have outlined social institutions that discourage men from wondering what others are thinking even as they press women with the imperative to anticipate others' thoughts or feelings (Hochschild 1983; Ochs and Taylor 1996). In this light, we can begin to ask what conditions motivate searching for others' "Theory of Mind" or that find that they lack one. To understand this would require some sociohistorical accounting for how theories are made.[18]

The linguistic anthropologists and other scholars I have just cited arrived at many of their insights about the ways social and political relationships condition the possibilities of speaking through analytical tools developed by Russian scholars—specifically Valentin Voloshinov and Mikhail Bakhtin in

1920s Moscow. That they were empowered to do so just as the twentieth-century Cold War peaked and waned tells us something about the politics of translation, conversation, and connection across rival borders that we have yet to understand.

POINT TO LINE

Our starting point in this chapter, from which we trace further circles and rays, was the Russian Academy for Theatrical Arts. Established in 1878 as the Shestakovsky Music School, it was renamed the Musico-Dramatic School of the Moscow Philharmonic Society in 1883, becoming a conservatory in 1886. In 1934 it reformed as the Lunacharsky State Institute for Theatrical Arts (GITIS). Renamed after 1991 the Russian Academy for Theatrical Arts (RATI), it remains known as GITIS. The largest and oldest theatrical arts academy in Russia, with a student body of about fifteen hundred, GITIS competes with a handful of academies in other cities and teaching studios affiliated with theaters, such as the studio at the Moscow Art Theater (MKhAT), the Schepkina (Maly Theater), and the Schukina (Vakhtangov). GITIS was the first to devote training to stage directors after the Revolution, and in the 1960s it began training special actor groups within each directing cohort, giving them acting students with whom to practice communication. Each cohort now brings together eight to ten aspiring directors with about twenty actors and actresses. I conducted fieldwork in that department from 2002 to 2003 and in 2005.

GITIS aspires to combine styles, to draw teachers and directors from across the country's theaters: Maria Knebel', for example, directed at the Children's Theater in Moscow. Even under the hegemony of socialist realism, each school was said to develop a trademark style: the studio at the Kamerny began with principles of ballet, the Maly with mimetic etudes. GITIS stands apart also through breadth: it encompasses all aspects of stage work, accommodating faculty in choreography, stage diction, circus management, variety production, dramatic criticism, theatrical history, costuming, set design, and so forth. The faculty for stage movement occupy their own low building, furnished with a magnificent, polished hardwood and a sprung dance floor, surrounded by risers and gymnastics equipment, where one can learn everything necessary to choreograph and perform elaborate combat scenes without leaving campus (since 2009 the campus has expanded to include a grand new facility across town). By the time students leave, they are expected to have forged enduring professional contacts—and later to find just the person to create the effect of soft rain on moss, or to play a theremin.

GITIS is a dense node of cultural and social production, condensing and concentrating resources and networks, admitting some while evicting others. In coldest winter at GITIS, someone had opened the *fortochka* to release excess heat. Such steady delivery of heat is not always the case across Russian territory,[19] but we were in the center of the center, near the avenue carrying government cavalcades each morning to the Kremlin. Few in the room were native to this place; more than half had come from afar, thousands of kilometers away, from Irkutsk, Ekaterinburg, Rzan', Surgut . . . and a handful from still other, farther cosmopolitan centers—Doha, Seoul, Paris, Stockholm. Small groups from America visited for a week or so. Many teachers hailed from the provinces, having settled in Moscow decades before. Now the cohort I know best has dispersed, working in Vladivostok and Riga, on film sets in ja Siberia or in South America; some return triumphantly to Moscow openings. Several have become stars, gone to Cannes or Broadway, choreographed in Hollywood. Some are not (yet) famous, but work steadily in television and theater, and some supplement this work with acting lessons for businessmen. A few have left the profession. But back then, in that studio, biographies from beyond the moment submerged, reemerging only in short bursts as we focused on making contact with each other here and now.

A *fortochka* works with a building's system of *kommunikatsija*, its networks of cables, pipes, and wires carrying water, electricity, sound, and data (the analogous English usage of "communications" can be found among U.S. building professionals). The Russian word *kommunikatsija* can be used to talk about human communication,[20] and metaphors about communication as infrastructure abound (Stalin likened language to railway tracks), to inflect the ways material conditions in Russia are ideologically burdened.[21] Russian pipes built above summer bog and winter ice, over and under streets, come under foreign critique as ugly, too visceral. Such criticism demonstrates disregard for sound reasons to build above marsh and permafrost; fuel and water pipes rupture underground, as America is learning, and we might learn better. Russian communication, too, comes under too quick criticism. In this light, a telepathy lesson that opens a *fortochka* is bound to be misread unless we cross borders drawn during the Cold War.

1. Do We Have Contact?

This book connects and contrasts hitherto separately treated places, practices, and situations, following actors and psychics and those who cross their paths. Others have written about Soviet theater or about telepathy science as distinct topics, and in rich and insightful ways. This project instead sniffs along the edges where fields of expertise converge and diverge. Some of these overlaps are easy to see, such as when American security forces hire psychologists like Paul Ekman or when Russian detectives quote Constantine Stanislavsky.

In 1996 I started to collect books from street vendors near Moscow metro stations, books that forged hybrids of theatrical and criminological knowledge, branding technologies for intuition, like *What Is in His Subconscious? Twelve Lessons in the Psychotechnology of Penetrating the Subconscious of Your Interlocutor* (*A chto u nego v podsoznanii? Dvenadtsat' urokov po psikhotekhnologii proniknovenija v podsoznanie sobesednika*). The author, psychologist Aleksandr Panasjuk, begins by challenging the Russian proverb asserting that one must "eat a pound of salt" together in order to know and then to trust: "That is what they say who do not know the science of psychology. For science maintains that one can decipher another person in a few seconds!" (1996, 12).

Panasjuk then voices the retort of an imaginary reader: "But what if they are acting?" He reassures us that even the greatest actors have limits— even Innokenty Smoktunovsky, the Soviet-era star whose repertoire ranged from Prince Hamlet to Prince Myshkin, could never pull off a decent Lenin. It follows that ordinary people find it even more difficult "to act" all the time. Therefore, if your interlocutor does not want you to intuit what he is feeling, he must work quite hard. Diplomats, yogis, professional actors, and the like may have taken the time to train themselves to limit and control their gestures and tone, to tame their automatic tells—but rest assured, most mortals have not mastered the control: "If your partner has not studied in special schools or internalized Stanislavsky's system in the theatrical institute, then it will be incredibly hard for him not to manifest, through unconscious behavioral reactions, his true stance" (Panasjuk 1996, 46). Readers are promised specialized techniques from psychology and theater for penetrating an other's subconscious—if not to read thoughts, then at least to discern attitudes.

Scholars working elsewhere have theorized similar intersections across scientific experimentation; art; demonstrations of the magical, occult, or paranormal; and to some extent criminology,[1] demonstrating where similar aesthetic and technical conventions regulate attention and focus in ritual, in the lab, and behind the proscenium arch. Lights go on and off, doors, curtains, and windows open and close, sorting and separating senders from receivers, setting up barriers to some senses and channels for others, and segregating or linking actors and audiences, subjects and experimenters.[2]

It is commonplace to assert that just as modernity produces tradition, science produces the occult,[3] and that new forms of media motivate and empower mediumship.[4] Such claims warrant more thinking at the intersections. Luckhurst (2002) argues that telepathy is magic gone modern. In making this claim, he and other scholars identify junctures among formally distinct, public arenas ("law," "ritual") and more diffuse forms of sociality. They describe the nineteenth-century turn to spiritualism and hypnosis as echoing fears and hopes about messages crossing once inconceivable distances. Telepathy, psychokinesis, and all the paranormal powers did more than merely run alongside the novelties of mass printing, trains and telegraphs, radio and film, and now the cell phone and the digital image.[5] Strong feelings both for sounds transmitted along thin wires and for voices from the ether animated the extension of empires and states (see especially Galvan 2010, 2015).

Perspective matters a great deal to this story: because perspectives are both many and limited, I do not claim to paint a general landscape of fields, even within one country.[6] As a sociocultural, linguistic, and historical anthropologist, trained both to be attuned to interactions and to search the archives, my goals are not to catalog taxonomies, to distill origins, or even to posit causal explanations. I am motivated instead by questions like this one: As people move among situations, from the bureaucratic to the magical to the mundane, for whom do which channels seem clear? For whom are which channels invisible? Who aims for, who avoids, which contacts? How do these social facts constrain and enable human actions or even a sense of the possible?

In this book I move among settings in which professionals encounter neophytes; skeptics meet so-called naives; and outsiders and insiders trade places, mixing metaphors and trading tools as they debate and imitate, invent and borrow. Literary critics on talk show panels accuse telepaths of acting. Sociologists claim that fortune-tellers are no worse than telephone therapists. Stage magicians collaborate with film actors and consult with former military paranormal researchers on reality shows that debunk "bad psychics" as "just good psychologists."

Other scholars have brilliantly described Russian and Soviet sorcery, orthodox miracles, shamanism, folk healing, the occult, and the paranormal in local and regional terms, demonstrating complex relations and connections to economic patterns, regime change, and local scientific history.[7] Such works address literary and scientific struggles around the occult before and during Soviet times, the needs of late Soviet and post-Soviet clients seeking alternative treatment or spiritual counseling, the controversies surrounding UFO sightings, the legality of licensing nonmedically trained healers, and other topics.

Likewise, other scholars have explored theatrical movements across Russia and the Soviet Union, linking avant-garde, realist, and documentary work to political formations and social changes[8] and situating theatrical agents and projects in fascinating ways, while giving them their due as creative aesthetic projects—for example, exploring Soviet amateur theaters (Mally 2000) or twenty-first-century ventures such as teatr.doc in Moscow, whose participants draft scripts verbatim from interviews with homeless people, migrants, and prisoners (Weygandt 2015). Many have argued that aesthetic struggles regarding performance in Russia, and performances themselves, have shaped events and social patterns, as Russian artists hoped they would do, vesting lines of poetry and stage props with revolutionary—and even occult—agency.[9] Regimes both deify and destroy poets and directors, journalists and scientists, because they, too, worry about the effects of communication, even in play and fantasy,[10] in changing the world.

A U.S. Department of Defense report on telepathy science cites *Pravda* as describing the "showmanship aspects of some psychic subjects" (Air Force Systems Command 1978), a comment pointing to actual overlaps of expertise among personnel in the Soviet experiments. In the 1960s, when telepathy, telekinesis, and dermo-optics emerged as topics for public debate in the USSR, the newspapers prominently reported the results of tests with people like actor-director Boris Ermolaev and actor Karl Nikolaev (né Nikolaj Gurvich). Ermolaev had started life following in his father's footsteps, studying psychiatry with Leonid Vasiljev, a researcher of psychic phenomena and hypnotism since the 1930s (Vasiljev 2002). Encouraged by a neighbor, famous Soviet stage director Georgii Tovstonogov, he switched to the film institute in Moscow, following a childhood dream nurtured in Alma Ata, where his family had rubbed elbows with wartime evacuees such as Sergei Eisenstein. Ermolaev's networks spliced together theatrical and paranormal work.

Nikolaev's interest in psychic work was sparked more accidentally, at a working intersection of stage and magic. During World War II, while on leave in Hungary, Nikolaev attended a performance by hypnotist and telepath Orlando. Once he had returned to Moscow, he read everything he could find on psychic phenomena, seeking out Wolf Messing, the Soviet Union's most famous magician. Messing, born in 1899 in a Jewish village in Poland under imperial Russian rule, toured European stages until he moved to the USSR in the late 1930s. He worked onstage as an *illjuzionist* (magician) for *Goskontsert* (state concerts) from the 1940s until his death in 1974, with a specialty in exhibitions of mind reading and hypnosis. By the time Maria Knebel' spoke of the theatrical work of intuiting contact through analogy to telepathy, connections among the paranormal and the theatrical were not just metaphorical, but historically linked professional specializations.

In 1968 American writers Sheila Ostrander and Lynn Schroeder made a pilgrimage to the USSR to meet a number of these psychics, doing research for *Psychic Discoveries Behind the Iron Curtain* (1970) Nikolaev is the second person they introduce to readers in the book (after their host, the organizer of an international Moscow conference on extrasensory perception [ESP], rogue biologist and parapsychologist Edward Naumov). They report Nikolaev as saying that his extrasensory powers "made me a better actor. I find it easier now to get into the lives of people I play. I tune in better to other actors and am more sensitive to the audiences," and that "anyone can learn to develop it." Nikolaev recounts how he taught himself, with help from his friends (fellow actors, quite possibly, as he describes tasks that recall theatrical academy drills): "They'd think: 'Light a cigarette.' . . . 'Ok, change your mind and crush it out.'" Nikolaev was keen to draw historical threads between his acting and his work with scientists, linking them through a common lineage, stressing that both psychic and theatrical labor relies on practices from yoga to relax mind and body: "Did you know that Stanislavsky developed his famous acting methods through the study of yoga? He believed an actor must eliminate all muscular tensions before going onstage. Stanislavsky thought that tensions or 'clamps' on the nerves block real freedom of motion and expression" (Ostrander and Schroeder 1970, 23–25).

One of the resident experts on early seasons of *Battle of the Psychics*, psychologist and criminologist Mikhail Vinogradov, by his own account has lived across all these professional intersections. Over the years I had several opportunities to meet experts like Vinogradov, who repeats much of what he says on air in biographical publications.[11] In the 1960s and 1970s he worked in government labs running experiments on thought transmission, hypnosis, and modes of extrasensory perception such as tactile vision (feeling color as heat) and other claims to synesthesia. He appears now on twenty-first-century television shows that repurpose the Soviet-era experiments, embedding in television performance both the experiments' conventions and recollections of the personalities who undertook them. Vinogradov developed his specialty in detecting psychic channels when, as an intern in medical school, he was called upon to evaluate self-proclaimed hypnotists who showed up at the lab. He later discovered his own talent for clairvoyance and worked on a team of psychologists screening people who asserted that they could see U.S. submarines. His age, smooth gestures, measured tones, and credentials add gravity to the seasons in which he appeared, administering trials to hopeful contestants and sounding out final judgments. ("She is a strong *ekstrasens*"; "No extra-sensation was involved in this contact.") He sometimes spoke against the other experts on the show, setting them straight about how probability works or about the physics of brain waves. Editors would intercut his face and words after tests to stress the historical connection to Soviet-era research: "We used to see this all the time in the lab." After a few seasons on air, Vinogradov expanded to collaborate more with law enforcement, opening the Vinogradov Center, where past winners of the show work as associates, devoted to finding missing persons. At its sister center, Volshebnaja Sila (Enchanted Forces), other protégés focus on healing.

THE PHATIC FUNCTION

It is common for Americans to describe the Soviet Union in terms of failed contacts: diplomatic snafus, postal failures, radio interference, and media censorship. Less common is to attend to ways the Iron Curtain generated excess communications, contacts, and channels, even beyond the little openings created by official exchanges, shows of contact among heads of state.[12]

To work in a more robust way, we need the concept of the phatic. The Greek *phatos* simply means "spoken" or "that which is spoken." English and other languages carry the root in words like aphasia (loss of speech) or apophasis (the device of feigning not to speak about a subject while doing so: "I hope no one brings up what happened last time."). Scholars have used the term *phatic* to address conditions for communication, the channels, media, and practices that open contact or cut it off.

Anthropologist Bronislaw Malinowski used the phrase "phatic communion" narrowly, to describe language that affirms or establishes social relations, "a type of speech in which ties of union are created by a mere exchange of words" (1923, 315), such as weather talk and greetings and questions such as "What's new?," which are best answered not with information but with acknowledgment: "Nothing much. You?" (Those of us struggling with literal mindedness stutter, trying to recall what is truly new; others are smoother with phatic niceties.) Similar difficulties are matters not only of personal inclination, but also of rank or social distance, as they affect expectations about phaticity in specific contexts.

Russophone-Anglophone-polyglot[13] linguist and formalist critic Roman Jakobson differentiated the *phatic function* from other speech functions, which he labeled referential, expressive, conative, metalinguistic, poetic. Linguistic anthropologists influenced by Jakobson have added more functions to the list and have demonstrated that when people speak, they usually activate more than one language function at a time.[14] If the officer at passport control says, "Show me your passport," the words both refer (to papers and to you), serving a *referential function*, and also prod a response, serving a *conative* function (in this case, as a directive). If the officer were to say, "Pass your passports, passengers!" the phrase would cover those same functions and might also activate the *poetic* function (with repetitions of sound drawing attention to form). Playing with tone and volume to hone and deliver attitude would add *expressive function*.

Words or gestures that establish, check, or close a channel or the media for transmission fulfill a *phatic function*. "Hello!? Hello? Do you read?" If you stand still and unresponsive in the passport line you may hear something sharper than a polite, "Are you listening?" If a colleague decides that this definition of the word *phatic* misses something and tells me so, then we are working through a *metalinguistic function*.[15] While metalinguistic acts are peculiar to humans, other metacommunicative acts are not. Gregory Bateson saw practices of metacommunication among all sentient creatures: "If we were to translate the cat's message into words, it would not be correct to say that she is crying 'Milk!' Rather, she is saying something like 'Ma-ma!' Or perhaps still more correctly, we should say that she is asserting: 'Dependency! Dependency!'" (1972, 372).[16] The cat is concerned not with naming milk (the referential function) but with drawing attention to the relationship here and now, with affecting the nature of contact.

Jakobson's meta-functions—the poetic, the phatic, and the metalinguistic—are among the means by which people communicate the forms and conditions of communication and by which they address expectations about what language can do or how signs work; and about which means of communicating are moral, which are appropriate or inappropriate, and which ways of speaking, writing, signing, or being silent are thought to indicate what about people—or about certain people and not others.[17] Matters of linguistic and semiotic ideology become political matters.

Perhaps because it is associated with certain forms of contact over others, the phatic is often neglected, its expressions downgraded as "mere" and "empty" words (see Nozawa 2015; cf. Elyachar 2010; Kockelman 2010; and Lemon 2013). Perhaps the phatic is neglected *because* attention to it is so telling: to speak *about* efforts to open or close communication can be discouraged as rude or awkward; like pointing out the emperor's new clothes, questioning a greeting (or its lack) can draw attention to hierarchies or to rifts running through social encounters. It can be difficult enough to question the definition of a word without debate and insult; even more so, discussing phatic acts brings social and technical arrangements for communication into focus, potentially clarifying coercion and conflict that are usually left unexamined, are part of doxa or dogma, or are even taken as natural.

If acts that deny contact can seem injurious—even a brusque "Huh?" at least acknowledges what the blank stare disregards—too much checking in can intrude, grate, or be read as micromanagement, disrespect, and nagging: "You never write! You never call!" Richard Bauman (1998) addresses exactly this issue, relating struggles over phatic language to political struggles, showing phatic acts to be political acts, by documenting seventeenth-century Quakers' refusal to utter greetings. They called them "idle words" that did not describe God-given reality, recoiling from "empty" formulae like "good day," and repudiated vain titles of address and honorifics like "sir." Their refusals to utter anything but words displaying pure referential functions irritated and enraged the non-Quakers around them, earning them hostility and beatings.

Attention to the phatic—especially to competing *claims* about contacts and channels for communication—sheds light on how some interactions become more visible and come to be regarded as more important than others, which are submerged or neglected as mundane or private. It also helps us to see which kinds of channels or contacts pose problems, for whom: Why does person A listen to person B only when person C is not present?

How do outsiders learn the right small talk (the right topics with the right ironic attitude, etc.) to scale professional ladders? Debates over phatic issues bring ideals about social configurations into relief: imperatives to seek a "liberal democratic form of phatic communion involving citizens and state alike" on equal footings (Slotta 2015, 132) aim at different ideals than do exhortations to avoid "going over the boss's head," violating hierarchical report channels. When newcomers or former underlings have demanded honorifics or insisted on equal time at the microphone, others have dismissed such moves as "political correctness" or have even grabbed microphones, confiscated typewriters, or otherwise cut channels.

One question that arises when we leave face-to-face methods to communicate is: Are these functions relevant when words stretch across space and time, in print text or in film? I posit that they are, working by analogy from the observation that even nonworking channels thread through or cut across our lives and that even language functions that seem to fail make something happen. If I call soup "ice cream," the referential function is still active even if its aim is off. Similarly, if I write, "Can you see this font?" you may never answer me—here too is an apparent failure, attributable to time and space conditions. That silence, however, negates neither the phatic attempt nor the material channel. In fact, the ways people attribute or deny channels or the possibilities for contact regardless of time and space limitations are matters of social and political contestation and control. Even when no contact is made, phatic attempts and judgments tell us something important about the shapes, materials, and experiences of social connections and rifts.

To prevent contact can intensify phatic communications, or multiply them across jammed channels and cut lines. "No one is home." "Don't bother talking to them." "No one can hear you": such statements are as often social judgments as they are descriptive meta-communicative statements. To better capture the meanings and effects surrounding and spun out by apparent failures or blockages, I turn to the category of *interpretants*, as formulated by pragmatic semiotic philosopher C. S. Peirce. An interpretant happens whenever a sentient being takes anything to be a sign. Peirce distinguished several kinds of interpretants, from ideational concepts and symbolic associations to responses: goose bumps and laughter can count as interpretants. Any interpretant can be taken up as a sign by still another (or even by the same) sentience. The initial sign-vehicle, be it a word, a gesture, a plume of smoke, can not fully determine possible interpretants. Peirce's claims about intrepretants ring true across many interactions: outside rituals or stage plays people are less certain of how their own signs will be taken up. Your companion faces you with the "shadow of a quickly hidden smile," and you are uncertain about whether to take that flicker as a sign, and of what. Your uncertainty may be expressed, say, in a pause, that pause interpreted in its own turn as a sign of mistrust.

Even the clearest of channels within the most regimented ritual settings can scatter diverse interpretants across many perspectives. The category of *intuition* is evoked and claimed not only in response to communication "gaps," but also in answer to multiplications of interpretants. Stray interpretants seem all the more troubling when they cross politicized borders; indeed, Cold War fear focused on ways that failure to read signals might lead to final nuclear destruction: intuition goes geopolitical.

The idea of contact itself often serves as a "trope for communication itself" (Kockelman 2010; see also Hoffmann-Dilloway 2011; Nozawa 2015, 386), but it does not always do so. Zuckerman (2016) shows how, during sports competition, hecklers aggressively make contact not to communicate, but to distract. Even as conflict during play *can* fold into the weave of friendship (rival friends becoming favorite friends), communication is may seem ancillary to the game. Indeed, an open channel never ensures all forms of communication: the fact that you answer the phone does not mean that your caller makes himself understood.

What about the term *channel*? A channel and a medium can align, but are they the same? A machine, such as a radio, can carry multiple channels, which can even interfere with each other. A theater hall, can activate multiple types of media, each materialized along channels laid in wire or cast by breath. Metaphorically, an "open channel" between diplomatic parties might be said to activate multiple media, such as telephone and memo text. I do not insist on a clean distinction, but try to use "channel" to address specific material conduits (this radio wave or that subway underpass) as well as social ones. Social and racial segregations of space also forward or prevent communication; they form channels for certain kinds of mediations and not others.

With divergent usages in mind, I avoid purifying definitions of *contact, channel,* or *phatic.* People define communications differently than scholars may, and their reflexive definitions reverberate through and even rearrange social worlds. I begin with a concept of the phatic, for instance, that is formal enough to set out across differently textured terrains but that remains vulnerable to adjustment. As I contrast situations, the reader will register contradictions among ways people understand communication, contact, media and channel, as well as disagreements about whether communication or contact occurs or not, and about what that entails. The goal is not to outline a taxonomy of kinds of phatic events, but rather through ethnographic and archival attention to arrive at a historico-semiotic theory of *processes* through which people manipulate and encounter phaticity.

PHATIC EXPERTISE

Failed communication structures the plots in works by Sophocles, William Shakespeare, and Alexander Pushkin, as it did earlier in myths and tales: kings are felled by semantic tricks, rivals plant seeds of suspicion, and dogs forget to pass on messages to divinities. Europe in the nineteenth century gave us the despairing heroes of Henrik Ibsen and Anton Chekhov, who seem always to speak past each other (Williams 1958, 1968; Levinas 1947; see Peters 1999). Postmodern characters curled even further from contact, as if language itself were insurmountably to blame. Modernists blamed a death of communion on the mechanical forces of industry and alienated exchange, on media reaching further than ever beyond face-to-face talk, perhaps even serving instead as technologies for surveillance or manipulation. Some linked postindustrial metaphysics of communication gaps to discoveries in physics: knowledge of circling atoms and subatomic particles, matter never touching across spaces between, scaled up as metaphors for awkward sociability across urban societies of strangers.

Disciplines separated, too. Before the eighteenth and nineteenth centuries, scientist-poets and inventor-artists (like Mikhail Lomonosov and Leonardo da Vinci) pursued rhyme and reason at the same time; as Luckhurst has argued, the invention of telepathy did more than modernize the occult, it also addressed the new separations among fields: "The conceptualization of telepathy [in 1882] in fact defines its own mode of discursive interconnection: it sparks across gaps, outside recognized channels, to find intimate affinities in apparently distant discourses" (2002, 60). For this reason, to discuss the invention of telepathy Luckhurst traces "sociological pathways" (51) through "energy physics to neurology, from anthropology to the ghost story, from wireless telegraphy to hypnotic rapport, from imperial federationism to the *peti mal* of the hysteric" (3).

All the angst associated with modern communication gaps, separation from the divine, alienation from nature, divisions of knowledge, fraction of kinship, divisions of self, and so forth affords a compensating pleasure in demonstrating interpretative or descriptive command of these gaps. To work with communication gaps is to claim a critical vantage, the kind of encompassment equated with intelligence or power, the status of sage, theorist, or mage (see West 2007; Palmié 2002). To force a rupture and then visibly work to suture the gap has become a way to claim not only to be modern, but also to *make* modernity.

Theater and telepathy research are two sites at which people work with gaps, making them in order to bridge them (only sometimes to unmake them); the space between audience and actor and the metal wall between telepathic receiver and sender are made in order to then demonstrate contact or communication across them. To consider them together allows us to contrast not only their working schema for contact and gap but also the relations among people who make and judge contact and those whom they judge. I call the former *phatic experts* (Lemon 2013). Societies divide linguistic labors (Irvine 1989); they also divvy up the work of talking about talk, the metacommunicative labors (Lemon 2002). The lawyer, the news editor, and the marriage counselor all master metacommunicative skills and specialize to different degrees in qualities of contact and conditions for communication, learning different skills to account for the most troubling gaps.

I came upon this category in the summer of 1997, when I began asking friends in Moscow, Perm', and Jaroslavl' what they made of the newly resonant term *transparency*, and in a more personal register, how they decided whom to trust. A banker acquaintance averred, "Who can tell?," suggesting that I ask "the experts among theatre actors and KGB agents."[18] In Moscow as in Chicago, surveillance experts and detectives, therapeutic psychologists and linguistic anthropologists, drama teachers, business communication consultants, psychics and their skeptics work on ways to recognize, manipulate, and represent contacts and channels: Are they warm or cold, open or closed, working or broken, veiled or revealed, lacking or excessive? Some phatic experts—people like Dale Carnegie and Constantine Stanislavsky—even brand coherent systems of "contact qualia" (Lemon 2013) to pass on their expertise.

My banker acquaintance had a point: I had long found common ground in Russia among people trained in theatrical work, because they loved discussing the pragmatic semiotics of minute behaviors in real-time situations, not just onstage. Like me, they actually enjoy discussing the ways tiny gestures point to relationships, both those in the moment and those beyond. At that point I had already lived for some months Perm' with people educated at the theatrical and musical academies in Moscow and Jaroslavl'; everyone was cash poor, some living rent free in the actors' dorm even into their thirties. It was this phatic expertise that they could sell when paychecks from the theater were sparse: they gave acting lessons to businessmen, teaching vocal skills to managers to improve their intuition for market and social encounters (for self-preservation, for rapport) that still seemed new.

Phatic experts take an interest in similar forms and details, in the quality signs (or *qualia*) of human sign behavior ("a spark in the eye," a "shift in tone"). They may do so to different ends. Some subsume phatic labor under other language functions; for example, police might take a flickering muscle around the eyes to indicate a blocked facial expression and deduce that the flicker indexes a lie. (Paul Ekman would caution that micro-expressions merely signify a shift among emotions.) Police need to monitor channels for signs of false reference; they use the phatic function to abduct the referential. Actors, by contrast, need to suspend reference to run multiple channels of contact in order to animate a "what if" inside a world of "not possible." American radio psychologists do something similar when they mix layers of memory by mixing tenses ("Where were you when daddy goes away?").[19]

Phatic experts often draw from other disciplines and places; doing so itself signals proficiency in crossing gaps. They are like brokers, accumulating value by working back and forth over the borders of nations, institutions, and disciplines. Their authority can accrue even in times of competition; some such work shades into the dark sides of contact, intercepting channels for intelligence or forcing words in interrogation. Phatic experts constantly engage with those who are not (or not yet) experts. Their expertise emerges historically, grounded not only in local organizations, but also in disciplines and institutions whose purposes entail crossing borders, both between states and within them.

REFRACTIONS OF EXPERTISE

When phatic experts judge whether contact has been made, channels have been broken, or communication is flowing, when they name good or bad acting, when they call out strong or weak psychics, they rarely work only with words, but also with materials, even with signs visceral to touch that are less than visible or audible to eye or ear. They also work with social divisions that channel who wields a stopwatch, who takes up a pencil, or who handles the X-ray or the energized gems.

Phatic experts are interested in similar forms and details of interaction and its conditions—but not always for similar reasons. Again, detectives succeed when they look for indications of truth or sincerity, but many actors cannot fret too much about verity (even offstage; as one student told me when the cohort was nearing graduation, "Our profession does not allow one to freeze out a person just because of mistrust"), as that would detract from collective labors to contact the audience.

Some sorts of phatic expertise ascend over others; to understand where, when, and for whom, we need to investigate how they intersect through divisions of labor.[20] Expertise accrues value when people, even starting from institutions that silo them (theater school, psychology department, film set, police academy), appropriate or debate others' schema for contact, others' technologies for intuition. Intersections with psychology, for example, are common. One film director advised me in 2001 to visit a center in Moscow where substance abusers received theatrical therapy in order to relearn how to connect with family members, as well as a group that, to help homeless dogs, staged role-plays to practice communicating with the police (he called these "psychodramas," adding that "the woman who runs this group sublimates herself through these dogs . . . she runs a pioneer camp for dogs"). American director Norris Houghton, who traveled to Moscow twice, once in the mid-1930s and again in the early 1960s, reported that the Moscow Children's Theater wove developmental psychology into rehearsal practice (1936, 230).

People continue to cross these fields. In September 2002 I audited a college course at the Russian State Humanities University, Experimental Theater for Psychologists. The department catalog explained that this class, required for the major, illustrates Soviet psychologist Lev Vygotsky's stages of development through theatrical techniques. As students, we went through abridged versions of drills in use at GITIS. By way of introduction, the instructor put us in a circle: we were to hold hands, imagine a color, then squeeze the hand of the person to the right. At the end, we reported results ranging across the rainbow. We had failed, the instructor said, because we had "not yet established contact." Next we were to close our eyes as she described a rural landscape, then open them to take up poses representing some part of the landscape: a tree, a flower, and so forth. She likened the activity to a "shared dream. . . . [W]hen you filled in the picture, you *obshchalis'* ('communed,' 'interacted'), yes? The text itself is not important." Then we repeated the circle—this time, colors linked, ranging in greens and blues: "There, you see!" Having made this point about contact, the lesson plunged into Vygotsky's theories of the social processes of mental development, whereby interaction with others leads to "internal speech."

At our next meeting we made another circle; much as at GITIS, students waited, "gathered energy," and then, all together, were to step forward in unison. The professor informed us that this, too, was a theatrical technique and seemed to know that at GITIS, the point of the drill is to develop attention, to convert phatic energy between working actors into connection with audiences. Her purpose, however, was to demonstrate how children learn to subsume and to differentiate the self and must switch among these positions before thought emerges, before the mind feels itself to be individuated, charting on the blackboard how interactions can oscillate among senses of you/I/we.

Even where ideologies and practices converge, actors still aim for different points, to produce different knowledge from those points. GITIS teachers used drills to criticize sociological generalizations, while the psychology professor made analogies between the contacts we were making and "cultural mentalities." She asked us to ponder uncanny contact phenomena, moments when "two people suddenly find the same word! How do *we* do these things?" She continued: "Maybe *you* do most things like a European realist painter—you look at nature a bit, then paint a little bit. A Chinese painter, however, will look and look and look and look, and then, *suddenly*—an impulse."

So, while phatic experts develop authority not only within institutions or disciplines but across them, actors who pull drills from books on social psychology and drama therapy and vice versa, having borrowed terms or tools, sometimes vociferously discredit the very field they have borrowed from. They can evoke intersections to undermine, such as when Soviet newspaper articles in the late 1980s discredited Gypsy fortune-tellers by calling them "good psychologists" who "read faces" and "track eye movements."

Even in a single rehearsal hall or lab, people might engage not just one but *several* sets of expectations about contact or technologies for intuitions. They might work to synthesize them, put them into competition, or use one to arrive at another. Were we to attempt to tie threads of expertise under a single profession, habitus, ontology, or ideology, we would miss these collusions and conflicts. To follow phatic *expertise* means to cross professions, schools, networks, and even countries to witness not only tangles and misfires, but also fresh interpretants that refract from even the most faithful attempts to translate.

CIRCLES: EXPERTS AND CIVILIANS

Good places to observe all this include those where phatic experts engage with people who are not, or are not yet, experts. Conflicts percolate through such places about how to gauge contact, how to evaluate communication, how to pick out signs and make channels, with which materials, connecting these people and not others. Among such places, GITIS is relatively insular while also communicatively dense, with constant interaction and discussion of interaction, in classrooms and corridors, onstage and backstage, before exams and after, in the café and in the dormitory, with its late-night chores and midnight meals and rides to and from on the metro. There is no question that GITIS is a "dense node" where resources and people cluster.[21] Entire ethnographies could be set within the institute or the dormitory alone; people described the situation as being "as though we live enclosed within a space capsule." Working, sleeping, and eating with the same people, from morning to midnight, every day, people said they felt in a world apart. While acclimating to the "space capsule" in the first year, for the customary midsemester variety show and party (*kapustnik*), the cohort rewrote beloved Soviet film song lyrics to convey the melancholy of cutting channels to past relationships, to "Moscow beyond GITIS' windows."

Time passed, and people graduated; "GITIS spat us out," laughed one actress in 2008. Some graduates work together, others meet rarely, to attend an opening or greet a new child. They Skype, some even with me, to practice an American accent or for help with Sundance festival instructions, a few just to talk. Most work steadily in theater; a few are now film celebrities. I am not surprised; their work is riveting. Some take acting techniques into different fields, teaching dramatic skills and theatrical appreciation to businessmen. One has founded a school for the arts in Germany, along the lines of a Steiner school, drawing together international connections from Paris, Hollywood, Moscow, and Tokyo.

I first witnessed how people shift expertise in 1997, among directors and actors in Perm' who contracted seminars for businesspeople, teaching acting skills to improve communication, and later investigated similar endeavors in Moscow. One that has achieved stability is called Shkola Obraz (Image School or School of Ways, as *obraz* can translate as "image" or "appearance" as well as "mode" or "manner," as in *obraz zhizni*, "way of life"). The play of meanings is fitting, as the school advertises theatrical skills as techniques for *living* better—by refining intuition.

A graduate of one of the smaller theatrical institutes founded Shkola Obraz in the mid-1990s, soon after the USSR had dissolved, a time in which bursts of self-help courses and books heralded new ways to make contacts and to read others. It was, as so many trumpeted, a new world of new signs, new partners in new markets. The school moved facilities several times in the 1990s and by 2000 had found a long-term space. As a part-time night school, it challenges the hierarchies of theatrical and film production in Moscow, offering entrance to the profession through a back door, with a shorter course of study and without auditions for admission; anyone who can pay may attend. It sells itself also as a path to solving everyday problems in a world where, as the website sympathizes, we all learn to compress our true selves under the gaze of others. There, acting skills (drawn more from Mikhail Chekhov than from other Russian masters) are taught to "housewives and businessmen," to help them "succeed through play." The school espouses a ludic, protean philosophy of theatricality (rather than theater as artifice) and touts monthly "happenings" at which students hit public transit walking on their hands or wearing dog collars to free themselves of public inhibitions. Every few months, sandwich board wearers pace central squares, passing out flyers and pinning them on bulletin boards—even in the entryway to GITIS.

The school also delivers lessons in how to relax, the better to channel new intuitions and energies. Shkola Obraz states explicitly that it links psychological knowledge, stage skills, and psychic capacities, offering dual learning tracks to merge learning to act and to meditate. Shkola Obraz, it turns out, is related to the Texas-based José Silva method. With franchises around the world, the Silva method offers "a unique combination of Alpha and Theta level mind exercises, creative visualizations, habit control, and positive programming methods has been endorsed by various thought leaders and scientists." Trained in electronics, Silva later turned to study of hypnosis and brain waves, dubbing his system the Silva Mind Control method in 1944 and going commercial in 1966. Shkola Obraz forms another turn in the circles of influence that once brought yoga to Stanislavsky's attention. This time, circuits of expertise cross borders and ideologies to create a hybrid of neoliberalism, occultism, and socialist technological infrastructure.

About midway between Moscow's center and the suburbs, at the Elektrozavod metro station, Shkola Obraz rents space in the building that houses a school for the Moscow Metro Builders (MetroStroj). Around 2007 it expanded from one to four rooms: three small ones nested together on the ground floor and a larger room for acting and movement on the third, next to Metrostroij's classrooms for mass transit accounting. A far cry from the grandeur of GITIS, with its grassy courtyard, curved wooden benches, iron gates, imperial heralds, and marble staircases, at Shkola Obraz's space people practice on gray carpet under acoustic tiles or listen while sitting in office chairs. The downstairs rooms are within view of the building concierge and turnstile where one shows a passport. A small bulletin board announces a low-budget session with a photographer to compile headshots to send to Mosfil'm or the new casting agencies. The innermost room serves as an office, with room for a desk, a shelf displaying several books on acting and psychology, and about six chairs. The middle room is for meditation training, with chairs around the edges. Shkola Obraz advertises a free introductory lesson every Thursday evening in either psychology or acting. Both lectures are available on tape and on the website.

I visited the school several times, attending the introductory lecture on acting in September 2005. Also in attendance were two teenage boys in jeans and a slender girl in stiletto heels with waist-length blond cornrows. They were just as beautiful as any beginning student at GITIS, but they kept so still and quiet that they hardly emitted any signs at all beyond their attire. I imagined that the course might do them some good; however, while Shkola Obraz is itself successful, its graduates have yet to penetrate far into professional filmmaking or theatrical work. During the lecture we learned that the cost for each three-month cycle of study was 7,000 rubles (about U.S. $230 at the time, about one-quarter of the average monthly salary in the city) and that one could attend either Monday and Saturday or Thursdays for a few hours a week: "No one in America studies acting at a five-year institute as we do here! They just take a few night classes. . . . *Anybody* can work in the theater after a few weeks training, just like driving a bus." The schedule and fees, the lecturer said, were signs of democracy.

By contrast, Leonid Heifetz, director and master instructor at GITIS, in his autobiography justifies closing the ranks to provide free education and training single-mindedly from 9:00 A.M. to 11:00 P.M., seven days a week. He addresses aspiring applicants by contrasting the theatrical to other professions: "One cannot simply select theater as a workplace. Theater is a calling. Say you are unemployed, but there are openings in a theater: 'I'll just go work as an actor.' Not an option. You will not make a single step onto the stage if you have no calling. . . . You need not only innate characteristics, but also a specific school, a set of abilities and masterly skills without which work in the professional theater is impossible" (2001, 5–6).

Our lecturer, Shkola Obraz's founder, laid out a different reasoning. He swiveled on his chair and spoke as if extempore, often reciting from the school's website word for word: "Let me tell you about my friend who was upset: 'WHY did I buy this thing that I don't need?!' I told him, and I'll tell you: 'Because somebody needed to lean on you to buy it, because somebody else was leaning on him to buy something else.' And so it goes, the whole world in a circle, . . . [P]eople won't tell you this, they won't admit it, but I will." He promised to teach us to prevent others from controlling us. Through meditation and play, we would learn technologies for intuition dedicated not only to contact, but also to jamming channels, to liberate ourselves from forces that make us puppets or robots, that *nas zombiruyut* (zombify us).

CRISIS?

At this point some readers will be intrigued, ready to ponder both how theatrical and telepathic projects intersect and how psychics and actors diverge. Others, before continuing to the specific cases, will want to learn about the kinds of explanations that have been given for surges of interest in or suspicion about theatrical skill and telepathy, as well as about the interests that hold stakes in those explanations. For now, let me identify some of the stakeholders. The first, which I address in this section, finds cause in crises, especially those during which unknown actors seem to draw curtains to hide their machinations from the rest of us. The other stake-holders I address in the following sections, to sketch the arc of a long game among world powers to demonstrate their own capacities for intelligence and intuition, attributing such capacities to enemy political systems, for instance by claiming that socialism or capitalism forces theatricality and represses authentic intuition.

One line of argument for crisis sees occult surges when seismic politico-economic shifts challenge familiar technologies for intuition, as when economic crises intersect crises of representation, or when distributions of resources change directions by seemingly opaque mechanisms or mysterious actors. This anthropological thinking runs from Max Gluckman through Jean and John Comaroff, from E. E. Evans-Prichard to Nancy Munn. For example, when South African apartheid ended in 1994, an oil boom rewarded certain people in such unexpected ways that others tried to account for it in terms of "occult economies." Drawing inspiration from Gluckman's 1959 essay "The Magic of Despair" (in which he cited Evans-Pritchard: "New situations demand new magic"), the Comaroffs assert that people imagine "arcane forces are intervening in the production of value, diverting its flow [and sparking an] effort to eradicate people held to enrich themselves by those very means" (Comaroff and Comaroff 1999, 284).[22]

Other scholars have convincingly linked the occult with political and economic crises (Taussig 1980; Geschiere 1997, 2013; Ashforth 2005; Morris 2000; Sanders 2008; Kivelson 2013). Many who specialize in Russian studies claim that the paranormal filled a spiritual vacuum created by the sudden collapse of state ideology.[23] Others have described the popularity of hypnosis during the 1980s (the period known for *perestroika* and *glasnost'*) as a symptom of "an unstable time of apocalyptic expectations" (Etkind 1997, 119). Others assert that, "[t]he occultism that has flourished in Russia has been a response to acute societal stress, like pain or fever" (Rosenthal 1997, 418), or ask whether such phenomena "suggest a terminally ill body politic, both in the physical and in the spiritual sense . . . [an] illness that is steadily eroding its grip on reality, this body politic searches for a way out—a portal into another dimension" (Geltzer 2011).

Across formerly Soviet spaces, changes in markets and market policy affected how people experienced and imagined social connections. Soviet-era networks for mutual aid did more than fulfill favors (Ledeneva 1998); people knit bonds of concern that extended the pleasures of consuming cookies, tea, or vodka together (Pesmen 2000; see also Farquhar 2002). Even the most practical such ties came to seem, retrospectively, both warmer and more comprehensible than the 1990s manipulations of *brend* and *imedzh*.[24] A lens of crisis illuminates that period. However, what about increases in interest in the occult during periods of stability, when paranormal surges do not correlate with acute crisis, such as in the USSR from 1961 to 1972 or in Russia from 2000 to 2007?[25] Even during the so-called stagnant, economically calm 1960s and 1970s, Soviets populated films and fictions with mesmerists, magicians, fairies, and sorcerers.[26]

CAPACITY TO FEEL: EMPIRE AND INTUITION

After crisis, another line of explanation puts the stakes in citizenship or belonging in imperial or nation states. Claims about European cognitive capacities and sensibilities have frequently justified rule; comparisons of national or racial capacities to think and to feel shaped logics of imperial ambition long before the Cold War. In the eighteenth century Montesquieu famously exposed a tongue to air at various temperatures, noting the constriction and expansion of its external fibers to extrapolate distinctions among nations:

> [In] cold countries the nervous glands are less expanded: they sink deeper into their sheaths, or they are sheltered from the action of external objects; consequently they have not such lively sensations. . . . In cold countries they have very little sensibility for pleasure; in temperate countries, they have more; in warm countries, their sensibility is exquisite. . . . It is the same with regard to pain, which is excited by the laceration of some fibre of the body. . . . [N]ow it is evident that the large bodies and coarse fibres of the people of the north are less capable of laceration than the delicate fibres of the inhabitants of warm countries; consequently the soul is there less sensible of pain. You must flay a Muscovite alive to make him feel. (1748, bk. XIV)

Montesquieu's text activated both early colonial hierarchies and imperial competitions, kicking off the long conversation about Russian capacity for feeling. Published in the years after Peter the Great's Russian imperial expansion, the text made an impression in Russia.

Russian imperial rulers were well-read; French, German, Latin, and English posed few obstacles. Empress Catherine, hailing from Austria, barely spoke Russian when she first arrived but carried on extensive correspondence in several languages with continental philosophes. Russian elites were always aware of European perceptions of Russia (see Layton 1994),[27] and as Soviets and now Russians continue to study other languages, they continue also to consider how Russia is viewed from elsewhere. It does not escape notice when foreign sources anchor policy to claims about Russian capacity to feel. It is noticed when depictions zigzag between extremes, northern stoics giving way to Dostoevskian maniacs or Hollywood depictions of cold-faced bureaucrats being eclipsed by Khrushchev removing his shoes at the United Nations to bang one on the table (some argue that those 1960s photos were faked).[28] The world switches between Orwellian visions of a state stifling passions and romantic images of a culture of feisty philosophers and emotional ballerinas. Russians get caught in these compelling oscillations; they echo the shapes of historical accounts of survival between other imperial powers, East and West.

Anglophone Cold War writing on Soviet telepathy and extrasensory perception rarely mentions crisis and instead privileges capacities to feel. When Americans Ostrander and Schroeder published their paranormal travelogue of encounters with Soviet telepathy scientists and telepaths, they took care in the introductory pages to note that people, such as actor Karl Nikolaev, greeted them effusively, belying images of emotionless, brainwashed Soviets:

> [A] major thrust of Soviet ESP work is to develop machines capable of monitoring, testing, and studying ESP. But the Soviets are also eager to study the human, people-to-people aspects of ESP. "We believe ESP is enmeshed with all of everyday life," they told us, "We believe ESP affects any group situation." And perhaps with people as warmhearted and volatile as the Slavs, ESP does flow more easily. Many Westerners seem to have the idea Soviet citizens are robot-like people, gray automatons in a well-run machine shop. An American we met in Leningrad confessed, "I thought the sun never shone in Russia and people never smiled—boy was I wrong!" (1970, 8)

They followed these words with examples of extravagant and spontaneous hospitality, descriptions of flowers and gifts of poetry, and accounts of sudden embraces from elevator operators.

Nevertheless, soon after their book came out, Ostrander and Schroeder appeared as guests on *The Amazing World of Kreskin*, a television program broadcast in North America from Ottawa, and zigzagged in the other direction, discussing how little Russians smile in public. These kinds of shifts happen all the time. One person might claim that the Russian people are more closed than smiling Americans, but in another context will say that winter frosts protect emotions deeper than any westerner can fathom. And yet these claims are often couched with one eye looking out for evaluations from elsewhere: on an October morning at GITIS, one of the acting teachers exhorted his students, "go look at faces on the Metro, you will not see a smile—foreigners notice this all the time."

I have indeed heard the refrain on absent Russian smile many times from Americans, since first visiting Russia in 1988 as a student on a study tour and then later as a professor leading such tours. "Why don't they smile?" This question, ten times out of ten, prompts someone else in the group to speculate: "Well, they never had the freedom to smile," or "It's trauma from Stalin's cruelties." The histories of the corporate campaigns in the United States to train the service smile seem yet unknown to most of my fellow citizens (see Hochschild 1983). American guidebooks to Paris, by the way, mention an absence of public smiles, attributing that not to political regimes, but to refined French sensibility. In any case, foreigners claim that Soviet-era rationality and rule shut down feeling—and many local people also say that Soviet modes of communicating chilled the space between souls, left a gap between false, official, public words and real, underground, or private expression. Words, some say, were born in a Soviet "culture of dissimulation" (Shlapentokh 1984; Sinyavsky 1991; Seriot 2002; Thom 1989) that barred citizens from "living in Truth" (Havel 1987). By the 1990s, such views no longer smelled of dissidence, and by 2000 they were mainstream.

"THE ONLY SPACE OF MAGIC IS THE THEATER"

Some arguments combine the approaches just described while sharpening the stakes, attributing intuitive capacities to particular political systems. They extend beyond any particular period of crisis, the better to press people to discern friends and declare enemies. There are many who blame socialism for such conditions, arguing that Soviet habits stunted abilities to connect and blocked compassion and communication, leaving people closed and numbed, suspicious.[29] Czesław Miłosz (1953) ascribed the duplicity of Polish intellectuals to socialist conditions, which he contrasted with the streets of capitalist Paris where he lived, juxtaposing its variety to the drone of socialist cities, where people adjust to lifeless architecture and to "short, square" bodies, the "racial type well-regarded by the rulers." Like many observer and émigré memoirs, his colored socialist societies grey and gloomy, a twilight of windowless rooms, overmechanized, overrationalized, and monotonous. If a paucity of sensation drains socialist spaces of "magic," theater restores it: "The number of aesthetic experiences accessible to a city-dweller in the countries of the New Faith is uncommonly limited. The only space of magic is the theater. . . . [T]he tremendous popular success of authors like Shakespeare is due to the fact that their fantasy triumphs even within the bounds of naturalistic stage setting" (1953, 64–67). Exiled poet Miłosz never actually lived in *socialist* Poland, though he did visit when he was a diplomat. From 1946 to 1950 he lived in Washington, D.C., working as Polish cultural attaché, and was transferred to Paris in 1950, where he defected. Published in France in 1951, Miłosz's *The Captive Mind* starts with a description of intellectual life in Poland under the Nazi regime during World War II and extends to describe the nascent socialist regime.

Many representations of life in the socialist bloc well known to Americans were written by people who spent little time in socialist countries. When George Orwell crafted *1984*, he drew from experience with the English government and from scenes in H.G. Wells's stories. Earlier, Yevgeny Zamiatin based his dystopian novel *We* on close observation of how labor was managed in the *British* shipyards in Tyne during World War I, when he worked there for the Russian *Imperial* (not the *Soviet*) Navy. He wrote just as critically about Russian imperial responses to the 1905 Revolution as he later did about the Bolshevik's strategies and practices.

Perhaps this preponderance of limited and refracted accounts, often written by diplomats constrained by their missions to limited contacts, helps to explain why, as cultural historian Julie Cassiday has noted, theatricality is "all too dominant a trope" to describe Russian people, as if they all live stifled under masks of deceit and suspicion or enchanted by illusory mystery, building Potemkin villages under duress. What are the anchors to the repeated claims that Russia is exceptionally given to theatricality, that acting pervades social life there?[30] Many of the anchors turn out to be texts by diplomats; Marquis de Custine, in his 1839 travel diary *Empire of the Csar*, described the Russian imperial court as theatrical. Russia's aristocrats, he famously claimed, lived under a veneer of European customs masking an Asiatic essence, possessing "just enough of the gloss of European civilization to be 'spoiled as savages,' but not enough to become cultivated men. They were like trained bears who made you long for the wild ones" (quoted in Kennan 1971, 80). Historically comparative scholarship since the late 1980s has demonstrated that similar accusations structured European descriptions of subjects and enemies, imputing mimicry and masking to colonial subjects in order to maintain distance, claim intellectual superiority, and justify imperial rule (Bhabha 1984). It is no surprise that a visiting French diplomat reached for a similar metric, especially when accusations of theatrical masking and manipulation were swirling through de Custine's homeland *before* his visit to Russia. Historian Paul Friedland, discussing political conflicts in eighteenth- century France, explains: "There were reports that deputies to the National Assembly were taking acting lessons and that claqueurs were being planted in the audience to applaud their employers on demand. . . . [P]amphlets were written in which the entire National Assembly was unmasked as a troupe of actors in disguise and election results were printed in the form of a cast list. . . . Conversely, while politicians were being unmasked as actors, dramatic actors were themselves being denounced by both the political left and right as being secret agents of the other" (2002, 2).

Habits of imagining political others' communications—and increasingly, their *thoughts*—as repressed or masked had already left deep tracks by the time Miłosz wrote during the Cold War:

> Such acting is a highly developed craft that places a premium in mental alertness. Before it leaves the lips, every word must be evaluated as to its consequences. A smile that appears at the wrong moment, a glance that is not all it should be can occasion dangerous suspicions and associations. Even one's gestures, tone of voice, or preference for certain kinds of neckties are interpreted as signs of one's political tendencies. . . . Of course, all human behavior contains a significant amount of acting. . . . Nevertheless, what we find in the people's democracies is a conscious mass play rather than automatic imitation . . . [until a person] can no longer differentiate his true self from the self he simulates, so that even the most intimate of individuals speak to each other in party slogans. (1953, 55)

This book has long been cited by American politicians as a core text on the socialist world. Its strength lies in explaining the *attraction* of ideology to people who had witnessed the atrocities of World War II. However, it is more frequently cited by Americans to claim that others are puppets who mouth propaganda—or who at best live by concealing all opposition, a contradiction they resolve "by becoming actors."

To be sure, people in Russia can also animate this logic: at GITIS during my time there, one teacher commented upon student failure at a drill in ways that put the blame on Soviet-era conditions. This was another drill to develop intuitive technique, again by limiting the usual face-to-face forms and media for communication, to channel and limit contact and its purpose. A student stood in the center of a circle of other students who had been assigned to play either "friend" or "foe" and had been directed to repress any sign to indicate which they were. As the instructor remarked, "In real life, such sentiments may be the very ones not expressed." The student in the center was allowed to shake each hand and exchange one word, "Hello." Based on that minimal interaction, she was to decide "friend or foe?" "Friends" were sent to one side of the room, "enemies" to the other. The poor student could not make up her mind. Flustered, she sent nearly all her cohort to the enemy line. As she shot each one with an imaginary bullet, they dropped to the floor, most declaring, "How I loved you!" Watching her desperate indecision about which signs to trust, her failure of intuition, one of the teachers, shaking with silent laughter, whispered to me: "Look at this—this paranoia is our Soviet, Stalinist mentality."

This bit of ethnography does not prove Miłosz correct—in other moments, the same teachers blamed markets, postmodernism, and Hollywood. Historical and ethnographic attention to specific claims indicates that we do better not to reduce (say, by deriving a statistical average among claims), but to situate each claim as such, as a claim, as a turn in more than one ongoing conversation. The magic of socialist theater owed less, perhaps, to contrastive glamour, fantastical color against grey landscape, than it did to the political drama of such claims. To follow enchantments of contact conjured by phatic experts, through technologies for intuition, it will help to look at where and how claims of intuition give way to those about perception. This is because each sort of claim—to sensation or to intuition—can be wrought and unwrought with reference to battles over materialism, over the matter and media for sensation and communication. Those battles simmered among imperial colonial powers from the time of René Descartes and continue within and across ideological oppositions, wreaking too tidy separations between capitalism/socialism, science/art, mind/body, self/collective, and inspiration/automatism.

2. Energy and Extrasensation

ROBOT SLOTS

American cold warriors depicted the Soviet socialist enemy as at best a robot-minded slave to be pitied and at worst an agent intent on invading other minds. If Russian literature, music, opera, and ballet were received as passionate tours de force, whence the portrayal of a people as robot-like? To be sure, the Soviet state imprisoned poet Osip Mandelshtam, executed director Vsevolod Meyerhold, and tried and exiled writer Andrei Sinyavsky; these moments complicate but do not negate Soviet-era creativity and fantasy. Some argue that it took concentrated effort to depict Soviets as if they lacked these qualities. For instance, some claim that it took CIA funds funneled through foundations (yet another sort of channel) to promote American forms of abstract expressionism as manifestations of individual creativity,[1] intending, by contrast, to prove Soviet rule toxic to human imagination and feeling.[2] Never mind Harry S. Truman's hostility to abstraction, tinged by racial slur ("If that's art, then I'm a Hottentot"); American accounts of twentieth-century cultural politics usually focus only on Nikita Khrushchev's philistine pronouncements ("Dog shit!" "A donkey waves better with its tail.").

Still other possibilities might explain why or how the "first world" described the "second world" (Pletsch 1981) as a land of robots. Perhaps depicting the USSR as a land of brainwashed ideologues projected more general fears about mechanization everywhere. Perhaps it expressed American guilt over dropping the atom bomb.[3] Whatever the diverse reasons, the result has been to score out a *robot slot*, not unlike Trouillot's *savage slot* (1991), a discursive matrix that, he argues, structures European accounts of colonized peoples. *Slot* is a metaphor for the ways strong discursive patterns call for repetitions, for filling in blanks as one does when making a metered rhyme or filling in a menu. Like most tropes about others, the savage slot projects colonial mythology and does not describe the colonized.

Worry about automatons may not have started within America; witness the ways women, colonized people, and people of color are described in many places as if they are capable only of imitation (see Bhabha 1984). But the American robot slot is a treacherous version; anyone, from middle manager to boss, can fear falling into it without leaving home. Consider all the 1950s office fictions mourning the sad, gray-suited, city conformists, sold-out souls working for pay instead of following Jack Kerouac to Big Sur.[4] Modernist aesthetic movements from beat poetry to punk sought to recover vital energies, awaken perception and will, and release the modern person from civilizing sublimation and submission, but the ironies multiply: white Americans turn to rock music or jazz improvisation to awaken from robotic emptiness, even while ignoring legacies of slave labor that still affect everyone.

There is precedent for another twentieth-century, paranoid, American Cold War version of the robot slot in *Dracula* (1897), in which projections of vampiric mind control from the East ominously threaten British imperial stability. In nineteenth-century Britain we also find the fear of automation expressed via suspicion of materialism—a suspicion that would carry over into the ideological enmity between socialism and capitalism in the next century. This was all clear particularly in studies of the mind that championed individual creativity and took an absolute moral position on freedom and will. Lorraine Daston notes that in Britain at the end of the nineteenth century, psychological approaches to mental phenomena were riven by worry over the moral implications of creating a science of the mind, "in particular, the possible encouragement it might lend to materialist or fatalist theories of human conduct" (1978, 192). Suspicion of materialism, especially materialist accounts of the mind, seemed aligned too closely with a fatalism that lent itself to automatization and to loss of an inner, active self to drive attention and sensation, a kind of self, Daston remarks, that was central to Christian morality grounded in free will.

Suspicion of materialism later infused American accounts of Soviet paranormal science as closed minded. A U.S. Department of Defense (DoD) report prepared by Air Force Systems Command remarked on "the strong tendency of Soviet and East European researchers to emphasize the physical explanation of the phenomena they are dealing with." Claiming that this materialism hampered creative thinking, the report continued: "In the Soviet Union . . . ambiguity cannot be tolerated in paraphysics research, and there is a strong tendency on the part of all paraphysics researchers to assert a presumed physical basis for their observations which does not violate known physical laws. . . . The effect of this may be a premature closure of options" (1978, 36). That is, they criticize the Soviets for being closed to the possibility of immaterial channels for consciousness and communication, even though elsewhere in the document the authors themselves, squeamish about terms such as "spirit," recommend positivist methods. The DoD report writers thus claim for themselves a properly modern, free, and democratic position between extremes, a Goldilocks perspective from which to subsume all others, to assess just how much materialism is too much, too little, or just right.

The Department of Defense report summarized mainstream Soviet print publications, providing a bibliography of newspapers and popular science journals from the 1920s through the 1970s. Upon reviewing these sources and many others, I found that the DoD writers minimized the breadth of Soviet opinion and expression on the topic, which ranged from the statistically grounded to romantic, from the comic and skeptical to the wishful and whimsical. The DoD report, while briefly acknowledging that Soviet publications sponsored debates,[5] depicted those debates as if they were spun so tight around the axis of ideology that the only relevant issues involved whether scientific experiments hewed to Marxist materialism or not, as if communist ideology had burned out the last bits of fuel for curiosity:

> Like other scientists, paraphysicists have had to spend considerable effort in justifying their field on ideological grounds. The first attempt seems to have been to assert that the phenomena were mediated through known, if not exactly demonstrable, material mechanisms. Electromagnetic waves became a favorite explanation for telepathy, despite the argument that electromagnetic effects caused by physiological processes were much too diffuse and weak to cause the noted phenomena. The other major attempt has been to acknowledge that the information or energy transfer mechanisms are not known, but to assert that this simply reflects the imperfect state of contemporary scientific knowledge. Lengthy sections devoted to ideology and quotations from Lenin are frequently found in the works of paraphysicists, particularly in the early and mid-1960's. (Air Force Systems Command 1978, 36)

As a matter of fact, in the sources mentioned in the report I have yet to find a single quote from Vladimir Lenin.[6] Leonid Vasilev, for example, opens his writings not with Lenin, but with Russian imperial neurologist Vladimir Mikhailovich Bekhterev, British physicist and parapsychologist William Barrett, and Italian psychiatrist Ferdinando Cazzamalli.

To recognize this breadth allows us to relate Soviet telepathy science to the ways people encountered and celebrated concrete materials for contact or communication, moving from those forms not to become robots, but to question how to live, with whom, and to what end. Bolsheviks had ardently hoped to make people true agents running the means of production, rather than cogs in the capitalist industrial machine; many Soviet people continued to worry about automatization and conformity, actively devising ways to nurture creativity.

THOUGHTS WITHOUT THINKERS?

To these ends, Soviet materialism was interesting and productive, even across the body of texts that the DoD summarized. Consider the essay by E.T. Faddeev, reporting in 1961 on a seminar at Moscow State University that had gathered philosophers together with natural scientists (1961, 60–63). Faddeev advocates a materialist explanation for thought transfer, positing yet undiscovered frequencies for rays, imagined sometimes as lines, sometimes as circular emanations of waves. At the same time, he describes the idealist position, whereby thoughts move without medium, in sufficient detail that those who might want to ponder that alternative. More to the point, his own, materialist speculations are in fact complex and intriguing; he posits the existence of waves—perhaps radioactive, perhaps microwave—that might penetrate the skull while skipping over the body's sensory organs.

During that 1961 seminar, V. Tugarinov objected to Faddeev's brand of materialism because, he asserted, it falsely located thoughts within *individual* brains, neglecting the possibility that thoughts cohere socially and through technologies to manifest ideation *in* material media, such as paper or bodily theatrical gestures: "as when actors mime an entire scene that is coherent to everybody." He agreed with Faddeev that thoughts are not strictly autonomous from the brain—in the sense that they do not empty from the skull like water from a bottle. But neither are thoughts shackled to their "first" or "original" media. Rather, they move along with materials: "Yesterday I sent a letter to America—which means that I sent my thoughts to the other end of our planet" (Tugarinov 1961, 22). Thoughts can even jump chains of media, or they activate several channels at once.

Where do thoughts begin, then? Friedrich Nietzsche famously refuted René Descartes's proposition, *cogito ergo sum*, which founded self-existence on awareness of thought, by remarking that a thought comes "when 'it' wishes, not when 'I' wish, so that it is a falsification of the facts of the case to say that the subject 'I' is the condition of the predicate 'thinks'" ([1886] 1989, 17) Tugarinov moved beyond the individual to assert that a brain is just *one* medium among others along chains of thought. Thoughts move beyond synapses, in flashes of matter in motion, sounds or signs brought by mail no less than by a dream.

The figure of the individual still overpowers social theory, despite anthropological counterclaims. Even after scholars inspired by Erving Goffman, Mikhail Bakhtin, or Valentin Voloshinov have demonstrated that speech does not emerge whole and pristine from within individual bodies, but distributes across people and situations,[7] we still have trouble imagining those phenomena we call *thoughts* moving anywhere but inside the braincase, barely hitching a ride to cross spaces riding signs or gestures, or betrayed only by outbursts, such as laughter.

It's no wonder the subtle complexity of Tugarinov's material-semiotic account of thought went over the heads the writers of this DoD report; it would be surprising to find many Americans who imagine thought or speech as other than individual, not bound to isolated thinkers or single speakers. To have done otherwise in this report would certainly have hindered the claim that Soviet materialism led to "closure of options" for research on thought transmission.[8] In fact, articles like the one by Faddeev kept company with a range of Soviet expressions of wonderment about communications as phenomena that escape the bounds of bodies, whether they move as electricity, electromagnetic waves, ink in a letter—or by less tangible media.

Throughout the 1960s and into the 1970s, scholars published on a number of sensory experiences in ways that encouraged wonderment about perception—and about the transmission of perception as perspective. For example, popular science journals informed readers that intense and shifting magnetic charges can cause glimmers of light to appear even when no light is present: the oscillations of charge create phosphenes, the simplest of which can be created by changing pressure (try tapping your closed eyelids). Along the way, they educated Soviets about how the chemicals in peyote activate kaleidoscopic effects, especially when the eyes are closed. Materialist methods continue to yield captivating techniques to render or represent sensation and intuition—and thus to artfully communicate.

Soviet stage and film techniques focused on sensation and matter in ways that really *did* "stir the imagination." The success of such materialism—to be interesting, engaging, worth learning—can be judged, among other things, by its works, by the accolades for cohorts who continue to come up through the theatrical institutes.[9] Whatever anyone might say about social realist film plots, the range and development of their actors is impressive. Institutions from acting schools to popular explorations of psychic phenomena continue to cultivate sensitivity to the material media that afford and channel contact and communication. Far from greasing robot cogs, they encourage exploration and speculation.

For Soviets, materialism deadened neither the will nor the imagination. Soviets were encouraged not only to explore the physical workings of sensation, but also to reflect upon the patterns and structures that produced different sentient perspectives, to ponder and compare complexly diverging points of view. Soviet popular science journal *Znanie-Sila*, for example, published pieces such as "How Does an Ordinary Fly See You?" (1966), featuring the work of Swedish photographer-scientist Lennart Nillson.[10] Still living today, Nillson combines aesthetic feeling for scientific rigor with the adventure of discovery; his later projects sketch the chemistry of love and photograph the stars at their most comforting. In the first photo in the *Znanie-Sila* piece, Nillson wields a fly swatter. The next photo, rather than zooming in on the bulging dome of thousands of compound lenses that make up a fly's ocular organ, instead arrays dozens of identical photos of Nillson into a kaleidoscope: the viewer is the fly looking at Nillson.

"NATURAL SCIENCE IN THE WORLD OF SPIRITS"

Truth be told, descriptions of Soviet telepathy experiments can be quite dry for some readers. In 1959, after the French press reported telepathy experiments aboard the USS *Nautilus* submarine, L. L. Vasiliev, a member of the Soviet Academy of Sciences and Order of Lenin Professor of Physiology at the Institute of Brain Research at the University of Leningrad, argued for increased Soviet funds for experiments in "thought transfer over distance." Soon afterward he published the book *Eksperimental'nie Issledovanija Myslennogo Vnushenija* (Experimental research on mental suggestion, 1962), recounting his experiments in the 1930s and those in the 1920s led by his mentor, Vladimir Bekhterev. Bekhterev's first telepathy labs installed special doors into cubicles holding slots to switch out materials known to block transmissions of various wavelengths. Day after day the materials were switched, doors opened and closed, while the receiver and sender were both kept blind to these changes. Bekhterev's experiments indicated that when screened by materials known to block electromagnetic waves, the receiver followed none of the suggestions mentally transmitted by the sender, but when screened by other materials, he or she did follow them, supporting a hypothesis that thought transmission was material in character, perhaps riding electromagnetic waves. In the 1930s Vasiliev obtained different results after placing subjects in Faraday cages more tightly sealed from electromagnetic radiation. This time, subjects responded similarly with and without the shielding, contradicting earlier results; perhaps telepathy had no material base, rode no waves, was message without media. Funding for the experiments was constricted, although Vasiliev maintained a prestigious post. The *Nautilus* affair put him back in the public eye, kick-starting paranormal experiments and debates about them.

In 1961 the Soviet Union's beloved science fiction writers Boris and Arkady Strugatsky published a story that situated mechanical laboratory procedures within a wide, astonishing world, or rather, solar system. In a collection spanning a future universe, *Noon: 22nd Century*, the tale "Natural Science in the World of Spirits" quotes the title of Engels's 1878 essay that acerbically thrashed spiritualist charlatanry. In the story, scientists have hypothesized a "field of contacts (*svjazi*)" that hovers in the atmosphere above Leningrad to explain the mysterious disappearance and return of the spaceship *Taimyr*. They have recruited "readers" (the story uses the English term, transliterated into Cyrillic, an internationalist twist) from among people who began openly reading minds several decades before. The story follows a few readers through a day in the life of science. The first one used to work as a natural scientist in the Yukon, a zoologist specializing in the genus Castor (the beaver). Every morning his nontelepathic assistant walks him to work, all the while reciting mental equations to jam the frequency, to shield his romantic obsession. As one might imagine, this makes verbal conversation awkward and a bit shallow, so as they walk, the reader falls into his own ruminations. His son had perished in a mission on Venus, never to witness humanity terraform that planet: "Oh, son, if only you could see the woods where we will resettle the beavers." A second reader emerges from his dwelling to join them. Now there is someone to "talk" to: they silently debate the burden of telepathy; the first man is all too aware that telepathy creates social awkwardness, but the second, a doctor, treasures the gift that leads him to those in pain.

When they arrive at the lab, dozens of readers enter insulated, isolated cells alone to listen for some sign from the field. For hours each day they sit in silence with no distractions, behind impenetrable walls. At the end of each shift, each door opens to the expectant face of one of the scientists holding a clipboard, hoping maybe this time. . . . Each day, each scientist adds "no data" to tables on a clipboard. This is the repetitive monotony even of ESP experiments inside a lab. But one reader, at least, is more absorbed by memories of family and forest, by enthusiasm for future beaver expansion across the solar system, than by scanning for channels. He listens for *dukhi* (spirits), cosmic, past and future all at once. The vitality of the research is not negated even in the recognition of the dullness of repetition in the method. Rather, just as the Strugatskys use the English word reader to indicate cosmopolitan conversations (about technologies for intuition) in the future, they combine characters' thoughts of elsewheres and elsewhens to complicate the relationship of science, and materialism, to the world.

The Soviet short story "A Lesson in Telepathy" (Soloukhin 1971) similarly reveals the scientific process as a social and material relation, folding romance around experimental method. Katja works for a distinguished professor as a subject in his study of long-distance telepathy. Every night at 10 P.M. the professor, sitting in the Arctic, randomly draws a Zener card while Katja, sitting in a Crimean port, receives it, drawing a square, triangle, cross, or double wave sign, then mails the results to him the next morning. But one day Katja meets a navy man strolling about on a day's leave. True love? Time is short . . . but she dutifully says good-bye to fulfill her obligation. She spitefully draws seagull check marks instead of triangles that night, thinking, "Take that!" A week later she receives a letter from the sailor confessing that he had "decided to enter the game," hoping that his mental transmission of birds at sea might beat symbols sent by an arrogant scientist.

The victorious, creative telepathy of the sailor is no anomaly among strands of romanticism across late Soviet art, literature, and film. If Cold War paranoia or rivalry structures the characters' given conditions—military ports, funded research—the story turns on the different perspectives from which the scientist and the sailor relate to the state, through divergent schedules for duty and love, seagulls challenging Zener symbols. These differences, fictional as they are, cue us to attend to ways actual people also craft contacts and channels that run askew and through geopolitical lines. Telepathic rays even refract against each other.

Kira Bulychev's book *A Hundred Years Ago in the Future* (1976) and its serialized television version, *Guest from the Future* (1984), render just such an antidote to paranoia in the trusting, curious character of a little girl named Alissa who lives in late twenty-first-century Moscow. Her father has invented a technology for intuition, a machine, the Mielofon, that enables its operator to read the thoughts of any sentient being. The rare device is a black box that, when opened, reveals a glowing crystal. We first meet Alissa with the apparatus in hand, as she entreats a silent crocodile (an ingeniously designed puppet) to stop joking around and cooperate with the linguistic task at hand. With the help of the device, she has already studied

Dolphin, at least its Mediterranean dialects.[11] In the wrong hands, of course, the Mielofon could be dangerous; sure enough, two bumbling, space-pirate shape-shifters attempt to steal it. By accident, a Moscow boy named Kolja from 1984 has happened into Alissa's century through a secret portal, and just in time—he recaptures the Mielofon and takes it to his own Moscow for safekeeping in the early 1980s. Alissa follows, spending a few weeks in Kolja's world and joining forces with him and his classmates against the pirates.

Oddly enough, the protagonists hardly ever use the Mielofon; they prefer to express their curiosity in words or eye gestures, to pose earnest questions. Only after Kolja is taken captive do they tune the machine to amplify thoughts: behind an apartment door, a husband grumbles silently, it is not his turn to go out for milk; a girl wonders, will he telephone? Only a nervous stranger, one who sweats so much that they can sense he is lying, prompts them to use the object to find Kolja. Otherwise, Alissa wears the thing on a leather strap dangling loosely behind her or leaves it lying on a sofa or hanging from a branch, with less care than other characters use to carry school portfolios. She hands it, with no hesitation, to any kid who wants to hold it. She is not jealous of its capacities, guards nothing, loves everyone, and listens to all. Before returning to her future, as a parting gift she satisfies students' curiosity about their own futures, naming each career path like a fortune-teller: who will become an athlete, a poet, or a scientist; who will write fantastical travelogues.

Late Soviet genres of popular science and science fiction wove materialist universes *with* lyrical, romantic characters, scientists, and others who were motivated by affectionate curiosity. Late socialist telepathy fantasies, like their literary analogs in the United States, bonded technical aspirations for civilization building and cosmic exploration with romantic expressions of imperial extension in scenarios common to both: "The ship has lost contact!" "These aliens speak nothing like the languages we know!"

The film comedy *Operation Y, and More Adventures with Shurik* (1965) depicts telepathy associated with inquiry for its own sake, the hunt as game, especially a romantic game. In one scene the sometimes feckless, sometimes clever, always adorable hero, Shurik, has been studying with his schoolmate, Lida, at her family's flat. He experiences déjà vu; she proposes that this strange sensation might be a sign that Shurik is gifted with telepathy, "just like Vol'f Messing!" She devises a test: choosing a stuffed mouse, she hides it underneath a soft sofa pillow. He does not find the mouse—instead he ends up kissing Lida. Failing a telepathy test, he scores an emotional success, contact in another register.

FIGURE 2.1. Partners on a thread. Photo by author.

BE THE RAY

Characterizations of Soviet paranormal science as insufficiently open to immaterial "options" tightly paralleled other Cold War claims that Soviet Russia had infused its sciences and arts with excessive materialism. Let us pretend to concede that Soviet materialism did close options in the lab, as if paranormal science in other places more readily admitted immaterial causes. Even so, outside the lab Soviet materialism allowed people to craft contact and conceive of communication in engaging and productive ways.

Consider a contact drill at GITIS, one formed around a material. Pairs of students each take up a length of thread and stretch it between them; their task, as they move together across the floor, is to make sure that the thread neither goes limp—*vjalo*—nor becomes so strained and tight—*zazhat*—as to break. While the drill seems to focus intensely on the here and now of interaction, the students and their watchers might always bring associations from other moments to bear on these shifting qualities. To describe stage dynamics in other lessons, some teachers spoke of "limpness" and "tightness." The master might query sharply: "Why so compressed? Get her to relax." Or, "Why is she over-acting? A very limp beginning." One instructor assessed a performance as "emotionally limp," making an analogy to a famous pair of cerebral antiromantics: "What is this?! Lenin dumps Inessa Armand?"[12] The thread stretching between actors is a material sign whose tactile qualities, looseness or rigidity, figure the intensity and constancy of contact itself.

Like Montesquieu, the French philosophe who exposed his tongue alternately to heat and then cold to examine its changing textures, the pairs and the audience focus less on that which is sensed and more on that which does the sensing. In this case, however, that which does the sensing has extended beyond the body, along the thread, which becomes both sense data and sensor. The drill trains actors to feel partners ever more sensitively through the thread, even as they render the string increasingly imperceptible, into "a medium that performs so well it becomes invisible" (Eisenlohr 2009), as teachers coach pairs to: "Feel your partner, feel their every impulse . . . now try it with the string tied to a less sensitive part." Their goals contrast, however, to cases in which people erase mediation under conditions of matterphobia; GITIS-made ideology of communication presupposes that contact is possible *because* we live in a material world, and actors must overcome squeamishness about this fact and embrace the willingness to be material, not to erase but to become the thread, to merge with media, to be media.

Neurologist Oliver Sacks describes how people extend the sense of proprioception—the sense of the body's parts in relative position, movement, and balance—from the brain and sensors in the ears and skin (the vestibular system) to the tip of a cane (see also Lende and Downey 2012). We do this all the time with objects, but we forget; the proprioception involved in parking a car arises to consciousness when we drive one larger or smaller than usual. The thread task joins two bodies via proprioception: sensors register, extend through body and thread to another body, and then back again, through the thread. Contact, note, is not a matter of transparency, not a matter of reading thoughts through a veil, but a matter of merged materiality.

At GITIS investment in the materialism of semiotic action best pays off onstage when actors are aware that attention to individual or pair-thread mediations is collectively organized. While the thread seems to channel concentration within a pair of individuals, the room is in fact intersected by multiple circles and rays for attention. The aim of contact from stage to audience falls short when envisioned simply as opening a channel for individual thoughts—even the playwright's, much less those of the actors. In this drill the work involves orchestrating and maintaining attention to the attention of others, including that of the teachers and other observers. Much of the entire first year at GITIS is devoted to learning to feel and to harness "impulse," "energy," and "tempo-rhythm" in the body and *among* partners. Sensory drills build physical and mental responsiveness among troupe members, their "reflex excitability," as Meyerhold put it. Training targets the senses as material resources for collective action: once pairs have mastered the thread, students move on to triads and quartets.

At GITIS contact by thread is a technology for intuition. In other settings, however, thread works as a metaphor for signs of contact. Consider a section from a late Soviet documentary, *9 Years with Psychics/Extrasensates* (Kiev 1989; dir. Olender), released shortly before the dissolution of the Soviet Union, which features interviews filmed between 1974 and 1986 with psychics across the socialist bloc, people made famous by local, national, and European print media, staged demonstrations, and word of mouth. The documentary features, among others, Vera Zrazhevskaja, who claimed to channel poetry dictated from beyond the grave by Soviet-era musician-actor, the star Vladimir Vysotsky; Albert Ignatenko, who began demonstrating telepathy on Soviet stages in the 1960s alongside the illustrious Wolf Messing; Nina Kulagina, who moved matchsticks in home movies shot in the 1960s (by her husband, say some; by actor Boris Nikolaev, say others; and by the KGB, claim still others); and an academic who conducted telepathy tests but who declines to show his face—we see only his hands.

The section featuring stage hypnotist and telepath Albert Ignatenko begins with shots of equipment that measure and monitor electrical impulses and heart rates, tracing peaking and falling lines of ink or light, threadlike, across screens and paper printouts. Once the camera establishes the arrangement of equipment and locations of observers, it closes in on the two research subjects, black-bearded Ignatenko and his partner, a blond woman in a black robe. The narrator's voice informs us that the psychic needs to "tune in to his partner": eyes closed, the woman sways just a bit as her partner passes his palms in front of her forehead. A few minutes later we cut to him sitting backstage, framed by a three-way mirror, describing energy moving through threads of the nervous system and the "need to tune."

Throughout the eight-minute section, visual image and voiceover are echoed by sound—the long drones produced by a theremin—the electronic instrument invented by Leon Theremin (Lev Termen) that is played without physical contact, by stroking the air above it. (Ignatenko himself often played the theremin onstage in his virtuosic demonstrations of brain power and memory.)[13] The filmmakers have chosen sounds that evoke the relative tautness and looseness of violin strings—but without touch. Each droned note discordantly replaces another at erratic intervals, higher then lower. All the while, voice-over maintains a searchingly agnostic mood, entertaining *both* the successes and failures of telepathic tests of contact. And regardless of each experimental outcome, those details identified to be visible and aural signs of contact sync and unsync.

REFLEX EXCITABILITY AND BIOMECHANICS (MEYERHOLD MATTERS)

What the thread, the theremin, and the line on the graph share is not a specific physical or chemical composition, but a material capacity to shift and show opposites: taut-lax, high-low, rapid-slow. Recall Moscow director Knebel', who in drills training attention and intuition had disallowed telepathy; it was attention to these kinds of shifts that she worked to teach. A good materialist writing in the Soviet 1960s, she stressed instead students' work with minute, barely discernible flickers, shadows "of a quickly hidden smile." The process of sharpening attention, especially to quick shifts and small details (learning to read them as signs *and* to convey their readings *as* signs), is valuable in itself, even "if sometimes they did not guess" (Knebel', 1967).

C.S. Peirce suggested something similar in 1884: that our perceptions of changes in sense data are more fine-tuned than we judge them to be (Peirce and Jastrow 1884). He and his colleague Joseph Jastrow, inspired by German psychophysicist Gustav Fechner's work on sensation (1861), demonstrated that minute shifts in weight are registered by receptors in the fingers more quickly than by reflexive brain processes. Peirce suggested that these findings might account for what people spoke of as intuition; like many at the time, he was interested in how information seems to move without apparent channel or physical contact, and he studied the protocols for telepathy experiments reported by the Society for Psychical Research: "It gives us new reason for believing that we gather what is passing in another's mind in large measure from sensations so faint that we are not fairly aware of having them, and can give no account of how we reach our conclusions on such matters. The insight of females as well as certain "telepathic" powers may be explained this way. Such faint sensations ought to be fully studied by the psychologist and assiduously cultivated by every man" (Peirce and Jastrow 1884, 83).

Peirce articulates a need to research the biomaterial mechanisms of intuition. Of course the "minuteness" of any shift in sensation is relative; it requires orientation to a conventional scale of measure, a problem about which he has inspired much research.[14] Perhaps this relativity accounts for why, a century later, claims about the mastery of perception of small shifts proliferate—and contradict each other. For every Maria Knebel' teaching the theatrical arts of attending to subtle changes across a room of persons, there is a Paul Ekman teaching the craft of lie detection by interpreting barely discernible shifts among "micro-expressions" on an isolated face (for further discussion of micro-expressions, see Lemon 2013).

Lecturing on the artistic importance of awareness of shifts in sensation, Russian director Vsevolod Meyerhold put this in formalist terms to his students, in lectures during the early days of GITIS. He asked them to imagine a doll onstage whose face never moves, while the audience perceives it one minute laughing, the next crying—the secret is not in the doll's expression, which cannot change, but in changes in relational angles achieved through choreography of bodies and objects.[15] A good actor, Meyerhold advised, should know to make his first entrance with his eyes level to the horizon; that way, any small change in the vector of gaze or tilt of the head would register as meaningful to the audience. The actor should also learn how a shift in position of her own body will relate to other bodies onstage, to how such material relations can incite audiences to make emotional and cognitive connections, the director remaining ultimately responsible for arrangements as seen by the audience (see Meyerhold 1969, 2001).

Meyerhold has frequently been miscast as advocating robot-like, mechanical performances. Alma Law argues that Western treatments of Meyerhold's system of gestural training, *biomekhanika*, often misinterpret the evidence, sometimes relying a solitary photograph (Law and Gordon 1996). To be sure, photos of his students at work do look as if a body had been posed to address a viewer. The trouble is that during training the pose in fact addressed others. The camera, we might say, opened a channel to the future viewer that was extraneous to the training in process. It captured a moment in one sense but not another. It did not capture the ways students were apprehending their own bodies and those of others as they put those bodies through movements that were not habitual.

The idea was that by estranging themselves from natural movements, they would achieve reflexivity about the body's seeming physical limits. The poses—and shifting between the poses—would also train them to awareness of just how and when the body emits excess signs. Onstage, the barest exertion of attention, the turn of a shoulder or the angle of a gaze, can read as intended to mean something (consider all the television punditry devoted to analyzing the body language of politicians).[16] Actors' "excess of non-purposeful" signs, inviting audiences to interpret them, frustrated Czech semiotician Jirí Veltrushky and directors like Gordon Craig, who fantasized the *uber-marionette* to take the place of actors. Meyerhold, by contrast, presaging Roman Jakobson's insights on multiple language functions, valued the multiple kinds of meaning available in nonlinguistic signs, in gestures and poses, in rhythms and tempos. A slight shift might even convey metaevaluation of ongoing stage communication and point to ironic or other alternative readings. A sweep of the hand, a slowed step, all can work as metacommunication. His training aimed to rouse what we might call a *biomechanico-poetic function*, in which shifts in bodily motion can reflect on bodies as they communicate, gesture as ironic diacritic, for example.

Meyerhold anchored early claims about bodily movement and contrast to the "most ancient" of forms (much as symbolist Vjacheslav Ivanov evoked ritual Greece, theosophist composer Aleksandr Scriabin turned to Indian art, and Russian futurist poets turned to Scythian sounds). After the Russian Revolution in 1917, Meyerhold mined scientific discourses on the body, reading Frederick Taylor, Aleksei Gastev, Ivan Pavlov, and Vladimir Bekhterev on nervous energies and kinesiology. He also continued to refer to the East, to Kabuki kata, drills for work on movements and relations among movements. Kata and biomechanical drills—like jazz scales—*prepare* repertoires of potential response.[17] Performances never just replicate these drills, when good players respond to other players' twitches—perhaps especially the accidental ones! Meyerhold's actors might modulate even in response to the rustle of the audience. This modulation among possible material shifts in speed, tempo, and intensity, for Meyerhold, generated a sense of energy onstage—as Hollywood would later discover in changing length of shots before switching camera perspectives.[18] Biomechanical training brought this sensibility to the ensemble: as actors practice unfamiliar movements, they sharpen their sensations of them, even with their eyes closed (e.g., to learn the limits of proprioception), becoming able to react quickly to others' also unusual, theatrical motions. For Meyerhold, this nervous reactivity of and to material bodies, to the tempos of their shifting signs, was itself a creative energy, a capacity that he called *reflektornaja vozbudimost'* ("reflex excitability").

PSYCHOPHYSICAL ENERGY

The terms *psikhofizika*, *psikhotekhnika*, and *psikhosensornaja* ("psychophysics," "psychotechnique," and "psychosensory") share intellectual genealogy with Meyerhold's reflex excitability. In contemporary practice at GITIS, as at other acting academies in Russia, they resonate across courses from acting through diction through stage combat.[19] An instructor, in warm-up before acting class, directs students to mime digging holes in tough, hard earth. Moving about the room with a broomstick, he asks each one to compare its wooden feel to his or her own mime. In a velvety timbre, as if voicing a stage hypnotist ("You are getting sleepy . . ."), he intones: "Now it is getting warmer, the earth is getting softer."[20] Some of the boys take off their shirts. Two go on strike. "Dig!" he shouts. "We *are* digging!" They are sweating. Finally he stops them and sends them to imaginary showers. "It is warm, enjoy it. Now contrast the feeling—cold water now." The instructor tells them to rest, to listen now, and probes: "Well, did you feel it? Did you enjoy the shower?" They are nodding. He pronounces: "We call this psychophysical": the drill conditions a dialectic between haptic knowledge and physical memory, to hone an intuitive body-mind, reactive to materials and their imprints.

Stanislavsky exhorted his actors to learn energy not only by doing, but also by watching, especially watching the points from which other beings make sensory contact with the world. During a rehearsal in 1932 he urged: "You have seen how, when a dog or cat gets into stance, all their energy is in their eyes, so that they can direct all that energy just when needed to the muscles. But *you* have all your energy in your stomach" (2000, 197). Energy and sensation still combine as vital metaphor at GITIS. Before beginning a day's acting classes, instructors might charge students this way to shut down certain senses and open others: "Eyes closed. Banish all thoughts about lessons, lateness, little problems. Let your face and mouth slacken, even become stupid. Say the sound 't.' Imagine a state of warmth and happiness. You are filling up with happiness, comfort . . . energy is gathering . . . a complete confidence in concentrating for today's lessons" (Fieldnotes September 2002). "What is acting?" the teacher asks rhetorically, continuing: "The ability to accumulate energy and radiate it to the audience."[21] Gather and fill, accumulate and radiate—the actor is like a battery, the mind like a circuit whose contacts must be cleaned before it can catch and arc energy, the eyelids and the sound "t" acting like material switches, or like the handles that open a *fortochka*.

This is one metaphor of energy, as riding with a substance collected into a body that is both container and conduit. When people at GITIS point to stage communications, however, and judge "here is energy" or "this scene lacks energy," they diverge from that metaphor and come closer to what Meyerhold had in mind. At GITIS they focus on shifts in attention and action that produce *temporitm*, temporhythms being understood as not just rhythms and tempos of actions, but intensities, tones, and frequencies of affect on stage, from sluggish apathy to feverish mania. GITIS students learn *temporitm* by working together: they are the material bodies that make and break physical contacts or that synchronize or desynchronize energies. They are told to mill about the room, to seek out who has the coldest hands. Then they are directed to rub their own hands together rapidly, to gather energy: "Now, try again, and look for who has the hottest hands, hold their hands tightly." Next they stand close together in a circle and are told, "Wait, wait, wait . . . ok, all step forward in unison! Clap! Then step back together." Whoever initiates an energetic movement, the rest are to "catch the impulse." The instructor narrates their wordless action, as if providing inter-titles to a silent film: "You are gathering energy . . . all together. . . . You explode!" They run through the first rounds in jagged asynchrony, but with repetition begin to manage without narration, in cleaner unison each time. They laugh and look at each other, impressed and pleased.

The teacher praises them; they are "giving good pre-signs, good telegraphs, as happens when people understand each other." Achieving energetic contact or synchrony effects alignments that are read as good communication. They are learning, again, to become the mediating material. Late in the academic year, a former student of Knebel' gave a master class on psychophysical energy as a means to understanding, a technology for intuiting the nature of even the most alien forms:

TEACHER: The energy of any object influences our bodies.
Psychologists have confirmed this. This is a game of "as if,"
but behind the game lie psychological realities. It is *as if* you
climb into another's hide. Have you ever been around someone who clears their throat, and then you clear your throat
. . . or you pick up their accent?

STUDENT: That is their energy?

TEACHER: Yes. Not everything has strong energy, though. Ok, before
you we have a stick.

STUDENT: Should we imitate its shape?

TEACHER: Of course. The better you can, the more you can reproduce
its energy. Now I am a stick, with completely evenly distributed energy. It is the same with observing animals—even if
you cannot crawl into the cage, sub-consciously, at a certain
moment you *can* crawl inside [after you] think of it moving
(Fieldnotes, October 2002)

For the novice actor at GITIS, all this work precedes any kind of character building. Here, acting has little or nothing to do with tropes of masking or ideals about authentic expression; the first training goal is to notice and then to embody shifts across material forms as energy.

Russian theatrical institutes begin by training hopeful actors less to express emotions than to pay attention: to the angle of an other's gaze, to the tempo of that person's footsteps, to shifts in changing postures.[22] Before moving on to character work, they have spent many hours over many weeks drilling recall, for example: "Eyes closed! How many ashcans are in the courtyard? Who is wearing which color shoes?" This is rigorous work, intimidating but fun—and they master it, improving quickly at noticing details they once passed by. They learn tactics to hone attention by experimenting with the *tempo-ritm* of sensation; for example, slow your pace when walking in Moscow, learn it as a city both of speed and sudden stasis. They hear a parable: a student rushed to class, was asked to describe his path—he remembered a few harried jostles, some angry words. His teacher had come by the same path but described rich details and interactions. "How could we have come on the same path?" "When you move at different speeds, you traverse different worlds," was the reply.

SEE THE EYE

The aesthetic philosophy of acting as energy exchange is not unique to Russia; Stanislavsky and his colleagues credited Eastern knowledges, creating drills like those above to apply the principles of *prana* to theatrical art (see also Weygandt 2015). Performance studies scholar Zarrilli (2007, 2011), among others, also approaches stage acting in terms of "energetics" rather than representation,[23] especially when writing from the vantage of the actor. Such philosophies are present in the United States, although American professional actors come upon them later in their careers, in special master classes. We live in a world in which forms of energy rule the rulers. Small wonder that political economy and infrastructure shape visions of not only biological processes, of life and healing (Barchunova 2007; Farquhar 2002), but also of sociality and communication (Chudakova 2015; Kruglova 2014).[24]

Romantic thinkers in the eighteenth century drew upon performances of famous actors, such as David Garrick, to project a science of vital forces in the body, driving sensation and animation;[25] a century later, Stanislavsky turned to nerve science. How can we repeat a scene for the hundredth time as if it were the first? Where mechanical acting is the result of fear, how can we relax, in order to concentrate through the stage fright? How can we reinvigorate what repetition deadened and refresh sensitivity and intuition in ways that make acting more compelling for audiences, not just for actors? He developed his approach to these matters while reading, for example, Ivan Sechenov's 1863 work on reflex inhibition and the startle response; Fechner's writings on the thresholds at which humans register changes in sensation; and Théodule-Armand Ribot, in *Psychology of Attention*, on emanations, radiations, and exchanges of energy. While reading both romantic natural science on electromagnetism (Friedrich Schelling's *Naturphilisophie*) and psychophysical studies of sensation, he also studied yogic ideas of *prana*.[26] These were the broad inspirations for Stanislavsky and his colleagues to develop drills to send and receive communicative energies, alternating terms like *prana* and *rays* to describe them:[27] "What to do? Communicate with your gazes. Because in life we often communicate with each other by our gazes. If we imagine a photograph of this moment, then rays are being emitted between you, fluids are being sent, an invisible conversation is carried on just by the eyes" (Stanislavsky rehearsing *Figaro*, 2000, 196).

This focus on the eye and its emissions requires a detour from scholarship on the gaze, the techniques and infrastructures of surveillance that structure prisons, land surveys, and patriarchal orders. The issue here is less how the gaze can see (or is imagined to see) so much as who perceives the gaze and how. For Stanislavsky, intuition requires delicate attention to others' organs for sensation and to lines of eye contact. Montesquieu's experiments similarly isolated the tongue, exposing it to hot and cold in order to chart changing qualities of the tongue's nervous fibers as they expanded or contracted— to hypothesize difference in the feeling capacities of nations north and south.

The phatic experts I have come to know also learn to analyze and then to focus attention around points of perception: eyes, ears, hands, tongue, nose, fingers, and toes become media for sensory and social contact, as well as diagnostic signs of contact. The eye—or rather its shine—the hand—or rather its warmth—is claimed to exhibit the essences of capacities to feel relational contact.[28] The gaze thus becomes itself an object for surveillance, such as when one teacher at GITIS chastised a student for shutting off contact: "You are angry, your eyes are dull, you don't even want to hear what I am telling you" (the student complained later in bitter terms, confirming the read).

"Where are the eyes!?" cries an instructor. He has sent students to the Moscow zoo to observe differences between the stare of the owl and of the gorilla. The results, as yet, disappoint him. Instructors more than once boasted of times past when intelligence agents used to visit, hoping to learn the hermeneutics of the eyes, the better to conduct detection work or interrogation after training in these technologies for intuition. They would always take at least the first steps in the acting courses, visiting the zoo to watch the animals: "Those agents went and sat in the cathouse and learned to do their work [by observing] lion's eyes." Activating this onstage, however, requires sustained effort well beyond a few trips to the zoo. The lack of "compelling eyes" was a constant focus for instructors' criticism: "It was interesting, earlier, to watch you, but watching you play a shoemaker now is not. Where does this happen? And not once, no eyes. Nowhere is it clear. It is all, 'here is how I walk, here are some boots.' I want to see variations in the eyes, a person who *looks* first at the boots, *then* at the bottle. . . . [H]ow do they mean different things? What is more, bottles mean different things to different people—and so, whose boots are these?" (Fieldnotes, November 26, 2002). Without studied attention to the movements and aims of looking—attention to physical sense organs (and eventually to material, historical conditions that channel the character's perception)—nothing is interesting, nothing will hold the audience attentive to channels for theatrical contact; phatic efforts across the proscenium fail. There is no energy.

By the end of their five years at GITIS acting and directing students learn to fill out haptic and recollected knowledge of sensation with other forms of historical and social knowledge. In 2005 I filmed a rehearsal of Gogol's *Nose* at GITIS during which the student director and his actors devoted hours to staging two minutes of dialogue, testing, adjusting, and discussing tiny shifts in gaze, volume, and gesture. They were working over the beginning: barber Ivan Jakovlevich has accidentally shaved the nose off a customer the night before. Just after throwing the nose into the Neva River, he notices the gaze of a militiaman. On a bare stage, the student director and actors worked through a dozen ways to play the barber's perception of another's perception, combining coughs and boot squeaks, pauses and quick shuffles. To depict a common sensation—that one has attracted the eyes of authority—in ways specific to the characters, they moved in discussion back and forth among the script, the geography of bridges in St. Petersburg, and differences among kinds of encounters with police.

SOCIAL DIVISION OF THE SENSORY FIELD

Extrasensory powers are expressed materially, through sensory deeds. The psychic's intuition is proven by material means; skeptics marshal objects and structures to create randomness and double blind, and they master observation of material shifts: the direction of a gaze, the tempo of a gesture. Each season of *Battle of the Psychics* begins with auditions, narrowing the field from a few hundred hopefuls to about thirteen.

Battle of the Psychics stages parades of failures. The first episode of each season always documents a maximum of botched trials and awkward screen tests. After preliminary casting in the provinces, promising contestants travel to Moscow, where, on the first day of auditions, cameras document their convergence in motley streams on the park near the casting hall. They

FIGURES 2.2 AND 2.3. Publicity shots from auditions on the set of *Battle of the Psychics*. Hopeful contestants stretch their hands to "see" behind the black screen set up on the auditorium's stage.

pass through a series of trials, the first beginning always in an auditorium, where a black screen is set up onstage. Once it hid a ballerina, once an owl; once the screen concealed dirty dishes crawling with cockroaches. Nearly everyone fails to describe anything close to what stands behind. The editors produce a montage of absurd misses; a ballerina stretches behind the screen as someone claims that whatever is there is "definitely not alive" or "emits a sinister energy." The camera pans a range of paranormal techniques: some draw, some sit quietly, some stare intently; one woman stands in the aisle howling, hands stretched up; another fixes a dowsing rod to her forehead; somebody tries to build a fire onstage; a guy in a headband traces signs in the air with a knife; and a young woman waves an antelope's furry foreleg.

A few miraculously succeed, but most fail. Some entertainingly rationalize their failures. As each season proceeds, failure talk fills episodes. Each season begins with a flood of failures, which produce dramatic conflict as accusations of cheating meet justifications, and arguments or tantrums are layered over by expert commentary. The experts convey opinions on the strength or weakness of each psychic, not only by speaking but also through physical gesture. The magician brothers roll their eyes and exchange glances when contestants falter or brag too much. The editors scatter shots of such reactions throughout (possibly layering them with events with which they did not co-occur). One season devoted an episode just before the finale to the experts' recollecting the auditions, revisiting the behavior of psychics who had flunked early onl they found especially hilarious a woman "from the south" who would twitch her head sharply to the right when speaking to her source in the astral plane. They said that she switched too rapidly between addressing humans and spirits, robotically, like a businesswoman more dedicated to her blue tooth than to the present company. One expert pronounced her phony, another "not quite right."

After the test of the black screen, the next always occurs inside a large warehouse, where the crew has hidden a person in a trunk among around thirty parked cars. Like most tests for extrasensory powers, this one blocks senses "extra" to *ekstrasens*; here, metal blocks vision. Each hopeful passes through security, his or her limbs and torsos wanded with wireless metal detectors as each strips off electronic communication devices, placing them in transparent plastic bins, just as at the airport. Contestants are, however, allowed to keep older media, devices made of wood or stone, such as dowsing sticks, divining pebbles, or matches—these are valid prosthetic extensions, feelers and amplifiers for psychic extrasensation. Contestants are not to use ordinary senses like vision or hearing; media such as cell phones in this setting are, albeit new, also too mundane, compared to the media of, say, gems energized by spirits.[29]

Before those auditioning enter, the crew sometimes creates false extraneous sense data, pressing hand prints into the dust on empty cars. In early seasons, passersby from the street were enlisted first, as a control, the camera recording their reliance on ordinary sense data, but their attempts at Sherlockian logic led them astray: "This car shows fewer fingerprints, so it must be that one"; or, "That car's trunk is much too small," or "I think I heard an echo, so logically, it must be that way."[30] Contestants who do well, by contrast, stand silently, never attending to *those* details, and if they demonstrate the usual senses, they do so in unusual ways: they tilt their chins at some unheard sound or feel for information in the ether with their palms. A close-up on a face depicts a "sharp gaze" aimed not *at* objects or bodies on set but *through* them. Most contestants are savvy enough to avoid speaking about material qualities that usually distinguish cars, such as paint color or engine size, and avoid mentioning the traces in the dust. When the experts notice such deductive detective work, they call it out; this is an excess of sensation that signifies failure. By contrast, to speak of sensations not normally associated with cars—human heat emanating through the trunk—is perfectly fitting. Successful *Battle* contestants may not evoke ordinary sense data, but they must depict sensation; they just have to do so via unexpected routings, unusual materials, and forgotten sensory channels.

While they are not to *sense* the usual material details in the usual way, contestants still must *speak* of them. One test every season places them blindfolded in a room with a "Mister X," usually a celebrity (male or female, regardless of the "Mister"). The psychics start by venturing generalities: "Somebody in your life is named Olga"; "You almost died once." Whether they hit or miss the mark, the camera cuts to Mr. X performing the oscillating agnostic, looking either impressed or unconvinced, raising eyebrows or shaking his or her head. One Mr. X, particularly enthralled by the psychic's accuracy, in an intercut praised her for speaking of "many lively details," such as the way he touches his beard when he smiles.

Meanwhile, video crew and editors provide *the audience* with materially saturated grounds against which to witness psychics' interactions and efforts. We watch the crew select objects inside an apartment (a tea kettle, a row of stuffed animals) upon which the psychic is to focus and hide other objects that "tell too much" (family photos). We listen as the master of ceremonies narrates a car crash, the occurrence of which the psychic is to divine, while the camera inspects each dent.

These spectacles recall the aesthetic arrangements and pleasures of the laboratory: anthropologist Joseph Masco (2004), for example, discusses how twentieth-century nuclear testing in the United States pushed further underground, distancing researchers' capacities to perceive the sound or light from a blast, shifting instead to virtual sensoria to animate blast scale and intensity through numbers and screens. *Battle of the Psychics* separates participants from some sensoria, but even more important, it situates different participants to differently *engage and disengage* the senses. To watch is less to play a game of "now you see it, now you don't," than it is to play "now you see him see, now you see him not see, now you see her see him not see." The show tests for extrasensation by distributing *differences* in sensory excess and sensory lack *across a social field*. The labors of sensing and extrasensing are divided from the work of speaking about acts of sensing or not sensing.

Spectacular aims of *Battle* partly converge with those at GITIS, where core projects also cultivate and manage differences among relations to sensation. All teachers there, across classes in acting, stage diction, song, dance, and stage movement, exhort students to attend to alternative senses, those usually neglected. Drills are set them to detect movements using only hearing, to imagine moving about in a forest as if all they can sense is odors. They are urged to extend sensitivity beyond the canonical five,[31] to attend to the senses of gravity, of temperature, of time and tempo, and of kinetic impulse or psychophysical energy. One teacher, from a city east of Moscow, told a story about a 1990s demonstration on Pushkin Square (for human rights for prisoners), forwarding a sense for crowd vitality: "15,000 people—I'd never felt such an animal herd before. A terrifying energy, especially when the police pushed. I simply felt the instinct to pick up a rock. Awful, that kind of energy! Like in a stadium. This, too, is a kind of sense, the sense of energy" (Fieldnotes, October 2002). *Battle* and GITIS both foreground the problem of phatic obstacles: screens and blinds, skeptics and hostile audiences who distract (students even practice communicating over hecklers). Both distribute distinctions in sensation across social fields. But they do these things to different ends. To illustrate, let me offer examples from both places in which the topic is the unusual application of touch instead of sight, or skin-vision, to read the paper.

One resident expert on *Battle*, psychologist and psychic tester Mikhail Vinogradov, often recollects on air the heyday of Soviet telepathy science in the 1960s: "They even discovered a woman" who, having been temporarily blinded by injury, could see colors through her fingertips, and even, as he told me and a friend of mine invited to his dacha, "excuse me, also with this soft part [pointing to his right buttock]." That detail never made it into international accounts of Soviet studies of dermo-optics (see, e.g., *Life Magazine*, June 12, 1964) or into central Soviet press accounts (regional papers may tell another story). In season eight of *Battle* (episode 3), a male contestant refuses to finish a trial in which, blindfolded, he was to read a newspaper in front of the seated jury of skeptics, asserting that this was not his strong suit (*"Ne moego masta!"*) and griping, "What's the point? You might as well have me read colors through my buttocks next, like they did back then to that lady, Rosa." The magician skeptics scoffed at such an experiment, but during jury critique at the end of the episode, as they labeled the contestant's excuse "ridiculous," Vinogradov interjected: he had been there, and the woman who could read paper with her buttocks was named Roza Kuleshova. Still, his interjection strengthened the argument against the candidate, who clearly lacked this extrasensory ability.

Analogy to skin-vision arose at GITIS during a rehearsal for a semester exam that combined sketches students had been polishing over the semester. One of these, titled "Classroom," pulled together character studies based on student observations of street life, children in playgrounds, and animals at home or at the zoo. At the conclusion, a student playing a little boy is left alone in the classroom, amusing himself with his chewing gum, mittens dangling on strings. Deciding to stick the gum under the desk where he sits, he gropes underneath, and his fingers encounter a folded piece of paper. He pulls it out; it is shiny and colorful. Eyes big, he opens it so that the audience can see a colorful montage of breasts and buttocks, and reverently begins turning the tabloid pages. The head teacher halts the action: "NO! STOP! It is as if you had already read it with your fingers! It is as if all at once you could sense: 'Oh-ho, pornography!'"

Reading paper *as if* blindfolded, like Rosa Kulesheva, discerning content *without* sensing it in the usual way, without the usual gaps, confusions, and double takes, is exactly what an actor must *not* do. If it is compelling for a psychic to smoothly and quickly decode letters on paper with the skin of her buttocks, but it is boring for the actor to detect buttocks on paper without showing us troubles that channel perception of the unexpected. He should let the audience watch *how* his expectations are undone; perhaps he takes the paper at first for a note or a grocery list. Because he circumvented ordinary sensation, like a psychic, in displaying knowledge too soon, he has failed as an actor. The teacher advises him to work with less surety, to reveal the stumbling of blind fingers, the fog as virgin eyes pick out a texture here, a form there, take on sense and shape. He is to depict maximum involvement with the material, letting viewers linger on his sensing organs as they encounter a world. To make contact with them, to communicate, the audience must see the eyes see.

Phatic projects at GITIS and on the set of *Battle* depend on collective work and divisions of expertise, and both are concerned with regulating contact points and channels. But they are not equally invested in maximizing communication, and not in the same ways. In both spaces, phatic experts oversee divisions of sensory labors, and editors or master instructors oversee their oversight. One concrete difference is this: most theatrical work focuses attention on how stage characters move *between sensory deficit and excess*, while *Battle* follows divisions of sensory labor *among participants, including crew, observers on set, and projected audiences*. The difference is not absolute, and there are genres from reality show to avant-garde theater that resemble *Battle*. Moreover, both are material in ways that belie the DoD's characterization of Soviet or Russian materialisms as narrow and repressive.

SENSATION MEMORY

That characterization lines up with Anglophone claims that Stanislavsky turned to a dull materialism under Soviet pressure. During the waning Cold War and afterward, in middle school, high school, and college, in private courses and under amateur and professional directors (in Nebraska, New York, Illinois, and Michigan), I encountered acting and teachers claiming to have links to Stanislavsky, but not psychophysical stage pedagogy.[32] We performed mirroring drills and improvised in groups, but with different metaphors, emphases, and goals that stressed emotion in memory and expression, less attention to energy and sensation. For all we knew, what was said about Stanislavsky was true.

American romance with Russian acting techniques flourished even after McCarthy and the arrests of the Hollywood Ten in the late 1940s; we lionized Stanislavsky all the more as a champion of inner emotional expression. However, ideological limits and the demands of translation constrained what Americans took to represent Stanislavsky's thinking. Method acting made for interesting theater, but its main adherents trafficked in mistranslations that affirmed prejudices about Soviet communication and myths about acting in general.

While American professional actors may be aware that Method radically distorted Stanislavsky's work, most Americans, if they ever talk about acting or Stanislavsky, speak of "emotion memory." Theater scholar Sharon Carnicke (1998), carefully contrasting English translations with Russian manuscripts, tracks the movement of Stanislavsky's pedagogy into an American Freudian register.[33] This is the source for Method insistence on remembered feelings, surging from deep inside each individual actor, like a life force to animate a character. Director Lee Strasberg,[34] credited with deriving Method acting from Stanislavsky, admits as much when he describes hearing Richard Boleslavsky, a student of Stanislavsky who emigrated to the United States in the 1920s, say in a lecture: "'We posit a theatre of real experience. The essential thing in such experience is that the actor learns to know and to do, not through mental knowledge, but by sensory knowledge.' Suddenly I knew, That's it! That's it! ... That was the answer I had been searching for. The point is, I had already read Freud and already knew the things that go on in a human being without consciousness" (cited in Carnicke 1998, 144–45). Boleslavsky opposes "mental knowledge" to learning by "sensation"; Strasberg hears him, but jumps rails, to describe things going on unknown "in" a human being.[35]

Translators cut Stanislavsky's writing about physical action and energy, instead foregrounding passages about affective memory. They inflated such memory from its status as one resource among others and deflected the original stress on specific, embodied memories of sensations or feelings to instead encourage meditation on buried childhood trauma. For Stanislavsky, affective memory could come in handy in a pinch, as a lure to flagging inspiration, but was not to infuse performances; with Denis Diderot, Stanislavsky feared that, like drugs or alcohol, too much passion gives the actor the illusion of deep experience even while ruining communication with the audience. Stanislavsky also warned against *aiming* for emotional results and advised focusing instead on specific actions, little material tasks. Entire pages of such warnings in the Russian manuscript are reduced to a few vague sentences in the English. As Carnicke notes, "personal substitutions [of emotion], so familiar from the American Method, do not appear" in the original text at all (1998, 3).

The English publishers eliminated words stressing "outer" conditions, such as events, substituting terms to suggest that actors explore "inner" memories and feelings. Thus, where Stanislavsky's language exhorted actors to live *the role*, American Method urged actors to animate the role from their *own* lives. A deceptively simple reversal, one foreign to those who read the Russian originals. Soviet psychologist Lev Vygotsky (who published theatrical criticism before turning to psychology) in his 1933 monograph *Thought and Speech*, quotes Stanislavsky to support his own argument that it is "external" interaction that constitutes "internal" selves,[36] stressing how the director exhorted actors to *first* research social relations and material conditions implied in the script *before* beginning to craft a character's "inner life" ([1933] 1986, 250–52). Stanislavsky, Vygotsky highlights, did not excise the category of "inner life"; rather, he urged artists to attend *first* to the materials and relations that afford it. Working to shape theatrical ensembles, Stanislavsky pursued this relational materialism decades before Soviet-era ideologies and practices nurtured a socialist brand of the individual, with an "inner life" developed in relation to collectives (Kharkhordin 1999; Oushakine 2004). Many Americans—critics and social commentators—have claimed that English translations of Stanislavsky's writings salvaged an authentic emphasis on emotions, that his work on "given conditions" and "physical actions" was a late-life capitulation to Soviet materialism, an obligatory bow to Pavlovian science. Such conclusions rest on ignorance of Russian participation in continental European research on nerves and psychophysics and contributions of

Russian neuroscience long before the Revolution (Carnicke 1998). Claims that the maestro switched to materialism late in life, and under Soviet pressure, do not hold up to scrutiny of his drafts and reading notes or of notes on rehearsals and lessons (see especially Roach 1993).[37]

He was a materialist well before the Russian Revolution, enchanted by Bekhterev's correspondence with Jean Martin Charcot on the energies of the nervous system, and by the early writings of Taylor and Gastev on task definition and management (Pitches 2006, 31; Benedetti 1990, 164). Stanislavsky saw his system as dual, enabling work from two directions at once: actors should train bodily reactivity as they simultaneously conduct documentary, ethnographic research on "given conditions" implied in the script.[38] The system would converge from two ends into a *psychophysical* unity of living action.

A century later Russian media still recognize Stanislavsky for psychophysical techniques such as breathing and concentration exercises to develop and sustain creative energy. Here is an example from the mid-1990s, in reply to a letter from a reader of the Russian-language version of the glossy magazine *Cosmopolitan*. The magazine's advice columnist suggested that the letter writer do "as in the Stanislavsky school," that is, attend to her bodily reactions, to her own breathing when in a comfortable situation, and then reproduce that breathing when stressed ("Krik dushi" 1997, 32). Ideologies of theater as masking have little purchase at GITIS. The techniques by which actors learn to separate from or meld with the characters they voice[39] do not craft expressions to arise onstage from within each individual, but instead rouse energies to ride multiple channels for contact, organized by collective phatic labors and expertise.

At GITIS there is little use for metaphors of the actor as hollow puppet or room for treating them as such. McCarthy era attributions of Russian origins to aspects of Method acting such as emotion memory dissolve. Its ostensibly enemy methods for communication (like those of the unions, whose meetings, pamphlets, and strikes the House Un-American Activities Committee tried to label as un-American) turn out to be homegrown. Cold War paranoia about Manchurian robots was manufactured without the Russians; it may have deeper roots in Anglophone gothic fiction than in the actual movements of people, methods, and ideas over recent centuries.

HERDING MATERIALS AND INTERPRETANTS

In the USSR, stage psychics and magicians appeared alongside variety acts and educational lecturers[40] as long as posters advertised the finale to

FIGURE 2.4. Messing performing telepathy in front of both an audience and a jury in 1966. Reprinted in *Sovershenno Sekretno*, February 1, 2012.

demystify with materialist science. Wolf Messing, performing in local theaters all over the Soviet Union until the 1970s, was allowed to demonstrate telepathy as long as he explained his skill as "reading muscles, not minds," sensing changes in motion and tempo, breath and gaze (1961, 6; Lungina 1992). Some attendees recall that he would skip that part.[41] Newspapers and biographies tell us that even when he did debunk immaterial explanations, audiences were impressed by his virtuosic ability to perceive "ideomotor impulses," those minute psychophysical shifts in pulse or eye movement. This was hardly less impressive than telepathy, even more so in a crowded hall among many distractions (though sometimes the more people, the more movements to read).

Soviet stage psychics, like their European colleagues, professional magicians in suits and gloves, waged rationalist combat against spiritualists, mediums, and mages.[42] Like them, Messing shared the stage with juries of skeptics recruited from audience volunteers and local authorities (journalists, teachers, collective farm heads, scientists) and also from among fellow magicians, trained to perceive illusions and sleights of hand (see also Wooffitt 2006; Jones 2011, 92). Magicians, after all, are phatic experts alert to distraction techniques onstage: sleight of hand for physical illusions, "cold reading" for mental ones.

Anglophone skeptics of the paranormal use the phrase "cold reading" to describe discursive and observational techniques by which psychics create the appearance of knowing things that "no one else could know."[43] The magician specialists who sit on the jury of *Battle* are supposed to detect when telepaths are cold reading, or sometimes describe muscle reading as an aid to cold reading, and to point out such violations. A Russian phrase meaning "cold reading" (*kholodnoe chtenie*) exists, although the *Battle* experts use other language to maintain that this or that psychic is "really just a good psychologist" who has "merely" trained to attend to all the little signs in stray interpretants.

Cold reading calls upon a conversation partner to fill in blanks in a fashion that seems to put private details into the mouth of the psychic; it induces a sense of projection,[44] "as if" the psychic voices the subject. In effect, subjects read their own minds, coaxed to use channels that they do not recognize as communicative or to speak in ways that elide how and when information passes. It is a technology for intuition that claims to work without material mediation but in fact relies on specific forms. It is not difficult to master, especially when working in teams. They share aspects with poker skills, improvisation skills, and skills that many of us learn who perform emotional labor (and most emotional labor requires phatic ingenuity). One tactic is to look for aural, visual, and kinetic "tells": signs that people give off despite themselves (the very ones that frustrate certain theater directors). An intake of breath, a blink, a hesitation, a slight movement of the face, a correction in grammar—any small reaction can be taken up, even *as* an ambiguous or excess sign, to demonstrate intuition even as words do not cohere: "I can see this does not make sense to you yet."

In essence, cold readers manage those initial proliferations of interpretants—proliferations that are almost inevitable when making first conversational contact with a stranger in public—and herd them into streams, some of which are bound to cohere into shapes, into meanings that feel like telepathy or clairvoyance. More concretely, to begin, a cold reader might make a few high probability guesses, drawing on available materials such as clothing or gestures as signs. Fingernails can suggest questions to suit a person identifying as tomboy versus a femme, a carpenter versus a musician: "Why have you stopped playing guitar?" "I don't play guitar, my wife does." "Ah, that explains it!" This is basic inductive reasoning, with the additional strategy to make use of those mistakes that induction can introduce. Such mistakes do not derail a practiced cold reader. Vigilant for tells of surprise or doubt, she can deftly change course or keep fishing: "No, no, it wasn't you, but *someone* in your family knows a Thomas" (see also Randi 1982). In such moments, many subjects will fill in the blanks or make corrections, thus fortifying the channel for the information as the psychic hones in around the near misses.

One effective opener is to deploy opposites: "You can be very chatty with the right people, but sometimes you feel silenced." This works when statements that balance opposing categories can pass as robust truisms (scholars do this, too, but at times cannot). Another is to make statements that can be true of anyone: "You feel like you never get caught up with all your e-mail," or, "Someone at work is making things difficult for you." Having spoken a general truth, the psychic invites clients to fill in the specifics. Failures in cold reading are expected; they are productive precisely because they invite correction and detail.

THE PUDDING IS IN THE PROVING

Judgments about failures, conversations, and actions that unroll after such verdicts open to further effects. Some failures do unsettle the reputation of a single psychic subject, while still affirming the conditions of the test. Its procedures reinforce some channels and split others. Maria Knebel' insisted that failing at telepathy spurred students to attend better. More to my point are structures of participation: when students line up "boys on one side, girls on the other," in order to cross a gap they first have to create one. To practice contact *they first practice social division*. In the telepathy lab, failure to send thought through a Faraday chamber wall affirms the materiality of the wall—as well as a social division of research labor around the wall. Certain conditions are placed under scrutiny ("Is the blindfold opaque?") while social arrangements around those conditions remain unexamined. The failures of one set buttress the authority of the other.

Battle of the Psychics could not exist without failures. At the end of each episode, the jury of experts, magicians, invited skeptics, and occasionally witnesses selects a winner and a loser. The announcement is but a denouement, for in each episode the pudding is in the proving, the pleasure in the testing and the criticism, the reasoning of failure; fan blogs take things even further, debating expert calls and trashing both losing and winning psychics' techniques, expressing more schadenfreude than wonder.[45]

The social and political stakes of boosting skepticism can be quite high. Consider again Olender's 1989 documentary (*9 Years with the Psychics/ Extransensates*). The film opens with actor and film director Nikolai Ermolaev touting his fame to a small group of visitors in his apartment: "They wrote about [what I could do] in *Stern*, in *Match*." The academics studying him, A. P. Dubrov and V. Pushkin, had named his powers biogravitation; he would sit on a chair and hold an object, a cigarette, between his knees. As he pulled his hands away, it would seem to stick to his *biopole* (biofield) as he slowly extracted his hands until the cigarette dangled, as if in gravitational orbit. Just three years after Olender's documentary was released, the Soviet Union was no more, and ABC World of Discovery made its own documentary, *Powers of the Russian Psychics* (1992). One section claims to reveal Ermolaev's method, visiting him in Moscow not long before he emigrated to Montreal. The lighting conditions, explains the American narrator, differing from those to which Ermolaev had been accustomed, allowed editors to spot a fine thread fixed between his knees. In the same year, the BBC produced a parallel documentary featuring American former magician and professional debunker and skeptic James Randi. In the first half, Randi debunks horoscopes and television mediums in the United States; in the second, he debunks psychic healers and stage telepaths in Russia. Translator in tow, he visits a center for brain research, where experiments on stage psychic Ignatenko (the same person as in Olender's film) are underway; a center for nontraditional medicine; and a pair of sister clairvoyants. Randi presses the researchers to adopt randomization and double-blind methods; the Russians are not materialist enough for him. He keeps a blank poker face when the sisters attempt to cold read him. He pronounces failures all around.

These American and British documentary reporting missions began almost immediately after the Soviet Union dissolved, reviving the thrill of books like Ostrander and Schroeder's 1970 *Psychic Discoveries* while also running a Cold War victory lap, clamoring to teach Western rationality. Both films imply absence of critical thought and debate,[46] not only in the present but also in the past—as if Soviet-era calls for standardized methods and randomization in Russian telepathy tests had never happened.

In 1967 a group of scientists had complained that the Soviet press reported too many experiments that affirmed psychic powers and not those that did not. In response, the editorial staff of the journal *Literaturnaja Gazeta* organized a test to challenge those experiments reported on by other papers and gathered a multidisciplinary panel to ensure checks such as randomization and double-blind techniques. Two teams, one for the sender in Moscow and one with the receiver in Kerch, were isolated for several days, with no access to telephone, radio, or other channels of communication. Fifty pairs of identical objects were split between the two teams and numbered. At predesignated times, the Moscow team would roll dice to select an object for mental transmission, then write down: #2 champagne cork, #17 axe, and so forth. The sender would then concentrate on the eraser, sole of a shoe, or anniversary kopeck to transmit to the distant human receiver.

The receiver (actor Boris Nikolaev), sitting in a rehearsal room in the Kerch municipal theater, was to select among fifty analogous objects laid out on a table; his team would then write down the name of the object and its number. Three days later, back in Moscow, envelopes containing the two lists were opened in front of both teams and still more observers. The paper published all the transmissions side by side.[47] Of the ten material objects sent and the ten received, the number of matches was exactly zero: an axe was sent, a wooden soldier received; a ball bearing was answered by a plastic doll leg. The commission agreed: they saw no signs of telepathy but supported further study "as long as both negative and positive results" were published.

Randi and his Soviet-era counterparts were operating in the same tradition, performing scientific skepticism, claiming modernity by asserting others' deficiencies in reasoning or evidence. Such claims have a long history among techniques for justifying state rule and industrial divisions of labor (see Jones 2009; Morris 2000; Meyer and Pels 2003; Wiener 2013) in both capitalist and socialist systems. French powers discredited wizardry in the colonies, and early Soviet atheist campaigns dislodged the angels, taking peasants by airplane into the clouds.[48] To stage a debunking is also to call upon audiences to join in, "to exercise their individual powers of objectivity" (Jones 2009), to be enlightened, pragmatic, savvy, and hip. Meanwhile, the skeptic can still freshly enchant with "technical virtuosity" (as in the Messing performances), where science seems to generate a "technology of deceit as impressive as any 'real magic.'" (Morris 2000, 466; Lachapelle 2008; see also Gell and Hirsch 1999).

Plenty of Soviet-era critics were alert to this irony, as they were to the artful use of scientific imagery and language. A. Kitajgorodsky, an opponent of pseudoscience and strongly skeptical, explained 1960s Soviet fascination with telepathy in his contribution to a series in *Literaturnaja Gazeta*, arguing: "Science, in the last decade, has introduced amazing discoveries: atomic energy, rockets into the cosmos, miraculous medicines, the genetic code . . . [but] many, without thinking, have lost caution, and too easily digest and adopt any revelation served up under a sufficiently scientific sauce" (1964, 9). Most privileged visitors to Russia, even including Mr. Randi, never learn basic conversational Russian, and certainly not enough to perceive debates on these or other matters in current times, much less Soviet times; this is one reason that we reduce complex issues to the simplicity afforded by our own limits. Kitajgorodsky's piece did not end the discussion; it was answered in the same thematic section of the issue ("The Debate Continues—What Is Telepathy") by a piece just after it, "No Need to Fear the Facts!" by psychiatrist A. Roshchin. Roshchin accused Kitajgorodsky of the same closed

mindedness that "just ten or fifteen years" before had targeted experimental genetics, resulting in the excesses of Lysenkoism, and he challenged
Kitajgorodsky to work through all the data, not just the negative, including
information emerging from studies of synesthesia and dermo-optics.
Urging his colleague to temper that critical edge with open, agnostic skepticism, he turned to materialist wonder, likening the ability to sense colors
printed on paper by fingers to the ways octopi sense light through the skin.

   During late Soviet years many called for balance, for open-minded skepticism about skepticism itself. Olender's documentary film narrator
expressed that very mood when pronouncing that the blindfolded stage telepath's tests "showed 80% accuracy—and cannot be explained by science."
The editing accents this tone with the minor, glissando notes of the theremin
over the narrator's soft voice, using none of the staccato tempos or major
notes associated with declaration and command. In that documentary
questions such as "Do they believe?" or even "Why do they believe?"—
questions still hegemonic in the social science of magic, religion, occult, or
the paranormal[49]—have little purchase. Soviet agnostic modernism elevated
the curious over the strictly rational subject; acknowledging this project
unsettles our stable vision of opposites whereby Soviet-era hyperrationality
represses Russian mysticism and whereby the West judges both extremes
lacking. In fact, however, this mood remains in the repertoire, audible when
post-Soviets declare their willingness to be convinced or not, for either way
they will partake in the pleasures of testing itself. *Battle,* in scenes that
encompass skeptical criticism with wonder and then in scenes that do the
opposite, claims to proudly balance agnosticism, to test perspectives.

3. Phatic Evolution: Race and Geopolitics

Claims to rational skepticism. Claims to critical thinking. Claims to genius. Claims that mental skills are inherent, inborn. Claims to superpowers. Such claims underwrite the tactics of both psychic and skeptical practices on the psychic stage. They both draw and dissolve lines dividing species (consider speculation about the psychic abilities of dolphins as "more evolved than we are") and peoples, figuring even in ideological struggles to define geopolitical relations.

Anthropologist David Samuels (2005, 104) notes that telepathy—the ultimate clear channel—is frequently figured as characteristic of highly evolved beings (as in Robert Heinlein's *Stranger in a Strange Land*). In the 1960s world of *Star Trek*, where contact with aliens such as Vulcans has ended warfare on Earth, half-breed Spock can achieve the Vulcan mind meld, while the human crew on the *Enterprise* makes do with language and mechanical translators.

Samuels notes that telepathy is also depicted conversely as a lost sense that once linked humanity with all of nature, as in William Golding's *The Inheritors* (1964), in which telepathic Neanderthals are replaced by Homo sapiens.[1] The film *Avatar* (2009) does similar work: humanoid and other fauna communicate telepathically by joining pony tails and upload memories through the fibers of the World Tree. The power to make mental contact marks opposing ends along scales of both evolutionary progress and regression. A late Soviet comic film playing off them by negating them both is *Kin-dza-dza!* (1986), in which inhabitants of the desert planet Pljuk immediately understand earthling Russian via telepathy, while the spoken Pljukan lexicon is coarse and sparse (about ten words), and Pljukans themselves practice trickery and crooked trade.

In person, even in a single conversation people are quite able to switch up evolutionary values. In 2009 in Moscow, a celebrity psychic expounded to me in her office: "Nowadays we all have cell phones, we call each other and what do we say? We say: 'Where are you?' Compare that to the days of Atlantis, back then people were more advanced, because they *had* to feel each other." By that logic, Soviet people untrained to the prosthetic cell phone channel, who stood in line at the post office to make calls, might have better commanded telepathic contact. Still, some minutes later the psychic spoke proudly about having appeared on a television program the year before devoted to the discovery of "meta" powers in specially evolved humans.

In Anglophone and Russophone worlds alike, writers and filmmakers have crafted characters who stand above and apart, especially when the superpower is mental. Such heroes may protect the dull masses (like the unfortunate Muggles in the Harry Potter universe) or work to improve the lumpen idiot classes (see Kukulin 2011; Lipovetsky 2013).[2] In the United States, science fiction often lionizes a chosen one, usually a man, endowed with extrasensory capacities, fighting for freedom ("Use the force, Luke"). The genius raised above the rest strides through Ayn Rand's *Atlas Shrugged* and Orson Scott Card's *Ender's Game*, both on the recommended reading list for the U.S. Marine Corps: "The few, the proud!" If American Ender is sadly alone in his brilliant awareness, so, too, is the Soviet hero whose mental powers outstrip those around him. In the Strugatsky brothers' novel *Hard to Be a God* (1964), the protagonist is forbidden to reveal his advanced thinking or tools to inhabitants of a planet lower down the rungs of social evolution than his own; he is not to interfere in their progress (much as *Star Trek* fleets accept the prime directive, to make contact but not to interfere). Literary scholar Lipovetsky argues that the Strugatsky brothers called on readers—Soviet intellectuals—to fancy themselves as like the hero, as champions of liberty and of higher level thought, evolved over "the social/cultural/ethnic Other: 'uneducated scum,' immigrant workers from Central Asia, people from the Caucasus, etc." (2013, 129). Science fiction in the United States closer to the Left, on the other hand, fears for the safety of the isolated, telepathic mutant—Octavia Butler's *Mind of My Mind* treats genetic inheritance of telepathic ability as an allegory for postslavery systems of labor and kinship that re-create structures for exploitation. In the *X-Men* comics and films, psychic outcasts stand among other avatars for people who struggle for disability rights. Telepathic superheroes and outcasts starred in stories read on the Kansas plains and in the Urals hills.[3]

The evolutionary scales applied to telepathy parallel those apparent in evocations of phatic expertise. About twenty years ago a Moscow friend of mine, a designer, asked me for my thoughts on a book by political scientist Francis Fukuyama, a 1996 tract on trust, especially among strangers in markets. The thesis contrasted Russia to other countries as "less trustful," aligning this deficiency with "lower levels of civilization," as measured by GDP, election statistics, and infrastructure. The book projected something like phatic evolution by linking national cultures' degrees and kinds of social trust to economic growth and electoral practices. Many in Russia during the late 1990s saw Soviet-raised persons as lacking both tools for accountability *and* skills for communication in the new markets and saw opportunity when Western nongovernmental organizations (NGOs) bustled to introduce these skills.[4] At that time Fukuyama, like other political scientists, seemed to offer traction for changes my friend and others wanted to see. In decades to come, however, weary of foreign condescension, and as Western training failed to work magic, such assessments shifted.

MAGICAL ORIENTALISM AND IDEOLOGIES OF CONTACT

What can disturb phatic evolutionary scales? In 2012 an American who goes by the name Veet Mano (born in 1956 in Michigan) competed on *Battle of the Psychics*.[5] A large man with white hair down to his shoulders and a short beard, who favors shimmery tunics over his teddy-bear frame, Veet was well liked by Russian viewers for his words of encouragement and warm hugs—exotically "American" styles of communication and contact. The show's panel of phatic experts, however, described him over and again as no mage, reading the words and hugs as signs that he was merely an empathic, spiritually minded person and "a very good psychologist." The summer before the season aired, one of the producers told me that everywhere they were filming, Veet was greeted with skepticism: "What kind of magic," villagers near the small city of Tver' had remarked to the crew, "can a Westerner do?"

By contrast, friends in Moscow asked each other (and me, as "our expert on Gypsies"), "Why do so many Eastern or Southern peoples win that show?"[6] The orientalism conditioning these questions would sound familiar to scholars of European imperial and colonial expansion, who have argued that in order to claim rationalism, "Colonialism *required* native magic as its foil and ground" (Wiener 2003, 140; see also Latour 1993; Chakrabarty 1995; Khan 2008; Meyer and Pels 2003; Palmié 2011),[7] while at the same time spiritualist, occult, magical, and paranormal performers and thinkers mined the East, the South, and the Primitive as sources for "human potentialities unknown to the West" (Jones 2009, 89). Not surprisingly, the show's Moscow editors frequently reminded viewers that Veet had learned to channel energies in the East, not in America, through apprenticeship in Osho meditation with Indian mystic and guru Chandra Mohan Jain (aka Acharya Rajneesh in the 1960s, Bhagwan Shree Rajneesh during the 1970s–1980s, and Osho from 1989).

The producers of *Battle of the Psychics* also draw from Soviet magical orientalism, which was itself never fully freed of imperial versions. Over the seasons, the show's producers and editors have foregrounded contestants' national, ethnic, and racialized identities by drawing from the images that once advertised Soviet internationalist and affirmative action policies, known by the shorthand *Druzhba Narodov* (Friendship of the Peoples). That project, even in its earlier, Leninist articulations, appropriated Russian imperial categories of nationality and race ostensibly to subvert them; raising the status of national minorities ultimately was supposed to undermine the pull of nationalism, rendering national distinctions merely decorative while building solidarity across classes. By late Soviet times, *Druzhba Narodov* had extended as an ideal beyond the USSR, promising, through socialist technical progress shared with all, to extend the reach of humanity—*all* of us—to explore the Arctic, the oceans, and outer space.

Since the inception of *Battle of the Psychics* in 2007, producers and editors of the show have arranged signs of regional and national identity to reflect the demographics not only of the current Russian state, but also of the former USSR, featuring psychics hailing not only from distant Russian cities but also from former Soviet Republics. The parade of Asian energies, Siberian shamanisms, folk magics, and paranormal sciences performed on *Bitva* stretches across the formerly multinational empire. Viewers easily draw parallels with Soviet-era slogans and imagery, fluently pointing out and making use of the very national categories and signs of identity solidified and even created during Soviet times,[8] as evidenced by passionate participation in Internet conversation threads about the show and its contestants.

On screen, the supposedly exceptional magical skill of easterners and southerners does not go unremarked. Producers and editors of *Battle of the Psychics* script commentary to stress "national color/variation." Narrative voice-over names certain contestants by nationality, claiming them: "Our Daghestanka." Melodies and instruments made familiarly ethnic in Soviet film and radio play for Burjat, Kazakh, and Romani contestants. Russian-identified psychics are labeled not by nation or place, but by specialty or *mast'* ("suit"), as "self-taught psychic and former lawyer" or "witch by

FIGURES 3.1 AND 3.2.   Publicity photo for *Battle of the Psychics* taken early in a season. For comparison, a photo taken in the 1960s to document a celebration of Soviet-era Friendship of Peoples.

heredity." The editors also highlight unscripted comments made on camera. In an episode from season 12, two of the magician-experts sit with witnesses at closed circuit video monitors. They register various shades of anxiety about the movements of a *tsyganka* ("Gypsy") psychic. They watch the master of ceremonies announce that each contestant will take a turn standing inside a ring of fire; as flames slip closer, they must divine which of several fire trucks parked outside the circle is actually loaded with water. When the "Gypsy psychic" takes her turn, she asks the magician handling test conditions to give her his hand. His brothers watching mutter, "Oh! She will snatch his wedding ring." Later in the same episode, contestants are escorted into a room where a baby lies in a crib in front of six seated men; their task is to name the father. When the "Gypsy psychic" leans closer to see the baby, the mother, watching on closed circuit television, takes fright, asking to stop the trial.

Over the years people in the United States, Russia, and European countries have warned me to take precautions against the "hypnotic gaze" of Gypsy women, said to manipulate with gesture, gaze, and even flashes of color—with inborn, magically dramatic flair, as if combining native performing skill and sleight of hand with real sorcery.[9] Russian and Soviet books, poems, and films have long linked Gypsy magic to visions of imperial extension and Russian soul (Lemon 2000a). These links, like those made on *Battle*, reveal less about Roma and more about social ideologies of contact and avoiding contact: Beware her eyes! Don't let her touch you!

While *Battle* mobilizes imagery from Soviet anti-imperial and antiracist policies, some viewers and contestants deploy Friendship of the Peoples to criticize the show. Challenging the show's contestants on the Internet—their credentials and abilities—provides its own entertainment. On one website devoted to *Battle* and its stars, the blogger (a previous contestant) describes one season as it winds down by speculating about the pregnancy of contestant Tydyv, a clairvoyant from Central Asia. Below the text, he inserts a screen shot of the show's main expert on psychic powers, Professor Mikhail Vinogradov. Over the image, the blogger has superimposed a white frame and a caption that reads: "Return of Budulaj. Who fathered Tydyv's child—the secret will be revealed." The joke assumes the reader remembers late Soviet media: Budulaj was the protagonist of a 1970s film and television series, both based on a 1960s novel titled *Gypsy*. Budulaj, a World War II veteran whose wife was felled by a Nazi tank, now travels the Russian countryside seeking army comrades and kin, fighting prejudice and enlightening Gypsy nomads along the way. The well-known story both incorporates progressive images of "New Soviet Gypsies" *and* typecasts the

Gypsy as natural performer, with magical musicality pulsing under the skin; in the television series *Return of Budulaj*, Budulaj loses his memory until he plays a harmonica and recalls his true Gypsy self. It turns out that Budulaj has a son, a fact concealed because the adoptive mother has claimed that a Tatar grandfather gave him a "swarthy face." The boy betrays his blood when he learns to dance from visiting Gypsy youths, picking up the steps immediately. The secret—who the father is—is revealed to be Budulaj.

The blogger's montage layers *Battle of the Psychics* with Soviet televisual intertext: Tydyv's unborn child is equated to Budulaj's son. But why is this mixed up with Vinogradov, who recruits psychics from all over the formerly Soviet world to work in his investigation group? Are we to imagine that a former researcher for the Soviet military is the secret father? Or will he detect the secret? Is this a jab at the show, at phatic expertise? Are the targets Soviet nationalities policies, the absurdity of Soviet utopian dreams in the present? Does the joke play off propaganda about the birth rates of "non-Europeans" in Russia?

Veet, even representing a rival state, arouses less controversy, perhaps because the show mobilizes local political contexts more than it does the Cold War axis in much telepathy science fiction. In any case, the West lacks magic. All the same, the American Veet won several episodes and made it to the season finale. The Romani contestant was likewise judged against type and was eliminated for allegedly using ordinary senses and logic rather than extrasensory channels. Formulae that map Gypsy and American to extreme ends of magical evolutionary scales could not have predicted these outcomes—and these are not exceptions to prove a rule. Interactions—even mass-mediated ones structured by reality shows—*always* riddle racial logic with apparent contradictions. Racism remains active not because it is consistent with practice, but because its logic finds circular proof in material encounters that have, in fact, already been structured by legislative and social processes.

RACE, MATTER, AND INFRASTRUCTURE

Infrastructures *seem* to exist for anyone, but they do not. Contact with them is regulated, and infrastructures themselves regulate contact. In this we see the everyday workings of racism and also can begin to ask: *What else*, besides racism, does racialization activate? In this way we see how racializing forces affect domains not usually considered racialized, people not usually treated as raced. How does racialization affect *everybody*? Institutions that racialize—industries that divide labor, city streets that

FIGURE 3.3.   An early scene from Tarkovsky's *Solaris* (1972). A world conference decides the fate of the space mission. Americans watching this scene have been puzzled—"But aren't Russians white?"—not recognizing that in the Soviet future of cosmic exploration, as in some American versions, to be the world has transcended nation states.

outline neighborhoods—also modify the ways any contacts come about, the ways any channels for communication work—or fail—and for whom.

Such successes and failures afforded the superpowers competing ways to claim "freedom of speech" versus "equality." Americans were able to claim freedom by erasing the making and maintenance of channels that segregate— even while describing Soviet censorship. As meanwhile the Soviets targeted American inequalities.

After World War II, European empires disintegrated. Both the United States and the Soviet Union courted former colonies, competing to promise both infrastructural development *and* racial equality.[10] They painted similar futures for peoples across the world: mechanized irrigation, moving sidewalks, talking computers, and rapid space travel would one day lift all humanity equally from conflict and toil.[11] In the 1950s mainstream Soviet and U.S. science fictions alike peopled this cosmopolitan future with international interstellar crews, as if competing to depict diversity in space. On board the SS *Tantra* of Ivan Efremov's novel *Andromeda Nebula* (1959) we meet the African man Mven Mass; on board the USS *Enterprise* we find Uhura and Sulu.[12] While scholars have detailed the corresponding promises for modernity across the United States and the USSR, journalistic writers and political speakers still prefer to erase similarities and connections; in the early twenty-first century, it remains expedient to forget how Soviet and American public relations shared goals, methods, and styles. It was not only Coca-Cola who wanted to "teach the world to sing in perfect harmony".[13]

With decolonization, racism became a key term in Cold War ideological battles. Each superpower asserted its rival's violence and repression—white racism here, anti-Semitism there, each side calling out the other's proxy war moves, denying its own. On the level of diplomatic competition, both deployed artists, musicians, ballet troupes, and chess players, each claiming its own system better sparks creativity and freedom.[14] Such a measure of civilizational advance preceded the Cold War, having already crystallized in G. W. F. Hegel;[15] the USSR and the United States both drew from movements of emancipation and suffrage begun in the eighteenth century, inheriting moral and political philosophies written by men whose governments touted freedom for *some* through institutions that restricted others—through land-tenure and literacy laws after serfdom and slavery (Buck-Morss 2000a; Trouillot 1995).

Processes that *cross* periods, institutions, and territories amplify the force and appeal of racism. Becoming "white" or "European" has depended on transregional manufacture of race: circuits of Atlantic and Ottoman slave trade fed North American versions, and the networks and institutions that racialized there did not terminate, but unfolded across still other borders. More recently, both Moscow *skinhedy* and Chicago skinheads align with white supremacists farther away, be they West or East, downloading graphics and strategies from the Internet.

One way to track how racism moves and settles in is to concentrate on infrastructures,[16] divisions of space and access to material objects, such as tools that configure ways people experience limitations of action and interaction—who handles the keys, who holds the steering wheel, and who immerses their hands in hot dish water?[17] How do these handlings interface with social relations?

Cold War era racializations involved organizing human relations to material objects, tools and infrastructures, commodities and dwellings. In Moscow as in Detroit, not everyone encountered public transit or water supplies in the same ways. American Jim Crow shared similarities with the rules of Russian imperial pales of settlement, echoed in Soviet *propiska* (residence permit) rules, systems that concatenated with institutions (educational committees, medical clinics, editorial boards, voting places) and materials that anchored them (buildings, furniture, tools, decorations, identification papers). Similar as they were, systems also diverged. Both black automakers in Detroit and Romani metro builders in Moscow encountered their cities differently than did people marked "white" or "European"— and yet differently again from each other. Well-worn debates about which economic system produced better material goods, who crafted pavement, tea, or blankets of higher quality, are only partly at issue. What matters more is attention to *who* handles what.

To make useful contrasts and comparisons has been difficult because scholars of and in the region long declined to recognize racial categories in Soviet or imperial practice.[18] Soviet policy treated race as a construct belonging to capitalism; the government barred racial categories in policy language. Despite the intentions of the state, Soviet people, like those anywhere, signaled racializing thinking without racial terms or even corporeal signs (such as complexion), deriving signs of race from objects (gold teeth, dollar bills) and practices (dancing, hunting).[19] We live race through spatial practices that join and separate activities, material things, and bodies—and that channel communications. To return to the comparative task: the intersections of matter and race in each state differed for historical reasons, and those differences have generated still other effects. These effects are especially apparent when things break down.

Both states promised to erase segregation and discrimination not by enlightenment alone, but also by achieving automation. Through better infrastructures. On the starship *Enterprise,* a machine delivers meals on command; one supposes that the toilets clean themselves (I assume the same for the teenage starship crew searching for alien contact in MosFil'm's 1973 *Moscow-Cassiopia*).[20] Eventually, however, both socialist and capitalist realities faced a similar problem: neither actually achieved computer-delivered meals or self-cleaning latrines; neither reached "full development" or "world communism." The things that each system built—the dams, reactors, bridges—started to fall apart, contradicting modernist dreams in both the first and second worlds. In Gary, Indiana, and in Sverdlovsk, the Urals, flights crashed and roofs collapsed, housing towers crumbled, and nuclear reactors leaked or imploded. During the same decades, broken public telephones dotted Chicago and Perm'. Similar material crises posed similar doubts about the promises of either economic system to deliver smooth, clean infrastructures—and about the capacity of infrastructures to deliver social equality, justice, and freedom.[21]

Things break down everywhere. In the Urals and in Arkansas alike I have seen people improvise engine belts with string; in Detroit and in Moscow, entire cars are held together by duct tape. Similar material ruptures, however, have not had the same political and social effects. Nor has knowledge of such effects been distributed in the same ways. Elites in each place encountered ruptures differently than did nonelites, but those differences themselves differed markedly. First of all, we need to acknowledge the obvious point that being elite in the United States could involve much larger accumulations of individual and family property in land (along with things like multiple cars and access to quality education) than did being elite in the USSR. Being elite in the USSR involved living in the centers of large cities, shopping occasionally in special stores, or knowing the people who ran factories, hospitals or other institutions. Or being approved to travel abroad. Even among the Soviet-era elite, there were those who did not, for example, own a car, but who might attend tomorrow's ballet by making a phone call (and there were also nonelites who might manage both to own a car and acquire ballet tickets). The following discussion clarifies differences between the elites by contrasting the separations in each society between elites and others.

During the late Cold War U.S. elites could easily separate their experiences from those of people living close to broken factory gates and ruptured pipes. In the USSR they could not. In the 1980s Chicago dwellers of means could organize daily trajectories to circumvent housing projects, to see their dark windows only from the IC train. Late Soviet *nomenklatura* lived well, more often in the sturdy, central buildings, but they were not cloistered in neighborhoods cut off from public transit or in cul de sacs (this began only in the late 1990s). Dwelling in a majestic Moscow Stalinist building did not shelter a person from using other structures, never ruled out visits to school friends living in communal apartments. Soviet elites sometimes frequented special stores and clinics, but not always, and they too encountered infrastructures falling apart. Even decades later, city powers have not yet banished nonelites from the center, and penniless friends still socialize with schoolmates who have moved up.

By contrast, in the United States, perhaps more so during the Cold War, prolonged exposure to infrastructural breakdown was a matter of segregation, by race and class. Soviet nationalities policies and practices enacted and defined ethnic, national, and racial identities (see Hirsch 2005; Martin 2001; Slezkine 1996; Weitz 2002) and forms of labor discrimination, but they did not segregate entire neighborhoods. While the American interstates and other infrastructures cut off such neighborhoods, the Soviet train did not channel elites away from points where Soviet modernity fell apart.

To be sure, discrimination shaped many lives in Soviet and imperial Russian urban capitals, through pales of settlement and permits denying residence within one hundred kilometers of the city to ex-convicts or people labeled "Gypsies." People living in Romani settlements faced violence and structural exclusion, as did Muslims in Kazakh and Tatar towns along the Volga, in the Urals, and in Crimea. All the same, experience of shortages and breakdowns impinged upon everyone, not just these people or the poorest, and in ways that gave everyone reason to complain. That is, Soviet forms of segregation articulated with Soviet infrastructures and access to material resources differently than did those of the United States.

PHATIC INFRASTRUCTURE AND DOUBLE VISION

Material infrastructures can act as phatic infrastructures that make it possible for people to communicate—or can merge with social forces that separate people. The latter sort especially affect which people learn or do not learn about material breakdowns and about their social extent. Here the superpower states diverge: the Soviet Union could not channel information about material failures away from the elite and along racialized lines at once, while the United States could. A full, book-length discussion of these processes would need to go further to compare each state's elites—what it meant to be elite, how elite was elite—but for the purposes of this argument, the distinction holds. For example, an elite Moscow student in the 1980s might have had little cash but free tickets to the symphony every week. Having lived among the poorest and wealthiest in both states, I could give many and numerous further examples of who is aware or not of how others live. The divergence in the very possibilities for perceiving and reflecting upon troubled infrastructure was itself productive, insofar as it also distorted the ways people opposed the capitalist to socialist worlds.

If anything can work smoothly across the United States, it is the interstates, moving cars through standardized systems of truck plazas and rest stops. My Russian visitors always marvel at the uniformity and the boredom of the interstates. The interstates, by the way, do not advertise which of their exits lead to sundown towns, places where one is afraid to be caught while black after dark. These towns are easy to miss from I-80, making it easy to imagine that racism does not exist across the wholesome Midwest. Many who drive through Nebraska believe it is completely flat. It is not; the interstate follows a river valley and has been graded, and beyond it the land undulates in waves that produce, from the top of some, a dizzying vertigo. Passers-through may think that everyone in the state is white, not tuning into Lakota or Winnebago broadcasts that belie claims of disappearance.

To be sure, plenty of white people know America from behind plastic bags stretched across window frames. Plenty of black and brown people live in homes of suburban comfort. Near army bases, old factories, and prisons, white and black and brown worlds alike are scruffy, peeling, drafty, and in need of repair. Yet wealthy white families rarely live in underserved neighborhoods, while due to a legacy of racist real estate discrimination, wealthy black families sometimes do. Thus, poverty and infrastructural inequality remain difficult for American white elites to see, or even to hear about, as classmates and neighbors do not move in those spaces either.

Journalists in the United States do publish stories about poverty, documenting struggles with tenement owners, sometimes titillating with glimpses of meth moms and cat hoarders. But here is another key difference: among the white wealthy in these journalists' audiences, print or video sources do not layer with additional channels for knowledge, such as daily sensory knowledge or face-to-face talk. The mere state of being in proximity can make people, too, into phatic infrastructures.[22] Children in elementary schools know full well that bodily proximity opens opportunities to whisper, to pass notes; this is why middle school teachers separate talkative friends. And this is one reason that property laws regulate where people can assemble. Unless U.S. elites become very curious or otherwise motivated, they do not learn how many poor there are, how they live. They are rarely forced to triangulate media accounts that would trouble what *they* see and hear, or work against their haptic awareness of comfort, to offer other knowledge through the body, the cold wind on the walk to school, the smell of a leaky gas line. They are cut off from social channels where knowledge of troubles passes through family talk, along circuits of neighborhood hospitality. They do not know breakdown through combinations of *multiple* bodily sensations, contact channels, and media, combinations that afford what W. E. B. DuBois recognized as "double consciousness" (1903) the ability, often thrust upon one, to perceive more than one social ontology at a time—and to perceive how others perceive the self, usually through a distorted lens, such as that of racism.

American elites might read about material conditions in prison, but few do time. It is a truism that to read an exposé of prisons is not the same as to live in one. This is not what I am trying to say. Rather, *some* U.S. citizens learn breakdown or poverty through *multiple* channels: a press report triangulates against an uncle's stories, one's own sensations, or the fact of the absence of a brother. Others learn *only* through a single source of mediation, such as a good documentary. During the height of the Cold War, U.S. elites lacked occasion to layer and contrast mediations, even to try to contrast footage of a fire across town to haptic knowledge of flimsy walls and the smell of leaky gas lines.

Within the respective superpowers, channels by which such knowledge might move crossed social fields differently. In the USSR, knowledge of ruptures in the promise of modern comfort, or knowledge of incarceration conditions, was not channeled by racial segregation. Soviet labor camps, harsh as they were, did not imprison Roma or Ingush or Estonians at rates higher than Russians. Both states saw comparable rates of incarceration and forced labor,[23] but it was in the Unites States that prison became a continuation of *racialized* slave labor. Moreover, while U.S. elites famously managed to avoid incarceration, Soviet elites were just as famously incarcerated, as during imperial times. Soviet elites and intellectuals ate prison food and breathed in bad prison factory ventilation. Prison also brought them into contact and conversation with people from other demographics. Many prisoners received amnesty in the 1950s and 1960s, and many (including Sergei Dovlatov, Yevgenija Ginzburg, Varlam Shalamov, and Alexander Solzhenitsyn) published prison memoirs and exposés. Even the best placed urban people had relatives or friends who had done time or lived in exile.

That is, people knew of troubles on the highway projects, in the factories, in the new settlements, and in the prisons well before people like Solzhenitsyn published about them. Contradictions to Soviet modernist fantasy could not be contained, as they could be in the United States, within "bad neighborhoods." Intellectuals, scientists, and cultural elites lived in communal apartments with engineers and street cleaners. Some won spots in special buildings, say, for writers, but still did not undertake daily errands, work, or school untouched by late socialist-era shortage or decay. Moscow streets could seem utopian compared to muddy village roads and rusting busses farther out, yet people *did* venture farther out, and often, to cultivate gardens or visit family in Ukraine or Siberia, for weeks or a month at a time; city people did not live only in the city. Naïveté about material lack, shortages, or breakdown simply was not possible. Urban registration permits only buffered communication; they prevented many Roma from living in the cities, for example, but did not sever all talk across most categories. There was no equivalent to the wealthy Americans who never ride the subway, who fly but never take the Greyhound bus, versus those who never fly. Soviet soft-class train cabins (two beds at ground level) sometimes separated *nomenklatura* from people riding in ordinary cabins (four sleeping bunks, behind a sliding door) or in *platzkart* (a dozen or more bunks across an open car), but the station latrines were for everyone. The USSR, investing in trains rather than highways, made Soviet long-distance train cars into another phatic infrastructure, bringing strangers into prolonged proximal contact, all the more so as passengers on Soviet trains expected to share talk and provisions—to do otherwise was impractical and not much fun.

To counter exceptional thinking about these matters, we have moved back and forth across the superpowers not merely to compare and contrast.

Our next task is to situate, in relation to these, more loudly proclaimed comparisons and their effects.

CHANNELS TO FREEDOM

In the Cold War–era United States, pockets of material lack, decay, and violent rupture that poked holes in American modernist dreams were disproportionately distributed across racialized spaces, infrastructures, and social networks that, even when they extended beyond one space to another, did not connect everyone in the same way. Roads, for example, offered mobility (to some) while also cutting vision: road grading and concrete walls channeled the perception of those who passed, windows up, through drive-by lands or fly-over country. In the Cold War United States, muckraking reportage did not reproduce layers combining sensory and mediated knowledges; such layers piled up for some, while others only saw the film or read the book.[24] These relatively local divisions of the known allowed elites to invest in flawed claims to American exceptionalism and to do so in ways that still disrupt diplomatic process and justify geopolitical aggression.

Moreover, segregation in the United States could impede knowledge *without particular agents,* such as censors, *and without needing to actively block broadcast or print channels.* Consider the uprisings in Detroit in the summer of 1967, which some called race riots and others named urban revolt, action for social justice. In the decades after the events in Detroit, no one had to actively censor accounts of them in schoolbooks, because those who continued to live there had little access to any of the presses that manufactured high school texts—or to mainstream broadcast media.[25] Elite white Americans noticed nothing missing; it still takes most a leap of effort to attend to such histories. White high school students during the 1980s did not ask why Angela Davis was not mentioned in social studies. If American kids did not already know about Detroit or Angela Davis from friends and relatives, they might not learn until decades later, if ever.

What need was there to censor black, brown, or "white trash" voices when segregating spaces and limiting access to media technologies prefilters them?[26] For all America's vaunted spatial mobility, to move North to work did not mean freedom to join the golf club and there to chat, face to face, about the need for regional public transit. In towns where black people could not (de facto, if not de jure) swim in white pools, what need was there to monitor communications among the kids? In our town, one could count on teenagers to beat girls and boys who stood in their swimsuits at the fence, talking through the links. Infrastructures—and rules for their engagement—could cut channels before any necessity to censor content. In the United States, those who did not experience the world as broken hardly spoke to those who did.

By contrast, in the USSR such things were passed along—in visceral, haptic terms, along social links, even through media subject to censorship. Again, Soviets who served time and knew prison conditions were not marked as descendants of racialized slave labor (even if their grandparents had been serfs)—everyone knew of these things, they simply did not speak of them in most settings (Platt 2016). Their number included many with higher education, people who worked in central bureaucracies, whose kin worked in publishing offices. They knew where to borrow typewriters, how to strategize manuscript circulation. Their words were censored in the mainstream press, but still such people had recourse to parallel networks leading to printing houses outside the country, such as Ardis Press in Ann Arbor, or to journals in Paris. They spread the very complaint *of* censorship far and wide. Solzhenitsyn, even after serving time, was vastly better connected than most people in the United States who have been jailed or imprisoned.[27] In the United States, reports of abuse of authority, corruption, bad prison conditions, military malfunctions, misappropriations of highway funds, and so forth did come out in leaks. The elites, when they read about them, could digest it all separately from their own experience.

These different intersections enabled Americans to figure the United States as a haven for freedom of speech compared to the USSR. We could even occasionally acknowledge racism while simultaneously erasing the means by which we limited perception of racist conditions. We could lionize the muckraking journalism that occasionally brought topics above ground— even while rationalizing structures that made overt censorship unnecessary. People *in gated neighborhoods* could look at the USSR as if *that place over there* were the source of all that is zoned, walled, and censored.[28] This is how many Americans could believe that we *all* had freedom of speech. Segregation obviated direct censorship. Privileged Americans could imagine themselves luckier than those poor, brainwashed, Soviet robots.

Conversely, the USSR could pretend to racial equality, but meanwhile (and perhaps as a result) left acts of censorship visible. Soviets could believe that they lived without racism, while abandoning any illusion of living without censorship. The two countries generated mirrored contradictions, as neither consistently championed either freedom or equality. In denying this, we have been trapped in competitive, Hegelian distortions, unable to sort out how our own repressions have fed others'. Sharing a genealogy, our blind spots overlap: twentieth-century Americans invested in believing "we are free" while calling out (in limited ways) racism; Soviets could believe "we are equal" while calling out censorship.

These blinders are still effective. In the first decade of the twenty-first century, I led several groups of American students to Russia. One year, our group finally included two students of color. They were shocked by comments about race that they encountered in Moscow and equally puzzled that such talk seemed to contradict genuine signs of goodwill. We encountered more trouble, however, when in a meeting with Russian students, the group was asked, "In the US, do you fear your own police?" The white students replied, "Of course not, we are free." One of the students of color interjected, "Are you KIDDING! Maybe that is how it is in YOUR family!" I made the same error when, while driving Moscow friends through South Dakota, a state patrolman pulled me over for speeding and let me go with a gentle warning. They asked me the same question, and I answered with the same forgetful, "No, we are not afraid, not in this state." Americans in the twenty-first century are becoming more aware of police surveillance and violence that profiles black and brown, of the destruction of water supplies on reservations and in industrial towns like Flint, but those who have not lived in such places have to work harder to see and then *not to unsee* them.

MATTER THAT CHANNELS

European modernists have been projecting unfreedom elsewhere for a long time, all the while relying on institutions of slavery and incarceration to build democracy and liberty—for some but not for all (Trouillot 1995; Buck-Morss 2000b). Cold War media institutions reinforced this tendency, adding new institutions that augmented the ways segregation obviated censorship in the United States—while increasing the visibility of censorship in the USSR. To proceed more attentively means to doubt whether *only* Western institutions allow open exchange of ideas and that socialist societies *always* mire communication in bureaucratic "wooden language" (Thom 1989; Seriot 2002), barring people from "living in Truth" (Havel 1987; for a critique, see Gal 1995, 2005).

After World War II the United States expended enormous resources to broadcast information to compete with local media in the socialist world, establishing Radio Free Europe/Radio Liberty in 1949 in Munich. RFE/RL, or just "The Radios," names an organization of two services, the first aimed at Eastern European and the second at Soviet territories. Its stated mission was to serve as a surrogate free press in places where the press was "banned, censored, or incompletely established." The Soviet state, in response, spent nearly as much to block these broadcasts. Such jamming, along with restrictions on travel and on currency trade, embodied those obstacles that together some call the "Iron Curtain." Once again, it is crucial not only to compare and contrast but also to acknowledge connections across borders—including chains of events and discourse founded in comparison itself.

For decades, radio stations funded by U.S. and British agencies (including the CIA), edged close to Soviet bloc territories. Occupying German and Japanese soil, the U.S. State Department was well positioned to beam waves from Munich and Tokyo. Moscow, by contrast, commanded fewer geographic broadcast points that could reach the Western Hemisphere farther than Alaska (my stepfather served there during the Korean War, listening in with his army Russian on military shortwave). Buffered by Mexico and Canada, the Pacific and the Atlantic Oceans, the United States had little occasion to worry about its people tuning in to Radio Moscow, all the more as U.S. citizens were educated with comparatively little attention to languages besides English. American citizens were insulated by oceans, continents, and language barriers—and also by a market that barely produced shortwave radios.

Short waves reach farther than FM or AM medium and long waves; they bounce off the globe's surface into the ionosphere (particles in the atmosphere) and then back down again, thus zigzagging across the globe rather than flying straight into the horizon (see Yurchak 2015b, 341–54). Radios sold in the Soviet market reached across all the wave lengths, especially shortwave. It was a gigantic space to broadcast over. As one historian of the Radio Free Europe project described this: "[I]n one of the most bizarre examples of incompetence in the history of the Soviet Union, despite the billions of dollars spent on jamming, the Soviet State itself saw to it that its citizens had cheap short-wave radios, which they used to listen to Western propaganda through the jamming" (Nelson 1997, xv); while "the salt in the wound was that in the United States, England, West Germany, and other countries, mass production of short wave radios, on which Soviet programs could be heard, had stopped" (ibid, 93). That is, Moscow broadcasts might have reached Americans (and perhaps then called for obvious jamming)—except that less than 0.1 percent of radio sets sold in the United States could receive shortwave. If the United States *had* produced shortwave receivers in surplus, would we have celebrated listening to stations from around the world? Would we have doubled down on lack of support for foreign language learning with domestic jamming? If not, would we have called that a chaos of freedom or "bizarre . . . incompetence"? The Soviet Ministry of Communications did propose to end mass production of shortwave radios in 1954, but it did not, although after 1958 some waves were trimmed from the dials.

Readers not raised in the Soviet Union may not realize that jamming was irregular, focusing on certain foreign programs and letting many others through. The state in fact *encouraged* listening to foreign broadcasts (Yurchak 2015b), encouraged learning languages and listening to global news (the Radios distinguished themselves by broadcasting versions of *local* news). No Soviet-era government, neither in the USSR nor in the socialist bloc, ever made listening to foreign broadcasts illegal; many did believe that it was, and testified to arrests for charges on other grounds, like black marketeering or holding foreign currency (Nelson 1997). The stakes of listening were sometimes high—but sometimes not. The point for contrast is that Soviet citizens were constantly confronted with radio waves, audible, offering themselves to be alternately tuned into and lost again to jamming or static. Americans were not. Radios waves were prefiltered by material supply; the channels were simply not available to most, and there was no material infrastructure, machine or waves, to tinker with. We could imagine ourselves free to listen because we did not encounter jamming to signal a channel underneath.

America broadcast messages to the Soviet world that were designed to heighten residents' perception of interference with information channels. Early on, the U.S. Congress tasked the Radios to "refute Soviet misstatements and lies more quickly" in order to encourage resistance (ibid, 36). Another of the Radios' mandates was to help exiles of those countries to broadcast back;[29] the CIA contacted Soviet émigrés specifically to amplify their perspectives on Soviet policies and to influence events and opinions back home (Kind-Kovacs, 2013). Radio Free Europe/Radio Liberty hired émigré native speakers to speak on the air, while American-born scholars and journalists joined them off air to structure broadcasts. A geopolitically inflected division of communicative labor took hold.

Broadcasts were designed to point out discrepancies, to maximally contrast with information given by local media, and thus to shape a *sense* of censorship. This style of information combat became familiar in many places (during the 2016 U.S. elections, many who accused news services like Russia Today of similar tactics clearly seem not to know the history of American broadcasting overseas). The Radios worked in two stages each day: first, the research department monitored local broadcasts, both for event news to pass up to the State Department and for points to refute. Second, broadcast groups crafted refutations for recognizably native voices to read alongside other programming. Sources that detail this work are few; I can provide a firsthand account, having worked at RFE/RL for a full year just after it moved from Munich to Prague, in the research department in 1995–1996 as it was being transferred to the Soros foundation,[30] renamed the Open Media Research Institute. Still partly under the jurisdiction of the U.S. State Department, we labored for two bosses at once. I was a new hire (the Soros Foundation, not the State Department, had requested an analyst aware of Romani issues, able to read Romani); my colleagues had worked at the Radios for years, surviving a culling in Munich. Our job, every morning, was to sift through international and local newswires from Prague to Bishkek, across a dozen languages. We were to paraphrase those texts for the English-language digest sent to the U.S. State Department and other elite subscribers. The digest allotted each country two or three separate items, a small paragraph each; as one might expect, only certain topics passed through the editorial filter. Romani news, rather than having its own dedicated space, was counted into the quota for the relevant state, and thus was often cut to make room for news about visits of ministers without portfolio, and so forth. While we might not call this censorship, these institutional practices channeled media via national and racial logics.

From 8:00 to 10:30 every morning, analysts raced the clock to read the wires, then sputtered through last-minute struggles with editorial staff over which chunks of text would make it into distribution by 11:00 A.M. Each morning our department would send a person to attend the meeting with the Radios' liaison for the U.S. State Department, held at the broadcasting headquarters in central Prague (our offices were further out in the city). State Department staff would have read the previous daily digest, and at this meeting the liaison would brief the RFE/RL broadcasters about which local stories they ought to respond to on air. In Munich, I was told, relations had been tighter among State Department, analytic department, and radio broadcasters, everyone united under one roof, one authority. Before 1990s restructuring, the process proceeded more efficiently, analysts monitoring and digesting local media, State Department staff vetting it up lines of command, passing guidance back down for broadcasters to shape. A lot of specialization is involved in crafting communications to stress flaws in enemy channels, painstaking work to find inaccuracies or misrepresentations, to counter even small details with alternative information. Many described this as a necessary antidote against mendacious Soviet media, and depicted Soviets who tuned in to RFE/RL as demonstrating the will of the people, the will to listen themselves to freedom, from which an objective view of the repressive forces of socialist censorship would become clear.

The Soviet state was not positioned to make similar assaults on U.S. media (there were as yet no proliferations of warring Internet sources spinning the same video in seven directions, no Russia Today television network). Very few Americans encountered any foreign media, much less foreign media that purposefully echoed back to them the inconsistencies and omissions of local media day after day, over decades. There was, in corollary, no need for the audible, obvious noises of jamming.

In contrasting political conditions for media, phatic infrastructures, and the divisions of labor that maintain them, I am not proposing that the Soviets did not censor. Nor would I deny that people living near U.S. military bases or nuclear test sites could sense that *something* was being blocked (see Brown 2001; Masco 2004; Lepselter 2005). The point is that the Soviet state could never render censorship practices invisible, while the United States did not need to; it could rely on naturalized conditions—from racial segregation to the absence of shortwave radios—to limit media from elsewhere, without having to exercise overt censorship. And so it is not really so ironic that, a decade after the USSR had dissolved, it was the International Monetary Fund that subsidized consolidation of post-Soviet Russian media into oligarchs' hands.

STATIC AND THE TELEPATHIC BODY

Claims about censorship under socialism arose not only as channels were blocked, but also as channels multiplied. Varied experiences of different overlays of channels and obstacles created diverging anxieties about and hopes for communication, about contacts desired and dangerous. For a teenager at the radio dial in Surgut, both to succeed and to fail to tune in made distant barriers into closer and more tangible things-to-be-overcome. Citizens of socialist states were made all the more aware of foreign broadcasts, waves sometimes palpable when jammed by competing broadcasts. Excess radio noise demanded to be interpreted. Television crackles did not generate the same interpretants for people in Paris or Moscow or Omaha or Kungur. The noises of failed or blocked transmission might evoke *similar* hopes and fears, but not the same ones in the same combinations for the same sets of people. People in the USSR and in the United States expected different engagements and effects even from similar media.[31] For some, static signaled fears of siege or infiltration, while others hoped for jazz trivia, and still others for alien messages.

The topic of telepathy opens a fresh vantage point onto the making of media expectations in the USSR, both because it manifested through transnational communications and because it was itself subject to censorship. In the USSR, telepathy was among the topics subject to restriction, along with nationalism, man-made disasters, violence, sexuality, and religion. While in 1923 Bernard Kazhinskij had published a book arguing that telepathy rides electromagnetic waves, *Thought Transfer* (printed alongside early Soviet-era fiction on mind control like Alexander Belyaev's 1926 *Lord of the World*), from the late 1930s until the 1960s the topic almost never surfaced in the papers or television, only in live performances. Then, in 1985, when Soviet general secretary Mikhail Gorbachev introduced the reforms known as *glasnost'*, these were the very topics that bubbled into print and broadcast. Starting that year, media producers were encouraged to allow more debate and to produce investigative journalism. The state loosened procedures governing access to media, including face-to-face channels for embodied mediation, lifting rules regulating numbers of people who could assemble in outdoor spaces (which have since been reinstated).

During *glasnost'*, hypnotists such as Anatoly Kashpirovskii and healers such as Evgenia Davitashvili (aka Dzhuna) made their radio and television debuts. They had achieved fame through other media—posters, local papers, stage appearances, chatter—although even in the early 1970s the Soviet press had reported on visits to Bulgarian clairvoyant Vanga (Vangelia Dmitrova, speculated to have been close to Zhivkov's government) by Soviet celebrities; Brezhnev was a rumored client. Throughout Soviet times and across the Soviet Union, paranormal demonstrations in variety show entertainments (*estrada*), such as those staged by Wolf Messing, played to full houses, advertised by local concert posters and word of mouth. As Soviet-born, Swedish-trained anthropologist Galina Lindquist also reminds us, Soviet people sought healers and shamans long before *glasnost'*.

And yet the period amplified occult and paranormal performances, broadcasting them through more media, allowing psychics and shamans to buy print advertising (subject again to regulation in 2012). Mass healing sessions moved from provincial stages and factory cultural clubs onto television screens and into hockey stadiums (Lindquist 2006, 36–37). But *glasnost'* did not *spark* these practices, nor did it initiate Soviet curiosity about them, and older people now well recollect the 1960s and 1970s films, the print debates about telepathy tests.

Still, in the 1980s many did attribute the intense interest in the paranormal to *glasnost'* and asserted, "We couldn't talk about this before" (see Platz 1996; Lindquist 2006). The narrative that repression was being followed by new freedoms dominated (even while other topics became more difficult to air in public). Consider one of the famous televisual psychics of that period, Allan Chumak. One morning in 1989, Chumak appeared on television performing a silent gestural mime, offering healing vibrations to cross the screens. He continued for many mornings afterward, beginning always with a brief statement on the day's focus: "Today's energy is directed towards the digestive system . . . but anyone can benefit." Viewers took up the broadcasts in differing ways: some called the station with effusive thanks, while others ferociously accused Chumak and all the others of charlatanry. Some saw in these psychics harbingers of freedom, in broadcasts amplifying the potential of *glasnost'*: "I welcome the television spots of Djuna, Raikov, Chumak, Kashpirovsky. And not because they might heal one and all, or charge us up with bioenergy and so on. Still, if it helps even one person, then such séances are necessary. In their mere appearance on the television screen, I see a gratifying instance of the real democratization of central television.—V. Zhukov, Novosibirsk" (letter to editor, *Izvestija*, 1989). Interestingly enough, U.S. journalists at the time read Chumak's work on the screen in opposite ways. If for Mr. Zhukov from Novosibirsk, the television psychics manifested democratization of media, the American journalist reads Chumak's gestures as miming the mental state of a drowsy public, perhaps no longer robots, but still caught in the amber of Orwellian stasis:

> Early every morning across the Soviet Union, thousands of people rub the sleep from their eyes and sit in front of the television set, waiting to be healed. About 7:15 am, Allan Chumak appears on *120 Minutes*, the Soviet equivalent of the *Today Show*. Sitting behind a desk, the owlish, middle-aged man with a mane of white hair stares at the camera and flings his hands about, as if he were petting an irritable cat. . . . *Glasnost*, miserable medical care, and a certain naive belief in extrasensory powers have led to [his] remarkable success in the Soviet Union. (Remnick 1989)

In thinking about these appearances, to avoid tacking between willful freedom and weak-minded hypnosis, I want to focus less on Chumak's healing message and more on his phatic work, his silent and spoken references to contact (with viewers) and to channel (the televisual waves imagined between camera and screen). Chumak's verbal silences amplified other sounds; during those stretches when he requested viewers to shut their eyes, as anthropologist Tomas Matza puts it, it was as if he asked viewers to "reshuffle the sensorium" from privileging vision to attend instead to other senses, to the "smell and crackle" of the TV itself (freq.uenci.es, January 6, 2012).[32] Can you feel the medium itself, and the static that envelops it? Static, sounds layered by jamming, noise from rough electrical connections—the energy generated by Chumak's silent gestures promised to reach along even the worst connections, flow over decayed wires, ride even static.

But as we have seen, static is no generic haunting by a universal media ghost, uniformly distributing equally points for contact to falter. What are the potential interpretants of static? Does it point to alien contact, government interference, bad weather?[33] Does it sound like voices of the dead, competing channels, mental projections? In the 1980s, static in the USSR signified something different than it did in the United States; moreover, its significations shifted across the USSR and over time.

In the Soviet 1980s, good telephone lines were not yet taken for granted. For instance, out-of-town calls were ordered in advance, connected by an operator. Many could not place such an order from home and went to the postal and telegraph offices to order out-of-town calls. When lines were crossed, every one standing in line heard bursts of words ("Platform 7! Noon!") belted out before the connection was lost. The frustrations of static were rarely confined to just two parties at each end of a single line; such channel complaints were audible, accessible for others to interpret as signs about the world. If Chumak had told 1980s U.S. audiences to imagine trying to "hear over a bad telephone connection" he would have been evoking different experiences.

Differences and changes in media technology evoke comparisons—but comparisons become ideologically bound when marshaled for abstractions like "freedom of speech" or modern "comfort and ease" (Sherouse 2014). In late 1980s Soviet imagination, Americans no longer dealt with mediate indignities; it was not known in Moscow that many Americans could not yet afford cable, tussled with static in television reception, rarely made what were at that time still quite expensive long-distance calls, and used broken pay phones. Bootleg Hollywood videotapes inspired such comparisons, and people like Chumak spun them into visions of a better future. Evoking the telephone *while* gesturing *as if* through the television screen, he layered phatic troubles with all the Soviet media still implicated as signs of backwardness, to transcend them all at once, staking a claim to communion through multiple mediations by machine and body.

Down the page from Zhukov's 1989 letter to the editor hailing television psychics such as Chumak as heralds of openness, the head of the Moscow City Telephone administration announced in an interview that new directories would include the telephone numbers of foreign embassies (a few years later, I would copyedit the English versions). More and better communications to come! Chumak signaled new relations to media, however, that could not be read as openness alone. His wordless broadcasts amplified not just the machine crackle of static, the aural quality of bare broadcast channel, but also the sounds of his every intake of breath, swallow, quiet grunt of effort, and moist lip smack. These sounds exuded from, pointed back to, indexed a specific physical existence: a particular body, the body of a male, middle-aged, former athlete and sportscaster. The sounds emanated from a corporeal position, from a body taking a place in televisual divisions of labor, as beyond, behind, and around the television cameras, other persons labor as camera operators, sound managers, and scriptwriters. The dozen or so extremely popular late Soviet films set in television studies or on film sets that dramatize such divisions of labor (e.g., *Moscow Does not Believe in Tears*, 1980) situate those biographical accounts that highlight Chumak's occupational journey from performance to paranormal.

Chumak had delivered sports news but got his start as a bioenergetic healer in 1977 while conducting research for a program debunking faith healers. His subjects convinced him that he himself possessed an unusually strong aura, or *biopole*.[34] When *glasnost'* began, he and others who executed new TV programming (or new telephone directories, etc.) were not new personnel; they had held their positions for years, and some would not retire for a long time. Chumak was a media veteran at a central television studio that decided programming content and broadcast times. So, while some read his silent blessings to reverse the optics of centralized media, or at least to bend its frames, it was long-term, Soviet-era social placement in the division of communicative labor that placed him to make phatic claims that his energetic channels rode televisual media.[35]

LOVE, LONELINESS, AND THE COLD WAR TELEPATH

In the twenty-first century, contrasts among new and old communications media no longer work to the disadvantage of Moscow; cell phones work there more consistently than in most of Manhattan. After the Soviet state dissolved, telecommunications were among the fastest of infrastructures to transform (mechanical upgrades to public transit, for example, took longer).[36] By 1993 international calls had gone to direct dial, intercity connections had improved, and detailed local telephone books were published. Urban expertise and everyday experience with wireless electronic media had leapfrogged that in much of the United States.

And yet the imperative to compete to develop communications technology could never quite override impulses to appropriate media for less competitive communicative ends, carving channels, real and figurative, alongside or over new media and communication structures. Efforts to remove wires, papers, speakers, all materials, from communications across greater distances could not erase the bodily labors to connect or to separate, not just in the making of messages, but in the dialing, the waiting for a reply. Cold War competition, aiming to detect and defeat enemy propaganda, to block mental manipulation, to develop means to influence, to win hearts and minds, informed state-sponsored research in telepathy and other paranormal powers, infusing them with the mood of paranoia.[37] Threat, however, did not exhaust all motivations, did not tamp out dreams for connection across troubled borders. Even government scientists and soldiers fantasized contact, even with the enemy others and especially with the unknown, as a good in itself.

Such sentiments color science fiction, such as when Soviet author Efremov's ship, the *Tantra* of *Andromeda Nebula* (1955), encounters an entire planet gone silent; the tragedy of missed connection hits the multinational crew hard. We can find examples also in the writings of those who participated in Pentagon research on telepathy and clairvoyance, former military men like David Morehouse, Ed Dames, Joseph McMoneagle, and Mel Riley, who produced dozens of popular publications and documentaries on secret remote viewing programs.

These authors insistently quote the canonical set of Department of Defense declassified documents on Soviet paranormal science—and each other.[38] Veteran officer Morehouse, for example, does so in *Psychic Warrior: Inside the CIA's Stargate Program: The True Story of a Soldier's Espionage and Awakening* (note the excess of colons, poetically mimicking the way the text itself enfolds earlier accounts). Morehouse (1996) was in fact criticized for quoting so much from other authors to make his own autobiography more cinematically vivid (Mandelbaum 2002, 168; Schnabel 1997), but his practice was not unusual. As they compete for best prior stories, and as each new author reinterviews the last tellers of the tale, an aggressive, competitive mood knits across the corpus of books and documentaries.

And yet other structures of feeling poke through that aggression. In a 1993 interview for *PSI Spies: The True Story of America's Psychic Warfare Program*, Morehouse, detailing the vantage of a psychic cold warrior with snatches of 1970s pop radio—and glimpses of the enemy as ordinary people who communicate via ordinary media—told Marrs:

> I went to one of the remote viewing rooms and listened to the Eagles' "Desperado" through headphones for my cool down session. Then I was read the mission coordinates, closed my eyes, and within seconds, I landed crouched on a rooftop. It was freezing cold with snow covering everything as far as I could see. I was on top of a three-story building which was part of a compound somewhere deep inside Russia. . . . I willed myself through the building's wall and was instantly relieved by

the warmth of the interior. . . . I saw people working at their desks. Some talked on the telephone, some simply were doing paperwork, and still others were conferring with each other. The office seemed to be for administration, not remote viewing. . . . I began experiencing trouble bending my legs and moving my head. The sensation became stronger as I drew closer to a small, flat, box-like device mounted high up on a wall. . . . I felt all my cells tingling. . . . [Mel Riley] too had seen the box, as had the other [remote viewers]. . . . It turned out to be some type of energy shield or screen, which the Soviets had been working on for years. This device recognized all forms of energy—extra low frequency, radio, television and the like. . . . The Soviets had mounted these shields in rooms where high-sensitive meetings took place or where their extrasensory [agents] were operating. (2007, 167–69)

Militarized tropes of energy and penetration pepper the account, the focus on internal sensation; "my cells tingling" draws attention to the enemy source of jamming energy, a static-making device that blocks channels to see and hear. But the actual people present all remain innocent—they chat, write, telephone, "simply doing paperwork," paying no heed to the invisible machine-channel of state buried in the walls: both Morehouse *and* the Soviet state are aggressive intruders on people just doing their jobs.

Morehouse's opening cool-down hints at hopes for human contact across paranoid barriers. The Eagle's song "Desperado" gestures to the Wild West, the free but lonely cowboy. Morehouse probably expected readers to be Americans who would recall the line urging the wanderer to let someone love him: "Desperado, why don't you come to your senses, come down from your fences, 'n open the gate." Morehouse voices a familiar character here, one branded by those American institutions that have militarized entire families, a masculine shadow who narrates war and love together, joining them through tropes of fences (albeit several steps removed from the way androgynous David Bowie sang about lovers at the Berlin Wall).

Along the very walls that we fortified, Cold War fantasies of contact germinated. American science fiction writers filled tales with Soviet characters who ignored lines of enmity to share discoveries—*especially* on topics like telepathy. Soviet science fiction writers projected an internationalized future, sowing stories with footnotes to foreign publications, their scientist heroes always off to international conferences.[39] Post–World War II fascination with telepathy cannot be reduced to warm and cozy motives, of course—still, even from governing perspectives, the competition was not waged in the terms of violent conquest. The state that could light the path to perfect peace would claim the high road to hegemony: to develop perfect media was a means to this end.[40] What better way to broadcast a worthy state than to compete to achieve the most evolved means to communicate with a worthy rival, one that also claims impressive modern advances along the scale of phatic evolution?

"WHY CAN'T THEY READ ME BACK?"

For the U.S. Department of Defense, while Soviet paranormal experiments hinted at modern advances, the figure of endemic mysticism demonstrated the failed reach of Soviet-style modernity. The appearance of the topic in the press indexed alternative channels, resistant communications outside "channels controlled by the government": "The ancient traditions and belief in the occult are passed down by word of mouth from generation to generation, outside the formal communications channels controlled by the government. . . . By channeling potentially dangerous, idealistic and spiritual popular beliefs into officially sanctioned channels, the government can in some measure defuse those beliefs" (Air Force Systems Command 1978, 39).

And yet for all that "beliefs" in alternative powers and channels are associated with informal channels, with the people plural, across their informal networks, the figure of the psychic stands alone. Science fiction of telepathy across the continents worries that reading others' minds makes social life painful, impossible, lonely.[41] One Moscow celebrity remarks publicly how difficult it can be for psychics to become intimate with anyone, *especially* other psychics. For her, "It worked out well that my husband is not an *ekstrasens*," for two psychics cannot make a good marriage. One might develop her own talent while the other lags, becoming mere "ballast," competition and resentment killing love. Her husband, luckily, was "a stable, ordinary, former KGB" bureaucrat "who grounds me" for her own flights. This contradiction of the lonely telepath bothers a good number of former Soviets: "How do you get along with other psychics?" "Can psychics marry each other?" were questions my friends suggested posing, and the topics always came up in meetings with psychics, without my asking.

This was the case when I visited the sister center to Vinogradov's Center, Enchanted Forces, which focused on healing. In a building tucked behind a line of trees alongside a metro station far from the center of Moscow, inside the back courtyard, up on the second floor, the office was secured by a brown, padded leather security door. Next to the bell, a long placard hung bearing the logos of MasterCard, Visa, and American Express. Inside, a corridor opened into the clinic, offices branching off it. All was tidy, attractive RussoSoviet décor—many, many lush, green houseplants, rubber plants, geraniums, jade, large and small, in every corner and every window, evening rays brushing leaves, well-watered, green. The psychic greeted me with a handshake and a steady gaze and led me into a Spartan room where a desk and two chairs buttressed a window, and a clinical exam table and sink lined the other walls. The only talismans were a pack of yellow wax church candles and a small brass holder for them on the desk. She gestured to the more comfortable chair, glanced at my business card, nodded as I explained my hope to begin a documentary film or project. Then she launched into her biography, hardly taking breath between sentences. She may have prepared some phrases for her ongoing auditions for *Battle* (she has since become a celebrity on the spin-off show, *Psychics Investigate*). I asked no questions. She started right off with marital status: "We are both from the area near Saratov, and moved here for his police work." Her husband fully "supports and believes in my talents—he comes home sometimes and asks for help with suspects." Nevertheless, she stressed, it is very difficult for him to live with her, and she with him: "I get impatient because I think that I have sent him my thoughts, so why doesn't he understand?! Always that feeling that others are not as smart. . . . I read them, so why don't they read me?"

Another celebrity psychic complained to me the next week that the people who phone her now, all day long, occupy her social life, that she has neither time nor inclination to find a partner or start a family. Her own parents had married in the Crimea the fifth day after meeting (he had been in the navy; all the men in her family had been navy). She described them to me as "an ideal pair. He never drank, never cheated," and fast-forwarded to her current romantic life: "This is what you have to give up in this profession. Sure I date, I might spend time with someone, but to be an *ekstrasens* makes womanly happiness impossible. That is what you have to give up. Also, I could not live under a man's rule. I am no feminist, but I could not do it" (written notes, 2009).

She went on to lament that it is also difficult to make friends with other psychics—not because they read each other (that is the fun part), but because they compete. "To show off greater powers?" I asked. No, no, this was competition for attention, over who got a press article, who a television spot. "We made a big mistake making all this public." She suffered from her fame; people were always grabbing her sleeves on the street, asking her to divine their future. One can find clips of her being stalked on YouTube and RuTube, posted by celebrity hunters. (Moscow is, after all, a city dense with celebrities.) Nonpsychic friends disappeared when they did not need help: "One is left with those who only want to talk to you because you are psychic."

Celebrity psychics complain of having trouble making contacts last, trouble reaching friends and spouses when channels run one way. One means to situate and understand the ways these ideologies of contact burden love and friendship is to contrast them with other kinds of "one-way" encounters, especially those that work against intimacy. The next chapter takes up the dynamics of contact in bureaucracies and at checkpoints, places for the flashing of credentials, in spaces where some people are read but are not supposed to read back—except for the psychic, whose acts of reading themselves serve as credentials.

4. Circles, Rays, Channels

The students who live and work at GITIS endure a challenging series of entrance auditions, then courses, exams, and other trials before they emerge with credentials. So many want to study here, in Moscow, in the center. The campus could not be more central, a pleasant brisk walk even in a wet November from the metro station at the Lenin library, from a spot overlooking the Kremlin walls just above the traffic node at Red Square. Americans hold the lease on this vista to the Kremlin towers and the river that flows by them; the embassy residence is here. I have never looked out from its windows. Most threads of American expat social life in Moscow are invisible to me; Russian friends, and even Moscow acquaintances from other European countries, know American diplomatic circles better than I do, have even been inside the residence. I knew the late Romani singer Olga Demeter, who writes in her autobiography about performing at there in the 1930s; that is the closest I have come. In large part, this is due to diplomatic rules about local contact, regulations that would prevent ethnography, but it is also due to the fact that in my American life I do not know the kinds of people who become diplomats.

In August 1991 at this same, central spot I saw soldiers stand at attention around their tanks. Called in by the leaders of an attempted coup, it soon became clear that they felt little connection with those commanders, and the people surging around the tanks pressed that point. These were local boys; an older woman poked one of the soldiers in the chest with the tip of her umbrella, knowing he would "never shoot his own people." By the next day their tanks were shielding her side, and the resistance had transformed the center into a festival. People poured in from the edges of the city to build barricades, to witness, to play music, and to paint. The resistance held, and the coup failed. A few years later, however, the city constructed a pleasant buffer zone at the foot of the Kremlin walls, with shops and fountains and paths that minimized the space where before huge crowds could gather.

Imagine that both the Kremlin and the American residence sit near the base of Moscow's thumb. GITIS is just above that, just where the thumb stretches across the lanes of old Moscow, toward a grand avenue of glass towers that rise still. The next fingers cross leafy boulevards and meandering streets to the trafficked avenues. A walker's dream with good shoes, an umbrella, and a metro pass. These avenues conduct social, cultural, and material capital through the central banks and the central theaters and academies. GITIS is certain of its own centrality and is reliably, if not lavishly, funded by the government. Even Hollywood, for all its marvelous technologies for creating illusion, has little to teach GITIS about technologies for intuition

At GITIS I was no professor; my American credentials did not register as important or central. I was to join the students and interns, those who stand up the moment an instructor crosses the studio threshold. They did not socialize with us, the maestro and the pedagogical team; they had other gigs, a show to finish. There were also unwritten rules limiting social contact across ranks. A few would greet me with a grave nod, but not all (one, earning an advanced degree, never made eye contact). By contrast, at the first daily encounter, students never failed to recognize everyone at least once, including me, with kisses on the cheeks. Once having greeted, we were free to ignore each other all day.

It was more difficult to claim the attention of ranking teachers, and I never managed to convince one to sit down for an interview, although they were pleased to be videotaped in front of the class. By contrast, even the most famous of Moscow's celebrity psychics quickly agreed to meet with me. Friends in Moscow were surprised that famous persons were so immediately accessible; even in August, a difficult month to find people in the city, my cell phone rang as secretaries for *Battle* celebrities returned my calls. Why would psychics be more eager than famous film or theater directors to talk to a foreign scholar? Is it because historically, scholarly (and sometimes foreign scholarly) attention has been useful as a credential, as university scientists so often were part of the juries for public telepathy tests? I have always found in Russia plenty of actors and musicians who enjoy collaborating with an American (someone who commands jazz standards or can show them how to pronounce Shakespeare), but those at the top, who stoke the furnaces of creative tradition, were not hungry for outside validation.

My situation could have worked out differently had I been introduced through different social channels, but my Russian acquaintances do not run along those particular elite social chains. At GITIS I had no prior contacts: I paid tuition and met the head of the department for foreign students, who then introduced me to the head of the first-year directors' cohort. Her introduction over, I was on my own; the teachers had to accept me in the corridors and classrooms, but no more. When it came to reaching psychic celebrities, there too I had no connections. In that case, however, a Moscow friend offered to make calls on my behalf, as an "assistant for a professor from Michigan," explaining in gracious formal Russian that I hoped to explore possibilities to take oral histories. Her mediation both buffered and focused first contacts—and like a good letter of recommendation, it implied that I warranted such attention.

Papers commonly anchor credentials, but so also do communicative processes such as these telephone introductions—along with other mediations that first buffer and then link new contacts, to delay contact while establishing a channel. To Foucault's governmental technologies linking power to knowledge—the archive and the gaze meeting in the credential, or the arrangements of prison cells—we should add those that block, delay, or skip over sensible contacts, over presence, techniques that involve a sort of phatic triangulation.

A first summer meeting with a star from *Battle of the Psychics* led through a series of spatial buffers out to the rings of dachas where people like to spend the summer. Deep green patchworks of pine and birch forest, river, and marsh circle the Moscow metropolis, and small wooden houses follow after large stone villas, each with its surrounding garden, or the occasional apartment block. Stores selling vacation and building supplies dot smooth highways. Once we turned onto dirt back roads, to wind past fences and thick brush, branches scraped the car. Everyone we asked recognized "that professor from television," *Battle*'s key expert and Soviet-era psychic researcher, but only after we circled for a while did a man on foot give us precise directions. This was our host's son. He called ahead from his cell phone, so that his father met us, opening a red iron gate that protected the courtyard of an immaculate wooden dacha with a mature orchard. He was wearing a tweed jacket and I, too, had selected professorial wear in the July heat, a green plaid shirtdress. His family—wife, son, daughter-in-law, and boxer dog—left us to talk in a cool inner room, sparsely furnished and dim in the afternoon shade. My friend tried to limit her involvement, placing her body out of our sight line, back to the wall, until our host, after politely swiveling his head a few times to address us both, asked her to sit closer. (Later, she confessed worrying that she might undermine my scholarly authority were she to get in the middle. Far from it—not only did she amplify my credentials, she noticed angles and details that I did not, about which she told me later.)

He asked me to explain my project. I began with my credentials, items from my CV—workplace and discipline, past writing, current interest in contact and communication—but the conversation did not start to move until I named our countries' oppositional positions. Up until that point he had listened steadily; then I added, intending to show friendly rivalrous respect, "Our government used to be afraid of Soviet psychic capabilities." "So," he finally interjected, "you are here for personal reasons, not reasons of state?" "Our government does not listen to ethnographers. And I promise not to ask where the secret labs are." He laughed, my friend laughed, I laughed; we all knew these phrases, which hit a pleasurable and familiar nerve, these geopolitical tropes of competition. They opened a vantage of coherent, almost comfortable conflict—the phatic work of monitoring a superpower rival itself projects an elite position. In recognition of rivalry, we credentialed each other as imperial forces.

"No, no, no, it's all open now," he continued, "though I *can* say that while Britain has just published their secret lab results, we still have not." Indeed, details of his biography are published in print media and on the Internet; he several times pointedly repeated that everything he was telling us about the old research is "all available in the open press." As he did on the air, he spoke languidly yet precisely, steadily holding eye contact. Back in the 1960s, his first discovery of "distance viewing" talent had gone like this: he had been called in to observe a fellow who was sitting and talking with a ball on a string. "Mikhail Viktorovich, we need to admit him to the psych ward." "No, no, no, let me have a look at him." He listened to the man describe submarine manufacture in "such and such a state in the U.S."; "cross-checking with the KGB" confirmed the information. "The Americans then worked to catch up with us—even using their psychics to steal our discoveries," he added, pulling out his cell phone to dramatize the example. These were familiar accusations—those Soviets/those Americans, they only imitate our genius, steal our thoughts. Our introduction slipped in and out of familiar tracks, comfortable but not too close. We mirrored the work of diplomacy among states as much as we did replicated mundane attempts to move up or into social hierarchies; in such work, certain channels must be buffered in order for even a few others to open at all.

EXPANDING CIRCLES, EXCESS CHANNELS

Paper credentials are supposed to condense and represent time and effort spent in the socially buffered zones where expertise is passed on. In the 1990s this assumption was challenged, as credentials mushroomed across new zones: colleges and institutes branched out of Soviet university faculties or sprang up as night classes, consultancies, dojos, studios, and correspondence courses offering instruction and diplomas for pay. Paths, channels to become accredited in *ekstrasensorika,* especially seemed to multiply[1] and to thicken branches that sprouted in late Soviet times when psychics offered themselves to be tested at universities in hopes of being certified authentic. This was not unique to the socialist world: in the 1970s, Uri Geller claimed to have participated in experiments at the Stanford Research Institute as a credential (his debunking occurred not there, but on television, on Johnny Carson's show).[2] In 1999 Doctor Kirill Leontevich, recollecting laboratory studies conducted in the 1960s, described the arrival of one such psychic from Khar'kov, Vladimir Rud': "He turned out to be a hard nut for Soviet science to crack. The University of Khar'kov, after a series of experiments, had acknowledged him a genuine telepath, which made Vladimir very popular. But the Ukrainian telepath wanted to conquer Moscow. From the Academy of Sciences here he requested an official certificate of his capabilities" (Vorsobin 1999, 7). Rud' passed a series of tests conducted at the Institute for Problems in the Transfer of Information, but then they found his hand drill for poking holes through walls to adjoining rooms.

In twenty-first-century Moscow a number of centers that teach and accredit psychic powers ground their authority in Soviet brain science. "The Bronnikov method," taught across former Soviet territories and beyond, is one such franchise, advertised by the approval of Soviet-era brain scientist and granddaughter of Vladimir Bekhterev, the late Natalja Petrovna Bekhterova, *akademik* at the Academy of Sciences and former scientific director of the Institute for Human Brain Study at the Academy of Sciences. In 2002 Bekhterova conducted an experiment with Bronnikov's child pupils and judged his methods effective.[3] His schools claim to develop ordinary physiological capacities, to train a person to see with senses other than vision—what he calls *neurovision.* Bronnikov's course advertisements offer "to form a new instrument for perception and for processing information—a *psychobiocomputer.*"

Like Bekhtereva's pronouncement, Soviet-trained expert appearances on *Battle of the Psychics* certify the show. Former contestants have used participation on the show to attract clients; this television production, aired as it is on a channel for broad entertainment (TNT), has joined the ranks of institutions issuing credentials. As Arina Evdokimova, a psychic who gained celebrity after appearing on the first season of *Battle of the Psychics*, told a reporter for *Vzgljad*, "I think this project has become a video diploma for our abilities" (Shabashov 2007). The winner receives a transparent, blue trophy in the shape of a hand, fingers open and reaching, and all finalists receive a paper diploma, text printed over the spectral blue imprint of the hand. Former contestants hang out their shingles, displaying the *Battle* certificate along with other papers on their office walls. Some embed the image on their websites, alongside event photos, video clips of successful events, claims to descent from "hereditary Scandinavian mages," and diplomas for completing NLP training or "a year of study at a U.S. business school."

Some find such numbers and mixes of credentials dazzling and impressive, while others describe them as contradictory and jarring. As means and media to accredit psychic talents have expanded, so have efforts to discredit them. Bronnikov's endorsement by a high-level Soviet-era brain scientist has not sheltered him from other scientists' efforts to invalidate his claims. The Commission to Investigate Pseudoscience and Falsification in Scientific Work was established under the Academy of Sciences in 1998 to counteract the growing appeal of the paranormal. The commission's director, Eduard Pavlovich Krugljakov (then director of the Institute of Nuclear Physics), spearheaded much of the work, exposing what he called the charlatanry and cupidity of people like Bronnikov and those who promote them. The commission works with organizations such as the Russian Association of Humanists and the Orthodox church, investigating, for example, people licensed to "adjust the biopole, which does not exist," as he explained in an interview with a regional Siberian newspaper in 2004:

> Our people really believe in all kinds of "epaulettes," in titles and ranks
> . . . It is a nightmare. . . . Unprincipled and basically open trade in
> diplomas is going on. The representatives of the Moscow diocese in Ufa
> approached me, asking me to evaluate the activities of the Russia-wide
> Professional Medical Association of Specialists in Traditional Folk
> Medicine and Healers, an association that has received administrative
> permission to work in Ufa. Their petition [for permission] was signed
> by a professor and doctor of medical sciences, Academic of the RAEN,
> V.A. Zagrjadskij. Naturally, I decided to verify all these titles and
> received this answer: no such credentials and titles are recorded for this
> person. There is only one conclusion: this guy is a shyster. (Notman
> 2004, 8)

Krugljakov also tells of a journalist acquaintance who, sent to investigate Bronnikov, discovered that the blindfolds used by his students allow peeking. That journalist, invited to appear on a television program featuring Bronnikov, stood up on camera and successfully demonstrated how the blindfold was designed. In the broadcast, however, "the journalist who had demystified the fraud disappeared, there remained only the triumphant doctor Bronnikov with his children and their fantastical *dermooptika* ('skin vision'). All I could do was exhale: yes, our television will do anything to hold viewers, who are losing interest in all the TV channels. Here 'skin vision,' there that hooligan Kirkorov. . . . How much farther will they fall in making fools of people for the sake of advertising?!"(Krugljakov 2009). For Krugljakov, fascination with the occult comes from above, as old bureaucracies metastasize under the new markets into something even more alarming; it does not bubble up from the people and is not a response to chaos or the opacity of power—it is a tool of power.

LOCATING LICENSE

Compared to Krugljakov, *Battle of the Psychics'* "resident expert-skeptic" is much less skeptical, asserting that some people master or embody *ekstrasensorika*. His training during Soviet times as "criminal psychologist and expert in extrasensory matters," authorized him to discern the charlatans from the strong psychics and even to divide psychics into kinds (clairvoyants, telepaths, spirit communicators, etc.). His own psychic talents lay in locating criminals and victims of disaster. At his Tsentr Vinogradov, past winners of the show, listed as working associates, focus on unsolved crimes, while at its "sister center," Volshebnaja Sila, the psychics concentrate on healing. I have visited the first center several times over the years. The reception area is free of the usual spiritual decorations; just a *few* certificates and letters in frames stand calmly against wood paneling and white walls, and desks and fax machines flank the waiting room, warmed by an aquarium and a resident kitten. A comforting notice informs patrons that fees are waived for people enduring "extreme situations."

Let us return to the first time I met him, at the dacha, where my friend had worked to minimize her own contact channels, her signs of presence, sitting silent to the side. He had summarized the press documenting his role in finding and arresting serial killers; it was this revelation that stirred my friend to finally join in, exclaiming: "People need to know about this!! If more criminals knew that *ekstrasensy* would find them, that somebody is watching, there would be less crime! We need to shout about this, show it on every station, and not just on TNT, but on Channel One!!!" Our interlocutor nodded with gratification to hear someone so passionately relate his mastery of technologies of intuition to law.

A few days later we recycled the conversation in a different setting, sparking competing interpretations that revealed the high stakes of these topics. We were sitting at the table in my friends' kitchen hosting others of their close friends. We already had told neighbors about our encounter, at which they had laughed, and so I prompted her this time also to "tell what we did this weekend." Seeing her cautious inhalation, I tried to backpedal, but before she managed to say much, the guests interjected, "You can go psychotic, schiz out!" and, "This is a sin, you have to decide what you *believe*!" Our very contact with such people put us at great risk. But my friend stood firm: using psychics to catch maniacs is a moral good for society, "If they just knew that they were being watched!" They countered: they did not question the *existence* of psychics, but their motives and ends. We went back and forth for a while until they asked: "Who told you all this, the psychic himself?"

"He is a professor."

"A professor of *what*?! What was his degree, where did he get it?" This is a common question after two decades of multiplying accreditations and specialties, rumors of degrees bought and paid for. What finally ended the discussion, however, was a story locating psychic credentials as an agent of tragedy in a concrete social world. The guest revealed that his father, who had worked as a technician at a central theater, had died after refusing surgical treatment because a psychic healer had told him, contradicting the medical doctors, that he did *not* have cancer: "That psychic! To whom the whole theater turned with their problems, with all his certificates!" he spat, furious. This revelation left us quiet. If proliferations of credentials signaled opportunity to some, they threatened others even with death.

PHATIC GLAMOUR

Diplomas attest to capacities acquired elsewhere in the past, indexing some timespace in which expertise passed to the certified. They specify a holder by filling a blank. The words around the blank point to sources for expertise, surrounding the name like a halo. People question the origins of many certificates, and the psychic holders of diplomas, knowing this, augment their authority with techniques and media other than papers or expert genealogies. They arrange the very conditions for communication, opening and shutting channels for contact via social and technical buffers: agents, secretaries, answering machines, and schedules do more than manage phatic work they also amplify authority. Obstacles to contact, waiting periods, and rules or spaces that dampen communications can effect a kind of phatic glamour, undermining ordinary expectations about contact and intensifying uncertainty ("*Will* she call back?"). Such moves can incite the very impulse to seek out psychic intuition. Advice on phatic glamour graces the book of Ovid (in a section on withholding attention for romantic success), and we know from the movies that phatic glamour is the principle at work when a secretary makes her boss's rival wait because "he is in a meeting."

Ms. D is a relatively difficult celebrity psychic to reach. When I first e-mailed *Battle* contestants, many responded, but she did not. Her website, however, is among the easiest to find. There one can read about her commitment to "white magic" (no husbands returned against their will) and purchase talismanic cell phone wallpapers. The site gives detailed walking directions from the metro station to her office and lists five telephone numbers. My friend and I took turns dialing each one for an hour; some rang endlessly, and others were answered by secretaries unable to tell us anything concrete. One of these women gave us yet another number that, she said, was Ms. D's personal cell phone number. At that number we reached a woman claiming to be Ms. D who made us an appointment for the following evening at 6:00 P.M.: "Should we call back to confirm?" I asked. "No, no, I have you in the appointment book." We conjectured that some people must give up trying by telephone and just follow the map.

The office was easy to find, far from the center at a station near the southern end of the purple line, which runs above ground past the textile and automobile factories until the air feels cleaner again. In an area dotted with green parks and red brick buildings, the office is entered through the back of a four-story structure, just yards from the station, fronted by a jewelry shop and a homeopathic drugstore. (The latter are not new; in late Soviet times they bore the generic shop sign "Homeopathic Drugstore.") I arrived at the appointed hour. On the third floor on a dark landing a guard manned a desk, not asking to see anyone's papers, just gesturing to the open doorway on the left, where one next steps over a dozing black-and-white cat. Lined with a dozen chairs, the narrow waiting room was half full; six women were waiting. Past them a red sign on the far door stated "Registration." To the right of that was another door labeled with our psychic's name, with still another sign underneath warning, "Don't open the door—the owl will fly out."

At Registration I addressed the secretaries quietly—clearly I was not the only one here at 6:00 P.M. for an appointment. They looked over my University of Michigan business card ("Oh yes . . . the professor, yes, yes

. . .") and asked me gently: Would I mind ever so much waiting just another half hour? Sitting in the reception area, I took in signs, hung one on each wall ("Please observe silence so as not to disturb the work of the specialists") and clients' clothing (manicures, heels, cell phone tassels) and ages (one teenager, two women well into their fifties, the others in between). A barometer. A poster: "Moscow from the Cosmos." A letter of gratitude from a local military unit. A sign pointing to the cashier's window. One woman was reading the colorful monthly newsletter published by the center, *Secret Force: Magic and Healing*. We waited. More people arrived. Two women finally broke the silence: "I heard that you can wait here for two, three hours." "Yes, yes, I've been here almost that long, my appointment was at 4:00." Fifteen minutes later a secretary called me back to Registration: "Ms. D is ready to collaborate with you on your project, but as you can see, too many are waiting today—can you come back tomorrow at noon?" This consideration, releasing me, I took as special treatment.

The next day, by 11:45 A.M., there were even more people waiting, now two men among them, and it seemed we all had appointments at noon with Ms. D, who had still to arrive. Forty-five minutes elapsed. People used the bathroom; there was no sink, so back in the waiting area we each demonstrably rubbed our hands with German-manufactured baby wipes. We held the silence. Someone asked the secretaries to turn on the air conditioning, someone visited the cashier, and a man tapped the metal chair legs to summon the cat, "kssss, kssss!" In Soviet times, even early post-Soviet times, this waiting would have been nothing, easy—people waited hours, all day long in all weather, with no chairs, no bathroom (much less baby wipes), just to buy coffee or bread, to see the doctor, to reserve train tickets, to tick their names off a waiting list for a sofa, to take oral exams. This was physically easier, more comfortable—but it was also more strictly policed; this new regime for waiting discouraged contact, forbade us to talk, to compare notes. And we were not responsible for our line, as we had been before; we could not establish among ourselves "who here is last?" No one here relied on others to "remember I was behind you" in order to step out for a while, to get other errands done. Those Soviet-era practices had been democratic, collectively regulated; that habitus for waiting still works well, by the way, in places such as the post office, though such waits are rarely as necessary as they used to be. Here, we could control how we waited, facing strangers, to be chosen next . . . or not chosen.

The secretaries called on clients in no order that we could discern; short flurries of hushed talk on the topic were followed by scolding from Registration. We watched each other wait. We were all subject to temporal manipulation as well as phatic monitoring and blocking that kept us distant from each other as well as from the object of our anticipation.[4] At about 1:00 P.M., a bustle at the door sent the cat running. Then an entourage filed through: a stocky man gripping a walkie-talkie, Ms. D herself, another stocky man ("probably bodyguards," a friend ventured later when I described the scene), and a woman carrying several plastic grocery bags. She glittered in flowing, blue and orange Dolce & Gabana skirts, hair spiraled in large gleaming coils, nails golden, stilettos golden too. *"Zdrastvujte"* ("Hello") she whispered politely to the room as she passed, making eye contact with no one. The door to Registration closed behind them. More time passed. Several were called; we craned our necks to watch each one go in. The owl stirred and made a noise. I was called in third or fourth. Close up, Ms. D blinded me: she stood at the secretaries' counter, a white owl perched on her left hand, feet gripping her fingers between rings. Would I mind waiting just a bit more while she received one girl first? Phatic glamour interrupted and then suffused the waiting, waiting to be named, called, greeted, seen, understood.

CHANNEL TEAM

An hour later, having been admitted to the inner office, I saw that only half was decorated for psychic work: icons, crystals, and candleholders were piled on one side, near the desk, facing an aquarium and a birdcage. The other side of the room was bare, with a dusty wardrobe and a coatrack. We took our places, Ms. D behind her desk in a tall swiveling office chair. She opened, confessing that parsing my credentials at the university website had been a bit complicated: "Of course, we understand English, but can you please explain your project in more detail?"

Later that night, friends would declare that question a proof of charlatanry: "It says on her website that the client needn't explain the problem—she is supposed to see everything herself and *tell* the client." I however, at least at that moment, had been more impressed that she had taken the trouble to tailor her words to "discussion with a scholar," never attempting to reframe the conversation as a reading. Most people, however, give no quarter for psychics not to be psychics; their talent should always be on, regardless of situation. This is something resented by psychics, who compare their work to that of an artist or a musician, who is rarely expected to perform without variations or failures, or they compare their extrasenses to the ordinary senses that wax and wane in good light and bad. Just as a shy singer or star athlete can falter in the spotlight, they say, the throat constricting, muscles giving out, a hostile crowd can cause all those yet undiscovered psychic organs or channels for sensation to constrict and fail.

Ms. D's ongoing success on radio and television (she appears on several series and has hosted at least two radio shows) owes a good deal, I propose, to her sensitivity to the pragmatic demands of contexts. With me, she showed familiarity with a range of sociological and autobiographical registers. For instance, to my broad question, "Why are people so interested in *ekstrasens?*," Ms. D agilely spun out embedded clauses to connect the stock market, jobless rates, social insecurities, and occult fascination, all the while twisting together two thin yellow church candles from a box on the desk. Her phrases echoed the political science language of Russian journals like *Ekspert* and *Itogi* (resonating also with scholarly arguments linking interest in the paranormal to crises). The tenor and tempo of her speech appealed to me, drew me in, and I found myself wanting to argue just for fun—to counter that the *krizis* of 2008, a year old then, had hit only after *Battle of the Psychics* had taken off, just after a long period of expansion in Russian employment and markets statistics since 2000—but then her iPhone jangled, opening another channel, and our face-to-face talk switched to standby. I examined the aquarium, curious about the caller.

Such talent to switch had not been manifested in Ms. D's earliest television appearances. Perhaps she developed it later, or perhaps such moments were cut. She later assembled a staff of consultants and agents who help to juggle her many channels—the sheer number of calls magnify her value: "Please excuse me, my phone will ring from time to time, a lot of people are calling today." We had been speaking slowly; into the iPhone she sped up, informing someone that the difference between television appearance A and B was that, "one is paid, the other is not," while looking at me from under enormous, black, false eyelashes.

Her eyebrows were powdered over, thinner ones painted on above. A lovely face. Ms. D leaned forward in her swivel chair. The owl started pooping a gray trail down the front of the chair's microfiber back. Hitting end call, she lifted the owl to the desk. "Her name is Sofia; it means wisdom. A psychic should have a familiar, you know." "Who picked whom?" (not an owlish pun in Russian: *kto kogo vybral?*) I asked. "It should be mutual," she answered. Having chosen, such familiars, alongside staff, also act as living credentials, part of the animal collective that makes a psychic psychic. Sofia hopped onto the branch of a large plant, which collapsed under her weight, depositing her on the floor. Ms. D pulled the owl, upside down, closer by the string around her scaled talons, flipping her right side up to set her back on the chair. "She is still learning. She doesn't see very well in daytime." I told her that I had a cat of the same name, and we regarded the owl in silence. This was our first silence. We were not here to talk about *my* biography.

Ms. D writes on her website, and detailed for me in person, that her gift first appeared during late Soviet times when she attempted to win the attention of older schoolmates. On the train to pioneer camp she had tried telling fortunes, and to her surprise it had worked; they told her that she had said true things. More and more people came down the train corridor to try, "even the school teachers." Ms. D asserts that desire for such attention motivates everyone, even "more than money, more than love." She offered an example, by way of responding to a final question. It was one that friends had asked me to pose, noticing that *Battle* stresses violent crimes and mysteries: "Are there never any comic moments? Is it all really so tragic?" Ms. D sat up and smiled and said:

> Sure! We have a cleaning lady here in my office who wants to be a psychic. One time I had to go outside to get something from my car—I have a Hummer, by the way—and when I returned she was sitting in my chair, receiving clients. Sometimes the secretaries pretend to be me. Everybody wants to be a psychic—it is some kind of vanity. It is just like a friend I have; she works in advertising, but tells everybody she is working for the FSB [formerly KGB] and is always rushing off "for the homeland."

Of course it had already occurred to me that the "personal cell number" the secretaries had given us had probably never rung any phone that was in Ms. D's hands. The impersonation that she described, and that we encountered, seemed built into her organization's procedures, a means to foil our usual technologies of intuition, to wonder, for instance, "With whom are we making contact?" My friends, untouched by the glamour, found the story hilarious, asking me many times to "tell about the owl" and "tell about the cleaning lady," sometimes stealing the punch line: "*By the way*, I have a Hummer!"

SENSE OF BEING SEEN

Does everyone want attention? Do not experiences of attention vary? What of those with no way to buffer attention or contact? Attention feels different to those whose mere efforts to get from point A to B are restricted, when attention threatens body or family. Success may expand some channels while contracting others, but how and how much depends not only on technological limits to media, but also on things like hierarchy or minority exclusion. To enjoy the sense of being looked at, much less to enjoy fame, is not a neutral capacity equally distributed. The communicative load of fame, the sheer volume of attempts at contact from strangers, is riskier for some.

In 2009 a friend and I visited another of the celebrity winners of *Battle*. Mr. M was an Iranian dentist married to a Russian in Moscow. After winning season three, Mr. M opened his own consultancy in a three-room apartment in a building housing the Benin embassy and Iran Airlines. We waited comfortably, just the two of us, in a white-walled conference room, and not for long. Two secretaries offered us tea and coffee at a long table and desk configured into a "T," standard in Russian administrative offices. A glass case held soccer medals, bronze gazelles, and daggers, and on the adjoining wall hung a Persian rug woven and embroidered with the story of the Ten Commandments, next to a portrait of Mr. M with an older man wearing an oversized gold medallion. That man, my friend informed me, was his best friend and rival on *Battle*, the deceased sorcerer Fed.

The trophy from the show stood high on the shelves, next to the diploma. On the wall alongside the *Battle* diploma hung a framed finger painting in the same colors and shapes: "Maybe it's a diploma from his children," joked my friend. I wrote her words in my notes; they seemed important. I thought of the placement of the child's painting as decorative play until a few months later, when my friend e-mailed me that Mr. M had left consulting as a psychic to return to dentistry—and to write poetry and spend time with his children. When we met, he had already expressed a respectful distance from other psychic celebrities and centers, explaining that while Vinogradov and his protégés devote themselves to unsolved murders, his talents are otherwise tuned: "I can't help those people, they are already dead. I can only help living people." In light of his later (temporary) retirement from the paranormal, I am tempted to read the child's painting of a diploma hanging in the front office as diluting the forces that usually animate credentials or deflecting psychic fame. As he gently told curious television journalists, explaining his transformation: "I just want to be just Mr. M, not a psychic, just Mr. M,"[5] refusing the defining words written on his trophy. Like Ms. D, he spoke of the wearying forces of fame, but while she refracted attention by multiplying channels (and avatars), to ultimately amplify its effects, he deflected it.

Mr. M did have a staff to buffer contact, a secretary to answer e-mails and phone calls, as well as a right-hand man present during office meetings, benevolently nodding. Before television, however, Mr. M, unlike some of the other contestants, had been subject to frequent document checks. Moscow neighborhoods may not be segregated, but police do stop people they determine look "non-European"[6] and ask to see residence papers.

Once he became a famous psychic, he was rarely challenged to prove that he belonged in the city, but he was called upon to display magical proofs, not just to the police but to everyone: supplicants, journalists, scientists, and skeptics. Perhaps, already familiar with surveillance in public, Mr. M came to fame already weary of the sense of being seen.

LUSTER IN THE EYE

The eye that does the seeing, the organ for sensation, can itself be taken up as a sign, one that signals or even credentials special powers. I once met a psychic celebrity just as she was stepping onto the ladder for television appearances who was concerned that her eyes would become such a signal. We had faced a failure of credibility almost immediately upon meeting when she tried to cold read me, guessing the wrong number of siblings. When I acknowledged the errors, she shifted immediately from that technology for intuition, appropriate to psychic-client situations, and began instead to reflexively explore the failure itself on a meta-level, asking me how I perceived her and our ongoing communication, to figure out why her psychic skills were letting us down. She suggested that national distinction was to blame: "Maybe because this is the first time I've tried to read an American?" This answer seemed comfortable, transforming a lack of capacity on her part into a normal obstacle; the failure thus normalized, we could even return bravely to this reflexive key. She switched to autobiography, recounting when her powers had manifested. She did not pause, and I did not pose questions. After an hour she began to wind down, shifting again to a reflexive stance, to ask in quieter tones: "Do I *look* like a psychic?" I stuttered that I was not sure what to look for. She replied readily:

"A penetrating gaze."
"Yes, you have that. What else?"
"A luster to the eyes, like they are shining."

Indeed, her dark eyes did shine. Her dark, curly hair also gleamed. She wore a luminous satin, red, sleeveless shirt with rhinestone epaulets and long, dangling, sparkly silver earrings. How did psychic accreditation and advertising come to favor *this* abstractable quality?[7] One can certainly find images of wizards, shamans, and telepaths in late Soviet and post-Soviet films who eschew bling, who favor, say, wood and feathers, water and mud. She was not unique in Moscow, where glitter and light have come to dominate an urban landscape that, before the 1990s, was nearly dark after

FIGURE 4.1.   Raya's gaze, framed in close-up. The film has just flitted through a montage contrasting the directed concentration of her eyes to the frenzied and sudden arrest of the horses' motion.

nightfall. Central Moscow's neon, shining plate glass, burnished Mercedes cars, and sequined platform shoes still contrast with cement and rust—and forest and mist—farther out.

In Ms. D's office, her glitter had impressed me perhaps differently than it did the others waiting.[8] Twenty years before, much less extravagant attire would have seemed freakish; in Soviet times, people said that one could tell a foreigner by his running shoes or Italian leather. Back then, changing clothes each day was a foreigner's telltale indulgence, a waste of soap, water, and effort. But Soviet times were two decades gone, and Moscow center, once nocturnally dim, glowed at night like Las Vegas. On the way to see Ms. D, passing underground metro kiosks, I estimated three hundred shades of nail lacquer filling the front windows of each one—a range certainly on offer in U.S. drugstores, but tucked aside in gendered aisles, not displayed on the street. By the end of the 1990s Moscow was wearing European *Vogue* before the New York issue hit the stands, and Russian travelers were blogging about Americans' sloppy dressing, "They don't bother to iron." Shine, along with color and other formal markers, had become a sign of attention to fashion beyond the Soviet-era offerings, of reaching for modern cosmopolitan, not just a show of wealth.

The contrastive value of shine was greater in the Soviet past, when the streets were lit by few neon signs, but glittering costumes and dazzling light displays flitted across Soviet fantasy films and variety shows, especially intensely for the New Year, always a period for pleasing children. Soviet-era nonrealist films especially for children (or claiming to be for children), set in past kingdoms, future utopias, or faraway planets, almost always maximized glitter and shine. Some did so by foregrounding the spark of a gaze, to create the piercing, mesmerizing eyes of magical folk such as Gypsies (like the lyrics of a famous ballad: *Ochi Chernye, ochi strastnye* [Black eyes, impassioned eyes]). Such characters' eyes signal magical depths and powers, as when Raya, Gypsy heroine in the Soviet-era *Tabor Ukhodit v Nebo* (Lotjanu, 1979) halts the Boyars' charging horses by drilling the ray of her vivid stare into their wild pupils.

Roma whom I know laugh at this scene; subject to frequent profiling, stops and searches, and worse, they are nearly immune to the romantic screen chemistry pretending that Gypsies are free and carefree (they also note that the actress playing the part is "not Romani"). For other Soviets, however, the fantasy of Raya more convincingly reverses the panopticon, flipping the usual vectors for attention when authorities stop drivers or pedestrians to check papers.

Early Soviet filmmaker Dziga Vertov begins the film *KinoEye* (1924) with a shot of a perceiving eyeball looking through the camera lens, calling out viewers to come witness, too. Late Soviet film sees the eye seeing differently than did early Soviet celluloid eyes. Gazes go magical not in only depictions of Gypsies, but in female characters like Alisa in *Guests from the Future*, Hari in *Solaris*, or little Monkey in *Stalker*.

Miracles and catastrophes poise to unfold as these women look. Their ocular gestures beckon toward Soviet dreams in a romantic mood, stressing tensions between male and female as women's lines of sight escape the camera or seem to probe through the screen. Many of us know all too well the effects of others' denials of our consciousness; many late Soviet films ask viewers to take the face as a call to intersubjective recognition. In these Soviet films, women gaze at us or into the unknown, proposing another angle, inviting the viewer to wonder what these eyes see, perhaps to long for the grace of attention, a touch from those eyes.

This issue is less to do with reading feelings expressed by the eyes, such as rage or happiness, than with the eye as a sign of capacity *for* feeling, knowing, and influencing *others*, a psychic capacity. Such sensory experience is not

FIGURE 4.2.   The male protagonist follows Hari's eyes, perhaps for the first time wondering how and what she sees. The planet Solaris's first draft of her, after all, had lacked a dress zipper, invisible to his mind's memories.

bare; rather, sensation layers with perception *of* sensation and even explicit talk about sensory capacities. Encounters with the look are thus a nexus not only for artistic elaboration on romantic awe, but also for representing state power, bureaucratic surveillance, and all the everyday ways that the look is regimented. Post-Soviet journalists were warned, like everyone, to avoid the Gypsy hypnotic gaze. One, describing a country healer in *Moskovskaja Pravda*, wrote: "She had unusual eyes: big, wide, open, with little black pupils. I would not say that they shot lightning or penetrated the soul, but her gaze put me out of myself" (Timofeeva 1992). A luster in the eyes is taken to indicate extrasensory or extrasentimental capacities. Classic Russian literature made much of this trope in the figure of the Gypsy (Lemon 2000a), in descriptions of women in love. Soviet-era film aesthetics amplified it, and it now sparkles bright in everyday aesthetics.

STAR AUDITIONS

Let us turn then to stardom. More prosaically, let us turn to processes for accrediting future Russian film or theater stars, in order to think through whether and how sensate qualities matter differently across fields that produce technologies for intuition. A diploma from the directing department at GITIS is awarded after five years of study. That study, as we have seen, is based on learning to attend to details like the angle and luminosity of a gaze, talking about what such details do onstage, and testing this or that means to channel the audience's perception. Besides looking for "a gleam in the eye," people at GITIS discuss, demonstrate, and test out varied configurations of sensory media, from phonological qualities (that index class or regional differences: "Draw out the vowel, drop your jaw, less palatalization—you are an Estonian fashion model!"), to expectations about the quality of volume or prosody ("Really? A man from Surgut would speak so loudly, so bluntly, on a cell phone to his new boss?!"), to the speed of a bodily gesture (called out for destroying the illusion of fresh dialogue: "You nod too suddenly, as if you already know what she will say"; the work of the actor can differ from that of a cold-reader psychic).

These conversations may begin from detail or quality and lead to meta-discussions during the course of theatrical training or production about the meanings and uses of details, then to meta-meta-discussions about *how* actors and directors ought to discuss these things. An instructor might chastise a directing student for overreacting to criticism of the way he had directed his actors to interact, leading to a generalized discussion about how directors ought to issue directives. This is to become their livelihood, after all, attending to multiple channels, including those for communicating about communications. Students spoke with appreciation and wonder about their new meta-powers, about drills that set them working to notice, recall, and rearrange their observations of communication. They remarked that both the assignments and the critiques motivated them not only to work better on stage, but also to change how they lived, to walk the streets with varied tempo (especially to slow down) and how to ride transport: "We have really started looking now." "We see such *kadry* ("film frames"), just in the ways people move their fingers while riding the bus!" (Fieldnotes, November 2, 2002).

Few working actors in Russia have not passed through years of this sort of training. An academy credential is essential for sustained work. Hollywood-style sudden discoveries of unknowns do not characterize the making of stars on a central city stage or in film and certainly will not earn one a place in an ensemble. The ensembles in Moscow draw from its theatrical institutes and a few others (e.g., in St. Petersburg, Jaroslavl'). Rags-to-riches stories—the miner who starred in workplace theatricals, encouraged to apply to GITIS, earns a red diploma, and makes good—are few. Leonid Heifetz, a student of Knebel' in the early 1960s, teaches at GITIS and at the Vakhtangov, but started out as a factory engineer: "I was not a bad engineer, but when I worked in the factory all the same I watched the clock . . . but when I went to the drama circle . . . I was happy and time flew" (2001, 8).

Once beyond the amateur drama circle, actors face many obstacles, funneled through first auditions and yearly exams, when they can be cut. The theatrical academies and musical conservatories have grueling admissions processes. Application is in person, over several days of oral and written entrance exams, interviews, and competitive rounds of auditions. If one lives in Irkutsk, that means that in July one rides the train to Moscow, a journey taking up to a week, to make the rounds on foot to each institute. Until very recently this was the case for all universities, institutes, and academies in Moscow; many a Soviet bildungsroman begins with the future scientist or actor spending the night in the Jaroslavsky train station between entrance exams. At the highest mathematical, engineering, and literature faculties, hopeful applicants would group outside the lecture halls, awaiting their turn to face oral examiners sitting on the lecture stage. This system began to be phased out in 2008, replaced by computerized applications for some schools. Theatrical or musical academies, however, continue to require applicants to arrive in person for auditions, running successive rounds of cuts to derive classes of about thirty from the hundreds of applicants for each department. In 2005 the administrators at GITIS built a white fence and gate to contain the growing numbers of hopeful applicants during July auditions, to keep them from overflowing into the courtyard where the current students take their breaks, and from, as one actress told me, "throwing cigarette butts everywhere."

Narratives about Soviet higher education swing between two extremes: we hear both that it was exceptionally rigorous, producing the worlds' best computer scientists and ballerinas, as well as the world's most literate population—and also that education was corrupted by influence, the best schools populated by well-connected children. On the one hand, high literacy rates, competitive research institutions, and Nobel prizes; on the other, bribes and family connections—not unlike how many in the United States talk about elite college admissions. Post-Soviet lore claims that it is difficult to pass entrance exams without connections, but at GITIS it was clear that without skill or talent—and motivation to work all waking hours, seven days a week, to develop them—a mediocre hopeful would find cold welcome at GITIS. This is not to say that children of actors, familiar with the theatrical dynasties, have no advantage from their early exposure to theater worlds. Still, unlike entrance exams for, say, an economics department, for which papers, pens, and even computer screens can be switched about, one cannot pay a substitute to recite Pushkin for an audition at GITIS.

The techniques involved where credentials for both theatrical and telepathic talents are assigned, and where they are demanded or shown off, all involve play with the forms of contact, as well as play with the sensate means for detecting contact. The next chapter starts from moments of checking credentials or documents, then moves on to demonstrate how such moments define contact itself, *as if* it were merely a matter of closing a gap across two points, like dyads across an electrical circuit, distracting from collective communications and multiple channels.

5. Dividing Intuition, Organizing Attention

BUREAUCRATIC MESMERISM

Wolf Messing, the most famous psychic of the USSR, narrated his budding powers to influence other minds like this: it is about 1910, and the boy Wolf is fleeing his natal village near Poznan. He has jumped aboard a train and hidden under a seat. A conductor approaches:

> "Young man" (his voice still rings in my ears), "your ticket!"
>
> My nerves were stressed to the limit. I extended my hand and grabbed some paper that was lying about on the floor, probably a scrap of newspaper . . . our gazes met. With all my strength and passion I wanted him to accept that dirty paper for a ticket. . . . [H]e took it, and turned it over strangely in his hands. I even squeezed myself, burning with this violent wish. Finally he stuck it into the heavy jaws of his composter and cracked it. . . . [H]anding me back the "ticket," he shined his conductor's lamp into my face again. Apparently, he was completely taken aback . . . and in a kindly voice said:
>
> "What are you doing riding under the seats, you have a ticket— there are places free . . . in two hours we arrive in Berlin." (1965, no. 7, 2)

Messing's first act of mental influence transformed a scrap of paper into a ticket—or rather, convinced an authority figure to treat the scrap as a ticket. He writes also that Joseph Stalin had ordered him to demonstrate similar skills; he passed the leader's guards by mentally projecting the phrase "I am Beria" and convinced a bank teller to read a blank check as a valid order for millions of rubles. Enchanting authorities who check identification cards and passes, currencies and credentials, he became a psychic hero for readers familiar with a bureaucratic world. His feats parallel numerous reminiscences of evading the attention of those who ask to see one's papers. His words cover the same ground as does less magical advice for passing under the sensory radars of ticket takers, security guards, and others who staff points of surveillance: "When you don't have your papers, look through them, just past their ears, but *not into their eyes*" (Messing 1965,no 8, 34).

Much has been written about the Russian Empire and the Soviet Union as exceptionally bureaucratic states, territories where people had to maneuver with documents, identification cards, tickets, passports, receipts, stamps, and diplomas. Soviet life did, and twenty-first-century Moscow life certainly still does, involve daily crossings at points where papers must be shown: every institute, university, archive, library, and government building, and many business offices are fronted with a combination of gates, guard rooms, concierge desks, or turnstiles. It is important to remember that Soviets did not bear this condition alone. I might list many parallels, but one case also illustrates that people evaluate and compare these most visible of state practices. One summer my Russian visitors were turned away from a Detroit-area bar because they had left their passports at my house. They were surprised to be expected to carry identity documents into a *place of leisure*; staff in Moscow bars never asked us for papers.

Claims that contrast *ideals*—rationalism, transparency, freedom—to Russian, Soviet, or post-Soviet *instances* of surveillance are not only inaccurate,[1] they preempt sustained conversation about how we have built interlocking regimes across Cold War borders. The arts of facing authority when papers are lacking are widespread; Carolyn Steedman (1987) recollects that in her a postwar London childhood her mother advised her to look straight ahead whenever the bus ticket collector came around. American audiences laugh in recognition when BBC science fiction hero-alien Dr. Who flashes his "psychic paper" whenever London police or galactic powers demand an ID. The paper, like Messing's scrap, is basically blank; the necessary name or title manifests as the situation demands.

Competitive nationalist discourse about whose state offers more freedom or less surveillance distracts us from seeing connections among historically twisted paths by which states have built a world in which people must show papers. To unhook bureaucratic process from national cultures or territories instigates more sustained attention to the movement of techniques and to the ways in which mundane, crypto-magical techniques, such as directing the gaze "just past the ears," work—and work *for some* but not for others. Victor Turner (1982) was wrong to characterize thresholds as liminal; very much on the contrary, doors, bridges, and passport booths are points for definition, places in which some feel the forces of segregation more than others, hesitating to ask, can I enter this place? The queue at passport control extends the zone of distinction as other queues have led to this one; tactics to evade the administering eye are possible only for those who have already passed through other sluices.

In this light, reconsider the train conductor's response to Messing's proffered scrap. It would not take a mind reader to deduce that a ragged boy hiding under a train seat wishes he had a valid ticket. As some of my Russophone interlocutors suggest, perhaps the conductor took pity, colluding with the boy to go through the motions, punching the scrap "as if" the bit of paper were a ticket in case there were onlookers? Perhaps the conductor counted on their collusion, wanting them to see him as the kindly kind of authority. Soviet train personnel were by many accounts capable and sometimes quite determined to show a capacity to care through "little human acts," without the promise of a tip.[2] So who was the magician, Messing or the conductor?

So far so good, but what broader structures (for sympathy, for verification) infuse the social and material conditions that make bureaucrat enchantments possible? Nikolai Gogol lampooned human machinations with documents, specifically records of serf ownership, in *Dead Souls* (1842). Foucault's discussions of panoptic power seem a bit naive next to Gogol's story of people who work attention and distraction even in the tightest of bureaucracies. Gogol was alert to the fact that few study advanced bureaucratic mesmerism to open or close loopholes, that most people just scan for luck, collusion, or empathy (except the lucky few who always have the right papers). Messing's story, like Gogol's *Dead Souls*, points to limits on panoptic power. Panoptic technologies and infrastructures watch and discipline, but their structures cannot explain the social distinctions that cull candidates to fill the watchtower with this man and not that one, and even more, cannot explain why and when the watcher is open to shifts of attention, to open a loophole or to close it, to make alliances or refuse them.

For whom are such alliances possible? Messing's story has been much republished, reenacted, dramatized, and retold in the last few years in documentaries and on shows like *Battle of the Psychics*.[3] The story still echoes common advice for passing security guards, coat checkers, passport controllers, and concierge desks, points for crossing into countries and into universities, archives, libraries, and now Moscow business offices. Some advice counters Messing's bureaucratic mesmerism, suggesting instead avoiding communicative contact: "When you don't have the right papers, look through them, just past their ears, but *not into their eyes.*" Not all can aspire to attempt Messing-style contact. Who can aspire to direct and shift such channels for attention?

During the years after the USSR dissolved, westerners flooded Moscow and initiated all manner of tricks with papers. I accidentally observed this occurring at the Moscow agency in charge of registering my visa. Ahead of me were a man from Texas, his Russian fiancée, and a person who was translated for the Texan. He faced a bureaucratic dilemma: he needed to give his passport to the agency to file at the central Moscow office (OVIR), which takes several days. However, he wanted to get married the next day, and the marriage bureau requires a passport. He had not planned ahead; maybe he thought Moscow was like Vegas. In a hurry to fly home with his bride, he started hinting, "Don't you have any friends there? Can't we solve this some other way?" The agents explained that OVIR was quite strictly ruled by regulation. He escalated the situation, protesting that were the passport to leave his hands, "This is a violation of my rights!" I intervened, reassuring him that this is standard procedure, that even if it were lost, he could get a replacement at the U.S. embassy. He snapped his fingers and offered high-fives: "That's it! I'll say I lost my passport today! That's what we're gonna do! I'm gonna get married tomorrow!"

EAT THE PAPER

Another story that Wolf Messing's autobiography recalls to Russophone colleagues and friends in Russia is Mikhail Bulgakov's 1936 novel *Master and Margarita*. This fantastically Gogolesque tale weaves encounters with papers—telegrams, theater posters, ID cards, book manuscripts—with themes of panoptic failure and strategic opacity. Quite unlike George Orwell's tightly regulated, totalitarian world in *1984*, Bulgakov's Soviet characters wade through a swamp of bureaucratic caprice, fogged by the vanity of those who manipulate credentials and currencies, telephone messages, and manuscript approval forms. In the fog, they change forms and even dissolve. Woland, a foreign stage mesmerist (who may really be the devil), has come to Moscow to wreak havoc on fickle bureaucrats who manage theaters and publishing houses. He turns their own channels against them: over the phone, he finagles his name onto the central stage's opening bill, then confuses management further with counterfeit telegrams. He evacuates value from all media, including money; during his stage show, in the magical finale he conjures loads of cash from the air, sending the audience scrambling to catch the bills, which, once they leave the theater, convert into mere paper scraps (reversing Messing's process on the train).

Bulgakov's vision aligns with observations made by historian of the Soviet Union Sheila Fitzpatrick (2000) and others on the ways, during the

1930s purges, people interpreted switches from one medium or channel to another, especially when messages were contradictory: a written petition to Stalin might be returned not by a matching written telegram, but by a telephone call. But everyone knew that the telephonic channel might imply intimacy and protection even as the police knock on the door. This meant that shifts from tangible, durable paper to transient sound waves become meaningful in part because they revealed relays for power (see Keane 2013), but also because they invited puzzlement and strategy. In these cases, the switch from paper to telephone posed an existential riddle (kiss of favor or kiss of death?), became animated by uncertainty because it was this leader, this leader known for capricious paranoia, and not just anyone, who demonstrated agency in making the switch in media.

Post-Soviet people do speak of chains of encounters at lower levels for transforming a shared bottle into a job,[4] much as in America we hear of those who can turn a golf game into a government contract.[5] Numerous memoirs trace the paths of rubles turned into a doctor's note, the note exchanged for another document, this one authorizing exemption from military service, which in turn affords registration at the wedding bureau, the marriage document being necessary to apply for a city residence permit.

Bulgakov and Messing—and BBC science fiction writers—are among many who have drawn such chains in fantastical terms, practical outcomes fusing with supernatural capture of bureaucratic contact points, as if someone has siphoned the phatic energy. Some narrate ritualized challenges, attempts to reveal the social links and institutional supports that invisibly surround any bureaucratic moment, which shifts all attention to the materiality of credentialing media ("Is this paper counterfeit?") or the deportment of those holding papers (e.g. for "signs of nervousness"). Such conditions make bureaucratic interactions especially fertile ground for tales of *ekstrasensorika* and for technologies for intuition.

Sentiment about ways people divine, influence, and imagine chains of documentation or movements of power became inflamed after the sudden dissolution of Soviet authority, especially in filmic genres of grim naturalism (*chernukha*) and its violent offspring.[6] Piotr Lutsik's monochrome film *Okraina* (The outskirts, 1998) violently traces the social sequences through which a single piece of paper—a land deed—has moved, at a time when the nature of both contracts and distributions of property was unclear. Far from Moscow, several farmers awaken one morning to discover that their collective has been sold to big oil. They take up guns to track the path of the sale, starting from the local collective farm leader, who traded the deed over a bottle for a favor. They go to town and tug the buyer out of bed, beating him until he points up the line. They next work over the town boss, who traded the deed for a job for his son, then through the former *obkom* regional head, who wanted an apartment, and finally to central Moscow, to the top of one of its towers. There, fantastical filmic violence forces the un-sensible—invisible, illicit, social alliances of intrigue—to the surface.[7]

In the office of the oil baron who holds the deed, the farmers' rage seems to subside as they stand quietly before him, requesting meekly, "*Pokazhite bumagu, pozhaluista.*" ("Show us the paper, please."). "Why of course," smiles the oligarch, pulling it out. But the farmers have hidden razor blades behind their gums, and in a blink they have slit the throats of the oil man's minions, grabbed the paper, burned the office down, piled onto their motor-bikes, and headed back East. The film ends with a sunny afternoon harvest, the men merrily steering tractors in a staggered diagonal line across the landscape—a creepily cheerful echo of early Soviet films. They, simple farm-ers, have *pounded* their way up the contacts of the hierarchy: violence is their magic; no intuition necessary to successfully invert the conventional bureaucratic directive, "Show us, please, the paper," usually issued from above, not just to convince power to deflect its spotlight, but to flash it back into its eyes.

The end of socialism corresponded with the global advent of the Internet and other links among computers;[8] a proliferation of channels changed how copies circulate and endure as transcripts, tickets, and police records began to replicate over digital networks at the turn of the twenty-first century. *Okraina* slides over the way legal papers can no longer be destroyed in the same ways as before; at the end of *Master and Margarita*, Woland utters the most famous line of the story, telling the Master, after the novelist has thrown his pages into the fire, that "manuscripts don't burn." Some quote the line as defiant commentary on censorship, as a claim that even after channels to publication and performance are blocked, an idea can live on. Possibilities to burn, spindle, or mutilate documents, to destroy them completely—or conversely, to conjure their existence—become harder to come by.[9]

In Soviet times, a carbon twin *might* lie somewhere in an archive or state register, but not always. The Western image of an omniscient Big Brother never dealt with the material fact that paper was in short supply, that bureaucrats made finite numbers of copies and filed them in idiosyncratic ways. Entire archives burned after the Russian Revolution, during recon-struction, during and after the Great War of the Fatherland. Files in personal folders got lost in the stacks. For all our Western fantasy of Soviet surveil-lance, Soviet people knew these material conditions, could see the spaces to take advantage of the ephemeral materiality of paper archives.[10] This is the case midway through a Soviet émigré autobiography titled *Metro* (Kaletski 1985): the hero (incidentally, an acting student at GITIS), in order to escape military service, needs a document that will identify him as suffering from hypertension and mental health issues. Just as he acquires it, however, he is given the opportunity to tour in the United States, and now he needs instead a clean bill of health. So he must "disappear" the first paper. With the collusion of a medical worker who leaves him alone in the doctor's office with his file, he manages to eat the paper. Those were years when the protagonist could tell a train conductor, "I left my ticket on the piano" and expect that she might take pity, at worst hint for a tip, for conductors were not issued passenger manifests, and train tickets at that time did not link to names of passengers. In these procedural gaps, some who held authority to block movement or communication would choose not to use it.

This story, recent revivals of Messing's story, and the last scenes in *Okraina* all evoke the means either to activate papers or to destroy them. Perhaps ironically, it is the networked multiplications of digitized copies, not the paper papers, that sharpens Orwellian practices into structural teeth.

DYADIC FETISH

The passport booth is both a technology for intuition and a segment of a phatic infrastructure that funnels people into queues, isolating persons (occasionally a family, bracketed as a unit, whose passports are handed over all at once) at a spot to make minimal contact with a stranger who looks at the face, the paper, a computer screen, then the face. This node reinforces circuits for verbal communication that seem to pit a sender against a receiver, a phatic configuration that makes contact with the state seem dyadic, as if it were made of two opposing parts. Such points model communication not only as a dyad, but as a certain *kind* of dyad: decoder reads sender, conceived as an individual who either hides or reveals information. It is not for the sender to decode passport control (except in revenge fantasy, as we have seen). The vectors for such functions within a bureaucratic channel are one way; to enforce that direction seals the ritual circle of the passport booth, and in just the way to obscure chains of actions, expressions, and conditions that shape the moment and extend beyond it. Bureaucratic mesmerism enacts the dyadic fetish.

Foucault sketched such spaces as technologies of individuation. In fact, confession, therapy, and the sociological and bureaucratic interview carve out not just individuals, but pair-units. Asad (1983) indicates as much,

arguing that historically specific (European) circuits of torture and interrogation created the very definitions and category of truth; truth becomes
a question within certain kinds of encounters, between accused and interrogator. From the chess match to the wedding, making two is as ritualistic
an endeavor as making one or joining many. I am not the first to suggest
that selling the dyad is a step in selling the individual, making individuation compelling and desirable: to earn freedom to choose the love of the
pair, the romantic must leave the embrace of the family network, abandoning collectives and companions in arms.[11] The individual is thus not the
lone harbinger of modernity; the pair secretly on the telephone, the lovers'
letters that console upon storming convention, are.

Linguistic anthropologists have been fighting the dyadic fetish for decades, drawing from feminist observations about power, as well as from
thinkers such as Voloshinov, Bakhtin, or Goffman, who all worked to subvert both the idea that the individual is the only kind of subject or agency
that matters and the dyadic, speaker-hearer model of communication.[12]
These scholars charge us to register the overlapping channels among and
shifting fields of participants, to see leaks between and effects across interactions, to hear echoes of past situations and projections of future consequences. They have demonstrated how even institutions that build nodes
and channels to assemble pairs—weddings, therapy sessions, courtroom
interrogations—cannot excise all who might rock the pair: those who overhear, interrupt, or distract, or who cannot insulate themselves from earlier
texts or actions from other times and places.

Messing described the conductor's lamp *as if* its halo enclosed just the
two of them, but it need not have. At passport control, too, even could we
could empty the lines and turn off the cameras; it is difficult to forestall
future auditors and impossible to extract the traces of past ones. Social life
unfolds not *despite* interdiscursive and situational (and national or cultural)
leakage, but *because of* it. The illusion that individuals add up to pairs, who
then create nuclear families, and so forth, must be maintained by institutions, rituals, and practices, in courtroom interrogations, romantic tragedies,
and telepathy tests. Ironically, channeling pairs works best when it draws
upon the very interdiscursivity, the hooks and links to other communications in other places and times, that it denies.

There are many ways communicative contact is *not* experienced as dyadic
even while it can be depicted as such. Say we film a meeting of five people
over dinner, and in editing, we choose shots to emphasize rays of mutual eye
contact—exchanges that really are limited to dyads; just try to hold eye
contact with two beings at once. We will end up with series of switching

pairs—intrigue! But if we privilege sound and stress convergences of laughter, we will end up with configurations that depict simultaneous contact among three, four, or all five. Dominant models of society that build, say, from an ideal mother-child bond or from an ideal romantic couple separated from families, have been constructed by scholars and others not only on paper, but also during research, for example by conducting sociological interviews that pull people away from usual interactions within a large family, a group running a theatrical production, or a network staging a political campaign—and then putting them into dyadic situations formally similar to police interrogations or job interviews. Yet for all the work of linguistic anthropologists pressing us to attend to real-time multiparty interactions, the dyadic model persists, seeping back into our accounts, especially via theories that treat intersubjectivity as if it were a matter merely of switching perspectives and as if communication occurs only along one directed channel at a time. Consider instead the cardioid microphone that captures sound in wide angles; our common sense about communication could use similar widening. My goal in the rest of this chapter is to suggest ways to notice *how* dyadic models of communication persist and what such models produce or enable. I now address ways people bracket space, train attention, and channel senses so that certain configurations structure interactions so that they seem dyadic, while certain other infrastructural and interactional patterns obviate the collective work to make this happen.

MATTER IN DYADIC ILLUSION

Messing's story evokes anxieties common to theater and to telepathy, to problems of trust in faces and in credentials. This is no accident; he was a psychic stage performer. Even when not combined in the same person, stage actor and psychic enact dyadic models such as "telepathy" or "the couple," using similar techniques and materials—shining lights, bits of paper—to organize certain channels for contact and not others and to organize attention around those channels.

Bureaucratic practices activate dyadic configurations—or rather, the illusion of dyads. To work border magic requires honoring this illusion while undermining its semiotic aim, directing participants to attend and then dis-attend, so that material props can work now as this, now as that. Amplifying some channels while jamming others—turning cell phones off before entering the customs area, before the stage lights go up—is only part of the process. Such outcomes require erasing multiple participants, reducing to two by dividing labor and then obscuring the divisions; the labor of handling paper goes to *this* official and not that one (even as another watches on a closed circuit camera or through one-way mirrors from another room). Now I contrast examples of phatic spectacle that help us understand the range of divisions across situations, in staged telepathy tests and classes in theatrical attention.[13]

About halfway through Olender's documentary, *9 Years with the Psychics*, the crew films a telepathy experiment. On a stage in a small house of culture somewhere in southern Russia, a sender-receiver pair is separated by about six feet and a curtain as the camera crew and investigators bustle to arrange measuring equipment. Once seated, the sender wordlessly goes through a deck of cards bearing the numbers 1 through 9, silently pondering each number. Meanwhile, the blindfolded receiver pronounces numbers that match, then do not match. A moderator, in black turtleneck and leather blazer, face neutral, takes each card once the guess has been made and turns it to face a panel of experts and then the camera, before handing the card to another assistant. Behind him the members of the panel scribble notes, while behind the panel technicians monitor oscillating waves of ink and light, graphs that map data from microphones and heart monitors on the two subjects (no other people present are monitored thus).

The experiment follows protocols familiar to international networks of paranormal researchers: randomly selected Zener cards are tasked to provide a stable anchor for reference, to determine a thought to pass between sender and receiver that they cannot preselect. In fact, the development of random trials in other lines of research owes much to these telepathy science protocols (Hacking 1988). Like ID cards, well-shuffled Zener cards act not only as a verifying control, but also as a means to claim a purely referential match of idea, world, and communication. These matches register not participants' thoughts as situated, coproduced streams of action that affect consciousness, but "thought" as a unit in a generalized system of options, represented as a relation of an individual mind to singular chances, chances calibrated to an arbitrary standard (the possibilities of the deck). Machine graphs further correlate correct and incorrect guesses to further systems, indexing them to measurements of noises, heart rates, and brain waves.

Throughout the twentieth century tests for extrasensory talent often isolated the ability to sense marks on specific materials or beyond them (often paper, the back side of a card, or a note through an envelope). *Battle of the Psychics* deploys the wood of a box, the metal of a car trunk, and an abundance of paper. The master of ceremonies (MC) might present the psychic with a legal document, such as a passport, and task her to describe its owner, who, as the audience can see, is a celebrity watching on closed circuit in another room, commenting with hostile skepticism on the psychic's failure to read through the cardboard cover. The contrasts among media are mobilized; for example, paper, situated on stage among machines and cameras, is often figured as central to proof.

While discussions of occult and haunted media usually deal more with worries and dreams about new electronic media (as had those surrounding spirit telegraphy and ghost photography in the previous century), on *Battle* the parts played by relatively old media, in combination or contrast with those seen as newer, are just as important. The familiar old affordances of paper become *more* salient, seemingly more unique, as machine media multiply. Psychic performances, as do stage enchantments from magic to cyber realism, put media into contrast, and do so *as if* different mediating materials *in themselves* determine capacities for demonstrating communication *without* apparent mediation.

Encountered live, the two faces of a sheet of paper are well-suited to foreground dyadic aspects of a situation by repeating the model of twoness (here we see iconicity, or resemblance, deployed to index or point), to condense a well-populated scene into what seems to be a simpler communicative essence. As a flat form, a single sheet of paper can be held between interactants to demonstrate those two sides: one written upon, the verso blank. As such, it may well index *one* ongoing contact channel, while seeming to represent and record (anchor and prove) a telepathic one. One side depicts the thought sent, the other remains blank, and both face a receiver with a barrier of opacity while also resembling her waiting mind, ideally relaxed and receptive.

New media cannot do the same work as quickly or elegantly (yet).[14] A computer tablet screen might convey markings on one side and not the other, but are there really audiences lacking skeptics to look for distant reprogramming, for rewriting of the screen each moment? To be sure, paper can be mutilated, destroyed, or switched out in a number of ways, invisibly or spectacularly—folded small and tucked away, burned, even eaten;[15] a skilled master magician can achieve such acts with one hand. All the same, paper retains its "old" affordances; it remains relatively more difficult to rewrite from a distance, and therefore, in high-tech stagings, paper is still a favored medium not only to test telepathy, but in the testing to naturalize and reinforce dyadic contact as the ideal for *all* communication.

PHATIC TRICKS: CHANNEL DISTRACTION

In 2008 the young *illjuzionist* Rafael Zotov appeared as a contestant on the television show *Fenomen* (on Channel Rossija), a show conceived in the

United States, where it broadcast for one season in 2007. Israeli celebrity psychic Uri Geller acted as judge on a Russian version starting in 2008 and on a Ukrainian version beginning in 2011, speaking in English, aided by simultaneous translators. Grounded neither in Soviet science nor or Soviet-era romanticist antiscience, Geller's authority banks on international celebrity. Zotov stands alone on an open dais. Blue and white spotlights crisscross the circular platform and over faces in the audience as the MC introduces the act. Zotov looks into a camera that closes on his face, a tiny microphone dangling on a wire from his ear, and asks, "Have you ever received a phone call from the very person you were thinking about?" He proposes an experiment in transmitting thoughts over distance: he will receive a telephone number. A celebrity pop singer joins him on stage to act as his transmitter. They make scripted small talk: "Have you ever tried telepathically to will a man: 'call me, call me'?" "Of course!" she replies, singing a few lines from her hit single, "Call Me!" She asks for volunteers to offer their telephone numbers, selecting a gentleman from the back rows. Rather than, say, asking him to call *her* phone (activating caller ID, this being the preferred way to trade numbers in Moscow), a long-legged, blond assistant wearing a tuxedo jacket with tails over shorts—and also wearing a bluetooth earpiece and microphone—walks all the way up the rows carrying paper and pen. After a few moments we see the assistant cross the stage, rip paper from the pad, hand the piece to the pop singer, and stride off the stage. The singer holds the paper in front of her chest, carefully folding her fingers across the back to hide any shadows of pen marks. So many media, so many channels, where to focus attention?

Meanwhile, Zotov ruffles a ream of blank white A4 paper and brandishes a black Sharpie pen. One by one, the singer mentally transmits digits, staring into the psychic's eyes until he writes something down and holds up each sheet of paper to show the audience, then his partner. He misses one! He approaches to hold the singer's hand for a moment "to reestablish contact," then backs away to retry. All but the last digit complete, he reaches for his own cell phone to type it all in—a phone rings in the volunteer's pocket! Channels are clear! The volunteer smilingly consents for Zotov to write the last digit on paper, even "for millions of viewers to see." The camera pulls back, then shifts to Uri Geller's smile; he pronounces the performance a success, speaking English: "I liked it. I liked the way you incorporated technology," using the phones over the paper.

This performance bears comparison with the experiment in Olender's documentary, discussed previously. Both are enacted on a theatrical stage: one in an empty community theater, the other on a television soundstage.

Both shift among performers and judges: Uri Geller versus a commission of observers with pen on paper. The commission, however, makes adjustments, especially regarding the materiality of the paper; the psychic, blindfolded and with his back to his assistant, seems to be doing too well. They switch from Zener cards to cards bearing more digits. They add physical barriers between sender and receiver. The narrator tells us that the commission has noted that the sender always carefully presses her finger and thumb at the edges of the cards; perhaps the receiver is listening for a code? So they assign an engineer to make similar noises periodically, effectively jamming ordinary auditory channels.

In the final shots of the sequence, we see several hands holding pens, moving across white sheets. Uses of paper overlap in each performance—cards display digits, guesses are recorded on paper—but the moorings of those uses differ. Olender's panel of judges, the instruments, and the papers are constantly, visibly at work behind the telepathic pair, while Zotov and his sender stand against empty blue space (we see the studio audience or Uri Geller only in cutaway shots). The voice of Olender's narrator weaves through the action, explaining, oscillating between wonder and doubt, while *Fenomen*'s MC disappears between the introduction and final congratulations. In the Olender experiment, the material affordances of paper—the way it rustles to the touch, as that might affect results—become a topic of discussion and adjustment to the interaction. Matter is salient to their phatic work to purify contact.

Geller, while remarking on the clever thematization of technology, does not address uses of paper in Zotov's act. This is all the better for the act, since paper serves not only as medium to convey numbers, but also as a channel to distract from the other channels (earphones, lights, gesturing hands) that combine to pull off the trick: telepathic contact between two. Wolf Messing and other Soviet magicians often spoke about channel distraction in stage telepathy demonstrations. They described techniques for misdirection to keep an audience focused on the semantic content (in directives, in banter) while using *formal shifts* (in register, morphology, syntax, volume, tempo, etc.) as code. For example, if a stage assistant wanted a blindfolded Messing to guess the number 3, she might cue him using a phrase containing three syllables, such as, "Okay, next." She might raise her pitch to indicate that a volunteer was male. Someone like Messing or James Randi might look at the fingers shielding the piece of paper with the telephone number written on it: a pinkie twitch might indicate 3, and so forth. An assistant might shift from making a directive (asking an audience member to stand) to greeting another audience member, with such a shift signaling the blindfolded Messing to turn left. In this last case, the team might use phatic communication to mask a very different semiotic function. Thus technology for reference masks as technology for intuition.

How much simpler such collective work is when the magician and off-stage assistants are all wearing headsets! Even if the audience volunteer is no shill, how simple it would be for an assistant backstage to overhear as the assistant takes down the number.

CIRCLES OF ATTENTION: THE THEATRICAL COLLECTIVE

Both actors and psychics learn to artfully arrange attention, to deflect the ear from one sound to another, the eye from a slow hand to a fast one, from the circle of a spotlight to a shadow, to lead others' eyes with a gaze. They also learn to use one sensory channel to direct away from another: to sound from vision, words from movements, and back again. And they work in collectives.

Some skeptics assume that psychics operate as lone players, but it takes a team to run a telepathy demonstration, to mark out dyads from multiple clusters and tangled channels. This can be better understood by means of contrast. There are contexts that do not hide such collective work, such as in stage pedagogy, in which future actors and directors learn to organize attention and people theorize attention *not* as a single ray between binary nodes but in terms of nested and intersecting rays and circles. GITIS students learn not only to gesture and declaim, to study a single script, but also to map an interdiscursive terrain of situations, texts and songs, films and biographies, and events and intonations beyond their own experience. And they are urged to see every single living moment, on stage and off, as a series of permeable, multiple, sometimes nesting circles of attention, or *participation frameworks*. They are pressed to unlearn ideologies of communication modeled on speaker-listener pairs (not to mention those that assume unified speakers who articulate a single voice). They learn to manipulate multiple vectors for attention and to layer those through multiple media. The craft requires studying the semiotic limits of the matter at hand, that is, learning the range of noticeable shifts among gestures, lights, words, eyes, tempos, nails, paper, and stage curtains that signal signs are being made of them.

One evening a GITIS master instructor gave the first-year cohort a memorable version of a classic beginning stage lesson in circles of attention: "how to enter a room." Introducing the task as a puzzle to be solved in many ways, he insisted on one necessary condition: "To get the audience's attention, *you* have to be interested." He demonstrated, walking around, gesturing, squatting next to students on the parquet, the latter still sweating after two hours tumbling over wooden tables in stage movement training. Students and other teachers formed an audience by moving to a corner, with students along the wall and teachers in chairs. Masha and Zhenja volunteered to try "entering the room"; they exited to the hallway, then they walked through the classroom door, stopped, and slowly peered at each of us in turn through narrowed eyes. The master chastised, "What mugs! Like two cops! And all synchronized! Too compressed and tight, too self-conscious." They tried again and again, but the master was never satisfied. Another student tried and failed, spurring the master to contemplate the pitfalls of attending directly only to facing an audience. After citing Stanislavsky's observations on how to simultaneously direct attention and forestall the mechanizing effects of stage fright, he commented on the attempt: "Was this interesting? No. It was really boring. You lost the hall. A normal person [enters because he] wants something, but you enter, and all *you* see is a hall that *might* be exuding a great stream of negative energy, and you think, 'How to survive!? Every gesture is visible, it works or does not; such a narrow corridor you create, 'this way stupid, that way unoriginal'" (Fieldnotes, November 29, 2002). "Such a narrow corridor," that ray of attention, as if only the audience were the necessary addressee. Several students tried, and finally Aljosha and Timofej made progress. Timofej smoked through his entrance and announcement, holding a glass. The master praised this: "Look how interesting, good job, now you are engaged . . . because you appropriated a cigarette and a glass. These kinds of things demand greater organization than you know." From the beginning of the semester, the master had explained how engagement with materials produces effects, once praising how one directing student had arranged little sticks on a table like this: "Everything begins with precise choices. If there is a glass and a spoon on the table, they must be a specific glass and spoon. It is the same with timbre, with emotions. There can be no sadness in general. And on stage, editorial choice is key. To deal an emotional blow, to draw the audience, you have to localize its attention. You have to organize the circle of attention. Just on that one little spot" (Fieldnotes, September 2002). He exhorted us to consider the films of Andrei Tarkovsky or Vasily Shukshin, to observe how they arranged even small items on sets to create diverse homes, shared spaces, and landscapes, with an attention to detail that could not be reduced to simple naturalism. On the contrary, those directors demonstrate ways that even a single actor (like Timofej with his cigarette) can channel, the master said, "streams of energy" by multiplying and refocusing relations of attention among people and objects.

At GITIS, instructors teach Stanislavsky's "circles of attention" as foundational to practice (much more so than affective memory). Early in the first semester, after twelve hours of acting and movement classes, students stretched out across the wooden floor, some leaning against their lockers at the back, to hear one of the acting teachers discuss differences among "circles of attention." (The need for English translation reduces Stanislavsky's discussion of these circles to the smallest one, the cultivation of "public solitude" for the actor, say, to read a letter alone on stage.) Students had heard a brief lecture on the topic a few days earlier and been assigned the relevant chapters in Stanislavsky. The teacher quizzed them:

> TEACHER: What are the four levels of circles?
>
> STUDENT 1: Is the first circle just the self? Or is it the self plus contact?
>
> STUDENT 2: Or, plus concentration?
>
> TEACHER: Fine, good, and what of the next levels? (Fieldnotes, October 2002)

The students talked all at once, puzzling over how to differentiate the levels: Do certain organs mediate knowledge of certain circles? The teacher answered: there is some basis to this, and "you can read Stanislavsky all you want, but our work is *shkurnoe* ['of the skin,' or 'of the pelt']," although "animals would not recognize" the circles of attention.

The students wanted to more clearly define and separate the circles, but instructors constantly reminded them that they overlap, and they can jostle each other. The students persisted: one of their other teachers had said in a lecture that the four "circles of attention are organized by distance from the senses," and that "only the 4th circle is imagined" while the rest of the circles are real, of the here and now, made visceral by material boundaries or signaled by gesture, movement, or other signs. The students pressed the teacher: *Are* the circles organized by distance, distance *as felt by* sense organs? Yes and no, this teacher responded. The system describes a set of laws accounting for the nature of theater: "If Stanislavsky had not discovered the circles, they would still exist." So, yes, the first through third circles can seem more proximate to sensation than the fourth, where we imagine but "cannot sense just now": "Close your eyes and listen to the sounds from the street. When you listen, do you also try to imagine what is happening?" Yet, the teacher allowed, all circles admit to imagination.

JUGGLING CIRCLES

"But don't confuse the fourth *wall* with the fourth *circle*!" Diderot's "fourth wall" referred to conventions that cue the audience to pretend that they are invisible spectators, separated from a world of action onstage. The fourth wall proposes voyeurism, peeking into some imagined globe of space-time, a woodland dance floor or domestic kitchen. The tricky part for actors to learn is that the fourth wall can be signaled by organizations of space or by other cues, and that some of those differ little from others that mark circles of attention. At any rate, the fourth wall does not usually belong with the fourth circle, but *between* the second and third. A fourth *wall* is subject to intensities of attention that also block out or jam what is in a fourth *circle*, or beyond.

A proscenium arch need not automatically frame action as a realist diorama box; it takes additional realist convention to anchor that effect. The Russian avant-garde made this point ferociously, insisting that their colleagues recognize the conventionality even in such claims to realism. Most famously, Stanislavsky's students Vsevolod Meyerhold and Yevgeny Vakhtangov had insisted that without this realization, realism becomes a trap limiting audiences to passivity at a peephole. Meyerhold for this reason urged that in his plays the edge of the third circle specifically, where the proscenium lies, *never* be played as a fourth wall.

A beginning drill for *combining* circles of attention might go like this: students are instructed to form their own half circle, with one seated in the break. The instructor hands that person a book to read while answering questions fully; no brief "yes" or "no" is allowed. The students pepper the reader: "What is today's date?" "What did you think up for your directing assignment?" "In what town were you born?" The student answers all the questions, but after several minutes of this, tasked to report the contents of the book, he can do so only vaguely. The instructor seizes on the failure, shouting, "*Two* circles of attention you needed to have maintained!" In discussing the drill, the instructor clarified the purpose: students were to recognize how hard they must work to organize just their own multiple lines of attention, much less those across the theater hall (Fieldnotes, September 2002). In this, he echoed Stanislavsky, or rather, the character voice of the maestro's fictional acting student:

> I got to class in time to hear a heated argument with Veselovsky
> [another fictional student]. Apparently, he had said that it seems not
> only difficult, but impossible to simultaneously think about his part,
> about technical methods, about the viewers (which you just cannot
> excise from attention), and several other objects all at once.
>   —How much attention is needed for all that? Veselovsky hopelessly
> exclaimed.
>   —You think you are no good for such work, but a horseback juggler
> in the circus does even more difficult tasks excellently, even risking his
> life. His legs and body have to balance across the back of a galloping

horse, his eyes have to track sticks of various weights standing on his forehead, big spinning platters on top, while juggling three or four balls. And he still manages to holler commands at the horse. He can do this because humans possess multi-planed attention, and each plane can work without disturbing the others. It is hard only at first. Luckily, much of what we do becomes automatic. The same with attention. So, if you thought up to now that actors work by inspiration so long as they have talent, you had better change your opinion. (Stanislavsky [1938] 1970, ch. 5)

The character continues, recounting disorientation as he attempts to track multiple circles of attention on the street, remembering the words of his director:

Coming onto Arbat Square, I took in the biggest circle that I could capture with my gaze, and immediately all its lines and boundaries dripped and ran together. I heard a mournful horn and driver cursing, saw the car's front grill as it almost ran me over. "If you get lost in the big circle, quickly compress into the small one," I recalled Tortsov's words. That's what I did. "Strange," I pondered. "How come, on this huge plaza, on a crowded street, it is easier to create solitude than it is on stage? Is it not because nobody here has any expectations of me, while on stage everybody has to look at the actor?" It is the unavoidable condition of theater. (Stanislavsky [1938] 1970, ch. 5)

All the world, it seems, is *not* a stage. The spaces, objects, personnel, and tasks required to channel stage attention differ enough from those managed on the street that only special training and practice teach us to sort and command them.

At GITIS, actors and directors learn that no single circle of attention is ever in play alone. *Any* communication involves layers and shifts *among* circles. To begin to illustrate this, the instructor asks the students to recall exercises they have been perfecting over the last few months. Which train which circles of attention? They respond with alacrity: to isolate and move parts of the body—that is the work in the first circle! To remember how many ashtrays stand in the courtyard—the fourth! Pretending to ski—the first! No . . . wait, imagination and physical memory is involved . . . the first and fourth and . . . ? Lining up in alphabetical order—the second circle! No, the third! They puzzle over ways circles interweave, challenging sensations with other sensations, with imagination or memory. Even first circle matters are overlapped by memory of sensations from other times and spaces. Imaginative and bodily rehearsal mix, as in one warm-up that students classify originally as the first circle, then change their assessment: "What temperature are the toes? Feel the impulse . . . as you move, feel how your feet want to argue with your spine—how do your toes speak, how does your spine answer?" Reflection, imagined dialogue, and metaphor can also split and cut circles of attention. Directors all the more need to juggle multiple circles and rays and to imagine their final combinations from the perspective of an audience. One genre requires something multidimensional, like a moving cubist painting (or like Wassily Kandinsky, working with color *and* shape to warp perspective); another needs something more unified, a tight mobile in which nested circles all turn in the same direction.[16]

CHANNELING COLLECTIVES

Stage actors and psychics make use of similar techniques for channeling attention, sometimes to similar ends, but only sometimes. Both learn to master changes in tempo, to artfully deflect the ear from one tone to another, the eye from a slow hand to a fast one, from a spotlight circle on the floor to a shadow across the room. They even learn to use attention to direct attention, to lead others' eyes with still others' gazes, to shift media to distract from movements and movements to distract from words.[17]

Like actors, directors, and their stage crews, Zotov and Ignatenko also labor collectively to reduce the appearance of labors (plural), to hide workers up in the catwalks so that the audience registers only the one ray between points. The most convincing result, moreover, looks as if the pair telepathically channels through invisible string, instead of broadcasting like circles of radio waves.[18] On the spare blue TV soundstage, Zotov does not stand alone, but fronts a staff of assistants who handle paper props *and* electronic devices—media they will contrast. Olender's film crew, for their part, discuss interference from the sounds of the shuffled paper cards, but do so in order to pare down to a dyadically anchored thread of contact, unpolluted by other channels.

What differentiates theatrical pedagogy and production from these acts is that it rarely rests on a dyadic line between two points. Stanislavsky's practical theory of "circles of attention" challenges closed dyadic models of contact in ways parallel to the thinking of linguistic anthropologists who have developed the insights of Goffman and Bakhtin into robust theories of interaction. Think back to the drill in which partners navigate a room stretching a taut thread between them (in chapter 2): it *seems* to represent their interaction as merely dyadic, the thread linking "sender and receiver." However, as instructors say, "these kinds of things demand greater organization than you know." The contact along the thread between two bodies recruits the viewers' attention, as actors become accustomed to paying attention to their own attention. Teachers persistently remind them that the stage, like the street, comprises numerous possible circuits. The thread momentarily proposes to reduce them because its materiality can link bodies in finite ways. However, as a pair move around among pairs, they become mindful that viewers are comparing them all, from more than one vantage at a time. A girl and boy seem to gaze only at each other, or at the thread, but simultaneously open their peripheral vision, hearing, skin sense of air movement, proprioception to other pairs, to instructor reactions, to murmurs or movement in the audience. Threads of contact between the actors' bodies index multiple circles and rays of attention even while each thread's qualia, its tightness or looseness, seems to represent the essence of a pair alone. While each thread may represent the quality of a contact, across the room a moving mobile of vectors for attention forms, like an artist's model of subatomic electrons.

Becoming savvy about these multiple, overlapping shapes for space-time is the heart of a GITIS education. Peeking through the studio door to watch others watch still others, students speak of forgetting that they move inside a walled compound, a majestic, imperial-era structure, in the center of Moscow, even when those political surroundings are in flux. Recall the drill "friend or enemy?" (in chapter one). It mirrors passport control and ticket booths, requiring students to discern others' intentions one by one. The instructor that day had attributed their failures to "our Soviet paranoia" but had also criticized the students for not opening *all* channels, such as peripheral vision or smell, for not monitoring reactions of people standing just outside the dyad of the moment. To correct this, he assigned a second student to walk behind the first, to observe reactions when the first was looking elsewhere. He said they had learned to unsee too much; their follow-up assignment set them to broaden their attention in more chaotic venues, to attend to ways people in crowds, in shops, and on the subway use their hands, fold their fingers, touch rails and grip bags, push past strangers, or hold their children.

Sometimes instructors brought threads of action and echoes of phrases from the world beyond GITIS even into lessons that stressed the making of paired attention in the here and now, penalizing those who could not command the attention of a counterpart. In this drill, a seated pair faces off; one must attract the other, convince him or her to stand up and walk over. They are allowed only the single phrase, "come to me." The other must sit silently until he or she can no longer resist the call. At first all the callers failed. They were criticized for monotonously "repeating desperate tones."

After several rounds, students who "began to pay attention to minute reactions" started to modulate their calls, alternating among teasing, curious, or sad tones—in effect experimenting with different ways to say the line in order to make firm contact. Teachers noted the improvement. Now the students were ready for competition: two girls would call one boy, or two boys would compete to call one girl. A Kuwaiti and a Daghestani student were set to duel for a Russian woman's attention. Up to that point the instructors had offered the Russian boys specific advice about how to modulate and experiment ("you need to adjust to her, gauge your volume, shift your tempo"), but now, when two non-Russians competed, they shifted from the here and now of minute contrasts, instead evoking distant national resources and amplifying broad stereotypes about invisible bodily essences: "Kuwaiti oil is surely better bait for a northern girl!" But: "Hot-blooded Daghestani men surely possess naturally sublime powers of attraction!" Perhaps southern men should not need technique or advice about attention—like Gypsies, southern and eastern peoples are also treated as natural masters of hypnosis. Thus a drill that seemingly channeled attention to the here and now opened a window into decades of war in the Caucasus. Hard as participants worked to concentrate on the here and now, those face-to-face interactions could not excise geopolitical alignments or military conflicts projected elsewhere.

Stanislavsky's circles of attention presaged Bakhtin's and Goffman's later attempts to craft layered models of communication, to challenge dyadic models of contact. In practice, however, like any model the theory can still be subsumed, for example, under an ideal like "dramatic conflict." Circles of attention, alas, can be subsumed in ways that create contradictions for some: in this drill, it was precisely people thought to command special, eastern forms of magic and intuition who were blamed for lacking technique to capture attention. These are the very people who, in Moscow today, would rarely have the chance to work Messing's brand of bureaucratic mesmerism in moments of trouble (consider, for comparison: Which drivers in the United States can even attempt small talk to avoid a fine?). Once again, people use the phatic—along with judgment about contact—to do things besides make contact.

To "organize attention" requires making decisions about which contrasts make a proper difference. Russian formalists like Viktor Shklovsky on estrangement in art and Jakobson on contrasting pairs in poetry were instrumental in bringing us to attend to the poetic forces of contrast. What I want to stress, in addition, are the social constraints upon semiotic evocations of structural echoes: it matters who decides how, where, and when to focus on what, as contrast, and it matters how those divisions of labor come about. Messing's face and paper scrap were framed *not* willy-nilly by just any light in the dark, but by *a train conductor's* lamp. Who is sent to hold the lamp, who is vested with authority to read a ticket—or read a paper scrap as a ticket?

DIVISIONS OF LABOR

GITIS advertises itself as a place constituted by openings to elsewhere. In June 2001, in an elegant café ten minutes' walk from the academy, near the park Chistye Prudy (Clear Ponds), I was approached by a former GITIS student. I had just met with the chancellor and was reading the color brochures she had given me. A woman approached my table, saying that she recognized the photos on the cover: "I graduated in the late 1980s, I loved it!" We talked for a few minutes then and met a week later for coffee in a gorgeous mini-mall built with Chinese funds. She had graduated from the dramatic criticism department, and while she no longer worked in the field, she had no regrets; GITIS had given her a foothold in the center of Moscow and "into the *intelligenty*," social capital and cultural that otherwise, she said, "really take three generations" of education and urban life to accumulate. Studying at GITIS had furnished her with a "cosmopolitan interior"— inside oriented to outside—so that she might imagine herself comfortable to travel, "to order a cup of tea in another country."

To "order a cup of tea" situates travel fantasy in urban elsewheres, the café cultures of Paris, London, Tokyo, and Istanbul—a particular way of being "cosmopolitan." There were, however, other trajectories for connection that meant a great deal in Soviet times and still do (Humphrey 2004; Grant 2010). Starting in the 1930s GITIS, like other institutions in key Soviet cities like Leningrad and Baku, worked centrifugally through extensive education and internship programs. Many, even most, GITIS students, then as now, hailed from places far from Moscow. Many trained in teams that returned to run regional theaters to raise the local "cultural level"; entire collectives of non-Russian actors were drawn to Moscow from the republics and regions, and then, after five years, sent back. These groups trained alongside cohorts who remained in the city, the luckiest in ensembles formed under the maestro who ran their cohort—and many remain in contact, reuniting at festivals and hosting companies that tour.

Back in the 1930s, in order to forward Soviet policies to advance national minorities, GITIS was reorganized into two parts (as a *kombinat*): the Institut, training theatrical producers and directors, and the Tekhnikum, with sections for acting, musical-theatrical acting, and acting for national minorities. In 1934 four cohorts populated the national minorities section: Ossetian (matriculated in 1930), Yakut (1931), Kazakh (1933), and Kara-Kalpak (1934). Norris Houghton, after having spent a year observing theatrical productions in Moscow in the 1930s, wrote about these troupes at GITIS:

> I shall always remember a class of Yakuts which I visited. . . . They were dressed in that pathetic approximation of western clothing which so ill-becomes the Bolsheviks and ill fits all of them. Their faces were strongly Mongoloid, and there was an Eskimo quality about their appearance, which shirt and trousers and cotton dress could not eradicate. They were rehearsing in their own Yakutian language a translation of Moliere's "Le Bourgeois Gentilhomme"! To see these tiny black-haired yellow-skinned young men trying to assume the airs and manners of the French 17th century was amusing and a little touching. (1936, 46)

Such openly condescending, racializing phrases do not appear in Soviet-era publications about GITIS. They might have been spoken; perhaps Houghton and a few of his hosts found common ground conversing about the Yakut student, or perhaps Houghton offended with his American-style racism. We do know that GITIS, combining Russian ensemble training with Soviet nationalities policies, was charged to improve national theaters and regional studios, but like similar projects, it both afforded opportunities while also creating structural inequalities and divisions of labor.[19]

Post-Soviet GITIS no longer mandates separate acting cohorts for non-Russians, but it does continue to assemble and to train such cohorts. During my fieldwork it had just sent a cohort back to Surgut and was preparing one assembled from South Korean acting students. The corresponding Korean and Surgut directing students, however, were folded into directing department cohorts, where those still learning Russian faced difficulties asserting themselves as directors.

People describe studying at GITIS both as like a quarantine in a space capsule and as like attending a summit that gathered people from the farthest reaches of the world. The purpose is to forge professional links to animate divisions of labor, to meet people studying everything from circus management and musical variety production to dramatic criticism. Directors, especially, are supposed to map the available talents and skills, to collect numbers to call. GITIS, for all its hierarchies, brings applicants from distant parts of the former Soviet empire, some of whom arrive penniless at auditions in Moscow (successful candidates receive stipends and lodging at the dorm and free kasha at school until 11:30 A.M.). Roughly a third of our cohort lived in Moscow, at home or with relatives, but most hailed from elsewhere, from Rjazan', Pskov, Ekaterinburg, Irkutsk near Baikal, Makhachkala in Dagestan, and Estonia. A handful represented points beyond the former Soviet empire: one from Kuwait, two from Korea, and two children of Russian émigrés, respectively from Sweden and France (these students paid tuition and dormitory rent). As one might expect, their diverse experiences provided material for stage work, as well as reasons to tangle with teachers about *how* to do that work.

Students found these confrontations both productive and frustrating. Since all students knew conflict with teachers, those conflicts related to national identity did not always stand out as more painful, yet they fed divisions of labor. To take up the role of director, to organize attention, is not merely a matter of learning to draw a circle around the stage, to speak to actors in deictic terms (left, right, up, down), or to point a light into the center. It requires collective work over time to make a director. These collectives are animated through hierarchies centered in cosmopolitan cities, and this animation also takes institutional work. These are the historical conditions for learning technologies for intuition, which are also matters of learning divisions of labor—specifically of semiotic and meta-semiotic labors, that is, the work of making meaning and communicating about meaning—divisions that elevate and demonstrate phatic expertise alongside models of communication and contact.

6. Textual Enchantment and Interdiscursive Labor

In St. Petersburg, in front of the solid and majestic Kazan Cathedral ruling the main prospect, two bronze statues stand commemorating the 1812 victory over Napoleon's invading army, one representing Field Marshall Mikhail Kutuzov, the other Field Marshall Michael Andreas Barclay de Tolly. De Tolly was descended from members of the Scottish Barclay clan, who had settled in what is now Estonia; his father served in the ranks of Russian imperial nobility. The first time I saw the statue of de Tolly, in the summer of 1988, new acquaintances, dancers from Mongolia studying ballet at the Marinsky, said nothing about this cosmopolitan patriot's deeds or origins, nothing to criticize imperial ambitions. Instead, they pointed out that from the side, the paper scroll in his hand resembles a penis. Ten years later, in the city of Perm', musician friends showed me how to see similar protrusions from the figures along the portico of one of their city's houses of culture. At that time it was common to speak of such moments as manifesting a peculiarly Soviet sense of irony. To me, these acts were not exotic; they recalled Nebraskans nicknaming the state capital skyscraper: "Dick of the desert!" "Prick of the Prairie!" After all, atop its dome stands the bronze Sower, casting seeds to the wind from a bronze sack.

We are similar in this: in the Great Plains and in the Urals, the thrill in shifting perspectives is better in company, in showing the next person, confirming the multiplicity of possible angles *together*. Laughter across social encounters around even the most rigid of ideological structures still points to the edges of a fresh situation; whoever "we" happen to be, this laughter now manifests a contact. Such laughter can generate a *sense of* creativity even when the jokes (and even when the angles) are as old as the buildings, because *we* have never laughed *here* together like *this*.

Laughter itself can thus work as a sign. Like any other perceptible phenomenon, laughter can be taken up as meaning something, as pointing to something, as manifesting something; laughter becomes a Peircean interpretant. Emitted by sentient beings, moreover, it can be read as a meta-sign about capacities to understand ("She gets it!") or about the quality of social relations ("He never laughs at my jokes!"). Laughter is also felt, it is material motion, moving through the lungs, throat, and belly. It can overtake unruly bodies and entire classrooms, be difficult to stifle, and in excess can even cause the body pain; for these reasons, laughter is often seen as if raw, or unmediated. When aligned this way with immediacy, it can seem to signal perfect understanding (belied by recognition of nervous laughter and of laughter to please authority). Laughter that signals a "we" who perceive the same thing from the same angle can thus be extrapolated to identity. And it can seem to distribute complex sentiments like cleverness or discovery across a collective. Synchronous laughter can even allow those of us not dubbed individually as "geniuses" to partake in the affect of protean creativity and to be in the know.

Laughing at a bronze Scot, even Americans and Mongolians speaking a Russian lingua franca can thus forge a *sense of* contact, if not a durable "we." Durkheimian concepts such as "collective effervescence" do little, however, to explain what people do with these senses, once they are interpreted. The feeling of laughing together involves and entails more than waves of reflex response and energy. Laughing can also mobilize phatic meta-capacities, to observe not only others' mirthful reactions to shifts in perspective but also the reactions to those reactions, of those who can't take a joke. Laughter can also separate and even injure.

Critiques of socialist communication have often discussed laughter and parody as a response to that hegemony. In doing so, they often focus on the ways *individuals* respond to official *forms* or *systems*, as if individuals face structures alone rather than, say, in laughing clusters.[1] It is as if there were nothing interesting or creative for collectives to do or that only individuals deserve creative freedom. From images of hive mind to fears of mass brainwashing, terror of collectivities binds many in the United States to defend individual thought and expression to such a degree that to champion collectivist approaches can be ridiculed or marked as dangerous. A teacher at GITIS, by contrast, will argue that the most compelling, original stage encounters are not those worked out by an individual actor rebelling alone against a formal genre. "You can do nothing alone," the teacher would tell us. Even a one-person show mobilizes *collective* play.

More than a century before social theorists began to describe multiple perspectives or ontologies via ethnography, theatrical and other artistic practitioners elaborated theories to acknowledge and create multiple points of view. Meyerhold theorized play with relations among angles for perception; evoking his name, twenty-first-century GITIS teachers continue this work. While most have read structuralists such as Saussure and Derrida, they moved beyond structuralism and its posts a long time ago. They are trapped neither by the image of individual minds crashing like birds against giant structures nor by worries that we all, in the end, swim alone among floating signifiers. Having read Bakhtin, Voloshinov, Vygotsky, and Jakobson (Meyerhold and of course his teacher, Stanislavsky, having influenced some of *them*), they in fact share more axioms with pragmatic linguistic anthropologists than the latter do with other Americans. First, we consider sentient beings actively to make meaning out of words, markings, objects, sounds, and more. Second, we note that they do so always *in specific* times and places. As one of the teachers would often say, "What are you showing us? There is no love in general, there is no boredom in general. There exist only this love, this specific boredom."

These singular encounters are never isolated. Not only are they embedded in social contexts, they also are crossed by memories of other situations ("They pronounced it that way") and projections about their uptake in future situations ("Might this be misheard as a slight?"). Because GITIS people work in collectives, with examples always at hand, they are even able to sustain and even propagate these ideologies about communication, more consistently than linguistic anthropologists so far have managed to broadcast aligned theories. Players strike angles in the here and now of the auditorium, but thereby also afford perspectives on situations or texts from other times and places. Even penis jokes well offstage have to resonate with other texts and situations—they work intertextually and interdiscursively; they are less funny if we lack knowledge of what is *usually* not said.[2]

GITIS phatic experts must also master the interdiscursive and intertextual expertise required to make strangers laugh and cry. Put otherwise, phatic skill in the here and now, they taught, requires agility with making connections across situations and texts. During my fieldwork, instructors daily repeated to the first-year cohort the need to "rid you of pre-thought schema," to react to the unexpected "right here, right now." Yet at the same time they urged, "You must read Pushkin, Russian folk tales, Tolkien, the Bible" in order to discover which combinations of texts would "strike a chord." The point, they insist, is not to generalize across encounters, but to recognize possible links.

Such links are imagined to live as notes struck across many minds at once, in memories of books, songs, places, and events. Directing students are put to work early not to reproduce Pushkin's lines, but to arrange them with actions in spaces already echoing with, say, Pelevin's heroes or Harry Potter. The audience, however, never presents a library of completely shared texts or remembered situations; the practical goal is thus to strike a *chord across* an audience, never just a solitary note in an individual. Compelling dramatic work produces harmonies or chimes interesting discordances. An actor voices a line from Pushkin not only to animate a character (or to criticize the character, depending on genre), but also to activate the audience as a reactive, protean body, a living piano with keys that can either resist fingers or amplify their touch.

This practical artistic theory of collective creativity seems more robust to me, more amenable to anthropology, than those bound to romantic or neoliberal individualism. All the same, I bracket my evaluation of the means to create interdiscursive resonance in order to focus on techniques by which people craft a *sense of* virtuosic, collective play and recognize this as creative. Again, a heavy pile of ideological boulders stands in the way, from anxieties about collective action that mystify allegedly mesmerizing group "effervescence" to warnings of "the madness of the mob." What others take as a path to automatization or to mass control, GITIS actors, directors, and artists see also as the way to real creativity. Often their words echoed the terms of affect theory, to track "energy," "forces," and shifts in "intensities." Remaining agnostic about those categories—common also to the discourses of paranormal science, we should note—I concentrate in the next sections on divisions of materials, spaces, and labor that channel circuits for joint creativity.

These are the conditions for a specific kind of phaticity, a making of contacts *through* mediations of mediations, rather than by the erasure of media or material. To conjure sensations of creativity requires media, relies on material techniques. I hope not to romanticize too much; cynical appropriations of the sense of creativity, as in advertising, do this all too well, fixing brand by hinting that to own a certain watch is to participate in creative design, as if new pants offer a frisson of belonging with those on the cutting edge.

PATTERNS OF PATTERNS

As in stage enchantments that cut women in half and put them back together again, collective work, as we have seen, can create the impression of pieces, or even of dyadic segments. Such work also creates wholes. It does so in part by dividing and hiding labor and by visibly producing fragments to then be united. Before we turn to divisions of labor, then, let us consider ways in which fragments and wholes have been understood by some of those who are most invested in creativity, text, memory, and magic.

While pragmatic thinking about communication aims to tangle with specific, historically located situations (how this statue, here and now, makes her laugh with these people and not those), a dominant countertendency is to wave words like magical or ineffable or inchoate language that seems not to fulfill an expected semantic function. It takes more trouble to tease apart functions or purposes that go unnamed or to track social usages or effects that seem to contradict semantic logic. To treat the ways words can do more than one thing at a time beside denote an idea—spark collective laughter, induce action, point to authority—as magical, or even as just too mysterious or complex to parse, however, would negate the possibilities of ethnography, or of any kind of sustained attention, as in theatrical work, to interactions as they unfold in spaces and over time.

Over the last two centuries, starting in late imperial and continuing through Soviet and post-Soviet times, poets, artists, and scholars in Russia have debated the power of words in productive ways, some illuminating the wondrous complexities of living, spoken language as they developed robust metalanguages to theorize political speech and artful action.

Around the turn of the twentieth century, Russian symbolist poets such as Aleksandr Blok and Andrei Bely lamented civilization's numbing effects on the forces for inspiration, the ways mechanization produced social anomie and dissipation, breaking and splitting what should have been left whole. They sought to recover enchantments to rewire links to creative energy and to other souls, and to do so through poetry, in the textures of sound, in vital correspondences among fresh patterns of rhyme and rhythm.[3] In works like Bely's 1910 essay *Magija Slov*, drawing upon the writings of gnostics such as Vladimir Solovjev and theosophists such as Elena Blavatsky, they joined a broader, transnational search for universal connections, for links *among* designs, for ways that orders of grammars overlap with the structures of trees or of sea organisms, or even of stellar constellations. They asserted the resonant powers of homologies *across* patterns and produced detailed commentaries on the ways words—in the right *combinations*—might transcend repetitive, banal *byt*, "the daily grind" of chores and automatic habitus. Such poetry would defend against chaotic unintelligibility; in the new world, everything would become commensurable, as if alignment among systems would close the gaps that Saussure and other early modernists had opened between signifieds and signifiers, restoring syntheses of humanity with nature.

A symbolist poet who could align such structures to orchestrate vibrations became a shaman, mediating not only messages, but also orders of reality by bridging times and spaces.[4] Like many others in the late nineteenth and early twentieth centuries, Russian formalists, symbolists, and futurists (and symbolists who converted to Russian futurism) were impressed by demonstrations of electric power and magnetic fields, as well as then-new theories of relativity. Symbolist poet Blok, forwarding a utopian hybrid of science and the occult like that heralded by theosophy, declared that with the discovery of hypnosis, the medicinal powers of folk incantations were recognized "even by exact sciences."

While Saussure was lecturing on linguistic structures in Geneva, symbolists in St. Petersburg, like Bely, saw the magic of poetic incantation as emanating not from individual sounds, words, or texts in themselves, but from their relations: "*Connections between* words, grammatical forms, and figures of speech are, in essence, charms" (Bely [1910] 1985, 93). Words in patterns allow an utterer to link, for example, "two ineffable essences: space, which is accessible to my vision, and that inner sense vibrating mutely inside me that I provisionally call . . . time" (Bely quoted in Gutkin 1997, 231).[5] The poet-shaman commands *patterns among* signs, sounds, and media to call upon nature, to call the future into existence, to extend life across space and time. This particular sort of power is generated not by any word or phrase in isolation, be it spoken or written on paper (as can certainly be so in other semiotic maneuvers for magic, as Keane 2013 demonstrates), but rather by arcs that cross between them, as in electrical circuit nodes or synapses.

Russian futurists differed from the Italian variety, in part because most had passed through a symbolist stage; they were revolutionary pacifists for the machine future. While critical of symbolism's mystical mood, they projected similar hopes that patterns among sounds, lines, shapes, and colors—form, not only semantic content—could recharge human thought and feeling and thereby change the world. They, too, argued that incantations, even of words that seem incomprehensible, could, through rustlings of sound pattern, enter many a subconscious at once, reuniting humanity.[6] Russian futurists idealized world peace in a time of war, experimenting with transrational language (*zaum*) to bridge differences and break down autocratic social systems, to usher in progressive futures. They dreamed that synesthetic *arrangements* of written text with graphic design (colors, typeface) might evoke the imagination to conjure new social and material realities.

While focused on patterns, Russian futurist poets aimed not so much to discover or plug into vibrant ur-structures (as symbolists had, as structuralists would, each in different ways) as to scramble their circuits. The title of V. Khlebnikov's poem "Incantation to Laughter" (it continues: "Laugh it up, you laughniks, laughingly . . .") gives a wink to earlier claims of supernatural immanence in symbolic patterns, but his work and others' vandalized grammatical conventions with competing intuitions about street spaces where single lines of speech are interrupted by shards of talk, rays coherent from some new perspective. Their poetic play pointed to the multiple functions of language besides reference and inspired Roman Jakobson, a close friend of futurist poets such as Vladimir Mayakovsky. He would later articulate poetic discoveries for an audience of linguists and literary scholars, contributing to thinking about the utility in communication of marked and unmarked formal distinctions and later about the nonreferential functions of language.

WORD SÉANCE: BLACK MAGIC INTERTEXT

Soviet times and socialist realisms did not disenchant the idea of patterns among words or texts, even while formalists and futurists were repressed. By late socialist times, even highly placed figures noted the importance of resonance among texts and communicative situations—even as they leaned toward conserving original orientations and relations. Drama critic N. Potapov, discussing the Taganka Theater's production of Bulgakov's novel *The Master and Margarita*, titled his 1977 review (a review that, some claim, launched a decade of controversy around the play and trouble for its actors and director), "A Séance of Black Magic." The title echoes events early in the novel, when foreign hypnotist Woland creates chaos, yanking stage managers, censors, and poets through parallel channels more absurdly tangled than any bureaucracy. Bulgakov drafted the satirical fantasy in phases between 1928 and 1940; it is said that he burned one draft in 1930, and that the text remained incomplete, passed along by hand in more than one version. The most famous line in the book, spoken by the visiting foreigner, the magician Woland, has been repeated in varying ways to reflect upon recent Soviet and post-Soviet histories of relations among texts and their destruction: "Manuscripts don't burn." Indeed, Soviet-era dissidents took up the phrase as a slogan in defiance of state confiscations of *samizdat* books. By the twenty-first century, Russian Orthodox church scholars would argue that since it is Woland, the devil, who says that "manuscripts do not burn," we ought to question his claim; manuscripts, they point out (like good materialists), *do* burn, and people do forget poetic lines, unless they memorize them with an eye to times when paper will not be available (as a number of Soviet intellectuals did).

The novel achieved cult status despite—or because of—deletions and changes to the text. In the mid-1960s it went into print, with about 10 percent cut, in the journal *Moscow* (1966, no. 11, and 1967, no.1). This was the version that an actor in the 2005 televised serial version recalls: a handbound set of photocopies of the journal in the library stacks that he read standing up, rather than studying for exams in foreign literature. In 1973 a version closer to Bulgakov's 1940 draft was published by the publisher Khudozhestvennaja Literatura, and soon afterward the stage version went into rehearsal.

Potapov begins his review with high praise, describing the prelude, during which actors emerged from the shadows to pronounce phrases belonging to the characters. This staging reminds the critic of an earlier Bulgakov text, which he quotes. These are "stars that remain even when our *tel i del* ('bodies and deeds') are gone. . . . These key lines are like facets of a crystal, scattering rays, the many-layered artistic thoughts of the author" (Potapov 1977, 6). The metaphor seems approvingly to echo the principle of refraction in aesthetic *luchism* ("ray-ism": a theme that not only marks the writings of avant-garde painters such as Natalia Goncharova and Mikhail Larionov, but also appears in Voloshinov's essays on reported speech).

Soon enough, however, the critic complains, the actors refract their lines in directions too crooked. He offers as an example the scene in which Woland showers dollars over his audience, cash that, once people go out on the street, changes back into worthless paper scraps. This scene is played, says the critic, as a "sociological experiment" to imply that people in *this* audience are shallow and selfish. As an expert authority in the intertextual, he accuses the Taganka of transposing the original author's judgments "from the time in which Bulgakov wrote onto the viewers now," to make a bad analogy between the 1930s and 1977: "[The character] Berlioz, speaking with a self-satisfied, victorious smile about atheism, states that, 'the majority of our population consciously, long ago stopped believing tales about God.' The discussion is painted in the theater in tones such that Bulgakov's irony directed at Berlioz, at his erudition as a dull pedant . . . begins to sound like irony about things and categories essential for *our* society. Woland's skepticism reigns over the play" (Potapov 1977, 6).

The Taganka crew did not disagree; social criticism was among their controversial, experimental aims, after all, a different order of magic. It is worth noting that what Potapov objected to most of all was the way the Taganka's staging isolated the Master, the writer, as the only one capable of true crea-tivity: "Having left the figure of the Master, and with it the philosophical theme of creative work, a little in the shadows, it exaggerates the legacy of the unknown artist— the manuscript. As a work made in solitude." Potapov's view in this matter has not lost support; while GITIS instructors maintain close and affectionate ties with the Taganka—its leading directors deliver guest lectures throughout the academic year—none recommend solitude as a condition for meaningful creative work onstage, instead press-ing for collective interaction, among people *and* objects, as the best condi-tion for creativity.

THE ART OF THEORY

In the United States, arguably, fewer spaces encourage thinking or speaking of creativity except as a product of individual freedom, dividing "individ-ual" from "collective" as if these labels represent natural antinomies, affix-ing them to opposing ideologies (capitalist versus socialist, among others). In Russia, these oppositions were less fixed, one to each ideology; Stanislavsky ran experiments for creativity among *collective* ensembles decades before the socialist state, while explorers and scientists in popular Soviet films sang lyrics extolling individual decisions in love and life. To be sure, in the United States people actually working in many fields make it good practice to "bounce ideas" in a group or say that "two heads are better than one." Americans also know how to create with an ear to echoes with past creations, to consider the intertextual echoes among phrases as well as interdiscursive references among situations. In Russia as in the United States, plenty of people not trained in such expertise crack jokes during a film by riffing in lines from others or mash up memes from news texts to comment, for example, on common workplace dynamics. Techniques that mobilize forces beyond the individual—relations to other persons, time spaces, and texts—along with theories about how they work, however, have been more often and more elaborately articulated in Russia, and in more contexts over time.

To those socialized to anchor expression to individuals and to overvalue description as the main purpose of speaking, collective acts of creativity often seem to work "without signs." Such socialization is familiar in most spaces in the United States. By contrast, Soviet middle schools addressed multiple functions in courses on rhetoric (college students, by the 1970s if not earlier, read Jakobson and Bakhtin). Others in Russia who have crossed my path over the decades also speak more easily about nonreferential communication than do even many colleagues in the United States. In the classroom and elsewhere, dominant American common sense matches definitions to words and voices to bodies and separates speaking from doing. All the above ideologies live in both countries, of course; the difference lies in the extent and power of their habitual evocation across fields and venues and their influence in shaping possibilities to communicate about communication (and ultimately ways to communicate).

Speaking historically, Russophone artists and thinkers have nudged Anglophone scholars to consider more deeply questions parallel to those raised by language philosophers from Ludwig Wittgenstein through John L. Austin, by ethnographers such as Malinowski, and, of course, pragmatic philosophes such as Peirce.[7] The more I read about the formalist and futurist avant-garde in Russia, the more I am convinced that the ideas percolating through linguistics, literary criticism, and philosophy from the mid-twentieth century onward were already being theorized by poets, directors, and painters. It was they who first directed ears and eyes, via abstract forms, to nonreferential functions, to the ways grammar refracts class struggle (Mayakovsky) and the ways sounds resemble substances or vibrate with affects (Osip Mandelshtam, Andrei Bely). They enacted what scholars distilled into linear print form as theory. Khlebnikov's "Incantation to Laughter" is a manifesto of multifunctionality; it demands that readers attend simultaneously to poetic play with morphemes and to shifting conative functions across a series of directives ("Notice *this* about the fragments of the word 'laugh-ter'—and laugh!"). This play, along with essays by Meyerhold and Mayakovsky, preceded Jakobson's diagrams; after all, they were friends, sitting up late into the night discussing plays and verses. In a similar fashion, Bakhtin and Voloshinov did not invent polyphony or polyglossia so much as figure out how to explain what was fresh about the way Fyodor Dostoevsky orchestrated and layered many character voices. The repression of the formalists after the 1920s could not snuff out their ideas; they were already circulating in too many genres and media.

Instructors at GITIS are even more familiar than most with key theorists of texts and intertexts, citing Jakobson, Propp, Bakhtin, Kristeva, Derrida, Umberto Eco, Wittgenstein, Austin, and John Searle. They describe and wield nonreferential functions that linguistic anthropologists have yet to categorize. They never question that speech *is* action, as they ponder the effects of this wink to chime against a text or that nod to echo what one might hear on the bus. Russians who do not read semiotic theory thus nevertheless encounter executions of pragmatic and semiotic principles at the theater that, in the United States, remain esoteric, almost occult beyond academe. They also come to them via literature: the Russophone reader who meets Dostoevsky is already acquainted with accents and styles, can locate shifts between formal and informal modes of address, and can relate both to depictions of class or kin or gender hierarchies, or hear characters voiced,[8] as Bakhtin elaborated, without translator's footnotes (see also Friedrich 1972). For such a prepared public, art can do the work that theory does elsewhere. The alacrity of students at GITIS to take on the professional mastery of interdiscursive expertise contrasts with the baffled resistance American scholars face when we try to teach about such matters.

BROKEN GENERATIONS? PHATIC LOSS AND INTERTEXTUAL ENCHANTMENT

Widespread familiarity in Russia with the principle that meaning happens across texts and discursive situations amplifies the uses and popularity of this technology for intuition, to the degree that some see it as even more powerful than it is, as intertextual enchantment. Post-Soviet author Victor Pelevin, by contrast, in his best-selling 1999 novel *Generation P.*, mocks the fetish made of post-structural intertextual theory, to hilarious effect, depicting a post-1991 Moscow dazzled by multiplications of product wrapper texts, book covers, billboards, and television ads. The protagonist, a translator with advanced degrees in philology, loses his job and must turn his poetic, intertextual talents to advertising work. Experimenting with a range of pharmaceuticals, he hallucinates paranoid resonances among street signs and reads pictures on cigarette packages through passages from Saussure's lectures on semiotics, hilariously divining them all as signs pointing him to jingles. How to sell Sprite to Russians . . . as the opposite of Coke . . . of the tsars! Hmmm, what if we make anti-Nicholas into *Ne-kola!* "Not bad, but 7-up already did 'the UnCola,'" his new boss informs him, hinting that he should broaden his knowledge of global advertising texts. The copy especially tickles those who, like most in Russian cities (and fewer in America), know *both* American and Russian literature and pop culture.

In early twenty-first-century Moscow, to wax nostalgic for times when one could take for granted which texts, statues, or slogans stood ready to serve at the party (if not *for* the party) was not necessarily to hanker for Soviet master categories or to pine for a lost sense of unified thought (see also Boym 1994; Pesmen 2000; Oushakine 2000; Yurchak 2015a). Lost, too, were common points around which people could project distortions and angles: this had been great fun, spinning around them even through gestural meta-discourse. It was loss not just of content—a statue down, a street name changed—but also of channels. The old texts did more than carry messages; they attracted collective attention, banter, and debate—all of which made live contacts around them more visible. Their absence was a phatic loss.

For many the events of the 1990s unseated a repressive order, but it also rubbed out some communication lines. In the 1980s *glasnost'* colorfully exploded in pages of print on the streets; stacks of new books (some reprints of old *samizdat*), pamphlets, magazines, and newspapers at every busy street corner and metro station signaled "freedom of speech." Beginning in the years just before and after the Soviet socialist state collapsed, sudden textual plenty and variety contrasted with the shortages of food and sundries; it was difficult to find something to eat, but at least books and papers had become more interesting. Ten years later, even twenty, even against allegations that the "Putin era" has destroyed the independent press, colorful flows of print continue.

Plenitude itself, however, began to signify differently.[9] By summer 2001, some erudite friends of mine in Russia were complaining that people "no longer connect" through books. One friend had always spent hours a day at the kitchen table, surrounded by piles of newspapers and books; she rarely finished a single book without reading several others simultaneously. Still, she lamented that now there were too many dizzying arrays of glossy magazines and pulp best sellers at every metro station, "not as many good ones, and we no longer all read the same book all at once," she said, gesturing to the stacks. Contemporary fiction mirrors her words, setting up plots to stress shortages and excesses of books.[10] The fact that there are so many voracious readers in this "most literate of countries" only feeds the theme that broken links among *texts* reflect broken links among *people*.

GITIS teachers complained that entering cohorts lacked orientation to "classic texts." This lack, they said, rendered beginning students shallow, deprived them of means to escape their own habitual perspectives, in order to orient to others' actions and conditions; a real handicap to collective improvisation. This lack made the students "not interesting." They needed to learn the very basics for intertextual enchantment; directing students especially needed to listen for other "there and thens" to animate "here and now." Instructors maintained that they, the first cohorts considered too young to recall Soviet times, could neither appreciate older texts nor yet distinguish worthy new ones. And because they were not training to be writers, but training to animate scripts as action, the needed to recalibrate not only to texts, but also to people who read texts (or who don't). They were simultaneously exhorted both to read more and to pay better attention to conversations unfolding around them among the people on the street. They needed to be retuned in more than one way in order to align phatically from the stage.

Similar observations are made about "generations" all the time. The problem is not always understood in term of lack, the past severed, but in terms of excess, intervening layers, competing channels in the present and near past. Michael Silverstein (2005, 13) describes a kind of "anachronistic interdiscursivity" among American college freshman who react to Shakespeare "with a sense of déjà vu from 19th-century and later literature with which they were familiar." Through layers of intervening texts, they read Shakespeare as if flawed by the "[hackneyed] values such over-adjectivalization has come to have in our Strunk-and-White era of modernist prose standard." They are "intertextually deaf" to sixteenth-century parodies of speech because forms similar to those Shakespeare played with have already refracted through so many other texts.

Russian author Tatjana Tolstaja has described a kind of post-Soviet intertextual deafness as a loss of the sense for the connections among texts and people made in other times, in fiction exploring the consequences after books themselves are sacrificed. In her 2003 novel *Slynx (Kys')*, an apocalyptic blast has left nothing in Moscow, nothing but the stone Kremlin and some paper books. Recalling Ray Bradbury's *Fahrenheit 451*, authorities confiscate these books as they find them, except that they do not burn all the manuscripts; they cart them to a central warehouse.[11] There, scribes produce abridged versions to redisseminate to the people, in a genre blending the Russian imperial-era *lubok* and the comic book. After a series of absurdly violent conflicts, the protagonist reaches the warehouse in a Kremlin palace bursting with stacks. There he reads and reads, in no order. He has no way to relate any book to another one, or to the world of people, so he wanders from sentence to sentence, cataloging books by color or by thickness of the spine, not recognizing that he remains illiterate in the ways that the books had once spoken to each other and beyond.

Texts slip in and out of coherence with their interdiscursive and intertextual surroundings all the time; it takes human effort both to set and repeat alignments and to break them. Such effort does more to *produce* generations, genders, genres, and so forth, than the other way around.[12] Preferred relations among texts, best practices for picking out patterns to strike an interdiscursive echo, correlate with social expectations about ways to communicate, be it in democratic or more hierarchical collectivities. The "power citation" at the beginning of a scholarly publication is a good example in an academic register, intended "to situate" the piece "in a conversation" and also to recognize the aid and influence of others; it can be an act of collegial citizenship and of exclusion all at once (and we worry about getting it right: Will I be sorry not to have cited someone in relation to this point? What have I missed?). We learn what a theoretical conversation once was through back formations that are written by scholars who align with currently dominant schools of thought. Bourdieu (1977) makes a similar point about the ways people structure accounts of kinship relations: in a world where multiple kinds of relations are always possible, a kinchart is always a situated back formation. Like that third cousin who might also count as an aunt, except during matchmaking or when the census comes around, the writings of women, colonized peoples—and artists—are both absorbed and erased by scholars when they call them anything but "theoretical."

At GITIS in fall 2002, the very first days of theatrical education concentrated on cultivating relationships of people to people, people to texts, and texts to other texts, in situations beyond the walls of the school. "Who remembers when people used to say ___?" Thus began training not only in intertextual, but in interdiscursive expertise, in learning not only how to riff with famous texts, but how to riff on ways this character or that might sound out some quotation while in the sauna, or on the telephone with a client, and so forth. Over the summer, first-year students had been assigned to accumulate found texts, bits of song, snippets of overheard conversation, and text from ads for rooms to let. They presented their found bits in ways that treated texts as if they stood alone; plays on words and verbal absurdities ruled the day. The head instructor saw this as a troubling indication that these young people were indifferent to those who generated or read the texts *for a reason*. They could not read beyond their own skin. He accused the cohort of rejecting the "depths behind the word." By "depths" he meant not layers of internal selves, as depth psychology would have it, but biographical trajectories that crisscross conditions, in circles binding specific events, spaces, and times.

RETUNING

According to GITIS instructors, even shared material surroundings still standing across Soviet-built urban spaces could not overcome a generation's loss of the means to connect. Students contested this judgment, insisted on knowing, but they were told that impressions were just that, and that they did not cohere. One afternoon an instructor asked the cohort to lie on the floor, to imagine that their bodies were flat, like scraps of material that someone was beginning to inflate. He walked around, poking: "The air got to this arm, no?" He asked several students which toys they were becoming (Fieldnotes, December 2002):

STUDENT: I am the "Melancholy Clown."

TEACHER: Why?

STUDENT: Just so. No choice. You know, "Soviet Union."

TEACHER: But the Soviet Union—*you* never saw it!

STUDENT: Hello! [*Zdrast'e!* "Give me a break!"]

TEACHER: Good morning! [*Dobroe utro!* "You give *me* a break!"] What year were you born?

STUDENT: '82.

TEACHER: Brezhnev died in '82 and the USSR was no more. You saw only remnants.

STUDENT: Well, you could get only two colors of tights.

TEACHER: That was not the Soviet Union.

STUDENT: Well what?

TEACHER: Remnants.

As Tatyana Tolstaya depicted scattered, disordered ruins and texts in *Slynx*, the teacher revealed seemingly shared material signs of the Soviet (tights, dolls) to be disparate scraps, remnants, not webs of social action or meaning. Contact with such objects, as with single texts, was not enough to repair phatic loss.

In an attempt to cure interdiscursive deafness and phatic loss, the teachers introduced another Soviet-era manuscript, not a work of fiction but a state-published handbook for everyday living. In December 2002 GITIS instructors created an assignment featuring the Soviet-era cookbook and table etiquette manual *Kniga o vkusnoj i zdorovoj pishche* (The book of tasty and nutritious food). The cookbook had had modest circulation until 1953, the year that marked its first mass printing in the hundreds of thousands; by the late 1970s edition, circulation had hit the millions. The teaching staff presented the project as an innovative way to incite a young cohort to feel the tender irony suffusing the 1950s, the tone of a time when "hungry people opened a book with pictures of ham in aspic." Perhaps they hoped to spark some intertextual magic.

"This book embodied ideology," said the head instructor. "Through food, it made people part of the system." Cultural historian Catriona Kelly similarly argues that the book represented an early attempt to present Soviet society as a unified whole through luxury goods—goods that (in time) were intended for all (2001, 287). She describes this book, first published in 1939, as the "most opulent" since the Revolution; while educating people about a "rational diet," it also extolled "elegance," "pleasantness," and "comfort." The head instructor introduced the book to the directing students in starker terms:

> This is a strange assignment. 2003 will mark 50 years since the first
> mass publication of *The Book of Tasty and Nutritious Food*. This is a
> phenomenally cynical book—it came out during a hungry time. But
> this is culinary poetry. Part sweet, part bitter. Our Russian history.
> About the text: one of our instructors had experience staging it out east.
> He juxtaposed readings with video of an old woman telling her life
> story—terrible experiences, but with such humor! Such a sense of
> counterpoint! You, then, are to select and stage recipes, one each for
> breakfast, lunch, dinner, and holidays, too. We take it up not merely as a
> book, or as a document, but as history. (Fieldnotes, October 22, 2002)

One instructor (the director who had staged the book in Siberian towns) passionately interjected: "It is second only after *Mein Kampf*!" The master, talking over him, complicated that perspective:

> Of course, there must be humor in theatrical play . . . but there must be
> a counterpoint, a metaphor or something else to burst the bubble of
> happy propaganda. *Do* this, but with one request: avoid politicization
> ("And sexuality," interjected another instructor). These things are
> beginning to be understood less in political as in aesthetic terms. The
> political is not interesting. The aesthetic phenomena of that culture is
> what is interesting. No political theater . . . we want you to *feel* the
> embellishments and curlicues of the Stalinesque baroque. Our problem,
> really, is how to acquaint *you* with a cultural layer that is now
> departing.

The goal was to ride the text and to reanimate relations to it, as a means to, as the maestro put it, to retune the students to the entire "*intonatsija* of a time,"[13] those years just after Stalin's death in 1953, but before Khrushchev's secret speech in 1956. Similar sorts of discussions were happening across spaces like this one, by the way, *before* state media in what came to be called Putin's Russia had amplified memories of that time, and the time just before it, of World War II and its losses.

RECIPES FAILED BUT FAMILIAR

It was important, the instructors said that day, to begin work not with abstraction from the text in general, but with *specific* texts, copies covered with notes and footnotes, with recipes or pictures stuck between the pages, with all their fingerprints and butter stains (index and icon of specific, past moments), as each book passed through hands and changed shelves. Here is some of the dialogue among teachers and students about the assignment, this time to stress the involvement that the topic of specific books aroused:

MAESTRO: Who has the book? Several must have it in their families.

STUDENT: [Says an early edition has passed down in his family now for three generations, with photographs, with layers of reactions penciled in.]

MAESTRO: What a great idea! Bring it in! [See] how we make wealth of our poverty!

TEACHER 1: You see in the recipes each family history!

MAESTRO: Send a telegram to Irkutsk, immediately! [They discuss where in the city to find old copies, the colors of different editions.] It's like the Bible. Hungry people would open it up—

TEACHER 1: The epoch is gone, but the book stays on as a monument!

TEACHER 2: I tried to make a dessert once; it came out inedible!

MAESTRO: It is a purely Russian book. France has tons of atlases of cheese; it is considered normal. . . . [F]or Russia, this book was not normal.

The cookbook, in its various editions, even very old ones, *was* a familiar object to nearly everyone in the room (friends, too, have shown me family copies since then). Hunger was also no stranger; the institute gave out free kasha every morning before 11:00, and for many students living in the dormitory on stipends this was often the only meal they could count on.

The instructors never seemed satisfied with the staged sketches that the students crafted from pieces of cookbook text. It was rough going through every stage. After he had introduced the project, the master gave the directing students an hour to leaf through the pages and select sections. The first read aloud a description of how cognac is made. The instructors criticized: this would never work on stage, too much "technical language." The student responded, "But what about the ending? The advice, 'In our country, drinking is—'." A teacher interrupted: "Yes, yes, fine. Take that part," declaring that section likely to strike a chord and to "find addressees." Another student read a paragraph about shopping for meat and produce, which the teachers dismissed immediately, quipping that the youngest students "will just not understand."

I could see what they meant; over the previous decade the contents, sizes, and locations of grocery stores had changed incredibly, as had the kind, quantity, and packaging of goods, along with habits for selecting vegetables or meat and comparing prices. Even I, a foreigner, then eighteen years older than the youngest students, better recalled standing in line for the single type of cheese in an otherwise empty store and bargaining for produce on the street. One evening after classes, around midnight on the way home, one of the students and I stopped in at the twenty-four-hour supermarket not far from our dormitory, and I came up against our difference. We had been chatting about films and the recent snow. In the store, he expressed frustration that while the shop stocked three flavors of gin and tonic in a can, stacked in a pyramid beside a giant tank of enormous live carp, they did not carry the flavor he wanted. He looked at me blankly when I laughed, recounting how we used to bring jars from home to siphon beer from the beer truck tank (you could still sometimes get milk and *kvas* this way in Moscow). The teachers had a point: Soviet-era shopping, the twisting rounds of relations in buying and selling, hoarding or gifting, had too many moving parts to handle just then. Even the texture of an exotic food seemed easier to convey; when the next student read a description of Roquefort cheese—no less foreign to these students than was standing in line—the master declared *"Pesnja! Chudo!"* ("A song! A miracle!"). As a body, the teachers approved a menu that included a dish of fried brains.

Over the next few weeks, part of each day was devoted to experimenting and debating in small groups: Where should we place the vodka bottle? Do we read a section on dumplings with a melodic Urals' accent, in a whisper? Clusters worked across the two rooms belonging to the cohort; acting students and directing students switched roles. Despite the fact that everyone was working from the same text, when students showed their first attempts to the instructors, the sketches showed even less unity in genre, tone, and sentiment than had other series of études (e.g., a series based on "personal ads" or "observations of animals"). "Fried Brains" came off as a grim, suicidal prison diary, the actor gulping water in order to swallow each spoonful of grey mush. In "Setting the Table," in contrast, six chirpy maids in uniform applied for a high-class restaurant job, parodying slapstick silent film. A student from Daghestan had been nudged to take up the section on Caucasian cuisine; between lines of mountain song, a rousing fantasy of rebellious and robust southern men, he savored lamb stew. Two female Korean directing students (who, said the instructors, "probably can understand nothing in this book") were encouraged to depart entirely from the text. They staged the discovery of kimchi and rice cakes by early *Homo erectus*, re-creating a Pleistocene cave with multicolored lights and echoes. The pieces did not come together; just one was selected to continue to the semester exam. Eight years later, while reminiscing about this project with several students at one actress's apartment, her mother (a film actress herself) quipped, "They did not know themselves what they wanted from you all." Certainly at work in the cookbook assignment was a "fantasy of cross-generational belonging," as teachers partook in the diverse forms and aims of nostalgia in Russia at the time (Nadkarni and Shevchenko 2004, 490). Our concern here, however, is less with nostalgia and more with how the dream of intertextual alignment around the cookbook hit the knottier movements though both interdiscursive relations *and* struggles to orchestrate such relations. Such knots in fact proved useful in dividing the labors of performance. Even if no unified production emerged, the teachers achieved other goals in asking the students to consider the links among specific copies of a text and the people who had read it.

DIVISIONS OF LABOR: TEXT AND ANTITEXT

It is not enough to separate or link words, lyrics, books, or even entire genres. Juxtapositions do not work alone to make theater; acts of division and connection work through standing social relations and hierarchies even as they produce divisions of interdiscursive expertise. The stage director, the orchestra conductor—these European roles within theatrical production solidified during the nineteenth century, as the large theatrical and musical academies were being founded across the metropoles.[14] The director and conductor embody positions that express the apical hierarchies and panoptic fantasies of empire, organizing communication from the distance of the hall, watching the timing and intensity of contacts among players and with props, with an eye to the perspectives of future auditors.

A director moves differently across the stage spaces than actors do, pacing the auditorium, climbing onto and jumping off the boards. Actors often prefer that directors do not close the distance too much. In Moscow and Perm', in town in Nebraska and in New York, while acting in plays and directing them, I have heard actors complain when the director gives direction *like* an actor; directors are to explain, to tell, while actors are to show. Actors can take too much demonstration as a sign of condescension. At the Moscow Romani Theater in the early 1990s such condescension could take on tones of ethnocentric superiority; as more than one actress recounted to me, the troupe did not appreciate directors who demonstrated gestures before trying verbal descriptions or metaphors, as if the actor were a puppet or a parrot, just a mimic with no knowledge of the world.

The Russian academies respect that division of labor in the curriculum. For the actors in the directing department, the first year is devoted to observations and attention, bodily flexibility, and speed of nervous response. Acting students begin work with scripts only in the second year; the first year involves only tiny snippets of found texts (personal ads, overheard street talk). Some lessons, as we have seen, abandon not only text and speech but also other material media—even facial expressions and eye gaze—to practice making contact with fewer and fewer media. The handful of directing students in the cohort, however, followed an additional, textual track. Each night after the actors were released, around 9:30, the teachers met separately with the directing students, until about 11:30 (sometimes, if the trip home on the subway seemed too daunting at that hour, some slept over in a classroom or behind some scenery). Beginning directors were exhorted in these hours to build "echoes among texts," especially along cosmopolitan literary paths, to be able to combine Bulgakov *and* Tolkien, Pushkin *and* Shakespeare, Limonov *and* Don DeLillo, *The Cherry Orchard* and *The Vagina Monologues*. They were told to read theoretical texts not only about the theater, but about texts, about style and form: Jakobson and Bakhtin, Eco and Kristeva, Shklovsky and Propp.

With acting students, by contrast, instructors foregrounded *bodily* forms of semiosis: the occasional quote from the Buddha or Pushkin or Meyerhold to exhort actors to "trust the body." Lessons in stage speech built awareness of the shifting shapes and moistness of the palate and throat, the size and strength of the diaphragm, as instruments for articulating all manner of sounds. Daily drills also trained awareness of others' bodily shifts, others' twitches and noises, the texture and timing of their movements and utterances; only such attention could open channels for compelling responses, make their contacts coherent as such to viewers. Drills foregrounded responses and collective imagination over individualized expressions, training sensory reflexes to quick relational shifts. Words were subsumed under these goals, for instance, serving to activate them. For example, every morning after stretching, students were to jog in place while imagining a run through the woods. The teaching assistant yelled out "Branch"! They ducked. "Scythe!" They dodged. "Stump!" They leaped. They had been doing this for a few weeks, reacting to these three words that signaled three distinct obstacles, when he threw in a new one: "Brook!" Some students, flummoxed, paused. He chastised them: they should be able to react energetically to *any* unexpected utterances, "Even the word *kosmos*! Let your body go, it will react by itself. You are too afraid to make a mistake. The body does not have to act correctly, just interestingly" (Fieldnotes, December 2002).

A week later, after a similar surprise switch in the lexicon of command, one of the students objected that they did not "have time" to respond creatively. They were told: "Your brain should not have to work. The body itself—the impulse, catch the impulse, don't extinguish it." A body must be trained into sensitivity to tune into the possibilities, to capture the whole range of impulses that a word like *kosmos* might trigger.

Instructors used the word *tekst* to signify several things: speech on stage, the trajectory of the script, and the world of texts and intertextual citations, from classics to boulevard romances. To clarify which sense was in play required attending to other cues. For example, instructors might urge student actors to "avoid schematic text and trust the body," while simultaneously instructing them to animate their own body parts as figures who speak to other parts or to "produce text" about the body. Such was a drill for developing sensory attention: a student stood in the middle of a circle, eyes closed as other students approached in turn to offer her their hands. As she took each one, by feeling the fingers she was to name their owners. As she began to work, the teacher cried, "Text! Text! She must formulate information!" He asked her to describe aloud her process of discernment, the details as each came to mind. She began: "This hand, this hand is male. . . . This one is not a man's—these are long nails—but wait, a ring . . . think, think! . . . Not ours . . . male." It took some trial and error for her to produce just the right balance of text versus touch and movement for the drill, but at no time did the acting student indicate that reaching for a book of Pushkin was being called for by the term.

CONFLICTING IDEOLOGIES

Separations of text from not-text, from bodily gesture, from silence, and so forth were neither pure nor consistent. Consider drills demanding that actors verbalize "inner text." For example, a classic task, familiar to nearly any actor in Russia from one's earliest training, is to ask the student simply to enter the practice room and decide where to sit while everyone watches. In our cohort, the first student to give it a try fixed his eyes quickly on a lone, empty chair, walked to it, and sat down. "Not interesting!" judged the master instructor. The student was sent to the corridor to try again, this time to "add text." He returned, uttering a somber: "There is a chair." The master instructor interrupted: "What is this, 'To be, or not to be?! You are acting too schematically," not "reacting in the present moment," merely quoting from Shakespeare without thinking about how to respond to the here and now. He sent the student out to try again, telling him to "concentrate your circle of attention" on the "given conditions" of *this* room. The student reentered: "Hmmm. . . . if I put the chair over there with the other students, then I'll be the only student sitting on a chair . . . but I can't really go sit with the teachers. . . . Hmm, maybe I'll just put it right here in the middle." This time his work was judged an improvement, "more interesting, do you all see now?"

In another warm-up, students were to treat their bodies as new interlocutors. They were to open channels among separate body parts, first creating clusters whom the student should observe and listen to before joining in as just another voice. To begin, students moved about the room while listening for sounds from within, sounds that captured "the body's feelings. Don't force it. Listen more attentively to your body, to how your body talks! . . . There will be counter-action. . . . This way, when you sing and speak, it will be with your body and not merely with your vocal cords" (Fieldnotes, 2003). To rephrase: acting students are not to avoid *all* speaking or writing on stage, but are to avoid enacting "ready-made texts," instead developing their articulations in concert with every other being and thing on stage, including their own bodies, which can also behave unexpectedly. To work with texts and to strategically stage a play in relation to other texts is the director's job, to arrange and orchestrate texts and bodies and objects and to achieve some effect through their resonance. To strike a chord.

GITIS teachers described the differences among the types of labor that produce stage productions in terms of that labor's relationship to text, and instructors often repeated this to actors: "*Ne tekst a* povedenie—*vot osnova nashej shkoly*" (Not text, but *behavior*—that is the base of our school) and "*Nashe delo—shkurnoe*" (*Our* job is under/in the pelt), and thus not for the squeamish, they might add (the last phrase echoing Stalinist and criminal registers, perhaps to signal the appealing danger of their work onstage, which must grapple with the pull of egotism). In every class at GITIS, phrases prescribing how actors ought to relate to words unfurled every day, cropping up also in quotations from master playwrights, from records of famous rehearsals with directors: "A word must ripen and warm before you send it out on the stage," said Aleksandr Kuprin. "As Meyerhold told us, 'Words are just the design on the embroidery canvas.'"

At the beginning of the school year, a list of required readings was taped next to the homeroom door. It included plays, literature, and of course, the writings of Stanislavsky, Mikhail Chekhov, and Meyerhold. At midyear an instructor drew attention to this list during an exercise focused on developing attention to and memory of details in one's immediate environment. He swept his gaze over each student, asking: "How long have you been meeting in this room? Three weeks? *Do* you know every object in it? Look around, what is to the left of the door?" One student responded: "A list of library readings." "And what is on the list?" They tried, one by one, to remember. One claimed to "see clearly" that the list was headed by a certain title, but upon checking, it was not there. The teacher quipped, "She looked but didn't see." Finally, one student admitted that he had "looked at the list but didn't read it." After this scolding, that list was never again referred to during acting classes (the acting students also took lecture courses on the history of theater).

Actors should leave the interdiscursive magic to others, to those trained to sound texts and situations for echoes. Directors, by contrast, learn to play with erudition, to juggle potential audience memories of many texts, to bring actors' work and other production elements into alignment (or interesting discord) with such memories. This division was made explicit one evening around 11:00, when students sprawled across the floor were discussing techniques for breaking conventional stage frames. One asked the teacher how he could *know* when he "was or was not *supposed* to make the fourth wall?" Where to draw such lines, the teacher replied, *can* be a question of genre, but ultimately the actor should "put the wall wherever the director says to."

But while the division was stated and reinforced, it could never be complete; teaching acting as one set of skills and directing as another was sometimes a sociotechnical matter of segregating media and mediators ("speech versus action," "text versus sense," "actors listen to directors") but at other times a matter of uniting them ("body as speech," "texts as energy"). Such seeming inconsistencies do not deflate the spells of theatrical enchantment: to attract and distract attention, as the stage magician knows, requires a palate of possible contrasts: shiny and dark, fast and slow, curved movements and straight, words and papers appearing and then disappearing. Theatrical pedagogy is itself theatrical, as it works through multiple, overlapping, and contradictory circles, stagings that call for quick shifts, as if making wormholes where students could feel categories of mind and body, matter and spirit, text and action, sounds and silence switch charges (this, I argue, is one of the reasons students enjoyed theatrical work so much, even while it made them suffer).

Meta-semiotic labor is socialized at GITIS in ways that reproduce *conflicting* ideologies about communication that are distributed across divisions of labor. Not everyone is enabled to switch among ideologies, but they all must learn enough about them all in order to work together. The institution licenses directors as meta-semiotic and interdiscursive generalists and meta-phatic specialists who mediate in several directions, between actor and script, actors and actors, actors and audience. Their socialization, acting and directing students together, cultivates actors' agility to oscillate in their relationships to signs and materials—to cleave to words and then reject them—a protean capacity that allows directors to direct them, and in many genres. Thus, when a teacher lionized a "classic text" in one breath and then in the next demonized overreliance on "literary schema," it was less a matter of uttering a categorical paradox than of dividing semiotic labors.

Both actor and director must be flexible, able to shift labors, but from different perspectives, in different ways. A directing student will try his or her hand at acting, but acting students hardly ever direct (until, perhaps, years after graduation). Directors need to learn the position of the actor in order to convince or even to manipulate. One exercise for the actors that I observed midway through the first year reinforced these divisions by allowing acting students to have a go at thinking like directors. Separating first by gender, students were to take turns reciting personal ads that they had collected for character studies. They were to listen to each other and to cut in when they "felt an interesting juxtaposition" or "a conflict between texts":

> TEACHER: Here's the game. We ask Julia to read her personal ad [as if] to some concrete addressee. If it fits, you can answer; if not, you can set up a conflict.
>
> STUDENT: Conflict how? I don't get it.
>
> TEACHER: OK, for instance, you read, "Seeking sponsor." So he might answer, "Seeking a girl. I am no sponsor." (Recording, November 4, 2002)

The actors had trouble with this one. After they had tried a few times, the teacher called a stop, reminding them that "behind every ad is a real desire," but what *that* is, ultimately, would be for their directors to help them to figure out. As actors, they should learn to "ask your directors a lot of questions." How *many* questions would vary depending on the director's preferences, so teachers admonished students to pay attention to signs that they were posing "two few questions" or asking "too many." An actor should expect this variance, be alert to accommodating the director, an expectation of deference that again points up the ways constraints on communication arise in and reproduce social hierarchies.

Students are even trained to expect and accept a director's opacity about such decisions for the good of the production. Advice to new directors on how to motivate actors, scattered through canonical masters' rehearsal records and echoed in lessons that I observed, claimed the strategic utility of indirection: "The actor must be gently drawn out. . . . If you say, 'Your psychological state at this moment is fear,' he will give actions that are artificial or exaggerated." In the late Soviet movie *Uspekh* (Success, 1987; dir. Khudjakov), a director leaves Moscow to work in a regional theater. There, he experiments with staging Chekhov's *Seagull* (a play about actors and playwrights) but encounters resistance, even hostility, from the troupe, entrenched in their ways. The film follows him as he brilliantly puzzles out how to manipulate each actor, sparking the reactions and emotions offstage that he needs them to animate onstage. They neither appreciate nor understand his efforts until opening night, when the pieces come together. As directors learn, directing can require keeping actors in the dark, that they *not understand* the production as a whole. Collective creativity is not necessarily egalitarian, and its joint labors, even animated as they are by contradicting ideologies about how language, signs, and media work, can reinforce the principles of hierarchy by showing their spectacular effects.

7. Intuition and Rupture

Remember Hamlet, trying to expose his father's killer? *The play's the thing wherein I'll catch the conscience of the king*. For Hamlet, it was the theatrical frame itself that would serve as technology for intuition: he would watch how his suspect watched, to divine hidden guilt. Play within play, film within play, play within film, films about directors struggling with actors, plays about failed actresses: these genres depict embedded frames as if their layers lure out hidden thoughts and motives, illuminating the shadows of hidden social ties. The generic meta-form itself, the play within a play, lends itself to serving as a technology for intuition for the prince because of the ways it organizes attention to attention. Consider also all the plays and films about making plays or films, which center dramatic conflict around production communications and conflicts, characters searching for authors.

Gordon Craig (1908) dreamed of the *uber marionnette*, the actor-robot who would not rebel. GITIS teachers, however, good Aristotelians, honored the principle of dramatic conflict—and dramatic conflict within the script did not suffice in itself to make good theater, so they constantly repeated the creative need for conflicts between actors and directors. Actors are supposed to push back and directors to complain about actors' stubbornness, vanity, and lack of agility; such conflicts were to be expected, not stifled (even if the director should win). To represent the actor-director relationship as rife with conflict is standard; books and films that do so are popular in Russia, appearing early in the twentieth century with the rise of the auteur director across Europe. With an eye to Socrates, Stanislavksy famously reproduced arguments between his own avatar, a director and his young acolytes. Nikolaj Gorchakov (1954) similarly recollected his own debates with director Evgenij Vakhtangov in dialogue format. Tairov represented his own rehearsals through dialogues and conflicts with actors. Rehearsal accounts multiplied in late Soviet and post-Soviet times, weaving into autobiographies by director-heroes like Yuri Liubimov, Oleg Efremov, Piotr Fomenko, Mark Zakharov, and Leonid Kheifetz. Of all these texts, only a few have made their way into English translation; within Russia they sell well. Nearly all of them involve conflicts that yield creative epiphanies and shifts in perspective.

When actors challenge directorial work, their rebellion itself is supposed to stir the creative process. It is as if the Aristotelian idea of dramatic conflict were transposed into the theatrical divisions of labor, a play nested inside that division such that conflicts between directors and actors generate energy to animate the story. In the curriculum, in key texts, and in sessions of critical advice, *konflikt* figures as a force for creativity. Behind the scenes, in rehearsal and during the process of learning to stage drama, *konflikt* opens perspectives, and demands improvisation. In a pamphlet marking the 120th year since the founding of GITIS in 1878, one rector asserted:

> GITIS should never be regarded as single-minded, single-voiced. . . . [W]e can easily discern different voices, dissenting, doubtful, mutually contradicting. . . . If your aim is to teach someone to be creative, you cannot achieve that without first providing a creative, totally new medium . . . while being in constant dialog with past authority, your own past or someone else's. We might call this a formula of creativity: the more tightly wound the inner spring of creative energy inside the pupil, the more dissatisfied he becomes with his master. . . . GITIS represents this long-standing, venerable theatre tradition of inner discontent and constant lack of stability. (GITIS 1998, 1)[1]

Theater and film projects, as collective endeavors, make struggle tangible in ways that, for example, painting does not (or not often these days; consider the teams who worked under the old masters). Directors cannot pretend to be solitary authors (when they try, actors and technical crews, like any workers, find ways to drag their feet—but less than one might think, for they rarely stop caring about the public outcome, in which their faces are the ones visible).

Forcing actors would be pointless except in the most rigidly choreographed productions: directors must learn to negotiate, convince, cajole, or manipulate, and yes, to argue with, actors. In an informal speech in the fall semester, master instructor and director Heifetz apprised the directing students: "You show up with a play, and you say, 'here is the main event,' and an actor will challenge you: 'But why?'" (Fieldnotes November 9, 2002). He recounted the first play that he had ever directed, at the Soviet Army Theater. The actors had all been given small roles, and several were dissatisfied. They contested his staging of provincial country life, even though they rarely left Moscow, "until I fought back with them."

To spare student directors too much conflict right at the beginning, their very first assignments at GITIS utilized no actors at all, allowing practice with syntheses of media and forms (music plus lighting, lighting plus scenery) before wrangling live people. For example, our cohort's directors for this assignment chose among five watercolors by proto-Cubo-futurist painter Petrov Vodkin: the students were to intuit a story behind the picture and create a corresponding atmosphere using only music and props. Later exercises gradually added actors, as the students developed means to give the actors convincing and compelling directives.

KONFLIKT AESTHETIC

The aesthetics of *konflikt* at GITIS also suffuse work to build theatrical collectives, as responsive assemblages of people and things focusing on sensations and contacts. Think back to the drill with the thread in chapter 2: as the students attend to the thread, they also learn that *maintaining* perfect contact, just right, between tautness and laxness, is impossible (and would be dull). It is better to manage inevitable oscillations, even to roughen their textures; as we ought to know from King Lear or Stanley Kowalski, failures to communicate sharpen dramatic conflict.[2] Conflicts and obstacles: that such sources for artistic enchantment exceed virtuosity alone is among the primary wisdoms imparted at GITIS. Drills focusing on contact and communication also taught about breaks and interruptions, juxtapositions and *kontrapunkt* (counterpoint). For example, a student strikes a pose such that the next can join with a connecting position; after managing this a few times, they were encouraged not simply to *continue* a theme or story, but to strike a *contradiction* to the last pose, to react agonistically with *kontrapunkt*.[3]

Konflikt has long held a central position in European theatrical production and dramaturgy; by Aristotle's definition, conflict is the pivot that makes drama dramatic. Russian literary scholar Propp elaborated on the obstacle, even in pure material forms, as a specific species of fictional conflict. Soviet considerations of what counted as worthy of thematic conflict shifted over time.[4] The "old" battled the "new" in Sergei Eisenstein's *Battleship Potemkin*; by 1960, during Nikita Khrushchev's "Thaw," successful plays featured a post–World War II generation struggling not with their elders, not against pressures of conformity, but to be understood (Houghton 1962).

Thematic *konflikt*—diegetic struggles among characters or world-views—also informs acting and training techniques that juxtapose materials, rhythms, and perspectives. In the early 1960s director and master instructor Maria Knebel' wrote about such techniques in a set of Stanislavsky's drills known as "Memory of Physical Action," intended to sharpen attention even to the most subtle of material obstacles as sources for creative *konflikt*.[5] A student might mime peeling a potato and then peel an actual potato—not in order to perfect the motions, but to hone awareness of those glitches that real potatoes pose, to wean the student of the generalizing forces lurking in the urge to perfection. Confronting any *specific* material object shows the student instead: "[A]ll the little obstacles unavoidably encountered in life when one makes even the smallest action. One object is too small, difficult to grasp, another slips out of your hands, one does not fit another, and so on. Objects stop being obedient: the thread won't slide into the needle, the soap slips, and so on . . . *[such]conflict always sharpens perception*, organizes and directs attention, mobilizes the will, and makes for emotionally saturated, internally dynamic action" (1967, 161). Conflicts constitute dramatic events, they "make for . . . dynamic action." In November 2002 I watched a young woman cut and butter a slice of imaginary bread as the instructor called out missed chances to play conflict: What about butter patties that slip to the floor, or a hard crust that deflects the knife? She was missing the little dramas that engage an audience and thus opportunities to make contact: "You do these pantomimes too schematically! Like an order given by the Party! Without the nuances and details that grab an audience with illusion!" Such events made drama even on the smallest scale: the more obstacles, the more interesting.

The aim of "Memory of Physical Action" is not to fix a standard for mimesis, for perfect representational accuracy. Instead, it is to alert actors to attend to the unpredictable posed by *any specific* material object or body in *any specific* space and time. Such awareness need not await the *failure* of tools or things (pace Heidegger, actually existing matter can resist at any time without detectable malfunction at all); practice in embodied attention to the singularities of materials is key. Conversely, even a reluctant prop or a clumsy acting partner might not restart the habitual inattention of an actor who, limited by stage fright, has not learned to run multiple tracks of attention and becomes too distracted in front of audiences to react to a partner's new gesture. To this end, students were frequently reminded, in every place they inhabited, to always seek something that they had never noticed before: a smudge, a wire, anything. And failing that, to change their own angle of vantage.

ESTRANGEMENT

The agile actor, as Diderot first wrote and as the director Meyerhold articulated often, runs more than one track of awareness at the same time; one of them observes the self. A good actor cannot operate with a one-track mind—even Stanislavsky wrote against full submersion (which some viewed as a draining sort of self-hypnotism) as being sublime to experience but dull to the audience. Actors and psychics practice similar drills to perfect juggling multiple rays of attention (although it is usually the psychics who stage demonstrations, reciting one hundred phone numbers from memory, blindfolded, while shooting an arrow at a target and playing piano with their feet). It takes not only practice, but also a willingness to hold disjunctures among perspectives within consciousness. Some genres run on such disjuncture: for the Vakhtangov Theater, the actor might play Turandot as if Turandot were played by yet another character, a "critical actor" who is nested inside (or worn over) the actor. Enacting such a-realist conflicts between actor and character has long been a favorite device on Moscow stages—even in Stalin's time, especially in fantastical and children's genres.

In Russian twenty-first-century theatrical practice, the term *konflikt* covers similar territory as has the term *ostranenie* ("defamiliarization," "estrangement," "alienation"). In a 1917 essay titled *Technique in Art*, Russian formalist critic Viktor Shklovsky elaborated on this coinage, arguing that artists deploy *ostranenie* when their work impedes habitual perception, makes usual modes of perception difficult. An artful poem slows the reader down; she does not simply recognize printed words, she re-cognizes their forms, their represented sounds (perhaps even questioning why they sound as if intrinsically belonging to high-class or lowbrow registers).

In the decades before the formalists published, Meyerhold had been drawing from grotesque master of fantastic literature E.T.A. Hoffman to develop a theory of estrangement (Jestrovic 2006; Possner 2016). Hoffman had identified a quality that he called "familiar-alien" (Meyerhold translates the German into Russian as *znakoma-chudo*) in seventeenth-century paintings in which musician-birds perch in tree branches while peasants dance below, as well as in drawings of saints' temptations in which little devils blow anus-flutes or fire from gun-barrel noses. Voicing ideas later amplified by Shklovsky (and also by Meyerhold's student Eisenstein, who modified stage juxtaposition into film montage, and by Brecht, who wrote about alienation devices after conversations in Moscow), Meyerhold wrote about the power of grotesque contrasts to provoke mental effort, to animate sentience: "The grotesque, in seeking the supernatural, binds opposites into a synthesis, crafting a picture that leads the observer to attempt to solve an unfathomable riddle. . . . Is this not the task of the stage grotesque, to constantly hold the observers in a condition of double relation to scenic action, which changes it movements through contrasting strokes?" (Meyerhold, *Balagan* 1912; see translation in Meyerhold 1969).

As a defamiliarizing impulse, an estranging prod, and a little shock of alienation to generate fresh thinking, *ostranenie* is often figured in terms of animation and sudden motility. At the turn of the twentieth century, like Stanislavsky and others, Shklovsky was concerned with refreshing the senses, counteracting the automatic responses and dulled instincts of industrial life.

For ways to refresh human energy, Stanislavsky turned to French psychology and Indic yoga; Shklovsky found a means to reanimate perception close at hand, in Russian literature—and not only in the avant-garde. In Shklovsky's view, Aleksandr Pushkin prodded at poetic expectations a century before the Russian futurist poets would take up grammatical deconstruction as political mission. And unlike other structural thinkers (Marx, Saussure, Freud), who aligned formal systems with the habitual and the unconscious, Shklovsky saw that even familiar forms and systems can be handled in ways to de-automatize thought and sensation, "to make the stone stony" ([1917] 1965, 2). *Ostranenie* need not destroy in order to work—play with perspective can activate the mind: if you can't move the mountain, look at it from a different window. As his very first example, Shklovsky offered a passage from Lev Tolstoy that deconstructs property relations by depicting the thoughts of a horse, who ponders the ways humans use possessive pronouns.

The concept that Shklovsky defined for literary criticism had already been theorized in theatrical circles: at the end of the nineteenth century Meyerhold was experimenting with ways to defamiliarize, and in 1907 he wrote that the realist theater had forgotten how much it relied on conventions, pretending to be raw representation. Mainstream theater, instead of battling with materials, with physical words, props, and bodies, had come to *rely* on them; orchestra pit and lights already separated stage dialogue from audience murmurs, dampening the possibility of the latter interrupting. Meyerhold dreamed of a theater capable of more surprises, with protruding prosceniums and revealed carpentry, movable platforms and pulleys. Treating language as matter, too, Meyerhold spoke of theatrical work through metaphors of industrial craft, much as his friends among the futurist poets did, treating language as matter, as Mayakovsky did in his

1926 essay "How to Make Verse," published in several Soviet papers that year, such as *Leningrad Pravda* (see also Lemon 1991). But his actors were not to become mindless cogs or robots; they were to analyze gestures, to break them down in uncomfortable ways, to hone the capacity to attend to ways the body engages with spaces, objects, and other bodies. The actor was to sharpen awareness (here Meyerhold owes Diderot) of simultaneously being both artist-subject and subject-object-character, to develop the ability to *zerkalit'* (reflect a mirror upon) the self.

Meyerhold's biomechanical exercises (e.g., in which students practiced patterns of stylized, acrobatic moves linked to a goal, like "shooting a bow") were practiced as forms of *ostranenie*. Their odd movements and artificial sequences disrupt, complicate, and slow down habitual embodiments, replacing them with other conventions to contrast with the usual. His actors learned in this way to re-cognize not only the stoniness of a stone, but also *the relations* among hands that feel stone and to other actors and the audience. In biomechanical exercises, strange movements aid the study of *rakursy* (from the French *raccourci* for shortcut or foreshortening), searching for angles that change perception, perhaps by shifting relative positions onstage. Their repetition is not to automatize, but to increase reflexive sensitivity. Meyerhold's biomechanics, far from instilling simple units of motion, empty, robotic repetitions, aimed for something like what Jakobson would later call the poetic function, only with the body, the ability to comment with the body about the body.

Many artists hoped during the first years after the Revolution that shaking aesthetic conventions might change minds, change the world, but not all of them were socialists or revolutionaries. And *ostranenie*, as Shklovsky defined it, did not remain the sole property of the avant-garde. Its principles continued to run through Soviet theatrical education (at times by changing vocabulary, avoiding the formalist brand), just as Meyerhold's sense of the animating potential of montage continued to influence even after his execution in 1940, through his student Eisenstein (and through the latter's students in turn). Within places like GITIS, people never stopped playing with shifting proscenia and angles, and after Meyerhold's rehabilitation in the mid-1950s, such play became increasingly commonplace, even on Moscow main stages.

TECHNOLOGIES AGAINST INTUITION

I am enchanted by the ways theatrical artists talk about *konflikt*. Their words recall the hopes for estrangement as a means to generate contingencies and juxtapositions, thereby animating new thoughts, even debates, at the very least renewing or engaging creative energies. They devote lifetimes to techniques that will capture the forces of counterpoint, whether to generate epiphany or simply to stage events that feel "interesting!" or even "*Chudo!*" ("miraculous, enchanting"). There is a problem, however, in ascribing too much to estrangement itself: there are degrees and directions of estrangement, to different effects. Clams about the efficacy of estrangement were developed at particular historical intersections of sociopolitical conditions and sociotechnical networks, where people pushed and pulled "[t]he historical metamorphosis of estrangement from a technique of art to an existential art of survival and a practice of freedom and dissent" (Boym 2005, 1).[6]

Attempts to estrange conventional barriers separating audience from actor can look similar while invoking different goals or playing out different results. Russian proscenium breakers Meyerhold and Evreinov, for example, both confronted dominant realisms by bringing spectators into the play, but *not* to the same ends (see also Boym 2005; Clark 1995): one aimed to reach social equality, while the other sought to reach higher metaphysical awareness. Debates about what art might change or ought to change shift ground from, say, 1930s Berlin to 1970s New York City.

Not all instances of *ostranenie* rock the world. We might hope that baring the device through fresh juxtaposition or montage or by breaking the frame or revealing conditions of production[7] will motivate new perceptions of the taken for granted, the conventional, or the habitual. When they have, it remains difficult to say which alienation device concretely nudged which social transformations. An estrangement can focus audience awareness on the aesthetic conventions at hand or draw attention to some habitual perception, and yet not draw attention to all the material channels and social structures that funnel relations suffusing each encounter with art. An estrangement technique can refresh perception along one channel, even while it floods or jams others. A case in point is Nikolai Evreinov's staging of the storming of the Winter Palace, for which he deployed masses of actor-spectators to disrupt conventions of scale, perspective, frame, and angle. While the 1920 event thereby made a statement *about* mass political agency to some audiences, many participants later recounted the performance as if it had been the Revolution itself (Clark 1995).

The shock of estrangement can even block, rather than spur, reflexive awareness. Stage magicians know this, but so do many agents of government, those who work out how to estrange one set of perceptions in order to install another.[8] In the interrogation room or on the stage, the spotlight is differently disorienting, differently displacing the same cup of tea. Cristina Vatulescu, writing on "police aesthetics," describes estrangement during Romanian interrogations of the socialist period. To make her point, she quotes from the 1963 CIA manual *Kubark Counterintelligence Interrogation*, assuming not so much direct and recent transnational influence on interrogation technologies as a logic shared from longer ago, whereby the interrogator works to undermine the interrogatee's sense of knowing anything: "The aim of the Alice in Wonderland, or confusion technique, is to confound the expectations and conditioned reactions of the interrogatee . . . not only to obliterate the familiar but to replace it with the weird . . . pitch, tone, and volume of the interrogators' voices are unrelated to the import of the questions" (2010, 178) The goal in interrogation estrangement is not to refresh sensations or spark creative response, but to shock and traumatize by manipulating sign forms, setting pitch, volume, and tone against reference. The point is not to draw attention to conventions that scaffold perspectives—and thereby social hierarchies. Alice in Wonderland technologies may detach the subject from his or her usual intuitions, but in order to animate the interrogator's logic, as in false confession.

Interrogators break out details from past narratives in ways not so unlike the way Meyerhold broke up classic dramatic scripts, staging them in a new order. Even before such an encounter, state agents need not organize "personal files" according to any particular allegation. The files fill up, as Vatulescu also notes, "without order": the name of a first dog, favorite ice cream, a hair ribbon, a theater ticket. Such a collection, before it is mobilized, can seem hapless or harmless: in 1997, one friend recounted to me how in 1983, in her early teens, after a small demonstration in Moscow against *American* nuclear weapon systems, she had been taken for a *beseda* (a "chat," euphemism for "interrogation"). She and her fellow arrestees, smoking in the holding area, had been handed a "lame questionnaire": "What soccer team do you like?" "What is your favorite subject?" She remarked that this experience had taught her "how badly the KGB was organized—it was a cardboard tiger."

All the same, montages of such detail can later arm the interrogator to bewilder the person interrogated, to simulate the state's omniscience, and to cast doubt on relationships that seem to have supplied the hair ribbon or pet names. Much as in cold reading, in which the client fills in details and comes to imagine that it is the psychic one who sees the connections among them, the interrogatee, faced by the interrogator even with unordered sets of detail, can imagine she knows their connections, asking, "How do they know this?" when in fact they do not, not yet. A key difference—primed by structures for policing rather than those for staging of telepathy—is also the enticements prodding the interrogatee to ask herself: "*Who gave* them this detail?" Here estrangement methods are tactical, neither mystical nor pedagogical, intended to plant paranoia, even to stimulate future counter-betrayals.

FRAGMENT AND WHOLE, BREAK TO CONTACT

Across Russia, historical narratives of rupture have torqued the ways people have taken up or rejected breaks in frame, montage, and other estrangement devices. Consider a few contrasts in ways that "fragments" have been made and been put to use. As scholars of colonialism have perceived elsewhere, there are fragments that challenge not only the idea of wholeness but the very idea of the "fragment" itself (for if there were no identified wholes, what would "fragments" be pieces of)? (see also Pandey 1992).

Much juxtaposition requires a recognizable break, pieces cut to be reassembled. Of all possible means of estrangement, juxtaposition was theater director Meyerhold's preferred; to achieve it, he split up existing texts into new units that he could rearrange. For example, he broke up Ostrovsky's classic *The Forest* from five acts into a montage of thirty-three "attractions" that no longer told a story, but instead resonated with each other as with conditions offstage (something like ringing intertextual chords, only with a technical focus on breaking out notes, rather than seeking them, and resonating with newspapers and events on the street, with less poetry). He did the same later with Gogol's *Inspector General*. Decades before thinkers such as Mikhail Bakhtin and then Erving Goffman would break down the ideal of the individual speaker to distribute utterances (or depictions of utterances) across texts and situations, Meyerhold scattered script and gesture across human actors and materials—as commedia dell'arte actors had done—repeating the words of visible prompters or using a puppet to depict the author peeking out from behind a curtain.

Techniques of disjuncture—like other methods for estrangement—are not alone sufficient to reanimate perception, to catalyze social awareness, or to animate agency;[9] they can renew perception on one level while dulling on another. Moreover, making breaks at quick tempo can create the *illusion* of animation, seem to motorize or energize, like stop-motion in cartooning. There is a fountain in the middle of Detroit Metro Airport whose jets converge at the center in smooth unity, giving the impression of solid and still tubes of translucent matter. Then, at computer-controlled intervals, the jets are interrupted to produce Morse code dashes of water and dots of air—

now the water appears *finally* to move, even though it has been moving all along.[10] Here disjuncture reveals movement, even while producing the illusion that it is movement that is new, not the breaks.

Conversely, the sense that a whole is broken is not always produced by fracture from natural continua. "Brokenness" is like dirt in Mary Douglas's (1978) sense; to break is to chisel or to startle "matter out of place," acts that require not only ideological maintenance and naturalizing repetition (habitus), but also the occasional recognitions of estrangement. Those same institutions that regulate entry at points for auditions or for showing bureaucratic papers both connect social assemblages and fracture pieces for estrangement, pieces that can be deployed in technologies both for and against intuition.

By extension, the conditions that set up judgments of the "broken" versus "whole"—that set them up as if they are natural, as if apprehended by intuition rather than by aesthetic means or through practical material habits—differ historically. We need not cross ostensibly hermetic cultural circles or national boundaries to encounter alternate motivations or working practices for claiming either condition. In my adopted home state of Nebraska, my mother's husband works constantly on a hay thrasher—one that she terms "broken." For him, since he first made its acquaintance in 1942, that thrasher has never quite constituted a single, individuated object to be broken; it is a technical node that has always demanded his bricolage, work that has evolved from asking around town to scanning Craigslist for similar thrashers made with similar enough parts. Whether thrashers are "broken" or should be replaced by new, "whole" ones is a point of gentle conflict. My mother sees strewn pieces and parts as signaling class: "We look like the Clampetts."[11] However, for him the world of objects is always already overlapping across materials that are more or less compatible to adaptation; to oppose broken to whole is, to him, a silly, useless binary. He describes an encounter with neighbor boys, laughing while quoting their description of a turbine roof ventilator: "'It's broken!' *Broken*? No, pay attention, look here, you can notice: 'This here piece is warped.' You look there, and then you can think, 'What can I use to shape another flange to fit it?' Then you go in the garage and get a Folger's can and . . . ."

My relatives draw on different expectations for durability and different allegiances to the ideal of wholeness. They also draw from differing experiences of material infrastructures and different ideological and moralizing ways to link materials and aspirations: Are the fragments signs of low class or of ingeniousness? To this farmer and former factory worker, material scenes that whisper "breakdown" to us city folk (for my mother returned to the country after being raised in a city, the first generation, her father and mother the only ones to leave the Appalachians, where all the aunts and uncles and cousins remained) speak of possibilities in a world *always ready for* thinking with and making with, in permanent flux for bricolage. Pace Martin Heidegger, people must pattern relationships to tools in certain ways before their "breakdown" makes sense *as* breakdown. How *those* relations come about and what they enable next are the more pressing questions. As anthropologists have learned, taking notes from thinkers from Franz Boas to Michel Foucault, people constantly break down and separate phenomena that could otherwise also be apprehended as continuous—to name colors, to segment sounds—and to claim separate "races," "languages," "selves," or even "events." Conditions must converge in still more ways for a perception of a break to bind to expectations such as purity, durability—or wholeness. In social worlds where durability of matter is not an expectation, broken tools do not force estrangement, and its inspirations follow other contingencies.

Efforts to maintain wholeness against brokenness—to bridge broken intertexts or to heal gaps between generations—thrive not because textual canons really make wholes or because generations naturally adhere, but because specific, historically motivated ideologies, such as capitalism versus socialism, charge wholes and fractures with moral power. Worlds that must never touch govern peoples who must not make contact. Like most ideologies when aligned with political goals to separate and rule, these become circular: contra the lessons of logicians, circular logic is all too often found beautiful in its repetitions, homologies across material structures standing as natural truths that mask the histories of built conditions (Bourdieu 1977): Why do water lines not reach this village or that town? The answer shoots back from people who have never lived in such places, be they in the United States or in Russia: "What for? Just look at how dirty they are; they would just steal the pipes!" The circles of such logics eat their own tails.

GEOPOLITICS IN BREAKDOWN

The stakes for defining what counts as whole and what as broken are high. The last century can be narrated through points of breakdown and ruin: real sufferings and material destructions have been told both from ideological perspectives that minimize them as well as from those that mythologize them. At the same time, the globe's civil wars, world wars, and proxy wars have left bullet holes, graves, and empty seats tangible to some populations and not to others. In just one set of contrasts, World War II took

400,000 American military lives; in school in the 1970s we were also told that this war lifted the United States out of the Great Depression, and that military manufacturing had triggered a burst of production and prosperity that lasted through the 1960s. Some kids were skeptical, but the losses were small enough, the destruction was far enough away. It was only by walking in Soviet cities in the 1980s that I saw traces of the war that had burned swaths of stunning devastation through Soviet territories, buildings still to be reconstructed, millions of civilians killed in the sieges and air raids, millions dead at the front still mourned. Americans suffered much less infrastructural damage and immensely fewer war casualties—at least twenty times fewer than those in the USSR. Even during the war the United States learned of sieges and genocide secondhand, if at all, and later through the words of camp survivors.[12] Twenty-five years after the end of the war, USSR firsthand, visceral knowledge of the war receded as the veterans and partisans passed away, although those born during the evacuations and bombings remain, as do those who were raised in the rubble. In Western Europe the U.S.-funded Marshall Plan built the West German autobahn, among other things, but no such deus ex machina from without came to heal the Soviet infrastructure. Repairs took decades.

Narratives of travelers to the USSR and Russia all too often stress material lacks (usually by unstated comparison to life in a green American suburb or quaint urban street). Worse, they portray these lacks as evidence that all promises of Soviet modernism were inherently bankrupt. These stories omit consideration of, among other thing, the long-term effects of war.

Soviet people related to luxury goods in ways much more complicated than Cold War American accounts depicted. (see Dunham 1976; Fehérváry 2002; Crowley and Reid 2010)—similarly careful work is still needed to understand material culture in response to the destruction of WWII. After the war, devastated infrastructure and diversion of resources to rebuild the military contributed to the famous snarls in Soviet distribution. By the 1970s it had become easy for socialism's detractors to criticize the state for easily broken consumer goods, the latter serving as material proof of the system's failure (Fehérváry 2013). But certain conditions remain overlooked: those European countries treated as a baseline for material normalcy either suffered much less war damage or received rebuilding funds and labor from the United States.

By the early twenty-first century the ideologies of ruin were shifting yet again. Two decades of marketization since 1991 had not spread glossy capitalist ease evenly across Russia; material objects and infrastructures broke down as much as ever. Hospital fires, plane crashes, and submarine disasters continued. Some blamed the ruins on the Soviet infrastructure,

which *was* built quickly, not planned to sustain twenty-first-century population growth or energy demands. Others blamed a supposedly passive
Russian populace, inured to tragedies. A small minority protested that special interests had been diverting resources that the socialist state had once
expended (e.g., to mitigate yearly freezing and thawing of pipes) and argued
that it was during the 1990s—*not only* during socialism—that the government stopped investing such funds and labor, and commercially minded
former bureaucrats took over maintenance. In this space, violent film and
stage genres, from the *chernukha* (dark naturalism) in the 1980s and 1990s
to the New Drama of the 2000s, proved both resonant and controversial.

Material breakdowns can never be fully understood as local; too many of
the structures of feeling and the ideological valences that embed them for
experience rely on comparison. By the time the twenty-first century was
under way, it had become clear to some that America had not won the Cold
War in 1991; rather, it had managed to evade exposure of modernist technical failures a bit longer. It was later that images of American collapse traveled
to the former socialist world; like other tourists, Americans included,
Russians saw the "ruin porn" depicting American cities from Detroit to New
Orleans. Socialist matter, it turned out, was not the only sort to degrade.
Material distinctions of quality, once imagined to distinguish socialist from
capitalist worlds, had lost their sharpness. The tendency of *all* matter to shift
state, to change under temperature changes or through contact with biomaterial, transcends any particular political or economic system, even one that
understands "breaks" as unexpected or contingent "events."

Philosophers, sociologists, and avant-garde artists, from Mikhail Bakunin
to the Sex Pistols, have hailed "creative destruction" (Ackerman and
Puchner 2006) as both a clearing of the ground for building anew and a
source for insights born of estrangement.[13] But again, the idea that to sun-
der parts is a technique to rouse consciousness (to awaken a drive for freedom, to unmask the patriarchy) gained followers in a world of competing
territorial powers. To those looking from an imperial vantage, breakdown
signals a return to raw chaos. But their ruptures are already cooked; to
experience a tool or structure *as broken* requires commitment to seeing the
world as separate sets of already claimed and bounded wholes (a culture, the
nation, the highway system).

DEANIMATED ANIMATION

For a break to estrange or to (re)animate, still other conditions must be met.
In a world of wholes, breaking can both animate and deanimate. Russians

have been typecast both as revolutionary avatars of destructive creativity (see Clark 1995) and as robotic, totalitarian automaton soldiers. Roma have also been doubly typecast through similar tropes depicting them both as avatars of freedom and as bodies empty of will, programmed by nature to dance or to wander. Black people in the United States face a similar wall of tropes that align freedom and slavery with animation and deanimation (see Ngai 2005).

To follow a few strands of ideologies that invest material breaks with meaning or agency, I turn to representations made in the United Kingdom and in the United States, both of which deanimate people by reanimating objects isolated as broken. Not incidentally, they do so as they impute belief in occult, monstrous, or ideologically lurid forces to others. One is a documentary filmed in Russia, and the other is a fiction film made and set in the United States. Both arrange and animate the broken to automatize people and can only do so by presupposing that humans move or think only by individual, internally generated energies—anything else leads to depictions of people drained of energy, existing without aim, puppetlike.[14] The British project purports to objectively document and even honor Soviet research on bodily reanimation, rocketry, space flight, and intergalactic communication.[15] All the same, the documentary manages to denigrate, framing subjects against a montage of broken objects and layering them under ironic voice-over. The American horror film sets its violence within squalor and decay, implying a materialist critique of capitalist, industrial labor relations before swerving instead to hint of immaterial but murderous forces, machine habits left behind after factories have closed, possessing the bodies of unemployed workers once animated by assembly lines.

In 2011 the BBC produced a documentary on the influence of Russian cosmism on Soviet rocket design and space travel, titled *Knocking on Heaven's Door*. The film sustains a mood of gently astonished condescension, alternating with wonder that fantastical dreams actually thrived in Soviet times, yielding productive advances in rocket science and communications research. The narrator claims to take us behind "the razzmatazz" of stage celebrations of Yuri Gagarin (the first human in space) and on a "strange journey into a Russian world where mysticism and science merge, and nothing is certain, not even death." These words appear over scenes of young women lighting candles before icons, then we cut to a lid being lifted from a cryogenic container in which, we are to know, deceased clients have paid to store their heads. The narration and camera work betray snobbery towards people who ostensibly lived in a vacuum, without knowledge, behind the Iron Curtain, yet bravely managed under repression to mystically reanimate the universe with brainwaves and UFOs. The film works to localize Russia to the extreme, as if the rest of the industrialized world had not dreamed similar dreams, sometimes in competition with the USSR. The documentary host interviews Daniel Medvedev, representative for a small "transhumanist" company that preserves brains and bodies for future reanimation. While the camera pans the location, just outside Moscow on country roads, the host quips upon approach, "Not exactly a gateway to paradise." Editors layer a seemingly real-time whisper (in fact dubbed) over a shot inside the lab, panning across piles of metal, bits of wood, and plastic containers: "Funny guy, refers to them as 'patients'." Adds the host: "Outside, it was like the set of some dystopic movie."

The objects on the screen distract from Medvedev's words about uploading souls in the future (motifs that would not long afterward structure U.S. productions such as *Battlestar Galactica* and *Avatar*). Montage points instead to materials in disarray, as if to claim these images as the real technologies for intuiting what is really going on here, thus animating materials to speak, elevating their agency to do so over Medvedev's. This move is ironic from the perspective of cosmism, the philosophy that inspires the transhumanists, which posits that the whole universe, all matter, is always alive: conditions such as life and death, broken and whole, are all temporary. In case we miss the BBC's point, the voice-over continues to undermine Medvedev's words expressing the dream of a future classless world, in which all will thrive: "It would be a world *of* rich, healthy people, not *for* rich, healthy people." Purrs the narrator, "That's revisionism for you," over an outdoor shot of empty blue water jugs, an old radiator leaning on a refrigerator, pots and lids around a metal table, sponges and a bottle of dish soap, a rooster visible behind bent chicken wire. A mess? Or tools caught mid-motion?

Russian-made news and documentaries cover similar topics and even film similar material arrays of objects. Some also use montage to frame and define people through relations to broken objects—fiction classics (e.g., Tarkovsky's *Stalker*, 1979) did this, as did much of the 1990s *chernukha*. Unlike the BBC filmmakers discussed above, however, Russophone makers of recent documentaries of the mystical, occult, and paranormal do not. For example, in one episode of *Battle of the Psychics*, contestants were interviewed in the vestibule of an apartment building in front of broken, graffiti-marked mailboxes. Such mailboxes certainly contrast, as Muscovites often themselves remark, to the genteel, clean decor inside the apartments—but nothing in the camera work used the mailboxes to reframe the story in terms of systemic ideological failures, nor was the camera work used to undermine the speakers.

Compare the BBC deanimation of people by association with broken things to that which unfolds in the 1974 horror classic *The Texas Chainsaw Massacre*. Both films say more about dominant ideologies linking materials, morality, class, and capitalism than they do about their respective subjects—in *Texas Chainsaw*, about the American working classes especially. This horror film lives on, by the way, as a familiar figure pointing to transgressions of right living in American pathologization of poverty as "squalor," as if broken things signal frightening personality disorders rather than broader relations.[16] Citations to this film pop up throughout popular culture, in reality shows such as *Hoarders*, in which participants liken their grandmother's rooms piled high with Tupperware to "old horror films like *Texas Chainsaw Massacre*."[17]

Most broken of all in *Texas Chainsaw Massacre* is the murderous, mute character called Leatherface, who animates his chosen instrument of death, the chainsaw, another thrumming monster. Or is Leatherface its puppet? His depraved "white trash" kin, we learn, are workers left idle when the old slaughterhouse turned off its lights. The slaughterhouse machines went still years ago, but their energy perversely continues to automatize and reanimate the old workers. While they have broken the factory down for parts, appropriating freezers and meat hooks the better to butcher unsuspecting teenagers, they are not agents; they merely carry on the labor the factory trained them to perform, its pieces (once means of production) still infusing them with a kind of instinctual second nature, mere living puppets (on why even stage puppets are, in fact, never merely passive, see Barker 2017).

The film compels disgust for the material experiences of labor in the United States, projecting fears of class warfare, of the working poor rising in murderous revenge. In both *Texas Chainsaw* and the BBC documentary, images of broken machinery or material disarray animate occult figures, evoking class warfare and the war against communism, neither of which, it seems, is over.

Within Russia, material disorder and poverty do not connect to decades of slasher film imagery (this is one genre that Soviet censorship definitively opposed). In cities that face the challenges of the permafrost line, where rust and weather beat hard on metal parts, more common than reactions of horror are expressions of pride in resourcefulness: a little duct tape, and we are on the road, like magic! There is a scene in the Russian blockbuster vampire film *Night Watch* (2004) in which the leader of the good guys (scruffy shape-shifters who run the energy utilities on old equipment) grabs a roll of duct tape and straps his head to the head of his scout, eye to eye, to create and hold a telepathic channel, to see what trouble is coming (from the sleek, shiny-new-car-driving bad guys).

In Russia (as in the United States), rejecting or avoiding objects deemed insufficiently new can be read as immature, as being too squeamish. And yet those who take such a stance may be increasing: celebrity psychic M., one of the youngest contestants on the first season of *Battle*, was often an outlier for the ways she spoke about objects put to use in the trials. In one episode, contestants were asked to distinguish which of two apartments in the same building had been the scene of a brutal murder. One was layered with decades' worth of Soviet-style furniture, wallpaper, rugs, and light fixtures. The other was newly tiled, painted white, with chrome fixtures, appliances, and an Ikea sofa—Spartan, monochrome "Euro-decor." The older contestants found the first apartment "cozy," "holding good memories." Only called it creepy. As it turned out, the murder had occurred in the new and glossy apartment; the blood had been cleaned up and the damage erased in the remodeling.

ENCHANTED WHOLES

In some cases, to disaggregate, to break and reconnect—as in film montage—serves less to animate particular beings than to rouse those abstract spirits imagined to drive nations or masses. German filmmaker Werner Herzog does such work in *Bells from the Deep: Faith and Superstition in Russia* (1993). A section in the middle of the film combines thespian with occult glamour: the camera sweeps along a narrow red carpet, cutting along the edges of polished stage boards. People filing past have lined up dozens of bottles, plastic and glass, large and small, labeled Klinskoe beer and Pepsi soda, all holding tap water for Alan Chumak to charge with cosmic energy. The camera cuts to pan a multitude of faces, people with arms raised up, palms facing forward. Chumak begins to speak, telling the crowd to imagine, "as if you are straining to hear over a bad telephone connection." Then the camera rests behind his silhouette. Chumak raises his arms wide and begins a gestural conductor's dance over the bottles while the people watch silently.[18] Herzog has superimposed over the crowd, with mouths still, a Russian church choir, with the sound of the song "*Pomiluj Gospodi, pomiluj Gospodi*" [Lord, have mercy], a montage that recasts audience as congregation, transforming Chumak into choirmaster and priest, making holy water. *Bells from the Deep* was marketed and reviewed as a documentary, but Herzog calls it his most effective visual poem. Like a poem, it juxtaposes pieces that echo—bits of scenery with props, sounds with signs, faces with objects—in ways that he feels authentically convey the deep mystery of Russia.

Herzog readily allows that some of the pieces were his own inventions. In the section that gives the film its name, his voice narrates figures crawling across the frozen Lake Svetlojar, telling us that they want to peer below, to catch sight of broken church spires of the lost town of Kitezh, said to have been submerged in the thirteenth century, like Atlantis or Avalon. It turns out that when Herzog arrived in the winter to begin filming on location: "I wanted to get shots of pilgrims crawling around on the ice trying to catch a glimpse of the lost city, but as there were no pilgrims around, I hired two drunks from the next town and put them on the ice. One of them has his face right on the ice and looks like he is in very deep meditation. The accountant's truth: he was completely drunk and fell asleep, and we had to wake him at the end of the take" (Cronin and Herzog 2003, 252).

Here, too, the director lays a track of choral music over outstretched arms and hands, animating a sleeping body as if reaching for communion through the ice. We can acknowledge the poetic virtuosity, the appeal to "deep mystery," as an appeal that some Russians gravitate to, even as a moral lodestar (see Pesmen 2000). Unfortunately, appeals to beautiful or mysterious national essences have fortified refusals—in many states—to extend basic infrastructure and security to, for example, people like the Roma. However, to turn a critical eye on uses of juxtaposition is complicated, as Boym (2005) has noted, by the ways techniques for *ostranenie* have become associated with enlightenment, liberty, and creativity. Herzog animates a landscape to depict opacity by manufacturing bits of footage before the montage has even begun; his pieces are cut not from a whole, but to comprise an imagined unity.

These tendencies are not immanent in estrangement itself; there is more evidence to demonstrate that they have been baked in, have come to seem natural semiotic affordances through historical encounters that enveloped artists' projects.

PERSPECTIVES

Avant-garde techniques—like any others—can serve repressive as well as liberatory ends. The original surrealist movement, among others, wed aesthetic commitment to anticolonial political conviction, arguing that Europe's forms of rule and conquest, like its art forms, were constituted by linear realism. To overturn them, the surrealists championed art from the colonies, believing that the native peoples had retained open channels to "wild

FIGURE 7.1.   Salvador Dali, *Slave Market with Disappearing Bust of Voltaire,*
1940.

thought," their art embedded in ritual and community, maintaining mystical roots that the West had poisoned. Surrealists, like many in the avant-
garde, thus laid claim to modernism and primitivism at the same time in an
aesthetic of associative symbolism, like dreams, they claimed, which might
bring us into contact with the recently discovered subconscious.

Surrealism aims to juxtapose "two more or less [distant] realities"
(Reverdy [1918] 1975). Many sorts of modernist montage and collage play
with incongruities in scale or perspective; surrealism in particular challenges
viewers to see such incongruities simultaneously as figure and as ground in
a symmetry that mirrors the political claim, demanding attention to perspectives. There is no negative space beyond perspectives in the plural, so
perception must keep shuttling—it is as if the viewer holds open more than
one channel for information at once, and as if the painted beings or faces in
both figure and ground are capable of taking perspectives themselves.

In 1925 the French surrealists declared furious opposition to empires,
claiming alliance with anticolonial political movements, endorsing negri-
tude in the 1930s and Algeria in the 1950s. Surrealists exhorted like-minded
artists and poets to channel the voices of imperial subjects into a politics
that would undermine the supposedly clear vistas of panoptic imperial

FIGURE 7.2. London World's Fair, Canada Exhibit, 1851. This drawing depicts viewers walking among exhibitions, suggesting possibilities for them to notice the perspectives of other walking viewers.

vision. Surrealists hoped to catalyze alternatives to imperial display, to undermine both old realism and skeptical, rationalizing modernism.

And yet in championing and claiming unconscious energies among colonized peoples, even in spurning the panoptic fantasy of transparent rule, the surrealists continued other imperial ways of looking: orientalizing juxtapositions of seemingly incongruous objects or ontological realms already ran through imperial dreams of extension.[19] Imperial aesthetics never did, in fact, keep purely to linear logics or sweeping objective perspectives, and also juxtaposed realities, oscillating between figure and ground. To be sure, World's Fairs' competitive displays of political and economic hegemony favored ethnographic naturalism, and the realism of material detail certainly dominated within single dioramas that re-created households or rituals.[20] To attend a World's Fair, however, was never a matter of gazing just at one diorama, but of moving about among *many* of them. The fairs were spaces to watch other visitors who were also moving among the frames that marked individual exhibits.

Postcards of single exhibits depicted viewers not only taking in a model of another world (a future world) from some panoptic position, but seeing how others see.

FIGURE 7.3. Peer at those peering into the future among other lookers.
New York World's Fair, 1939.

The viewers at the dioramas' edges suggest multiple angles; even more, who is viewer of whom is vulnerable to shifting and oscillation. This oscillation, in this case a quick switching across angles afforded by juxtaposition, is not, after all, what *makes* radical art radical. An effort of perception must be sustained, —and by more social forces than aesthetic forms or individual will. To see and to unsee may require effort, a learned oscillation of sensation (arguably more effort than to smell and to unsmell), but it can foster the opposite of revolutions, habituating persons to unsee sustaining labors, to identify a space as, for instance, all male or purely white.[21] As we have seen, work to create or claim communicative contact deploys similar sensory oscillations (the heard and the unheard, the taut and the loose, the clear and the jammed)— but so too does work to create gaps. Moreover, many of the most misleadingly Russophobic accounts of events in Russia depend on a trope of large-scale oscillations in historical forms; this enables many to convince themselves that they understand Putin and thus all of Russia's policy interests because, they are told, the current head of state reverbs from Stalin's time.

Journalist Peter Pomerantsev, in *Nothing Is True and Everything Is Possible* (2014), confesses to being enchanted by such readings while also insisting that Russian communications and media are best described as perversions, a kind of surreal approach to facts. By the book's end, however, he admits that the very media techniques under fire in Russia were developed in the United Kingdom, not in Moscow. Now you see it; now you don't. Indeed, some of the press tactics that Americans objected to during the 2016 presidential campaigns were blamed on Russian influence, but few are aware of specific tactics for undermining local news developed decades earlier by the U.S. State Department and the Radios. The ways the U.K., U.S., Russian, and other powers have divided communicative labors that block, open, and disorder news channels remain unseen.

BAD BREAKS

In autumn 2002 at GITIS, our first-year cohort devised a frame-breaking finale for the *kapustnik*: the boys unrolled a long red cloth across the front of the stage, scattering it with amber splinters of glass from beer bottles. The girls lined up behind in shimmery evening dress. Everyone sang in Latin: "*Gaudeamus igitur iuvenes dum sumus*"; on the last note, the girls slipped off their heels and stepped, in unison, onto the shards. The metaphor seems obvious: bare feet on broken glass; we suffer for art. During rehearsals, the teachers had denounced this ending—not because it broke the proscenium, broken glass against flesh at the edge of the stage, but as a "naturalist trick" that was "too sad and catastrophic" for a light gala genre. The students persisted, however, refining the finale for tragicomic effect.

They staged their finale not in some generalized space-time (such as "Russian culture") but in counterpoint to recent memory of violence in the city, launched from behind a theatrical proscenium. In Moscow on the evening of October 23, 2002, armed Chechen rebels took the stage of the Dubrovka Theater, disrupting the second act of the hit musical *Nord-Ost*, based on a much-adapted Soviet novel, *The Two Captains*, by Venjamin Kaverin. The musical, an ode to Russian and Soviet polar and military aviation, boasted a real World War II bomber plane in the finale. On October 23 this finale was never played, because soon after the first intermission men dressed in contemporary military camouflage emerged from backstage and declared: "You are all hostages!," clearing the boards of actors and blocking all exits. Confused audience members thought at first that the shots fired into the air were part of the show; as one survivor remarked later, "Everybody in the audience liked it, they shouted 'Bravo'!" The siege lasted three days. The 763 hostages were tossed candy bars and nuts from the theater café, and the orchestra pit served as a toilet. Until cell phone batteries ran down, hostages were encouraged to call relatives and reporters, stating one key condition for their release: an end to the war in Chechnja. After the third night, before dawn, government troops gassed the building and raided it. All 50 rebels died, along with 139 hostages.

Teachers at GITIS all lost former students, actors, in the siege. During class time they spoke of it only once, and they did not encourage more talk about it. The rest of theatrical Moscow, however, drama critics and others, described the event as a new and catastrophic convergence of spectacle with terror. In the 1990s, bombings in the city had occurred mainly on public transit and in pedestrian spaces: on buses, in the metro, and in metro underpasses (see Lemon 2000a). The selection of a theater as the space for violent protest was new, and it intensified worry about incursions of violence *and* of spectacle into everyday life. Barely a week after the *Nord-Ost* incident, the play *Terrorizm*, by the brothers Vladimir and Oleg Presnjakov, opened at the Moscow Art Theater (MKhAT). Reviewers vaunted its treatment of the "small, cruel ways we all terrorize each other" while also reengaging long-running debates about how the "real" and the "theatrical" ought to relate, lamenting both that representations accrued too much energy, beginning to catalyze social reality, and, conversely, that media had begun to dilute real catastrophes into virtual spectacles.

Staging a jagged, broken proscenium frame, the students worked in ways that paralleled those debates, without direct words. Their teachers did not identify the problem with the finale in terms of the unspeakability of violence (pace Scarry 1987): pain is no more or less incommunicable than pleasure; the problem in speaking of pain or torture is to find willing listeners. To speak of pain as inflicted is to attribute responsibility. Yet the channels for such attribution weave through familial and state institutions and structures (Hill and Irvine 1993), and thus there are nearly always stakes in speaking of pain in ways that identify agents.

The commentary about the Dubrovka events, like the students' broken bottles, gestured beyond pain, to concern that perhaps all those same technologies that make art artful and life livable—including frames for play and ways of playing with frames—are what kill us. But we are willing to keep trying, even when it means stepping on broken glass, making the audience wonder whether this is play or real. Like Chumak charging the water bottles lined up along the edge of the stage, in this way the students reached across the frame, if not quite breaking it. Of course, pressing their feet into shards, they knew that the right beer bottles break along curves, defanging the sharp edges. A bit of collective stage magic, this "naturalist trick" to break the frame.

8. Renegade Channels and Frame Troubles

Gregory Bateson (1972) famously described frames—or situational definitions—as labile, vulnerable to quick transformations. In previous work (Lemon 2000a) I have explored the social politics of framing: how shifts from serious to play communications are forced or contested. In this final chapter, I ask how, in this process, certain forms of expertise will out while others are submerged. Changes in frame can estrange perspectives in ways that spark creativity and pleasure, but they can also signal violence or power plays, as when recruits being hazed wonder, "*Is* this play?" Bateson saw a related suffering in schizophrenia, where nothing is play because every form seems intended as a serious sign, messages reaching out from late night television static. In this light, incapacity to discern a play frame tangles intuitions.

All the same, "the frame" is a trope, based on theatrical architectures that in their own turn had to be built and managed, like all made things, their shapes subject to struggle. European theaters built dividers and platforms, bolted rows of chairs into the floor to keep the proscenium stable—and later theatrical movements worked to undo all that. By analogy, people often struggle over different framings that delimit what is "going on." The stakes in framing and in disputing a frame extend beyond the moment. To define an act as "hazing" rather than as "just a joke" can be to assert perspectives upon a fleeting interaction that challenge even durable hierarchy. This is true especially in spaces in which the playful and the serious can quickly shift, where "what is happening here" remains a live and slippery question, but it can be the case also in places where the boss sets the parameters, and where meetings, auditions, exams, and checkpoints seem to run on automatic.

Situational definitions harden through divisions of communicative labor and other means to channel and restrict contact. The making of play frames differs from the making of lab walls, and the making of state borders and prison fences in terms of material process—but their purposes overlap, as do many of their effects in channeling possibilities to communicate, with whom, about what. The idea of the frame may be a metaphor, and a European metaphor grounded to European stage practices, yet, it is a metaphor that many have found all too useful to justify and to build national borders and prison walls.

Bateson gives us a clue to the hierarchies that historically bind frame-making when he claims that, the capacity to discern framing signals is revelatory of sentience. Animals, in his view, are more like humans in this way than we admit. Wolf cubs and kittens learn early to tell a teasing nip from a bite (actual pain speeding that learning) and to recognize "the nip" as a meta-sign, a signal declaring that ongoing communication is now in a state of play. Bateson noted that what comes fairly easily to animals (recognizing play signs) is more complicated for humans. A plethora of Internet videos depicting cross-species animal play, feathered beast curling up with furry, testifies to the ways that animals respect play signals made by other species. Humans can do this, too, but we also try to force frames. We are capable of inflicting pain for a photo, to make a game of torture to show high ranking trolls or bully buddies. To counter that a joke is "not play" becomes a matter not simply of batting aside a play signal, but of politics or social resistance.

Claims about *abilities to distinguish* frames are buttress claims to social superiority, especially where such abilities are thought to mark a modern capacity to reflect and to abstract, thereby to make reasoned moral and social choices. Jane Austen's wiser characters deserve good fortune because they *recognize* the conventionality of social dances as play, as but metaphors for marriage, emulating channels for marital communications without being them. Less wise characters, who take play conventions too seriously, accede to bad marriages with good dancers as if they were fated (Segal and Handler 1989). In this way Austen's foolish dancers resemble the insane, who treat television personalities as if they are speaking directly to them across the frames, and distances of broadcast (a relation that some broadcasts work to encourage. Peters 2010).

Literary critics and historians who focus on Russia have sometimes treated mastery of performance frames as a mark of civilization. Some have famously argued that awareness of (and reflection upon) theatrical frames suffused the elite in ways that affected events and distributions of power, shaping imperial hierarchies and revolutionary tactics. Thus it came about, some argue, that "theatrical" language and deportment saturated Russian imperial and Soviet daily life. They go so far to claim that theatrical play frames afford they very sort of estrangement that drives modern change: "it is precisely because the life of theater differs from everyday existence that the view of life as spectacle gave man new possibilities for behavior" (Lotman 1985, 56; see also Clark 1995).

Such logic, however, is all too often turned against nonelites. During my fieldwork with Roma in Russia in the 1990s, I often heard people claim that certain social types—Gypsies, villagers, uneducated people, children, the insane—"cannot tell the difference between life and art." My fieldwork demonstrated quite the opposite, bringing me into conversation with many Roma who reflect upon the meanings and uses of stage frames in society. In fact, the biggest case of frame confusion I witnessed was when a non-Romani audience member at the Moscow Romani Theater interrupted a play by crawling up onto the stage to converse with the actors (Lemon 2000a). To abstract moments of frame trouble, as if they manifest the semiotic naivety of a group of people, can intensify racial and other social distinctions. In the case of Russian Roma, the politics of framing art from life generated divisions between Roma and other Soviets as well as divisions among Roma.

Competing definitions of situation arise not only from individual perspectives, but also across institutions. The metaphor of "the frame" has spun out productive debates across elite cultures, in theatrical productions, in art studios, and in scientific labs where divisions of labor run through the ways frames and structures organize attention, whether to challenge reality on a canvas or to anchor it in a lab. These institutions compete to divide people—via education, via specializations of expertise—into those possessing and those lacking the right sorts of modern reflexivity to make theatrical or scientific discoveries. At one extreme of that project lies the genius, and at the other, the idiot bumpkin or even the criminal. Still, as thinkers since W. E. B. DuBois have stressed again and again, the nonelites, the servant classes, the colonized, and the racialized already inhabit conditions that require them to see multiple perspectives and frames all at once.

Meanwhile, the trope of the theatrical frame has come to echo and infuse the boundaries within and around institutions beyond those claimed for art and science, such as the trial, the court, and the prison. Likewise, the very practice of theatrical framing has historically become anchored to specific divisions of communicative labor that maintain and justify walls much sturdier than those that bracket the spaces of the stage.

ANTITHEATRICALITY AND ANTIREALISM

Efforts to purify frames for activity; to label communicative and physical actions within them; and to regiment and restrict ways of speaking, moving, gesturing, listening, heckling, and so forth merge with a European phenomenon that has been called "antitheatricality." Cultural historian Jonas Barish (1981, 118) outlines several other motives for antitheatricality in Europe: disdain for mere mimicry, concern about immoral imitation of sinful acts, fear of hypnosis or magic that might influence the audience, and unease about trickster or hybrid play with categories (e.g., when men dress as women). Specific institutions shaped distinct antitheatricalities; the stage competed with the church to capture imagination, to depict worlds beyond the here and now. As far as the church was concerned, good must not mingle with evil even in play; the commandments must be kept *no matter the genre*, lest sins be induced by imitation.

Plato's earlier antitheatricality saw danger to the polis in illusions that might influence the crowd. Hannah Arendt expressed parallel unease about mimesis. She saw danger in staging historical events as dramatic tragedy, for this not only reifies deeds, carving them out from fields of social interaction, but it also motivates excess political risk and violence, prodding individuals to inhabit the costume of heroic character, valuing the "immortal deed" over measured reasoning toward common good. "Tragedy is the amber, not the fly" (Arendt 1958, 188; see also Halpern 2011). Tolstoy wrote scathingly of Shakespeare that "having absorbed the immoral view of life that pervades all of Shakespeare's writings, he [the spectator] loses the capacity of distinguishing between good and evil" (1906, 123). Mikhail Zoshchenko's early Soviet-era stories also betray suspicion of theatricality as a bad influence: street traffic siphons bystanders into unwitting performances, and the decorum that theaters were to instill breaks down into humiliating chaos when plays become too real (Kaminer 2006). The protagonist of Zoshchenko's story "The Actor" agrees to substitute for a drunken player in a traveling troupe. When his character is robbed, real hands snatch his real wallet: "Help! Citizens, they are really robbing me!" But the audience does nothing except simultaneously call out his real name and offer advice to his character. Zoshchenko saw folly in the early Soviet project to deploy theater to civilize, refusing to see it as a space of refinement that, once workers were allowed to occupy it, would "raise their cultural level."

Antitheatricality is not universal, but historical, and not everyone who comes into contact with it is convinced by it. Barish elaborates on alternatives that thrived alongside European antitheatricality, activating conceptions of the divine not as original state or pure entity, but as emanation, as endless creative metamorphosis. To act on stage, then, was not to refuse God, but to partake in creative energy and to multiply possibilities. Writing their roles, humans made theater not in mimicry, but in protean potentiality, emulating the creator. In this view, the proscenium, as material form and as trope, changes value, becomes contingent, optional. Rancière (2011) differently celebrates how theater can disturb taken-for-granted distributions of agency. Workers gather in the square for the show; neither at work nor in domestic isolation, they become visible to each other in this "redistribution of the sensible": here we are, together. It is here where people—even in audiences segregated by ticket price, race, or gender—apprehend possibilities for collective agency. In the decades before the 1917 Revolution in Russia, some railed against the ways theatrical auditoriums separated audiences from actors and split classes into sections.[1] The avant-garde wanted to blur distinctions in the ways that Tolstoy and Zoshchenko feared; they wanted spectators to challenge words uttered onstage and to ponder actions suggested in the theater.[2] Directors like Evreinov and Meyerhold denounced theatrical realism trapped behind "the fourth wall" of meticulously decorated parlors, stage conventions dovetailing all too smoothly with domestic scales and patriarchal orders, inviting the audience to settle in as accidental voyeurs, "at the keyhole," as Meyerhold put it, captive to the frame illusion, inclined afterward to discuss the play no more deeply than to debate how well or poorly the crew had emulated the sound of rain.

It is common to recount demolitions of the fourth wall as creative subversions (of the state, of the church, of taboo) and as if they were limited to short periods. Soviet attacks in the 1930s against theatrical antirealism were, however, neither absolute nor everlasting; even when main stages avoided too much antirealist technique, directors and their protégés did not forget them or stop teaching them after that period. American theater scholar Norris Houghton, in Moscow during the mid-1930s, observed rehearsals experimenting with nonrealist, frame-breaking staging (1936). During the postwar 1940s and early 1950s, as directors' and actors' biographies testify, even large state theatrical institutes such as GITIS and MKhAT protected spaces, even "in the hallways," where people could experiment with framing conventions, even blending audiences with actors. During the height of Stalinism, from 1937 to 1953, people who publicly quoted only Stanislavsky nonetheless staged work that drew from the nonrealist methods of Vakhtangov, Tairov, and Meyerhold. Khrushchev's speech denouncing Stalin in 1956 gave the green light to publicly rehabilitate people such as Meyerhold. Houghton, by his second trip to Moscow, found that even large state theaters' main stages had been breaking the proscenium frame for some time, such as when the Moscow Satiricon theater staged Mayakovsky's *The Bedbug* in 1955 (Houghton 1962). In 1959 Nikolai Okhlopkov, actor, director, former student of Meyerhold and the artistic director of the Mayakovsky Theater, wrote: "The new world is too new and grandiose, too romantic and poetic to be shown within the frame of the traditional, [everyday-life play] and old theatrical techniques" (1959,60). In short, experimentation with framing conventions never fell out of professional practice or training in Soviet Russia. People in these circles work hard to claim and to mark gaps between genres of the ordinary and those of the poetic (Briggs and Bauman 1992). They do so while also building structures and institutions to obviate that work—and to channel, align, and justify certain kinds of social rifts, certain channels for communicative contact and not others.

FRAME TROUBLE

The theatrical frame is a metaphor for diffuse signs and techniques define and bind communications, and it is also a historical product, crafted for organizing sociality. Its tropes have been built into many diverse architectural schemes, structures that suggest conditions for encounter. As frames are exerted by gestural, linguistic, and more durably material means, metaphor becomes social fact; divisions among interaction frames cut paths for more durable divisions of labor. The theatrical frame suits certain communicative arrangements better than others. And some frame types bear breakdowns or leaks better than others, even folding disruptions, overlaps, and frame troubles, in Goffman's terms, back into a dominant scheme.[3] In the Athens of Plato's *Laws*, the tropes and technical structures for dramatic and legal spectacle overlapped quite easily, sometimes embedding one into the other. As literary scholar Julie Cassiday (2000) has described them, early Soviet courts, stage, and screen similarly leaked into each other shifting direction of influence over time.: in one decade people's courts agitated for performance of self-criticism (Wood 2005), and avant-garde theaters animated viewers like Greek choruses, urging spectators to actively enter the participation frame to argue law, while in the next decade directors shuttled audiences back into passive viewership.

Erving Goffman, in his later work on frames, footing, and participation frameworks (1974, 1981) gestured to hierarchy as a key factor in defining frames and their acceptable levels of permeability.[4] He opened the essay "Footing" with President Richard Nixon just after a bill signing (1981,

124). Nixon, putting down the pen, shifts tone, addressee, and topic all at once, by turning to journalist Helen Thomas to comment on her pantsuit (he finds it insufficiently feminine). He asks her to pirouette. She does. All laugh. Moving from official and serious to informal and playful topics, mimicking worlds beyond the moment, ballet and fashion, Nixon tries to change character, from head of state to good old boy (roles that, as we know, all too regularly align).[5] That is, he shifts his footing; he shifts his relationship, his attitude, his stance both to words uttered and those addressed. Because of his status, he succeeds also in shifting relations among others in the room, making some into overhearers of the play with Helen. Note that the shift to "play" was, all the same, a move that demonstrated authority; we wonder what would have happened had Helen Thomas refused to twirl.

Confusion or conflict over "what is going on" does not always challenge social hierarchies. People both collude and struggle to define "what is happening here." Many of us learn to interact competently with reference to a ruling consensus, even while rejecting the dominant situational definition, inhabiting a different perspective on it. Keep waiting those tables; complain when your shift is over. If some wrestle to change frames, others are too caught up in surviving, needing to figure out how to move within situations defined by those more powerful, by structures more durable, by reigning meta-pragmatic expectations.

These political conditions shape frames. At the same time, insofar as frames can differentiate participation structures, they constrain possibilities for contact. Some frames activate clear channels among some persons while cutting off others; in court, the lawyers may speak to the judge in turn, others not at all. At school, children are not to pass notes in class, and are instead to raise a hand to address everyone at once. Phatic infractions are punished. The politics of framing is thus always politics of the phatic. In some historical and social conditions, these politics are explicitly laid out; in others, they remain hardly visible or become "not worth speaking about."

FRAME IN FRAME

Battle of the Psychics is a spectacle that layers numerous frames that define situations and shows occasional collisions among the frameworks that distribute communicative roles. As it does so, it offers up the (no longer avant-garde) experience of peeking behind the curtains. Before the main action of a psychic test, television viewers watch the camera crew set up the shots, arrange props, and tell contestants where to stand; the magician skeptics hold envelopes to the light to make sure they are opaque, and the master of

FIGURE 8.1. Divisions of sensory labor, framed within frames on the set of *Battle of the Psychics*. A publicity photo: one professional magician-cynic watches his brothers watch a psychic trying to sense without the usual senses, without eyes or ears.

ceremonies dons a blindfold to check it for holes. In one episode, the crew members hang photos on a clothesline. Contestants are expected to approach from the back of the photos, then are asked to describe the images on the other side. The stage magicians check over the crew's work, and one spies the camera that will be facing the contestants: "What if the pictures are reflected in the camera lens?" He checks; that camera records his face looking through its lens: "No reflections, everything is OK." We, the television viewers, never see a close-up of *that* camera lens to check for any reflections on it; we are, of course, to believe the magician, we are only *as if* behind the scenes. This is "reality television," after all. We see *some* of the people who organize *some* of the relevant camera frames, not those who handle transport, for example, or the set managers who call for silence, or the editors as they cut (*Battle of Psychics* does not go the distance plotted out by Dzhiga Vertov in *Kinoglaz*, a film that made a subject of its own material construction).

Many episodes offer footage of magicians watching their brothers on closed-circuit monitors, in adjoining rooms, sometimes joined by civilians acting as hostile skeptics or the wondering curious. In an episode staged at the grave of Nikolai Gogol, a literary expert and a graveyard caretaker watch, commenting: "No, no, that never happened"; "Yes, yes, Gogol had long hair." Sometimes a whole neighborhood or passersby gather to watch those who watch the closed-circuit screen, which we watch on another screen. Episode finales invite viewers to watch the experts watch themselves and each other observing tests for extrasensation.

At one end of the spectrum, at the outer edge of the nesting frames being assembled, the crew trains cameras on people who watch still more people watching people being filmed. At the other end, the crew captures seemingly raw events that appear to disrupt interaction frames. Frame breaks are linked to contestants' flights of temper and tears, their refusals to participate, storming off the set, and their criticisms of the conditions of a test (all common fare in reality shows anywhere). Frame break becomes plot point or moment of character revelation (characters who accept the constraints on allowable contacts, channels, and media in respect to the camera are eliminated more slowly). Editors play a large role here, for example, retaining the shot of an irritable crew member on a crowded rural road directing others to "get out of traffic!" in order to draw out the sense that the production reaches all the way to raw reality, that its frames work in transparent ways. To privilege moments conventionally left "off-camera" is, of course, a documentary strategy that has fallen in and out of favor since Vertov.

In fact, those visibilities oscillate, as in a magic show—now you see the frame, now you don't—similarly alternating between cultivating wonder and sowing doubt.[6] In close-ups and in voice-overs, even the master of ceremonies alternates moods, skeptically sneering one moment, the next offering to believe anything if proof warrants it. Even the magician-skeptics, "professionals at fooling the public," as the narrator often reminds viewers, sometimes confess to goose bumps when capable psychics succeed. As the editors separate and combine shots, they also nest and switch perspectives *on* these attitudes; for example, they intercut incredulous facial expressions and gestures with skeptical ones. A magician raises an eyebrow, a camera captures that gesture, and the editor places it just after some failed contact with the informational ether or with the spirits. It becomes an unspoken reaction to the failure: a flicker of expressions unseen by contestants but caught by viewers, as if aimed for them, and thus inviting them to join the hip insiders backstage (the magician brothers are indeed young and fashionable). As the stage aside did for commedia dell'arte, Meyerhold's plays, winks, and eyebrow flickers are crafted to point inside and outside theatrical frames all at once.

This works so well because once avant-garde documentary frame-breaking techniques became familiar to audiences, perhaps especially in formerly Soviet states, long before *Battle* went on air. We have already seen that ruptures do not guarantee revolutionary affects. Estrangements, including those prompted by frame breaking, *can* afford possibilities to switch between figure and ground, between skeptical and open modes of watching. Recall again Olender's documentary on psychics, which began and ended with shots of the filmmakers watching footage together on a small TV screen. They smoke and drink tea as they rewind video interviews and point to gestures; the camera moves across their faces and over the walls of their shared editing workspace decorated with photos of celebrities. A cat tiptoes across the machinery. They narrator's tone is gentle, contemplative; there are no angry skeptics here, only curious agnostics. But when and where does framing become vulnerable to real challenge?

POWER TO PUNCTURE FRAME

At GITIS, learning to make and to juggle circles of attention within (and across) stage frames happens inseparably from learning divisions of communicative and metacommunicative labor—and learning hierarchy.[7] Only instructors break and enter performance frames, shake others' footings at will. It is their choice to watch a scene to the end and then conduct a Socratic interrogation or deliver a few critical notes. It is also teachers' prerogative to enter students' "given conditions" for a frame: "Where are you going, sir, are you lost?" After speaking with the character, the teacher can shift back to a pedagogical footing to address the student, commenting on the character as well as on the actor's relation to the character. Two instructors thus engaged a male student and afterward chided: "When we talked to him . . . your character rambled. There is no kernel [in him]—just aggression, as abstract behavior. Once the aggression melted away, there was no more character. . . . He's playing at James Bond, but where is the kernel? *Why* is he displeased?" (Fieldnotes, November 2002).

Later on, this student told me that he had taken Al Pacino in *Taxi Driver*, not Bond, as his model, but, he said, it would have made no difference to have said so; the instructors' control of frame shifting not only drove the terms of the critique, but also blocked an explanation that drew from more distant framings.

Teachers were always at liberty to break or to maintain more than one frame at a time. For example, one evening toward the end of the first year, students had spread across their two studio rooms and corridor to work on character sketches based in observations of people on public transit. A few asked me to film them so that they could critique themselves. One laid flat a cardboard box to play a beggar, tucking his left foot under his thigh to look like a war veteran amputee. An instructor approached the student,

FIGURE 8.2.   Corridor life at GITIS. Naps and chess between rehearsals, lessons, and exams—offstage yet never unobserved by each other. Author's photo, 2003.

cursed him, and reached for the cane at the student's feet. Not getting a rise, he began to kick the student's legs and buttocks like a street fascist, while shouting phrases like a theater instructor: *"Net glaz! Gde glaz!?"* ("No eyes! Where are the eyes!?"). The student flashed into a rage that seemed quite real (it startled me anyway), yanking his cane from the teacher's hands and, as the teacher walked off, sullenly turning away. Remembering the camera, he turned for a moment and gestured to me to aim it elsewhere. All the same, while showing the sketches to the maestro the next day, the student incorporated that conflict into his work, casting two cohort mates to do the kicking (all within a single story frame this time, not reproducing the previous day's oscillation and mingling of frames).

Rarely did students take it upon *themselves* to blend or mix frames, and when they did, teachers called the final frame. During December the youngest directing student triumphed with an assignment to enact a chapter from Stanislavsky. Late one afternoon we were summoned to a studio with the explanation that we needed to arbitrate a transgression. The young director lined up three students in chairs to face the rest of us (the entire cohort of thirty, plus three instructors and a few intern observers, like me). She announced that someone had broken a window the night before, that we needed to figure out who and decide what to do. Her words reframed whispers and tears that we had all stumbled upon in the corners of the corridors all day long; a few classmates exclaimed, "So *that's* why those three have been acting strangely!" The three in front began to confess even while others began to flitter skeptically: perhaps the whole day had been staged? It had indeed, as was clarified once a teacher halted us: "Good, good. Stop, we get it." The directing student admitted that the corridor events had been staged, while several other students continued to share notes on how they had felt disoriented since morning by a "strange tone in the cohort."

One student, however, stood up, declared with a loud tremor that he wanted nothing to do with such dishonesty, and stormed out. I wondered then whether his action was just another twist in the plan, even though he, a directing student, was not so convincing as an actor. I asked the student whose project this was about it; his reaction had surprised her, too. The student who walked out left GITIS several months later; his outrage about this and other episodes of frame shifting had not helped him. He had once reported to me with amazement his discovery of the Soviet film *Uspekh*, in which the director manipulates actors offstage in order to affect their behavior onstage. But GITIS requires people to learn to make *and* to break frames, to layer frames within frames, and to improvise when others initiate a frame. To succeed, to become an actor flexible in any genre a director may choose, one cannot be squeamish about frame leaks or pollutions across the proscenium. The teachers praised this experiment and the impulse to blur lines between "life" and "art"; their only criticism addressed the tells that betrayed the gap (What night custodian would not call the chancellor?).

Afterward, one of the actresses in the piece expressed surprise that the others had recalled so many details of her behavior throughout the day, even all her little attempts to avoid contact, keeping her eyes downcast as if in shame. In answer, the teacher stressed that they all ought to mark "how much you are, after all, always under each others' *nadzor* ("observation," "surveillance")." Before filing this comment away as a Soviet holdover, consider the following. To be sure, the students, born in the 1980s, were familiar with film depictions of Soviet tribunals (see Lerner and Zbenovich 2013). But they also came to learn the frames and forms for collective discussions of responsibility in schools and workplaces that did not mark them as past or as Soviet. This did not occur to me until I asked one of the teachers about possible continuity with Soviet practice; he replied tersely, brushing off the qualifier of Soviet, instead pointing to whatever conditions he imagined would motivate me to pose such a question in the first place, as if there were something exotic about the practice: "Well you probably do not have this kind of thing in America—you just spread malicious rumors, right?"

DOOR FRAMES: DISRUPTING INTUITION

In places and times in which situation and hierarchy are not clear, it can also be less clear who should initiate a frame or what to do if one is undermined. Consider a case in which two situation paradigms seemed to collide: a preliminary ethnographic interview with psychic client intake session. In the very first season of *Battle of the Psychics,* in 2007, Mrs. A achieved fame as a strong contender, and she continues to appear on television in Russia and in Europe. I visited her office near the Taganka metro station, an old Moscow neighborhood south of the Kremlin, in a tall, solidly square red stone building across from an Orthodox church compound. The main vestibule is fronted by a pair of heavy, carved wooden doors; as I pushed against the wrong edge of one door in vain, two women pressed behind. One said, "Go on through, young lady," then softening the tone, added: "Are you here to see Ms. A.?" To my affirmation she replied, "I know, I sensed your presence." Given our appointment time, I, too, had reasoned the same—to point out that logic, however, would have been to call out her bid to define the encounter. I am not the only person for whom such acts seem impolite or awkward; psychics the world over reinforce this when they complain that hostile skeptics "disrupt the energy." We are not machines, they say, but organic psychophysical instruments, delicately tuned. A bad audience, they claim, can ruin even a trained musician's performance—even just one person sucking a lemon in the front row. Professional skeptics like James Randi contend that a good way to throw off a fake psychic is merely to refuse his or her framing: do not reply to questions; restrict all reaction and uptake. Conversely, when interlocutors go along with bids to set a footing for a séance or make a frame for a reading, mere conversational politeness colludes to make psychic encounters succeed, even convince psychics of their own powers (Lamont 2013, 214; see also Wooffitt 2006). Given these felicitous conditions, framing itself becomes another technology for intuition, just as disrupting frames can subvert intuition—or at least some claims to intuition.

We rode a small elevator up ten floors to a suite of four rooms. Doubled metal doors gave way into a wide vestibule that opened into a large, sunny room displaying a few dozen icons resting on shelves and gilded easels, furnished with overstuffed, camel leather chairs. A corridor led left past another large room, empty save for a mural of a waterfall covering the entire back wall and two facing barrel chairs. One Orthodox-themed room, one nature-themed room: variations to match subtypes of intuition to diverse clients (a decorating principle familiar to me from New Age bookshops in the United States). A room at the end of the hall offered a much smaller, cozier, more secular option, bearing signs of Russian hospitality: a table set for tea, cookies in shiny cellophane, and a table under the window laden with *matrjoshki* (nesting dolls), small icons, and postcards. Beyond this room, in a busy secretarial space, telephones were ringing on desks. Mrs. A's cell phone, too, interrupted her from sitting down opposite me. Assistants came and went, asking about withdrawals of money, visa forms, photos, tickets—Mrs. A was preparing to travel to Colorado.

After about fifteen minutes, the rush subsided, the assistants went home, it being after five o'clock, and Mrs. A put her phone aside: "Tell me please, about your research." I was not in Moscow to test her powers, I said, but was hoping rather to conduct oral histories, to connect psychics' life stories with events and social contexts. "Yes, yes, yes. I understand. And I like ethnography. I am writing a book about Atlantis. Go ahead." Despite the sense of agreement at the point that "what is going on here" was something like a preliminary discussion, our conversation never settled into the conventions of "interview," but kept jostling with "psychic test" and "client reading." She complained first that *Battle of the Psychics*, then in its eighth season, was no longer what it had been, but had become an advertisement for psychics who had become celebrities, with whom she contrasted herself: "I don't have a stream of clients, like X does." She warned me against several such colleagues, who, she said, put too much effort into projecting glamour, perhaps even pretending to powers, "of course, the crew gave hints to all of us, here and there, but some went out of their way to cheat."

Soon Mrs. A began to shift topics, between speaking about her life and demonstrating that she could see into mine. As for me, I switched between requesting elaboration and trying to not respond, for example, when, after talking about her own husband, she looked behind my shoulder and explained that she was trying to see mine: "Your husband is light-haired?" I felt myself start to smile at this cold reading, for I had caught a mistake. Before I could tamp down the fleeting facial expression, she corrected, "Well, going silver, then?" Yes, I acceded. "He can be stubborn, in the middle of an argument?" I shrugged, struggling to balance minimal response (to a statement true of anyone) with a friendly demeanor—in a situation in which even cool neutrality has a history of being glossed as the withdrawn hostility of a skeptic. "He can't seem to save enough money?" I shrugged again. "Your back hurts?" Here I could not stifle a response: "No, not really." Such questions can *seem* specific because they gesture at common possibilities while inviting interlocutors to fill in—even in the imagination, without speaking aloud. To deflect such invitations felt rude, though she seemed to take no offense, and I tried to soften the deflections by reasserting interest in her life "as a person, not only a psychic."[8]

After about an hour, I announced that I was late to meet a friend who had recently graduated from GITIS. She walked me down the corridor, back to the double iron doors, embraced me with a kiss on each cheek, and reached for the knob—which did not turn. We had lingered past working hours, and one of her assistants had locked us in. She began to telephone staff, one by one, her voice rising as she paced the hall: "A person is late for television!" I fiddled with the iron skeleton key sitting in the lock, trying to help. More calls turned up the cell number of the building concierge sitting downstairs. The concierge took a few minutes more, and we stood uncomfortably, voices now lower, making calm conversation. As she was traveling soon to Colorado, she wondered how Protestants feel about icons (Would they make good gifts, would they offend people?). When the concierge finally rattled the doorknob, Mrs. A communicated through the metal: "We are locked in—and she is an American!" The outer bars scraped, pulled back, but the inner door still would not open; I must have relocked it when fiddling with the key. After another minute of fumbling, we finally passed through, and Mrs. A showered the concierge with grateful kisses all the way down ten floors.

The event embarrassed us both in the moment. That night, back home with my friends, we and the neighbors found it hilarious, as if she, in dealing with ordinary doors, had failed actual tests, as if all of her life were framed as psychic demonstration: "She didn't know the phone numbers!" "You had double-locked the door, she didn't see that." An ordinary mix-up for anyone else, but for her, the authenticity of her powers, her potential international reputation, and more were at stake in defining "what is going on here." A genuinely intuitive subject is expected not only to answer well, but also to foresee both the questions and the conditions for questioning.

THE PSYCHIC ON TELEVISION

As the preceding example probably indicates, the "interview with a psychic" is a tricky speech genre, and not just for me. In order to broaden the corpus to demonstrate this, I take this ethnographer out of the picture and offer now by contrast an interview staged not for me, but for television, on one of many interview and panel discussions programs with psychic celebrities that have been broadcast over the last decade in Russia. *Shkola Zloslovia* (School for scandal) was a Moscow talk show (2004–2015) that invited celebrities, writers, directors, and politicians to converse with two prominent hosts, filmmaker Avdotija Smirnova and author Tatjana Tolstaja, promising to reveal unexpected aspects of famous personalities, to peek behind their public masks. A 2004 episode featured Allan Chumak, the psychic who earned his fame on television during late *glasnost'* by charging waters and creams with healing energy, through the screen. Chumak had been barred from the airwaves for a time—or rather, as he likes to stress, he was forbidden to appear *silently* on television—a sanction that, he avers, only credentialed his potency. For some years he was limited to live stage appearances, pamphlets, and books. He returned to television during the first decade of the twenty-first century as a guest on shows where he passionately debated, with scientists and others, the reality of energy fields and of the shiny webs of information that he claimed to sense and to harness.

The show often began *as if* catching the two hosts already deep in conversation, as if the camera had been turned on midsentence. Editing proceeded to cut often between interview space and backstage room, before and after. Again, experiments with frames, once avant-garde, had passed through several cycles of retreat and resurgence and did not shock post-Soviet viewers, but this episode cycled a bit more than others, shifting among interactions filmed before, during, and after Chumak's interview, which was staged in front of a small studio audience. The broadcast announcement, moreover, claimed that the episode's guest had long stirred "wildly disparate reactions"—from hope for healing to rage at charlatanry—and credited the hosts for attempting "to model the situation of conflicting interests in and attitudes toward this phenomenon." As producers and editors shifted among performance frames, they also moved across skeptical, open, and faithful perspectives on the interview. Such oscillations have structured the rhythms of magic shows for so long that the decision to move them into backstage discussion about how to encounter a magician seems almost overdetermined.[9] What most interests me, however, is *how*, during the encounter, its participants folded struggles over perspectives and frames into the drama of the interview.

Before meeting Chumak, the two hosts sit at a wooden table set for tea in a cozy paneled room. Tolstaja smokes, listening to Smirnova denounce the "mad idea" of inviting this guest. Tolstaja twitches a hand defensively, but calmly counters, "You hold a stupidly rational point of view." The camera pulls back to capture assistants as they apply makeup to Smirnova. As her face is dusted, she objects; the issue is not rationality, but the awkwardness of the impending situation. She faces making a direct, public challenge: "So, how are we going to even talk? Well, can I just tell this person, straight to his face, 'I don't believe a single word you say'?" She names this a struggle over how to communicate, as both investigative interviewer and generous host, with a psychic on TV.

Tolstaja advises Smirnova to be frank about her doubts, but then also assails her for mistrusting "things YOU cannot see—do you disbelieve in radio waves, too?" Onstage, the interview itself unfolds on a glass-trimmed platform where Chumak faces his inquisitors in front of an audience of about twenty adults. Smirnova opens by asking him to explain: How is it that he senses what others cannot? He replies by directing everyone present to hold up their hands, palms facing him, as he closes his eyes and manipulates the air with three fingers of a hand: "Do we have contact? Who feels something?" A portion of the audience raise their hands in response to his words: "Information"? "Energy?" Repeating the phrases he has uttered on 1980s television and on provincial Russian stages, he explains why only some can immediately receive the sensations of energetic information, likening the effort to learn to "straining to listen to a bad telephone connection."

His response to the uneven success in the studio audience resembles GITIS teachers interpreting their students' initial failures, stressing the need to work on attention. It also evokes common excuses for failed telepathic feats in the lab. Decades previously, in California, Stanford Research Institute scientists took the failures of Uri Geller merely as demonstrating the imperfections expected of any biological phenomenon (Lamont 2013, 198). The trained speaker facing a hostile crowd is also an organism whose talent can fail under conditions of bad chemistry. With time and effort, then, anyone can learn to sense, Chumak continues, the many channels of living energies. That is how he heals: he makes sensate contact with others' aura patterns, the patterns "imprint" their "information" on him, and then he is able to reorganize others' fields as he would those of his own energies.

He claims to make such contact even across recorded media, across space-time gaps—be it two hours' delay between studio recording and broadcast or ten years' lag for watching one of his videos, even after his hypothetical death. He continues, describing texts and glasses of water alike as living bodies of interactive, motile information. The metaphors do not satisfy the hosts. At several points over the hour-long episode, the editor cuts to the cozy greenroom, where a screen replays the studio conversation behind the hostesses. They debrief, debating the proper ontological grounds for evaluating the staged interaction—and its apparent effects on them now. The camera hovers at the ceiling for a panoptic view: Smirnova is disturbed by a lack of explanation coherent to her, doubly disturbed because Chumak had apparently cleared up her headache from across the table: "What is this, self-hypnosis?" Tolstaya accuses her partner of failing to cultivate the right balance of agnostic realism: "You cannot verify a dream, can you? Would you dismiss dreams, too? Do they not also exist?" Such rigid distinctions make us *more* vulnerable to phony psychics, argues Tolstaya. In reply, Smirnova rips the microphone off her back, flinging it on a chair: "There is no more talking to you." End episode.

The episode brilliantly revisits debates of the Soviet 1960s and 1980s, animating the dual figures of the agnostic and the enchanted, the poet and the scientist whom we met in earlier chapters, but now places them in conflict, rather than merging them into what was a uniquely Soviet model for the curious subject.

SURREAL PERSPECTIVES

If many psychics trace the emergence of their powers by narrating themselves as figures who, like Messing, pass through a nexus of authority, Chumak had himself once played that authority, the skeptic, the verifier of credentials. At the end of the studio interview, Smirnova had baited Chumak: "Are you a sorcerer then?" He smiles, "I *work* as a sorcerer." Earlier in the interview, he had described his shift in work, and in professional expertise, as having begun while he was investigating alleged charlatan healers for the television station. When he began to see and feel shiny energy trails, mandalas of information patterns, "that was when the journalist died" (no one asked him on air whether lysergic acid had been involved).

Mrs. A had played similar positions in her own story—she, too, switched figure and ground, moved from observing authority to being observed. She had left *Battle of the Psychics* midseason, after winning several challenges—it was too demanding, she announced, draining her health; the psychic work exhausted her. Indeed, the filming required late night shoots, hours of waiting for setup or for other psychics to take their tests. Her reasoning echoed accounts of psychic toil elsewhere, of the physical toll that extrasensory labor takes. Later she revealed to reporters that she had received at that time a false diagnosis of tuberculosis. But all this was nothing compared to her backstory at the time (since faded out from her web pages). During Mrs. A's moments onscreen, a male narrator described her as a psychic whose powers had blossomed "after a series of betrayals and violent experiences, including a period in jail."

Nexus of authority indeed. She detailed the events to me in her office. She had come of age in the Soviet 1970s. Her first husband had been Chechen; they met while she was serving during the last years of the Soviet Union as a border guard where the USSR met Afghanistan. It was that first husband's betrayal, she said, that landed her in trouble ("the matter rose to a national search"), and she spent one and one-half years in jail. There, she said, "for the first months, the guards look you over, as if testing: 'She may *seem* like a good person, but eventually, her real character will emerge.'" She learned this because one of the guards told her so, saying that he could see that *hers* was a good soul and that he wanted to help her. Like Messing's train conductor.

Shifting tone, she then asked me, "Have you read the book *The Master and Margarita?*" I have indeed, said I (so have, famously, Mick Jagger and Patti Smith, while perhaps most of my former classmates have not, and I also know former Soviets who fear to read the book). I listened, intrigued that she would reach for *this* textual reference during her biographical remarks. I expected her, a celebrity psychic, to develop an identification with the character Woland, the foreign sorcerer (who some say was based on Wolf Messing). But she had another character in mind. Dropping her eyes, she said: "That prison guard felt sorry for me in those surroundings, and told me to imagine myself as Margarita at the ball, and to imagine everyone who comes before me as one of the characters filing past." At novel's end Margarita saves the writer who is her lover, The Master, by making a pact with Woland to hold court as queen of his ball, sitting naked on the dais to greet his minions, a receiving line of witches and monsters (a ball, some say, written out in imitation of the famous balls staged in the 1930s at the American embassy). As they pass, they see her bare skin, but Margarita, said Mrs. A, sees *through* each of them, as if to intuit their deeds, their natures. She only seems to be the one exposed, while in fact everyone is.

Taking up this perspective marked a moment when, Mrs. A says, her own extrasensory and intuitive powers began to unfurl (later, she would refine and purify those talents, adding clairvoyant abilities, learning from church elders in Moscow's monasteries). In prison, Mrs. A lived in her cell and from Margarita's throne at the same time. Seeing prison through this textual matrix—passed on by a prison guard—Mrs. A shifted her own framing, if not that of others, to experience herself simultaneously as ground and figure, object then subject and back again, both seeing and seen. She did not reverse the state's panoptic vantage so much as become a surreal consciousness, taking on something like DuBois's double consciousness, seeing others see her. But why should she report this as a magical moment, rather than a political one? Material technologies for audio surveillance might have offered a working metaphor; a good set of earphones can work as a microphone if you switch the output contact to an input. Perhaps when senses emulate technical media for state surveillance, to speak of them in terms of paranormal intuition instead is to distance from profane powers. At any rate, several years later Mrs. A had given up the story in public, no longer mentioning either her previous profession as border guard or the advice from the prison guard. Instead, biographical publications and introductions before television appearances began to credit her clairvoyant powers to inheritance from a grandmother, to list multiple degrees in folk healing and psychology, and to cite celebrity clients. She was moving up.

CHANNELS IN SHADOW

The ways prisoners see others or speak of sensing the world beyond prison walls may seem of little consequence from outside or from the social heights. In this story, it is precisely sympathy that breaches the walls; it is as if the mixing of guards' authority with affection, hierarchy with intimacy, had sparked her second sight.[10] These encounters build narrative frames that transect other interactional frames, even as they run inside channels built by empires and by superpower states. As thinkers such as Dostoevsky, Chekhov, Foucault, and Agamben have suggested, the infrastructures and logics of incarceration transpose pieces of other borders, techniques for keeping gates, and means of activating boundaries. The prison wall and the proscenium alike share principles with checkpoint and border, which act not only to frame illusion or reality, but also to constrain movement and to funnel populations, to move them out or up, or to hold them in place.

Contacts between guards and guarded, watchers and watched have been enacted and reframed in stories and performances many times over, in many places and times. A decent number are set in Russia and in the United States—no coincidence, as both superpowers together are the twentieth- and twenty-first-century masters of mass incarceration. Consider next an example of the contested processes for framing one enactment of such contacts, a film production that located Russia as the site and source of unfreedom, but was produced jointly with North Americans.

In the early 1990s, while waiting for funding to begin a second year of fieldwork, I was asked to help as a translator and an extra actress on a film set inside a women's penal colony near Perm'. The film featured an urban intellectual imprisoned for killing her husband (a familiar tale: the naïve among the bandits). The Russian director had negotiated with colony officials to allow filming on the grounds, to absorb the colony's authenticity and assure also the free labor of inmate extras. The colony lay in the Urals foothills south of Perm', a region of many prisons, labor camps, and closed factories. Our cast and crew lived in a hotel nearby, just outside the township of Kungur, which boasted five prisons, including one in the town center, a high-security men's prison housed in a former monastery, girdled by prefab cement slabs topped with curling electric wire; beautiful still, that landmark is not included in the Kungur souvenir postcard set. Minutes away by car, among rolling hills, is a men's labor camp, and across the road, the women's. The colony housed *retsidivisty* (repeat offenders) who were sentenced for Soviet-era crimes such as speculation (including small trade) as well as for theft and murder, and was categorized as a "medium regime" prison, as opposed to "ordinary" or "strict regime."

A North American actress had written the script and was coproducing it with the Russian director. She and two more North American actresses were to play the key roles. They would speak their lines in English, later to be dubbed into Russian. Secondary roles and extras were drawn from the inmates, and so in the weeks leading up to shooting, my job was to translate among the several English-speaking actresses and the Russian-speaking crew, director, prison staff, and prisoners. The director arranged for us to spend time inside, to eat in the dining hall to learn how inmates spoon soup, pulling out the bay leaves and fish entrails, to try a hand at the factory machines, to learn to make chifir' (extra strong undiluted tea), to see the tools for drawing tattoos or bleaching hair.

And so, when at least a decade later Mrs. A spoke to me about her prison time, I did not imagine American-style jails, but this camp with wooden barracks spread across a lightly wooded field, birds roosting in the cafeteria and in the factory. There guards had spent all their time with the prisoners, in the same spaces, not talking through bars or remaining in the admin building. One Sunday, for example, guards and prisoners all spoke about looking forward to watching a Mexican soap opera, *The Rich Also Cry*, which was massively popular that year. All the Roma, all the Russians, all the other post-Soviets I knew in Moscow, in Tver', in Perm', all knew the series, and only a few would not admit to watching it. In a room used for education, papered over with posters on responsibility, the television was set high in a corner; we could all see well without staggering chairs. Some women knitted as we sat quietly, settling in, adjusting the sound; one guard scolded us for silence, but need not have. The episode culminated this way: the heroine stood at the foot of a staircase before three suitors, the camera scanning quick takes back and forth across all their faces. Everyone, guards and inmates alike, roared: "Such a problem!!!" Prisoners and guards laughed and exchanged gazes. These sorts of little everyday crossings, contacts made across and through the structures of prison discipline, were never collected, however, for staging in the film, and where they turned up in accidental footage, they were not used. Only scripted crossings for love and for salvation (a guard helps the heroine he has impregnated to escape) were staged.

Several guards spoke to me of the trouble they had trying to think of themselves as alien to the prisoners. Some joked that the little moves of improving environment (like ordering books for the library or receiving care packages) prove that the inmates "really run this prison." Such joking marks the sense, I speculate, that they were all somehow deviating from the strict lines that power ought to draw. Working communicative contacts—never mind empathy and sympathy among guards and inmates—were taken as signs of potential breakdown of the system. They spoke, as did many post-Soviets, of humanity always trying to squeeze through limits and rules about contact. One guard whom we shadowed for two days clearly liked many inmates: "I try to hide that," she sighed, when we finally asked her directly about this. She recalled the wrenching difficulty of the first months on the job; she, too, had had trouble with the rules, the stones in the kasha, the soup floating with fish guts, the bad factory ventilation, the raw coughing all night in the dorms.

But what had really unhinged her, she said, was reading the reports describing the women's offenses, then trying to reconcile those texts with the people she knew; indeed, whenever I had to translate an actress's question about what a particular woman was in for, her face would redden. The actresses stopped asking, finally, after this guard took us to the storeroom where recently arrived inmates were issued prison blues (and the cast members were fitted for costumes): skirt, tights, shirt, jacket, slippers, and boots. In "ordinary regime" prison colonies, women wear whatever clothes they have, but here uniforms were mandatory, though almost everyone violated code somehow, hiking up skirts to evade modesty rules, wearing them over track pants to exceed those same rules. The storeroom floor had just been painted with thick, brown paint, so after climbing thin, knobbed metal stairs to reach its door (the height was a security measure), we had to edge sideways across wooden planks to avoid stepping on wet paint and upsetting women on their way out, arms loaded with textiles. The inmate in charge sat us down on benches, offered us tea and to show us her wedding album, which she kept with her always. We leafed through snapshots of her family, her wedding, and her husband, a heavy person who wore only black turtlenecks covering her chin. They had met through a personal ad in a local paper circulated among prisons: "I am looking for a wife. No nasty habits/vices." They had met just that year, married inside the prison walls, and then honeymooned for three days and nights in the house for family or conjugal visits (allowed once every four months). The rest of the year, several evenings each week, he stands across the road, in sight of barracks windows, to wave and blow kisses. Many men and women do this, standing in a row to signal to girlfriends inside. She spoke at length about their last such meeting while stroking the brown, leather cover of her album. Once back outside, the guard with us turned red again as we pressed her to reveal the woman's offense. It was clear that the criminal record, while gruesome, cruel, and sad, did not deter our guard from having affection for the woman.

SCRIPTS AND WALLS

The prison records seemed (at least to the actresses and I, during this period) less disruptive than the text of the script, over which several actresses argued with the director (through me), vociferously disputing discrepancies between the script and the ways we saw inmates working, eating, and trying to relax, the ways they described their lives.

About a week into our actor-ethnographic research, we were invited to spend the night in a barracks. Sitting on cots on the second floor, we were treated to extra blankets and a dish of potatoes with dill and butter and passed a guitar around for a few rounds. The highest ranking inmates had displaced themselves from their own beds; they would bunk with the guard, in the adjoining room. The actress began to ask, for me to translate: "In the script, women fight because they are jealous over a girlfriend . . . if your friend drank tea with someone else, would you be jealous?" The women acknowledged fighting: certainly, they said, but over completely other issues, over exchanges—tea or tobacco for instance—or the loss of a toothbrush, or someone sitting on your bunk uninvited. But romance? Hardly. We pressed: "In the script, the women are all thinking about sex . . ." The women in the room interrupted, laughing to tears: "Oh, who has time for that! We are too tired for that!" I had little occasion to doubt or time to wonder whether they were deflecting, because snoring began as soon as the main lights went out, one bulb weakly glowing from the ceiling all night long.

In the script, a character was supposed to stand, naked, before male officers, so we asked a few inmates how often such a thing happened. "Well . . . seriously, only a doctor would ever see you naked." Upon taking this objection to the director, he deflected, casting all prisoners as always and only dishonest: "Everyone in there is lying, you can't be so naive." Yet in his very next sentence the director shifted rhetorical tactics, now lauding meta-phor as transcendent truth that justified the figure of the bare woman—this one lacking the power of Margarita at the ball or even the mildest forces generated by contact, like that between Mrs. A and her sympathetic guard (or Messing and his conductor):

DIRECTOR: My movie isn't about this jail, here and now, it's about a jail that was and could be. It isn't a reality, it is a metaphor, a metaphor of an entire society, of a prison within a prison, of how twisted all of us are inside. I show a woman naked before the male officers because that is fascism—it is a powerful symbol.

ACTRESS/TRANSLATOR: Then why did you even send us in there, if you don't care what we see, or whether that differs from the script?

DIRECTOR: You need to *understand* us—us all—better. . . . Maybe today there are no guns, no dogs, no electricity in the wires, but the fear remaining inside these women, fear instilled by the twisted systematicity of Stalin's time, remains everywhere, inside us, too. (Fieldnotes, Kungur, 1992)

Here the director moves away from cinema verité, for example, toward a surreal docudrama aesthetic—having the institutional and financial sup-port to film inside the actual material conditions of a prison, gaining access to forms that afford the artist oscillations of frames, frames switching expected figures and grounds, generating surreal realism for the metaphors of open space and naked vulnerability, freedom and capture both visible through the barbed wire. Compared to the solid concrete bordering the monastery prison in town, the boundaries of the women's colony seemed translucent. Just one small structure housed the checkpoint and gates, briefly punctuating wire fencing and trenches. Women gardened right at their edges. Inside the grounds several rows of two-story, red brick barracks were more visibly separated by walls concealing the dining hall and facto-ries, the areas of work and rest less visible to each other than the birches beyond. These seemingly transparent borders, the director told us, had inspired him to choose *this* prison place: "Freedom is visible from inside—you can see the trees on the horizon—and that makes it more unbearable."

Chekhov, in his travel diary describing the porosity of exile towns and penal settlements across Siberia, depicts open spaces for incarceration:

villages run by the sentenced, exiles and their progeny uncounted by the census, claiming surnames like "Don't know" or "Just got here." Discipline did not work there through panoptic visibility or rationalizing systems.[11] Much had tightened since Chekhov's journey, but not, after all, every wall in every jail. All the same, in framing film shots, together with the crew we created that metaphor of illusory expanse while also erasing everyday, social, tacit knowledge of encounters with authorities who did not, in fact, block up all the holes.

As for our role, as Americans and Canadians, in the process, all our questions, our attempts to extract the real truth from prisoners, were also shaped by Cold War contacts and channels—and blocks on them—that, in the circular fashion of so many ideological claims to superiority, shaped Cold War claims to intuition *about* contact. We used techniques like those I would later witness at Radio Free Europe/Radio Liberty. First we armed ourselves by close reading of a script, then we sought discrepancies in the world (not a dishonorable endeavor, in itself; I might do it again). Next, facing the director with contradictions, we demanded replies (I do not regret those acts, either). The trouble was that we imagined only *two* sides, a locked dyad in which one saw clearly and the other did not. At the same time, however, like so many Americans in Russia during the 1990s, we sought signs of transparency and opacity in this newly post-socialist world as if we were not part of the equation, were not part of what was being seen—as if America had not played a part all along during the last century of building Soviet prisons and then representing them. Throughout the shoot, what seemed to be the director's sole effort and individual agency to frame interactions did not, in fact, begin or end with him, or even at Russian borders. Our conflicts left us feeling as though it did—but our emotions in those moments did *not* reflect the social realities, to which our own familiar worlds had also contributed (including the structures that afforded us time for this project). Colluding in this, we too summoned the prison as proscenium from which to project mythic oppositions of lie to truth, walls to expanse, free to unfree.

WHO FRAMES?

Looking at the people actually on set, we might also break down our differing capacities to frame. The early twenty-first century saw the rise of reality shows in Russia (*Big Brother, House-2, Battle of the Psychics*) even while new forms of documentary (e.g., verbatim theater; see teatr.doc) drew acclaim (see Beumers and Lipovetsy 2010; Weygandt 2015). Back in 1992, however, though familiar with documentary film, the inmates found unnerving the task of playing oneself in the place one lives. If they had not been anxious about the role of the camera from the start, the director gave them reasons to become so. Very early in the shooting schedule, before filming in the barracks had begun, the director staged a mass scene, a roll call. He wanted to capture inmates' reactions to an announcement that forty-eight requests for amnesty would be sent to Moscow. The women watched the camera and saw male actors dressed as soldiers watching them; they knew that a movie was afoot, but were still not sure whether to interpret this announcement as information or as part of the fiction. People may have hoped the two were connected, as rumors combining both options circulated: perhaps the director might later really convince prison officials to send individual requests to Moscow, and getting cast in the film would help to that end. The day before shooting began, two inmates who had just been cast told me, as we sat on their barracks steps late in the afternoon after their factory shift, watching the film crew pass through checkpoints just inside the wire fencing, that they hoped cooperating on the film would bring them amnesty.

The director planned to film inside actual living quarters, and on the first day of shooting brought the crew into a barracks, while the women were all at work, to test angles for natural light between the bunks. The crew made changes: they moved a philodendron and a begonia from two window sills, slid photos out of sight or into bedside drawers, and replaced bunk tags with paper bearing the names of film characters. At the end of the workday, the inhabitants started slowly filing back home. Initially curious, they began to mumble as they discovered changes to their space. Upon finding an unfamiliar name tag pinned to her bunk, one woman, picking at the paper, muttered quiet obscenities: "*Mudaki—nara moja*" ("Pricks—this is my crib"). The director had placed me on a bunk so that his cinematographer could calibrate a light meter, and another inmate, seeing me there, also began to swear. The director called a retreat, telling us that he "sensed some tension," and the next day the crew set up a simulated dormitory in an unused barracks—more stark than the other, with no paint on the walls, flowers, belongings, or family pictures. In this new territory, prisoners working as extras continued to object to violations of prison conventions for respect, but with even less effect. One scene required an extra to sit down on another's bed and ask for her palm to be read. The girl hesitated, while other extras commented, "She *can't* just sit there uninvited—it's like someone's house, a bed is." Every once in a while the director would heed them—the women shot him constant advice, shouting out details, asking questions:

"They should join in on the last two lines of every couplet." "I would never sit like that." "Can I wear my jacket like this?" In a scene documenting morning awakening, they declared the action slow and static; there is no time for combing a girlfriend's hair, singing, or sewing on buttons—what matters is getting in line for water or for a turn to sit on the board running across the communal latrine trench. He complained that they drove him out of his head. When he did not listen to them, they spoke anyway, to me, to each other, to the crew.

On set, even if not on camera, the labors of the crew and actors wove through competing perspectives. This work asked us all to shift frequently between calls to regard and then to disregard the inmates' perspectives. Even had debates about what to include not been ongoing, even if prisoners, directors, actresses, and crew had not constantly asserted differing sensibilities about "what is going on," it would have been difficult for everyone to converge even on the significance of making this performance frame. For the crew and directors, the camera pointed "in," to penetrate a hitherto unseen world, and therefore shooting actresses framed by real bunks in a real barracks imbued their figures with authenticity. Inmates' complaints about the authenticity of a shot participated in creating such figures. All the same, for them the camera invaded; it cut up their spaces or cut them out of their own spaces, distorting social and sensory relations—but in doing so, the camera, they hoped, pointed "out," beyond the walls. Rumors of amnesty had come and gone more than once during their internment, but maybe all this acting would lead to the real thing. The production raised the stakes of performance, amplified desires to perform not merely for contact, for fame, or for insight, but also for freedom.

The filming promised to open channels—but it also put sharp hooks into the prison economy, exploiting and disrupting rhythms of work and rest, interrupting old partnerships and channeling new sympathies (with co-extras, with us). The professional actresses were charged with selecting prisoners for small speaking roles, told to tell the women that for "a chance to be in film" they would also have access to unlimited tea and tobacco. In one barrack room a table bore a samovar and bags of loose tea, while crew members gave out cigarettes throughout the day, two at a time (one for now, one behind the ear). *Chifir'* and cigarettes were prison currencies, media both for exchange and sociability, both consumption commodity and cash, indispensable to relations of sentiment and of hierarchy, providing communal and solitary pleasure alike.

Women earned credits to purchase tobacco or tea by working in the boot factory. The most difficult and dangerous job was running the machine that drives nails through heavy black leather boot soles, but it was also a desirable job, one secured by taking less pay but worth it because the machine became hot enough to boil water, so one could brew others' tea for a small fee or favor. This was against the rules but was difficult to monitor because of the way that machine's intricate metal manifold curved around the worker.

Credits came out of wages, calculated according to how well the *entire* factory filled quota. The casting process and then filming interrupted the factory pace and sparked bad feelings beyond envy of those who earned roles. Sometimes extras were kept up all night shooting, so they missed shifts or slowed down the line, which threatened the quota and meant fewer credits for everyone. After a few days of shooting, one of the extras did not show up because another woman had bitten her arm, shouting, "So you think you are an *artistka* (an actress)!" A prison officer, wary of increasing conflict, put an extra guard outside the barracks.

The director and crew referred to incidents like this one to prove that the inmates were somehow naive, that they lacked the capacities and skills to perceive boundaries between life and art. In fact, they understood many principles of theatrical framing very well, and they were also quite savvy about recognizing forces that pressed them to define reality otherwise than they would have. They had long become aware, at a high price, that no single perspective could make sense of the conditions of their punishment—no matter which authority tries to center a single perspective. For prisoners, it was no mystery that the crew was bound to divisions of labor that centered the camera lens to frame a story, like a radius from a point that draws a circle around itself. Meanwhile, the crew members were not unaware that the prisoners saw the story and camera together to point outward, to extend as a ray to some concrete exit, but they spoke of that interpretation of the framing process as delusion, itself a sign of moral corruption.

Again, knowledge about the work of stage framing is not so very mysterious in Russia; school and amateur theatricals made the sociotechnical organizations of space-time in rehearsal and performance, as collective process, familiar to many. A number of prisoners were proficient in stagecraft; indeed, we first met prisoners after watching a poetry recitation and a Queen cover band in the camp's theater, which occupied its own small building. Moreover, on a film set even professional actors become disoriented about which frames are in play. Onstage, the divisions of space and labor are more constant: the crew tiptoes along catwalks, up in the light booth, running pulleys, out of the way if their aims are not avant-garde. Even avant-garde play with frames usually puts actors in more informed positions about what is to unfold next in real time than does ordinary film acting. In film, actors always share space with the crew; the cameraman, key grip, and sound crew are constantly close by, even touching actors, switching places with them for new angles. They do not share space in order to make a statement about framing, as does avant-garde theatrical staging; rather, such arrangements have become socio-material necessity for film genres. On- and off-camera spaces are fluid, and this fluidity is decreed from the top down, creating conditions in which people constantly alert each other: *Ukhodi, ty v kadr popala* ("Move it, you've fallen into the shot-frame").

Time, when filming, is cut differently than onstage, especially as some shots are as short as a few seconds. Narrative time does not correspond with interactional time or real time; if stage actors are given the entire script, which they eventually run through in order, film actors may receive only sections containing their own scenes, and they experience filming them in no narrative order, not knowing how the story ends or even how their scenes fit with others until the premiere.[12] Film work schedules by the economics and logistics of set building and location access, the vicissitudes of lighting (sunset scenes are shot all at once), and the calendars of the highest ranking or most popular participants.

PRISON AS PROSCENIUM

"It is a powerful symbol," said the director, summoning a "greater reality" in which this camp was but "a prison within a prison." The power of the symbol, however, could only be evoked tautologically, by circling layers of authority to focus each point in the shooting—expertise about running the set or the expertise that selected the talented from among the criminal.

The director, however, took steps to achieve the metaphor with juxtaposition of images alone, as if contrasting spatial perspectives or sensual qualities told the whole story, a conceptual vision of freedom as empty space, rather than, say, a vision grounded in any actual deeds, such as when several prisoners interrupted filming to go have a smoke or left dinner early in order to feed a kitten. "Freedom" was not, for the director, a matter of action or redress across already populated social fields, but a simple reduction, an erasure of certain people and their messy problems to allow a clean contrast of confined versus expansive space, naked femininity versus uniformed masculinity, trees versus barbed wire. He invested his efforts in organizing an extreme version of intertextual enchantment from stores of familiar imagery and text. The cliché "Russia as prison" stood ready to overshadow the lives of any particular women actually serving time, to strike the right chords with the right audiences, perhaps especially foreign audiences. Many have claimed, for example, that Tarkovsky's 1979 film *Stalker* symbolized the gulag; despite Tarkovsky's pronouncements to the contrary, many have read it to indict the entire socialist world (and modern industry) as a condition of perpetual incarceration. In that film, too, boundaries are invisible, and fences pop up across deceptive illusions of open expanse.

A decade later, collectives such as teatr.doc formed in Russia that counter techniques of montage and metaphor, substituting interview transcripts for scripts; these and other perspectives complicate once stable accounts of Russia as prison, Russian culture as riven through by prison cultures and conditions. Cultural historian Katerina Clark, for example, rightly bemoans the frequent link made between Russian acting and surveillance, likening actor and sleuth as master observers of human behavior: "Indeed, it is something of a clichéd observation that Stanislavsky's school had some affinity with the NKVD" (Clark 2011, 232).[13] Forms of this cliché are repeated often, with greater and lesser grounds for belief, both in Russia and elsewhere. Norris Houghton, recounting his second tour of Soviet theaters, in 1960, quotes from a meeting with the artistic director of the Moscow Art Theater, who described a letter in which: "A stage-struck detective ... wrote to Kedrov after reading an article by Stanislavsky's disciple describing an argument over aesthetics: 'You are right and the others are wrong. We have learned from police experience that a man's acts—his physical behavior—reveal his true nature. How he looks, what he says can deceive; what he *does* determines it'" (Houghton 1962, 65). Decades later, GITIS instructors also recalled agents coming to study the secrets of perception and the technologies for intuition, to learn from experts on communicative behavior, following the first steps in the acting courses, such as visiting the zoo to observe gentle herbivores and cruel predators, picking up tricks to use during interrogation: "Those agents went and sat in the cathouse and learned to do their work by watching the eyes of lions." Claims that KGB agents valued actor training work like credentials, of course, scaling up importance and utility through contiguity with state power.

To link theatrical practice to those state institutions that define criminality is to join not just any cultural spaces, but two that have become emblems of Russianness and then of Sovietness for the rest of the world: the Russian ballet, the circus, and the stage on the one hand, and on the other, imperial exile to Siberia and Communist labor camps. What actually joins these spaces, however, are not threads autochthonous or unique to Russian soil, but broader ones, that if not fully global, are certainly transimperial.

Many raised in Russia are weary of the pounding repetition both of prison tropes and tropes of theatricality. They know their world to be more differentiated, and also more connected, than such tropes allow. These specific clichés were a sore point for theater workers and students at GITIS. During the fourth year of the cohort I followed, several of us were taking a break in the courtyard under the warm September sun with their young dance instructor (later to become an extremely accomplished choreographer), who had been doing tricks all day with a steel, U.S. military lighter.[14] He showed us the English engraving: "Salamander Division," then switched between English and Russian to narrate a scenario tracing the path of the lighter to his pocket: a Russian soldier and an American soldier meet up as IFOR peacekeepers in Bosnia. The Russian soldier has little currency or much else on hand, so he says: "I trade you . . . this stone." The choreographer laughed, dropping a rock. That story led him to recount other international encounters, such as an opportunity to travel to Washington, D.C., to perform at the Kennedy Center. He had refused, *Ne khotel pozoritsja* ("I didn't want to shame myself"): the American choreographer who had invited him had visited Russia to stage a dance about the prisons, like everyone else. He continued in English, "It was so stupid! She shows like Russia is always in chains. Russia the gulag. Like we only suffer. I tried to explain that this is wrong. Yes, [there was] propaganda, but we were also happy, too. She tells us the first day, 'I have read eleven books about gulag!' So we all make faces!" (Fieldnotes, September 6, 2005).

His words countered those of our Urals film director (which, I should stress, aligned with those of the North Americans who wrote the script with his consultation). Both contrasted yet again with words of the inmates whom I met, as they reflected on being observed and filmed by Russians and North Americans. In the mid-1990s, almost everyone else I met in Russia wanted to compare and contrast laws, vocabularies, breakfast foods, and prices in Russia and America. The ways that prisoners spoke to us, however, did not orient to Cold War difference; that was hardly the framing that mattered most, as the days piled up. The prisoners never named a desire that we "understand Russia"; they were more interested in contacts, in acts of sharing a cigarette, in describing the bay leaf in the prison soup as "a letter," in showing us the spots to stand to wave at kin standing on the outside.

On our first walk through the factory complex, one North American actress and I passed through a building set apart from the poorly ventilated, noisy factory where women assembled boots. Here it was airy, pleasant, sunlight hitting the tables for sewing boot linings. Two women on a stairwell were painting the walls. We stopped to ask about the choice of color, a muted aqua that is a familiar color throughout Russia (maligned by some as institutional and ugly; I find it interesting and soothing). They laughed, snorting, and I braced for the counter question (which colors do Americans paint their prisons) but instead, one of the women exclaimed with bubbly mirth: "*They* don't know why this color, *either*!" We had been laughed at before, foreigners who did not know how to enjoy *chifir'*, but this felt like an invitation to laugh along. Or was that a misleading intuition? Did they laugh upon discovering our *shared* ignorance, marking a similar enough distance from the powers who make ridiculous decisions? Or were we funny just like the authoritative fools who choose paint colors without understanding why? Paint everything aqua! Shared bewilderment can certainly align people across many kinds of fence. But did we really share an angle, a frame? We were so caught up in preparing to film their lives for different circles, aiming cameras along other rays for attention, that that we surely scrambled local channels with our chosen technologies for intuition.

Afterword

EAT A *PUD' OF* SALT WITH ME

If I look you in the eye, do we have a clear channel? I have never forgotten the incident when a cameraman, after a week of filming interviews with me, with Roma near Moscow, declared with confidence that he could see their criminal minds, just by "looking into their eyes." During that week, he barely spoke to any of us. I suppose that it is easiest to maintain illusions of intuition about others by limiting channels. Interesting then, that the channel through which he evaluated Romani character was also that sensory channel so often judged enchanting, mesmerically threatening. When one attends to the eyes of others: does one look for luster or track the direction of gaze? Which ray to follow? Without putting in the time, we may never find out. Time to eat salt, sweat salt, shed salty tears.

One summer Moscow friends visited me in Michigan. We had already toured Great Lakes industrial and Virgin Islands plantation ruins and taken photos in abandoned Soviet grain silos and restored Orthodox churches. We had each seen the wrecks and triumphs of the others' states. We compared notes on our infrastructures: there and here always falling apart or needing repair, surviving Michigan after a storm blackout, Moscow when the hot water is turned off. We had yet to visit my parents, so we set out west on a genuine American road trip, sampling AM talk shows and satellite radio, switching from a London pet psychic, to Moscow evening news, to French electronic music. By sunset we sailed through the windmills fanning western Iowa, into the night that fell just before Omaha. West past Lincoln, off I-80, down a state road another good piece, we arrived deep in dark Nebraska, miles from the nearest light, where astronomers and stargazers meet under the thickest stars. I took a wrong turn, and we rolled in pitch

FIGURE A.1.   Radio dish at the exhibit for radio technologies at the All-Russian Exhibition Center in Moscow. The overgrowth reminds me of the disarray in an exhibit at the museum for Strategic Air Command in Nebraska of Cold War–era missile communications equipment piled in a corner. Author's photo, 2012.

black over gravel, corn leaves scraping the car doors, until the road ended in a stand of stalks. Improvising, I stopped, shut off the headlights for full effect: on cue, my friend, playing 007, voiced the character of Cold War suspicion: "So . . . *this* is where you have brought us." That moment barely ranks among the silliest we have made together; this is merely one of the few examples that translates quickly into terms familiar to most readers. But let it stand as a moment of alignment that built contact out of attempts to divide.

Back on the right road, we turned some minutes later up the drive, where my mother's husband stood in red suspenders, waving us past small tractors lined up for parts. Later still, on a scrubby slope between the steel-framed ranch house and the barn, we put a sheet over the clover to lie on our backs and contemplate the dense Milky Way. On the slope, we spoke of childhood longings to know the stars, to hear from life on other planets. Then we became suddenly alarmed—*a gde zhe luna?* Where was the moon? We returned indoors for my mother to school us, pulling out the almanac: a good dozen times a year the moon completes its rising and setting all during daylight. City people! That is, people raised under light pollution (I did not grow up on the farm: our mother brought us from Tampa to Lincoln in the late 60s. She always wanted to live in the country, like her fathers' people still did in the southernmost Appalachian ridges). "The things one has to visit America in order to learn!" quipped my friend.

Moments like this one united us in our ignorance, lost together in the dark. Our urban disregard for the orbits of the moon aligned us across the rifts of opposing superpower states—and because of them. We who can afford to travel across oceans share infrastructural, linguistic, and media channels closed to many of our co-citizens. Sometimes our crossings help us to see how those closings came about, sometimes they strike us blind. By the summer in which we lost the moon, we had traveled together in other countries, watched many films together, and read many of the same books. We enjoyed triangulating perspectives or pointing out respective filters or gaps in the media that threaded our landscapes. We enjoyed comparing the surreal angles afforded by our respective states' imperial positions, and sometimes it was the puzzles that multiple angles posed, the knots at their intersections, that always best infused the sense of contact, connection, and communication.

In Moscow in 2011 one of these same friends and I went together to visit to a free, introductory Sunday class offering telepathy and distance viewing lessons, held in a sports club tucked between the locker rooms and training areas built into Dinamo Stadium. Not far from home, it was a little place decorated in bamboo, combining dojo with café. We waited for almost an hour with about a dozen other adults, in fashionable hoodies and skinny jeans, who alternately played with their smartphones and dragged bits of string along the ground to entice a tortoiseshell kitten. Finally, the instructors arrived. They screened a video explaining the teachings of Soviet-era psychologist and brain expert Bekhterova. "Everyone can develop these powers," they said. They led us through a few exercises to sensitize us to feeling subtle energies, not at all unlike the drills at GITIS (or the drills a sensei in Chicago had taught me long before to warm up before sparring): rub the hands together, then move them apart to sense the heat emanating between them. My friend and I later confessed to being alternately bewildered and bored by the video and the Q&A after. Not so the other attendees, who eagerly asked about precise ranges of various energy fields. Said my friend on the way home, "They obviously managed to prepare ahead of time, to to think through reasons to learn to see colors through a blindfold. What would you do with that?" Wiser than I always, she blamed not the topic, but our own lack of effort.

We often found the incommensurable together, around the block, and in the sky. We located some puzzles *in* our respective places, in Moscow or in Nebraska—but in puzzling them out, we never thought to pit two nations' so-called "patterns of thought" against each other. That tactic, so familiar in many of the encounters and stories of encounters that I have in turn recounted in this book, falls away. For one thing, Over the years we have eaten too much salt together to reduce the situations and events that matter to each other to our respective Russian or American cultures, ontologies, or identities: as contact makes channel, we learn the many reasons for the other's trajectories, the rays of actions, if you will, shining out from kin spheres and friend circles, bending through ripples made by all the events that reverberate in the present. I fail and fail to remember this, and fall back too often on shorthand labels for American readers ("Russophone," "many in Moscow," etc.) who may lack access to perspectives drawn by people elsewhere.

For another thing, while states can saw at kin ties or friendship channels by censoring the mail or turning off the electricity, people keep tuning in, keep clearing paths. Ours moreover, is not the only enduring relationship formed despite and because of Soviet or Russian territorial borders—many friendships, scientific and professional partnerships, marriages, and artistic networks have coalesced precisely along superpower lines of conflict. For decades Ann Arbor, Michigan, housed a center for Russian language *tamizdat* ("published over there") to be printed and smuggled back into the USSR or read aloud over Radio Liberty. Russo-Anglophone scholars, increasingly over the last twenty years, have reviewed each others' research and argued at conferences in Kazan' and Washington, St. Petersburg and New York. And still other bonds have multiplied since 1991; more and more Russo-American families travel between New York and Atlanta and Moscow, on planes served by bilingual stewardesses and stewards.

Many who live or work along Russo-Anglophone channels see a world long entangled by contacts. Still, unless we are among the most wealthy traders in oil or land, or travel with the diplomats or the arms merchants, we usually live and work in one country, where other forces police against outside influence and limit channels from elsewhere. For scholars and others to work across national, linguistic, and media barriers can mean renouncing willful blindness to tangled connections and to the debts to people dispossessed by contracts forged during and after the Cold War, in proxy wars and corporate networks.[1] Building stages or jail cells, many instead put scientific labor and artistic energy into illusory technologies for intuiting (and misintuiting) that were invented during warfare in the first place.

FIGURE A.2.   "Love is telepathic" (Manhattan, 2014).
Author's photo.

To me, many people in Russia seem more inclined to seek other perspectives than we are in the US, more wiling to tilt the usual geopolitical
maps to define different gaps and connections. Those maps are not always
so malleable, of course: the day before classes began at GITIS, in the
office for foreign students, I explained my research plans to the official
handling foreign students and interns. She determined that I should join
the first-year directing cohort and phoned someone upstairs about me. In
a few minutes the master instructor of that cohort appeared. I gave him
my university calling card, stuttering that, not unlike directors, I too
wished to understand human interaction. He nodded. The next day began
with students in a semicircle facing a line of seated instructors, in chairs
and on the floor, in sweatpants and athletic tights (one of the female
directing students and I stood out, overdressed in heeled sandals and
skirts, standard feminine uniform in summer Moscow, but not in this
place). The master introduced each expert on his pedagogical team,
including credentials and specializations. Then he said: "We also have a
visitor, from the USA, tell us who you are." From my spot in the students' circle I repeated the very same phrase that had elicited his nod the
day before, but for this audience, he interjected: "Be careful, she works
for the CIA!" Catching the wave of laughter, he retook the floor. That
evening, visiting my friends on the way to the GITIS dormitory, I told
them dejectedly about the day, but they laughed: "You should have
retorted, 'No! Just FBI!'"

I never did try to joke with him across rank in that way—but neither did his words prevent new channels among me and the students. In any case, he was not the only one to stress suspicion. Americans like to warn about false friends "over there," and similar warnings were repeated within Russia. Amid shortages and the collapse of the ruble, feeling dollar wealthy, I did sometimes worry that people would befriend me to exchange currency or arrange a visa. Two conversations in the 1990s shook me out of those anxieties. First, one of my mentors, the late Sharon Stephens, suggested that making friends according to, say, similar topical interests, is a luxury, a first world privilege. "Maybe," she suggested, "people in hard conditions become friends *because* they do things for each other, not the other way around." I have since then had opportunities to feel the truth of this principle during illnesses and disasters, both here and there. The second conversation took place in Moscow, in a local telephone call with one of our rock band's guitarists, a fellow insomniac. He wanted to know what was the deal with those American films in which, "Some character says to his best friend, 'You were just *using* me!' Hilarious! Who else would you *want* to use you, if not your friends?" What *are* friends for?

Time and motion reveal the moon to move in circles around this planet, seeming magically to disappear to those who have not paid attention for more than one cycle. Farm people learn to read the moon by attending to tempo over time, never resting with intuitions trained to a single instant, a single sense. Technologies for intuition that actually seem to work, to achieve some kind of mutual tuning, animate multiple channels, and to animate them over and over again, over time. We can work with similar attention if we listen over time, to track both turns of the spiral and flights of thought when, say, years later, friends "in the field" volunteer a shift in perspective on "what we did back then," or when someone moves from championing dissidence to advocating nationalism, or when someone argues against both of their past minds on a matter. If I hold that thoughts shift, circle and come back through other channels, then Is love telepathic? Or is it what emerges instead, after having "eaten a *pud* (36 pounds!) of salt?" What holds is less a sense of finally intuiting the thoughts of others, or, finally learning to read through a mask or to see through a skull, and more a willingness to think alongwith others. Do thoughts start from one point, like a ray (as if light and sound were not also waves, that ripple spheres of broadcast)? Or do thoughts form and congeal in willingness to eat a lot of salt, willingness to channel together, with bodies and along many threads, not only within the lonely head? Salt is, after all, a crystal.

Acknowledgments

I thank first all of the people whose words, actions, or spaces are represented in this book. I have tried not to make you recognizable as individuals, following ethical practice in the discipline of anthropology, except when asked or where celebrity is inescapable. Thank you for your attention and care. The International Research and Exchanges Board (IREX) provided funding for research at the Russian Academy for Theatrical Arts in 2002–2003 and in 2005. Enormous thanks to the administration of the academy for allowing me to enroll and for encouraging ethnography by settling me into the dormitory and introducing me to chief instructors. To the cohort with whom I was embedded and to their instructors: I admire your art, I am grateful for every word and gesture, and am not finished writing about your deeds and achievements.

I presented pieces that would evolve into this book over a long period, between 1998 and 2016. I am grateful to all the former graduate students who tolerated my seminar rants during those years. Immense thanks to all the participants in workshops and symposia who commented on drafts that made it into this book: Rethinking Cold War Paradigms, SOYUZ annual symposium (Yale, April 2009); the Michicagoan research group (May 2009); the symposium Disrupting Disciplines, Breaking Boundaries (Interdepartmental Program in Anthropology and History at the University of Michigan, November 2009); The Uses of Performance in Russian Culture (Amherst, March 2010); *Qualia* (festschrift for Nancy Munn, University of Chicago, April 2010); Can I See Your ID: Personhood and Paperwork in and after the Soviet Union (Cambridge, U.K., September 2010); the conference Cold War Cultures: Transnational and Interdisciplinary Perspectives (University of Texas, Austin, October 2010); Linguagenesis (Brown University, May 2011); the panel Natureculture: Entangled Relations of Multiplicity (Society for

Cultural Anthropology Spring 2010 Meeting, Santa Fe, NM, May 2010); the panel Personification: Conceptualizing the Agency of Things (AAA meetings, November 2011); Anthropological Turns in the Humanities (hosted by Novoe Literaturnoe Obozrenie, XIX Bannye Chtenija, Moscow, April 2011); Medical Pluralism in Soviet and Post-Soviet Eurasia (Franke Institute for the Humanities, University of Chicago March 2012); Making Sense of Exceptionalism and Diversity in Composite Polities and Societies: Past and Present (The Ab Imperio annual seminar, Kazan, Russia, May 2012); and Romantic Subversions of Soviet Enlightenment: Questioning Socialism's Reason (Princeton, May 2014).

I am deeply indebted to the University of Michigan's Institute for the Humanities for a writing fellowship in 2010–2011 and to the Department of Anthropology at the University of Michigan for the opportunity to present drafts of chapters in the 2016 Rappaport lecture series.

Many individuals took the trouble to suggest useful angles. I am especially grateful to Shunsuke Nozawa and H. Paul Manning for recognizing my 2010 symposium paper on the qualia of communicative contact as a theorization of phaticity; special thanks to Lily Chumley and Nick Harkness for editorial comments on that work. For encouraging me to write this book instead of an easier one, for reading drafts, and for riffing with me along the way, huge thanks to Luciana Aenasoaie, Meghanne Barker, J. Bernard Bate, Richard Bauman, Anya Bernstein, Elizabeth Bishop, Summerson Carr, Lily Chumly, Susanne Cohen, Steve Coleman, Jason de Leon, Hilary Dick, Erika Hoffman-Dilloway, Paja Faudree, Krisztina Fehérváry, Susan Gal, Elena Gapova, Ilana Gershon, Alexej Golubev, Bruce Grant, Zeynup Gursel, and Nicholas Harkness, Matthew Hull, Judith Irvine, Graham Jones, Lavrentia Karamaniola, Webb Keane, John Kelly, Stuart Kirsch, Valeria Kivelson, Lara Kuznetsky, Mika LaVaque-Manty, Michael Lempert, Mark Lipovetsky, Sonja Luehrmann, Bruce Mannheim, Mike McGovern, Meg McLachan, James Meador, Barbra Meek, Marina Mogilner, Erik Mueggler, Constantine Nakassis, Serguei Oushakine, Susan Philips, Christian de Pee, Adela Pinch, Eugene Raikhel, Madeleine Reeves, Elana Resnick, Elizabeth Roberts, Daniel Segal, Perry Sherouse, Michael Silverstein, Nikolai Ssorin-Chaikov, Katherine Verdery, Margaret Wiener, Susanna Weygandt, Kristina Wirtz, Boris Wolfson, and Alexei Yurchak. Special thanks to Anna Genina for helping me test translations of video material and to Perry Sherouse for a careful eye to the final edits.

At the University of California Press I thank Reed Malcolm and Zuha Khan for conversations and patience. For the sustenance of play and much more besides, I owe the members of the Ann Arbor roller derby league, the

Ann Arbor Derby Dimes. For everything that matters most, all my thanks to Maria, to Lee, to Dean, to Rolin, to Alena, to Rhonda and Charlie, and most of all to Alex.

NOTE ON TRANSLITERATION

To make it easier for the reader, I use standard anglicizations of familiar surnames like Tolstoy or ethnonyms like Yakut and have dropped the extra "i" that strict transliterations can require in many first names like Maria. Otherwise I have followed Library of Congress rules, except that I substitute j for ĭ, jo for ë, ja for i͡a, and ju for i͡u.

Notes

1. Anthropologists writing on alien contact and communication include Battaglia (2012); Lepselter (2005); and Samuels (2005). On the enchantment of communication across species as part of a modernist project, see Bennett (2001).

2. On ideas about the fourth dimension in modern art and the influence of theosophy, see Ringbom (1970) and Henderson (1983). On theosophical and other occult influences, themes, and movements in Russia, see Rosenthal (1997); Bogomolov (1999); Carlson (2000); McCannon (2002); Barchunova (2007); Maurer (2011); Znamenski (2011); and Menzel, Hagemeister, and Rosenthal (2012).

3. Recall Bateson's ([1936] 1958) discussions of "schismogenesis" as a process whereby at least two parties create and intensify differences, in this case gender oppositions through forms and actions not previously gendered.

4. Vladimir Nabokov's Russian émigré professor, the character Pnin, discovers something similar when he gives a book by Jack London to a puzzled American colleague who does not share Russians' passion for that author.

5. Literary scholar Fliegelman (1993) argues that American ideals of transparency follow a similarly Spartan aesthetic: Jefferson's rhetorical style matches the Windsor chair with its open, slatted back, an icon for democratic accessibility. Lev Tolstoy's novels frequently judge the use of aristocratic French against similar ideals (on Russian aristocrats as foreigners, see also Lotman 1985).

6. In 1918 the Bolshevik state legislated to simplify the Russian alphabet by expelling the letter indicating no palatalization, the hard sign ъ, since blank space provides sufficient contrast to the soft sign, ь (Lemon 1991).

7. There is extensive literature on dissident and artistic opacity or silence not only as violations of sincerity but also as means for survival, from deliberate and coded "Aesopian language" (a phrase that Saltykov-Shchedrin coined to describe writing under the tsars) to surviving while treading the "epistemic murk" of a violent reality (Taussig 1984). See also Strauss (1988); Losev (1984);

Boym (1994); Uvarova (2001); Oushakine (2000); Katznelson (2007); Lipovetsky (2010); Petrov and Ryazanova-Clarke (2014); and Platt (2016).

8. See Stasch (2008) on worries about opacity (of a kind inflicted by magical or emotional forces) *to* oneself *about* one's self.

9. Thinking on Soviet sincerity parallels and engages that on Soviet cynicism and masking (see Fitzpatrick 2000, 2005; Prigov 1991; Lemon 1995, 1998, 2000a; Epstein 1995; Yurchak 2005; Nafus 2006; and Rutten 2017). See also Ssorin-Chaikov (2008). On alternative ways to understand categories and acts often presupposed to undergird sincerity, such as confession, privacy, or authenticity, see Gal (1995); Kharkordin (1999); Lemon (2000a); Pesmen (2000); Ries (1997); Yurchak (2005); Nadkarni (2007); and Hellbeck (2009) , Gapova (2017). It is useful to also link these ideas to discourses on authenticity that suffused the European twentieth-century avant-garde, in beatnik poetry, rock, and punk rock (see Marcus and Ferrua 1989).

10. Humphrey (1994) and Gal (1995) similarly theorize the kinds of sociological relations that embedded Soviet-era jokes, warning us not to reduce all play with socialist signs to resistance (see also Yurchak 2005). Humphrey, for example, depicts a world in which officials tell *each other* ambiguous jokes about officials. I add that people working in state institutions were more likely to joke about the workings of the state; people living in rural Romani settlements, for example, were more likely to mock the forms of racializing encounters with other Soviets (Lemon 2000a).

11. But cf. Margaret Mead (1951) on group confessions under orthodoxy, which the authors claimed distorted relations to truth.

12. Appadurai (1990) usefully questions links between "sincerity" and "individuality" by contrasting European and Indic "topographies of self." If the former, traced to the New Testament and then to scientific depth psychologies, mistrusts "outer layers" of expression, the latter, valuing bonds of dependence linking divinity and devotee, privileges them as a means to build a "community of sentiment."

13. Consider refusals to translate, denials of the possibility of translation as a means of resisting domination (see Chakrabarty 1995; Rafael 1988, 2016; and Spivak 1988), or communication breakdown when conveying pain or trauma (Das 2007; Daniel 1996; Scarry 1987).

14. See Hull (2003, 2008) on ways bureaucrats evacuate agency, distancing themselves from the state even while performing the state.

15. In 2001 an acquaintance educated at GITIS in theatrical criticism opined that theater performances achieve a heightened force when actors combine *glasnost'* (which she translated as "transparency" rather than "openness" or "voicedness") with *iskrennost'* ("sincerity"). Her insistence on the power of their *combination* indicates that she distinguished among claims to sincerity and to transparency. On Protestant notions of sincerity that do link to categories such as inner truth, visions of spontaneous expression, and metaphors such as transparency, see Keane (1997, 2002, 2008) and Shoaps (2002). On *uses* of opacity or incomprehension, see Briggs ([1996] 2016); Lemon (2000a); and Lempert (2007).

16. A number of American scholars have recently studied or even taught at GITIS and other theatrical institutes in Russia, writing with marvelous insight about curricula, students, aesthetic and philosophical commitments, and influence (see especially Carnicke 1998; Merlin 2001; and Weygandt 2015).

17. Some readers may think I ought to have not only insisted on participating as an actor, but also devoted more space to experiences of acting. One reason I did not is that several other authors have recently written accounts of learning to act in Russia (e.g., Merlin 2001). Another reason is that I have performed so often onstage that to write about it with any honesty, about the failures and hopes, the rivalries and attachments, would be very personal.

18. Mokhov (2016) details the grim side of *Battle,* its preoccupation with mortality.

INTRODUCTION

1. See Carnicke (1998, 179); Merlin (2001); and Farber (2008, 13). These scholars, respectively visiting theatrical institutes in Moscow and in St. Petersburg, witnessed and participated in similar exercises. Many of the pedagogical practices we all describe are known to the public; television documents them from time to time, reporting even from the smaller acting schools in Moscow, such as the Shchepkin, or schools farther out, as in Yaroslavl.

2. Here we find another link to theatricality: Stoker was the business manager at London's Lyceum theater, and he based Dracula's gestures on performances by the actor Henry Irving.

3. For analysis of the nesting trope of the "enemy within" and the "black box," in both Western and Soviet art and scholarship, with historical and theoretical insight into the workings and effects of such recursive articulations, see Ssorin-Chaikov (2008).

4. See Briggs (1986, 2007).

5. On ways that situations and conditions of interrogation and torture shaped the very concept of referential truth in Europe, see Asad (1983). On the ways participation structures can disadvantage some in the classroom, see Philips (1972).

6. See Luckhurst (2002) and Roth (2005, 50). The list of Soviet and U.S. science fiction of telepathy is long.

7. Bringing people physically together is only one such means: Pinchevski and Liebes (2007) argue that qualities of radio broadcasting made the difference where there were no televised images of Holocaust survivor testimony, and speech was separated from specific bodies, marked and tattooed. People did not come together in a space of reception; rather, radio interrupted and intermingled with daily routines.

8. See Raikhel (2013) on Soviet writers on hypnosis who connected clinical hypnosis with the methods of European fascism. See also Etkind (1997). For debates over the effects of theatrical and other forms of mediation that create publics or stir social action, see Ackerman and Puchner (2006); Ginsburg (1994);

Gordon (2001); Stewart (2003); Hirschkind (2006); Larkin (2008); and Jannarone (2009); see also Warner (2002) and Cody (2011).

9. There were those who opposed Method acting techniques such as "emotional recall" because they saw them as unhealthy invasions of actors' psyches (Carnicke 1998, 148).

10. I have attempted such analyses of race and of currency (Lemon 1998, 2000a; Fikes and Lemon 2002), and others have pursued connective, comparative accounts of modernity and media (Buck-Morss 2000a; David-Fox 2011) and of industrial structures and carceral spaces (Brown 2015).

11. "Psychics" is not the most literal translation for *ekstrasensov*, which means "those who use extrasensory perception." In that vein, we would get *Battle of the Extrasensory Perceivers*, or *Battle of the ESPers*. Others have translated *Bitva* as the English "challenge" (like the title of *America's Psychic Challenge*).

12. See Taussig (2006) and Levi-Strauss (1963). See also Raikhel (2013) on forms of skepticism that in fact advertise and market certain medical services in Russia, insofar as skepticism itself requires an audience.

13. See Wolf (1982); Tsing (1993, 2005); Appadurai (1996); Marcus (1995).

14. Events and interactions everywhere, in Yugoslavia, New Zealand, France, and Burkina Faso, have affected Cold War circuits; my training leaves me sadly unable to do them justice, and I eagerly await further studies.

15. See Stites (1990).

16. On capacities of thought to affect others' minds and hearts and on the ethics of "thinking of others," see Pinch (2010).

17. See Stasch (2008); Keane (2008, 478); Duranti (2008); Robbins (2008); and Throop (2012). Brocklebank aligns Victorian hopes and fears about reading books with those about reading minds: "It is in theorizing what it means to read that Myers first articulated the concept of telepathy that would subsequently revolutionize the ways philosophers and scientists conceived of consciousness" (2006, 233).

18. See, for example, Steinmetz (2005).

19. Humphrey (2005); cf. Collier (2011).

20. People do use *kommunikatsija* to speak about interactions, but *obshchenie* is more common. On uses of both these terms, see Cohen (2015b).

21. On ideology and fantasy in and about Soviet infrastructure, such as the Moscow Metro, Tbilisi housing, and Siberian monuments and buildings, see Lemon (2000a, 2015); Humphrey (2004); Manning (2009); and Oushakine (2009). See also Boyer (2016) and Larkin (2008, 2013).

CHAPTER 1

1. See Houdini (1993); Roach (1993); During (2002); Pitches (2006); Mangan (2007); Lachapelle (2008); Jones (2009); Solomon (2010); Natale (2011); and Wiener (2013). For intersections of theatrical work and telepathy experiments in Russian imperial times, see (Mishuris 2017). On ways professional psychics

in Russia advertise through the language and expertise of psychology, see Wigzell (2013).

2. See Winter (1998); Daston (1991); Jones and Galison (1998); and Masco (2004).

3. See Lamont (2013); Luckhurst (2002); Mangan (2007); Morris (2000); Noakes (1999, 2002); Meyer and Pels (2003); Sword (2002); Vinitsky (2008); Wiener (2007, 2013); Johnson (2011); and Cruz (2015).

4. Historians like Andriopoulos (2005) have contended that movements such as spiritualism and occultism were never merely foils against technological development or leftovers of tradition, but rather that imagination about communication with spirits through magic mirrors and crystal balls and speculations about telepathy and clairvoyance shaped cultural conditions for the later invention of technologies such as television.

5. Blackman (2012); Bonhomme (2012); Brocklebank 2006); Chéroux (2005);Eisenlohr (2009); Klassen (2007); Klima (2002); Luckhurst (2002); McIntosh (2010); Miller (2009); Morris (2000); Natale and Balbi (2014); Natale (2011); Noakes (1999, 2002); Peters (1999); Sconce (2000); Sneath (2009); Thurschwell (2001).

6. Kivelson and Shaheen (2011), however, argue for good reasons to resist "semiotic totalitarianism" in discussions of similar phenomena in earlier Russian times.

7. See Platz (1996); Rosenthal (1997); Ryan (1999); Bogomolov (1999); Carlson (2000); Chernetsov and Avilova (2013); Lindquist (2001,2006); Kivelson (2003, 2013); Kivelson and Shaheen (2011); Pedersen (2011); Barchunova (2007); Khristoforova (2010); Geltzer (2011); Forrester (2013); Nun-Ingerflom (2013); Pimenova (2013); Wigzell (2013); Bernstein (2011, 2013); Chudakova (2015); Peers (2015).

8. See Roosevelt (1991); Senelick (1991); Tsivian (1991); Wortman (1991); Clark (1995); Cassiday (2000); Casson (2000); Lemon (2000a); Mandel (2002); Wood (2005); Kaminer (2006); Wolfson (2006); Beumers and Lipovetsky (2009).

9. See Clark (1995). On state attempts to direct the avant-garde impulse, Cassiday writes: "Bringing drama into the public trials after 1917 was not intended to discredit the Soviet courtroom but rather to transform it into a powerful arena for propaganda, education, and legal mythopoesis" (2000, 5).

10. On the politics of fantasy and fairy tale, see Balina, Goscilo, and Lipovetsky (2005).

11. See Komlev (2013).

12. On surplus *materials* during Soviet times, see Oushakine (2014). On the productivity of censorship, what media makers, including censors, made and created (such as a sense of Germanness, of modernity, etc.), see Boyer (2005).

13. Jakobson was educated in Moscow, first at a gymnasium specializing in Transcaucasian studies that offered courses in Arabic, Armenian, Farsi, and Turkic and Georgian languages. At Moscow University, as a master's student, he worried that sound film would create new language barriers and joined a group that was reading Ferdinand de Saussure critically.

14. See Irvine (1989) for an elegant account of multifunctional utterances that stresses the materiality and efficacy of language.

15. To objections influenced by use of the word *function* in social anthropology: Jakobson's definition differs from that of British structural functionalism in that it does not presuppose a functioning system, and assumes variations and contradictions among acts and purposes.

16. Compare Bateson to Strathern (1988), who describes a phatic function of the gift to keep social channels *potentially* open (for they may also be closed, or cut). For recent turns on the subject, see Frosh 2011; Kosova 2015; Kulkarni 2014; Peace 2013.

17. Silverstein (1979); Irvine (1989); Woolard and Schieffelin (1994).

18. Secrets for Developing the Intellect in the Special Service is a website devoted to Stanislavsky's circles of attention (http://subscribe.ru/archive /psychology.secretintellect/200712/13034612.html).

19. Gaik (1992) describes radio psychologists who switch from factual to hypothetical grammatical modalities as a therapeutic tool.

20. Nicolas Rose considers the "social role" of psychology through expertise, rather than through fixed groups of professionals; expertise "amalgamates knowledges and techniques from different sources into a complex 'know-how.' Only later is the attempt made to ratify the coherence of this array . . . as a certain 'specialism'. . . . [T]he key to the social penetration of psychology lies in its capacity to lend itself 'freely' to others who will borrow it because of what it offers them in the way of a justification and guide to action" (1996, 86–87).

21. For theorization of discursive and mediated practice as embedded and entangled within political orders, see Brenneis et al. (1984); Fabian (1990); Ginsburg (1994); Verdery (1991); and Boyer (2005). Fred Myers (2006) on "nodes" and "intercultural fields" is especially helpful in rethinking culture as process rather than container and contents.

22. See also Taussig (1980); Ong (1987); and Parry and Bloch (1989).

23. Working in similar paradigms, historians, sociologists, and emigrés have described how the Soviet state, rationalizing a human need to deal symbolically with crises, switched out religious rituals for Communist holidays and atheist scientific spectacle (see Lane 1981; Husband 2002). But see also Yurchak (2005); Peris (1998); Fehérváry (2007); and Luehrmann (2011, 2015).

24. See also Shevchenko (2008); Patico (2008); Ries (2009); and Cohen (2010).

25. Fehérváry, writing on astrology in postsocialist Hungary, observes that crisis was only one of the factors in its popularity; astrology was also good for "'revealing' selves that had been there all along" (2007, 573).

26. See Kukulin, Lipovetsky, and Maiofis (2008).

27. On the politics of awareness of the international gaze in other formerly socialist states, see Graan (2010).

28. Taubman (2003).

29. On such claims, see Lemon (2004, 2008, 2009); Cohen (2010); and Zigon (2009). For descriptions of Communist "wooden speech," see Thom (1989) and Seriot (2002).

30. For extended arguments for exceptional Russian theatricality, see Fülöp-Miller (1929) and Lotman (1985).

CHAPTER 2

1. "We wanted to unite all the people who were writers, who were musicians, who were artists, to demonstrate that the West and the United States was devoted to freedom of expression and to intellectual achievement, without any rigid barriers as to what you must write, and what you must say, and what you must do, and what you must paint, which was what was going on in the Soviet Union. I think it was the most important division that the agency had, and I think that it played an enormous role in the Cold War." Tom Braden, first chief of the Central Intelligence Agency's (CIA's) International Organizations Division, quoted in Saunders 2001, 82. See also Stoner (1995) and Caute (2003). For factors in addition to financing and diplomacy that channel shows through galleries, making and unmaking connections in the art world, see Myers (2006) and Ginsburg (1994).

2. Saunders (2001); Barnhisel (2015); on jazz diplomacy see also Von Eschen (2004) and Davenport (2009).

3. See Smith (2010) on images of brainwashing in the "American nightmare." See also Masco (2002) on discussions of "mind control" in the United States, accompanying fears surrounding nuclear policy.

4. See John Frankenheimer's film *Seconds* (1966), released after *The Manchurian Candidate,* for psychedelic critique of that scene.

5. "The conflict of competing ideas, of course, can be a highly creative process, and there is no doubt that the attempt of the paraphysicists to meet the skeptics on their own ground has yielded some highly useful results. The debate has spawned improved experiments, sharpened explanatory models, and improved the understanding of both sides of the issue. In some cases, it appears that the doubts of the skeptics were well advised, and paraphysics has benefited from that discovery" (Air Force Systems Command 1978, 38).

6. The thread of the conflict is already present in earlier work (see imperial-era scientist Kotik 1907) and already identified as a material/immaterial "problem" (see Mishuris 2017).

7. Michelle Rosaldo (1982) criticized British speech act theory for its universalizing presumptions about the speaking self (with insights more influential within linguistic anthropology than even Jacques Derrida's detachment of authorship from texts). Writing against Anglophone ideologies that sought to match individual speakers' sincere intentions to words, she theorized the ways people may treat communication differently, for example, in terms of jointly coordinated actions, whereby signs are thus rarely dual, like sheets of paper, one side private and individual, the other public and visible.

8. See also Chudakova: "Both Western and some Russian-language accounts of Soviet science have tended to focus on the peculiarities of Soviet and post-socialist scientific rationales and practices, either by pointing to the difficulties of transitioning to a research and design model (Yegorov 2009), or by cataloguing

the scandalously irrational 'dead-ends' of a science distorted by the ideological demands of the state" (2015, 410).

9. Director Pyotr Fomenko's ensemble was among the best known; successes during the time of my research have included troupes assembled by Sergej Zhenovach and Oleg Kudrjashov.

10. See Kelly and Kaplan (2001) on national character studies, which promoted nationalism as a liberating antidote to (socialist) internationalism after World War II.

11. The scene might resonate for Americans who read science fiction such as Larry Niven's *The World of Ptavvs* (1966), depicting telepaths' conversations with dolphins.

12. Inessa Armand, a feminist theorist, corresponded with Lenin from Paris before and after the Russian Revolution. He sent her lengthy and pointed criticisms of her pamphlet on free love.

13. For a fascinating early Soviet depiction of electrification as energy to connect all the people, which interposes, among shots of telephone operators and electoral cables, images of hands stroking the air around a theremin, see Esfir Shub's *Komsomol—Shef Elektrifikatsija* (1932).

14. On scale, see Carr and Lempert (2016). On the ways in which nesting scales afford ideological erasure and conflation, see Irvine and Gal (2000). On detail as such, Carlo Ginzberg has explored problems of authenticity, linking criminal detection work with determinations of artistic forgery.

15. Meyerhold's student, Sergei Eisenstein, later adapted the concept to film montage. The same example echoes in descriptions of the Kuleshov effect (named for Lev Kuleshov) in film. Why his practices and ideas are commonly credited to his students and to visitors from farther West, rather than tracked through Meyerhold and his influences, even within Russia, remains a puzzle to me, complicated by facts and stories surrounding their common repressions.

16. For discussion of pundits and politicians, see Lempert and Silverstein (2012).

17. For recent anthropology on creativity and practice for formal improvisation, see also Wilf (2010); Brenneis (2013); and Chumley (2016), see also Sherouse (2016).

18. Meyerhold on energy and Peirce on intuition foreshadow Massumi's (2002) discussions of affect, with its attention to *shifts in* bodily tempos and nervous intensities.

19. See Merlin (2001) for a marvelous participant description of psychophysical actor training at VGIK, the film institute in Moscow.

20. On equations between hypnotism and acting, begin with Enelow (2015).

21. Theatrical work described as "dealing emotional blows" (Lemon 2004) might also be conceived in terms of energy, in this case the material force of violent contact.

22. On similar pedagogies, see Oushakine on Makarenko's aims in the 1930s to teach an ability "to orient one's self (*sposobnost' orientirovat'sia*), to "almost unconsciously" feel what is happening around one, "to sense in which

position [*mesto*] of the collective you are [at the moment] and what duties follow from this position for you" (Makarenko 1989, 263, cited in Oushakine 2004). The work at GITIS differs insofar as the aim is less to learn a position in a structure and more to learn to be reactive to others within and through a large range of narrative conditions and material structures.

23. See, for example, Gordon on Eugenio Barba's "energy as thought" (2006, 343), and on training the actor's body to "break the automatic flow of the body's energy." See also Hastrup (1998).

24. On specifically oil-based metaphors, see Etkind (2013); Kalinin (2015); and Rogers (2015).

25. Roach (1993). On ways that romantic techniques for performing science overlapped those for making art, enlisting similar metaphors and philosophies of energy and animation, see Daston (2004) and Galison (2004).

26. Later trainers were careful about how they described drills during periods when the Soviet state treated yoga with suspicion. By the late 1950s instructional books on yoga were again published, and by 1970 documentaries about famous yogis were broadcast. In between, the aims of yogic drills were easily translated into the language of psychophysical science—or demonstrated by means other than descriptive language. Hybrid psychophysical work continued even through the most restricted of Soviet times; it crops up in twenty-first-century instructors' recollections of their mid-century studies (as it does also in drills conducted by Jerzy Grotowski, who attended GITIS from 1955to 1956).

27. For analyses that trace influences to particular colleagues and students of Stanislavsky, see Roach (1993); Carnicke (1998, esp. 176–84); Pitches (2006); White (2006); Rozinsky (2010); Tcherkasski (2009); and Weygandt (2015).

28. See also Munn (1986).

29. See Manning (2009) and Gershon (2010) on shifting perceptions of media perceived as "new" contrasted to "old."

30. In a later episode, contestants were to discern which woman in a group was pregnant. A handful of "ordinary men" was first recruited "as a control." Again, they selected visual qualities or objects—"a rosy complexion," "wedding ring," and "breasts that look like they have grown recently" as signs—some claiming that they had acquired the ability to thus intuit pregnancy through "experience with women."

31. For recent overviews and collections on of the anthropology and the extra-senses, see of the senses, Howes (2003; 2009); and Laplantine and Howes (2015).

32. At advanced levels, American actors might learn more, for instance, in special master classes on the topic, by reading Mikhail Chekhov (or, say, Declan Donnellan, who staged productions with Russian actors), or by traveling to study elsewhere.

33. Closer to Freud in Russia was symbolist playwright Nikolai Evreinov, who in the 1920s elaborated that "man is a theatrical beast," coining the term "theater therapy" (quoted in Etkind 1997, 125). Drawing on Freud and Aristotle, Evreinov argued that theatrical catharsis had the power to effect deep, healing

transformations in patients. In other works, he extended theater therapy to embrace healing hypnosis—hypnosis as deep stage direction (see also Golub 1984).

34. Strasberg did not work alone to claim Stanislavsky to be the father of "emotion memory." As Carnicke has demonstrated, the textual translation involved chains of agents, entire enterprises. The Anglophone publishers trimmed pages for reasons of economy and popular fit, making major cuts to "whatever was meaningless for non-Russian actors" (1998, 87). In the Othello chapter, they excised comic moments and pruned student reactions and peer pressure. "Deleting such interactions has two effects": first, the translation seems more theoretical than practical, and second, it diminishes give and take between student and teacher, exaggerating the impression of directorial authority (ibid). Other cuts in content not only made the "actor" seem to overshadow the play, "opening the door for the common misconception that an actor deals primarily in self-expression," but worse, deleted details about the collective work of directors, designers, technicians, and others in creating "given circumstances" (ibid).

35. Theater scholar Jonathan Pitches maintains that Boleslavsky had *not* read Freud, but that concerned to "root his interpretation of the System in America," he often chose terminology "colored by the popularity of Freudian terminology, either understood or not" (2006, 105). As Roach and Pitches also argue, for Stanislavsky, the inspiration linking experience of sensation to sense memory is not Freud, but Ribot on the animating traces that feeling leaves in the nervous system (Bently 1962; Roach 1993; Pitches 2006, 113). Indeed, even before 1917, Russian psychology paid little heed to Freud, devoting more to research on the nervous system, to the psychophysical work conducted by Sechenov, Fechner, and Bekhterev.

36. Vygotsky writes that inner speech is not only soundless, but also abbreviated, pointing to action or motivation without naming. These qualities make inner speech incomprehensible to others lacking knowledge of the "conditions" that embed the subject ([1933] 1986, 248), even while, developmentally, inner speech relies on external communication. See also Emerson (1983).

37. Stanislavsky's work evolved; he never worked alone and was always testing ideas with partners and students, from Leopold Sulerzhitsky to Meyerhold, working in genres from realist Anton Chekhov to symbolist Maurice Maeterlinck. American director and theatrical scholar Norris Houghton tells us that Mikhail Kedrov, head of the Moscow Art Theater after Stanislavsky, remarked that his colleagues each claimed best to understand the system while each interpreting it in "different and often contradictory ways. And each one says he is doing what Stanislavsky taught. It all depends, you see, on when they happened to work with him." Writes Houghton, "I could not help thinking of the practitioners of 'the Method' in America, who fixed their technique on what Stanislavsky was teaching in the early 1930s (principally about the means of arriving at psychological truth) and have maintained its sacrosanctity ever since" (1962, 64-65). Others suggest that differences among

American interpreters—for instance, Strasberg's "emotion memory" versus Stella Adler's "active analysis"—do not represent "radical change in the System, as is often assumed, but rather a cross-section of the master's continuing experiments" (Carnicke 1998, 67).

38. Russia has seen strong social links among theatrical and ethnographic experts. Stanislavsky had an eye for the ethnographic; he and Gorky worked together to research *The Lower Depths* by visiting taverns and markets. Contemporary playwright Maksim Kurochkin's father was an ethnographer; in Moscow, the company teatr.doc works from verbatim recordings of ethnographic interviews and life histories. On documentary genres, see Lipovetsky (2004); Beumers and Lipovetsky (2010); and Weygandt (2015).

39. Goffman (1981); Briggs and Bauman (1992); Irvine (1996); Seizer (1997); and Lemon (2000a). On tracing methods and motivations for layering multiple characters, voices, or animations, see Hill (1995); Silvio (2010); and Nozawa (2016). On the workings of "speech without speakers," see Hastings and Manning (2004).

40. For themes, structures, and techniques of *Znanie* society talks, see Luehrmann (2011).

41. Elena Gapova, personal communication with author, March 2016.

42. See During (2002) and Lachapelle (2008). Jones devotes special attention to how Europeans erased evidence that certain audiences (e.g., Algerians) already did *not* construe magical performances in supernatural terms. "As a form of entertainment, modern magic requires audiences to implement a culturally specific interpretive repertoire—indulging in awe but imagining naturalistic explanations for the magician's effects. From the normative perspective of Western modernity, it is therefore a genre of performance capable of confirming the cognitive skills of modern subjects, and revealing the cognitive deficiencies of non-modern subjects" (Jones 2009, 96).

43. See Jones (2011).

44. For a fine-grained account of such techniques, see Wooffitt (2006).

45. Internet forums track *Battle* celebrity downfalls off the air, such as when, in 2013, a former finalist was kidnapped for ransom, and commentators across several sites delightedly mocked her for failing to foresee her own capture.

46. See Larson (2013).

47. Mishuris (2017) discusses similarly formatted experimental reports on Russian experiments with telepathic stage performers, carried out by Russian scientists such as Naum Kotik at the turn of twentieth century (1907, 1908), and claims by Bekhterev and others that such demonstrations are worthy objects "of scientific curiosity" even if not in their own right, but "as a sign of other conditions," such as delusion or self-deception (see also Beard 1882). I.R. Tarkhanov argues similarly in *Gipnotizm, Vnushenie i Chtenie Myslej* ([1886] 1905).

48. Stites (1991); and Peris (1998).

49. Fehérváry brackets belief this way: "[T]he content of horoscopes allows for a wide range of interpretations, and their appearance in publications from

the somber to the frivolous allows people to take up a variety of orientations towards them, only one of which might be termed 'belief'. . . . A conscious belief in the predictive powers of the horoscope or the cosmology behind it undoubtedly plays a role in how it affects people's lives, but belief as such is unnecessary for the structure of the genre to have the potential to affect consciousness, identity and action through regular exposure" (2007, 565–66). Miller (2011) demonstrates the significance of looking beyond belief for motivations to participate in the occult, as entertainment that builds social bonds. The anthropology of belief is large; see Favret-Saada (1980) for defining work on the social paradoxes of doubt and belief.

CHAPTER 3

1. Soviet scientist V. F. Porshnev (1974) developed a similar theory (see Etkind 2008).

2. On postsocialist attraction to elitist politics and social ontologies, see Rivkin-Fish (2009).

3. On earlier parallels across superpower dream worlds, see Susan Buck-Morss (2000).

4. See Dunn (2004); Larson (2013); and Cohen (2015b), see also Wang et al. 2012.

5. Anglophones from the United States, the United Kingdom, and Australia (e.g., Jennifer Wallens, June Field, Jayc Ryder) have competed more often in a Kiev-based franchise of the show, which titles itself *International Battle of the Psychics*. Uri Geller takes one of the resident expert spots.

6. By way of contrast: Romani friends have yet to pose that question—one who especially loves the genre even advises me instead to stream American shows such as *Paranormal* and *The Mentalist*.

7. As anthropologists have argued, the "radical distinction between magic and modernity is a form of purification . . . an 'invention of tradition' that does not create continuity with the past as much as it distances itself from it" (Pels 2003, 32).

8. See Slezkine (1996); Lemon (2000a); Martin (2001); and Hirsch (2005).

9. Compare to Hall (1990) and Gilroy (1993) on arts in the formation of a black Atlantic.

10. See also Alpers (2000); Blakely (1986); Davis (1960); Haywood (1978); and Robeson (1950).

11. See Lemon (1998); Buck-Morss (2000a); and Brown (2001). Matusevich (2012) gives a wonderful Soviet example: a poster of Africans commanding the means of production as *Sputnik* flies in orbit above.

12. See Golubev (2016) on Soviet images of androgyny in outer space. See Kevorkian (2006) on the "black technocrat" computer geek as a manifestation of racialized divisions of labor in Hollywood sci fi and film.

13. The 1971 Coca-Cola "Hilltop ad" campaign also resulted in a hit single.

14. For details of these discursive struggles, with more examples, see Fikes and Lemon (2002); Von Eschen (2004); Hessler (2006); and Matusevich (2012). See also Muehlenbeck (2012) and Johnson (1996).

15. For discussion of how Hegel's account of a rising world spirit, the urge to freedom, first drew from but then erased knowledge (via newspapers) of actual slave rebellions in the colonies, see Buck-Morss (2000b).

16. On materials in British colonial racializing encounters, see Comaroff and Comaroff (1992).

17. In 1986, with the encouragement of my BA adviser, Ann L. Stoler, I investigated the gendered divisions of labor on a Wisconsin dairy farm, with special attention to the ways gender conditioned access to materials: tools, clothing, even food. Who handles the tractor? Who cuts the steak? How did those acts matter in family hierarchies, in dreams of the future? Later, I considered how racialization of Roma in Russia was animated by public discourse critical of minority ways to touch cash money (Lemon 1998) and ways to handle pieces and parts of public transit (Lemon 2000b). Bourdieu (1977) suggests in similarly haptic terms that gender is made through repeated movements that divide people and objects (What times do women walk where?). For recent thinking about racialization along these lines, see Pursell (2005); Nelson, Tu, and Hines (2001); Sinclair (2004); Mack (2001); and Resnick (2016).

18. For debates on the utility of "race" in Soviet-era scholarship, see Weitz (2002). My stance is articulated in Lemon (2002; see also Lemon 1995). For the imperial era, see Knight (1998); Mogilner (2009); and Tolz (2014). For a biographical perspective, see Khanga 1992.

19. I continue to find materialist and Marxist Feminist social theory more capacious than most of the new materialisms, especially for semiotic-historical work to theorize both divisions of labor and resources and contests of authority. On ways physical objects offer semiotic affordances for making race, see Lemon (1998, 2000a, and 2002). For discussion of ways Roma are racialized in relation to "trash" in Bulgaria, see Resnick (2016). On multiple understandings of "blackness," see Hall (1990). On the "elastic" qualities of color as an ambiguous sign in racial hierarchies, see Khan (2008).

20. There is more to say about intersections of social categories with viscous detritus in later science fiction, from the puddles of *Stalker* and *Blade Runner* through the myriad textures of shit in Aleksej German's *Trudno byt' bogom* (Hard to be a god; 2013).

21. See Lemon (2000a) and Larkin (2008).

22. Manning (2012, 111), expanding on Munn (1986, 55–56) and Elyachar (2010), puts it this way: "In Tbilisi, after all, Georgian generals and journalists might mingle together at a face-to-face society function like a supra (ritual feast) . . . the category of hospitality plays a crucial role as a kind of *infrastructure* of circulation alongside, for example, roads."

23. Some argue that the modern prison was perfected on U.S. territory; some of its tools were imported to the USSR in the 1930s after a visit to the U.S. by Anastas Mikoyan, at that time a Politburo member and later chairman of the Supreme Soviet.

24. Since the 1980s the end of the military draft has divided increasing numbers of military personnel from people in the middle and upper classes; military recruits commonly understand themselves as economic refugees.

Some ask me for citations on this last point and some of the preceding remarks about material culture and poverty in the U.S. These requests are revealing in themselves, they demonstrate part of my argument; among my American colleagues, I am usually the only one whose siblings or younger kin have enlisted out of poverty. Conversely, while I spend time in elite professional venues where few know what it means to enlist for a warm bunk and three squares a day, the rest of my family does not.

25. Compare to Romani lack of access to media (Lemon 2000a, 2002). Useful for comparative triangulation are works like Becker 1999.

26. Critical engagements with Habermasian notions of public spaces for discourse have helped to undo assumptions about such neutral zones (see Gal 1995, 465–75; Warner 2002; and Cody 2011).

27. Aleksandr Solzhenitsyn's grandparents had owned a large estate in the Caucasus. His parents attended university in Moscow before the Revolution; he earned a degree in mathematics and physics before fighting in World War II. In prison for eight years after the war, upon release he took up writing, publishing stories while teaching math.

28. See Brown (2015).

29. The Radios stopped broadcasting to formerly socialist bloc countries in Eastern Europe as those countries took steps to align with the North Atlantic Treaty Organization or the European Union. On the world journalistic order from another transnational intersection of nations and institutions, see Gursel 2016.

30. George Soros's purchase of the Radios' samizdat archives was contingent upon maintaining the research department for a period of time.

31. On diverging media ideologies, see Gershon (2010).

32. Matza's broader claim is, "These new openings brought what anthropologists have documented retrospectively as sudden 'break of consciousness' and 'strongest shock' (*sil'neishii shok*)." That is, it is as if Chumak's silence indexed the fall of empire (see also Oushakine 2000 on postsocialist aphasia).

33. Lemon (2013). See also Larkin (2008).

34. Chumak's autobiographical narrative parallels Claude Levi-Strauss's (1963) account of the trajectory of the skeptical sorcerer (Taussig 2006). Favret-Saada (1980) develops the theme of being caught in those webs of discursive practice that pivot around stances of belief and disavowal.

35. See also Anna Geltzer (2011) on how Anatoly Kashpirovsky's "theatrical" rise and televisual reach was anchored in decades of experience as a psychologist in the very kinds of medical institutions that he discredited, and Raikhel (2009) and Raikhel and Bemme (2016) on how current narcology draws on the fame of Kashpirovsky's past successes. For accounts of his performances, see Vinogradova 1996.

36. See Collier (2011) on the continuity of Soviet heating systems.

37. See Velminski (2017).

38. See Coxhead (1976); Ebon (1983); Morehouse (1996); Schnabel (1997); Mandelbaum (2002); Redfern (2009); and Marrs (2007).

39. See also Stites (1990) and Kukulin (2011).

40. In 2010, when Russophone websites discussed switching to Cyrillic URLs, some worried that this would prove a problem less to their own Internet reading than an obstacle to being found by others.

41. Examples are myriad; here are just one each from the superpowers: Robert Silverberg, *Dying Inside* (1972), and Abram Tertz (aka Andrej Sinyavsky), The Icicle (1962).

CHAPTER 4

1. See, for example, Pimenova (2013) on Tuvan Shamans and their bureaucratization after the 1995 legalization of shamanism as religion. (Pimenova also cites Minister Ivanov's statement opposing "shamans and quacks" and notes the existence of such categories in Soviet times.) See also Thomas and Humphrey (1994) on shamanism as a register compatible with state power.

2. *The Secret Life of Uri Geller* (BBC, 2013).

3. Bekhtereva and her collaborators published the results in English, also, in *Human Physiology* in 2002.

4. On uses of waiting by state agencies in Romania under socialism, see Verdery (1996).

5. Morris similarly reports a medium (2000) who quit occult work to become an Amway dealer.

6. Such judgments could rely less on complexion than on other markers, such as clothing, occupation, even the type of cash on hand (Lemon 1998, 2000a; see also Reeves 2013).

7. I discuss this question of Peircean qualia, qualic signs, in more detail in Lemon (2013). For more on "shine" put to similar ends, but for different reasons, and through different divisions of labor and practices for sociality, see Munn (1986)

8. On sparkling decor in psychics' offices, on its meanings for Russian healers and their clients (e.g., in association with good and bad energies of money), and on decor (especially kitsch) as itself a kind of enchantment, see Lindquist (2002).

CHAPTER 5

1. See Nove (1961) on problems in comparing "model to muddle."

2. On such acts as ways to show "humanity" versus "system," see Pesmen (2000). I can attest to Soviet and Russian train personnel helping others by "finding" sold-out tickets or switching women to compartments without young men, all while refusing compensation.

3. Messing worked on Soviet stages throughout the 1970s. Early in the twenty-first century, his biography was replicated on print pages and screens, and in 2009 Mosfil'm produced a television series re-creating his life story.

4. See Pesmen (2000) on the "magic" of the Russian table (cf. Ledeneva 1998). See also Kruglova (2014) on bewilderment when such expected transformations fall through.

5. See also Humphrey (2012) on the ethics of filial favors.

6. See Borenstein (2008) and Beumers and Lipovetsky (2009).

7. In this film we might see a transposition of "occult economics" into a poetics of repeating and echoing images of violent acts.

8. See Peters (2016) on Soviet research on to create networked computing before the Internet.

9. See Hull (2012) and Keane (2013) on material affordances of paper versus other media. See also Reeves (2013) on "clean fakes" in Moscow and on ways of aligning papers, real and counterfeit, with computer systems.

10. On how the affordances of paper make a difference in bureaucratic contexts, see Hull (2012).

11. A favorite theme for Shakespeare; for an anthropological account see Ahearn (2001).

12. Erving Goffman began from a point beholden to tropes of dyadic interactions. He struggled to undermine them in the essay "Footing" (1981), in which he laid out how seemingly tightly bordered social mise-en-scènes are crosscut by competing foci for attention; one speaker may nest several others who are seemingly silent or report interlocutors from elsewhere to anticipate future judges and auditors. Latour (1993), among others, seems not to have read the piece to the end, where it fractures encounter, showing how people invoke multiple space-times; Goffman's examples proliferate to undermine the dyadic categories with which he began. The implications become even clearer in the work of theorists who followed, such as Irvine (1996).

13. In demonstrations of spirit writing and automatic writing, paper converts meaning from otherwise unknowable dimensions (Sword 2002; Keane 2013). See also Manning and Gershon (2013) on animations that hide the discursive labor of many as if one.

14. For more elaborate discussions of new media used for occult ends, see Behrend et al. (2015).

15. See also Morris (2000) and Keane (2013).

16. On connections of stage practice to cubist perspective making, see Lemon (2009).

17. See Jones (2011).

18. Following Jakobson, I locate such work at an intersection of conative with poetic functions, shadowed by projections of referential-indexical functions.

19. Lemon (1998, 2000a). On similar patterns and for generalization, see Hirsch (2005); Martin (2001); and Suny and Martin (2001).

CHAPTER 6

1. I write elsewhere against the structure/individual impasse by connecting articulations of fantasy and ideology about infrastructure to *social* interactions in it and above it, through examples set in and around the Moscow metro (Lemon 2000a).

2. See Briggs and Bauman (1992) on "calibrating interdiscursive gaps."

3. See Gutkin's (1997) commentary on Bely.

4. On Russian poets and other Soviets on language as material, as conduit for vibration, or as tool in the world, see Lemon (1991).

5. There are interesting echoes here with the ways filmmaker Tarkovsky would later write (in a polemic against filmic montage) about time as a pulsing flow.

6. Khlebnikov (1986, 633).

7. Quite directly, as Jakobson was graduate adviser to both Paul Friedrich and Michael Silverstein, who were advisers to many currently active linguistic anthropologists.

8. See also Hastings and Manning (2004) and Silvio (2010) on voicings that animate specific characters rather than general identities.

9. See Oushakine (2014) on forms of Soviet material plenty (against the usual analyses of Soviet life only in terms of shortage), the overabundance of certain products, and the means for piling them in warehouses and recording inventories.

10. In the science fiction blockbuster *Metro 2033* (Glukhovsky published the novel in 2003, which has since spun off video game and other versions), books are rare and precious, while the monsters who live at the Lenin library are called "the librarians."

11. Another work might align all these novels in the United States and the USSR in which books are burned or not burned, from Bulgakov, with timelines for actual book-burning events in both places.

12. For a summation of linguistic anthropology on this point, see Agha (2005).

13. The "intonation" of a time need *not* do the same work as Bakhtin's *chronotope*. Depictions even of very different times and spaces can still run according to similar *chronotopic* principles, textures that structure depictions of possibility, the nature of agency and event (Lemon 2009).

14. Winter (1998).

CHAPTER 7

1. See also Chumley (2016).

2. Elsewhere I question the ostensibly inherent efficacy of oscillation, which appears in many other discourses besides that of Russian theatrical work. It appears in psychology (as in Freud's account of games of *fort-da* and in research on eye movement desensitization and reprocessing, a trauma therapy that alternates points of sensation). In anthropology, oscillation has served to explain the workings of montage or of perspectival switching (Taussig 2008; Willerslev 2004). Levi-Strauss grounded his study of myth on the principle that certain binaries can never resolve, but rather their oscillation and recursion make the structural spirals of the mythic dialectic compelling.

3. Again, the process differs from Anton Makarenko's visions of education (Oushakine 2004): the goal is less for the student to find a stable fit in a

structure (say, to build a human pyramid or work on an assembly line) than to contact others in the most "interesting" way possible. Discordant but interesting solutions are valued over perfect "fit."

4. See Faraday (2000) and Carnicke (2010). Knebel' (1967) herself recalls being criticized for lacking conflict, *bezkonfliktnost'* (conflictlessness or, if we want to take such a critique seriously, as a viable stance, rather than assuming it to be a worn communist trope, we could translate this as making work that is "anodyne" or "taking no risks").

5. On Stanislavsky on physical actions and commentary on misunderstandings about his ideas on the material, see Carnicke (1998).

6. She continues: "In my view, the poetics of the Russian Formalists should be placed in the broader European context of literary, philosophical, and political reflection on modernity" (Boym 2005, 1–2).

7. It can be useful also to separate deliberate techniques for *ostranenie* from encounters that afford a sense of indeterminacy or estrangement, and also to distinguish among techniques such as montage and perspectival contrast.

8. See Jones (2009, 2011) on magicians' use of angles and even on using skepticism within the act.

9. Ngai (2005) argues that principles like stop-motion, when applied to living beings, can work to deanimate or to animate in the negative sense, to automatize from without.

10. Krisztina Fehérváry pointed this out to me in 2010 as we were traveling to the conference at which I delivered the heart of this chapter.

11. The protagonists on rags-to-riches television series *The Beverly Hillbillies*.

12. On the Soviet press being the first to document the Jewish Holocaust during World War II, and on the ways the United Kingdom and the United State censored the images documenting those atrocities, see Hicks (2012).

13. In their 2006 introduction to *Against Theatre: Creative Destructions in the Modernist State*, Ackerman and Puchner argue that, insofar as modernity projects do formulate concerns about that which resists representation (the inner workings of mind, certain divisions of labor), "The disputed boundary between representation and invisibility" persists in attempts to create and then redress separations, especially from an audience—for example, by making and then tangibly breaking frames for performance.

14. See Johnson's (2011) discussion of the ways the Atlantic slave trade and American plantation economy produced claims that rituals of spirit possession among the enslaved confirmed that they were no better than automatons, erasing the ways the conditions of slavery produced the rituals.

15. See Bernstein (2015) and Yurchak (2015a).

16. See Resnick (2016).

17. Consider also depictions of murderers in their abodes as depraved, genetically devolved, incestuous trash living in squalor, as in *Silence of the Lambs* or *True Detective*.

18. On nineteenth-century images of the orchestral conductor directing the energies of the crowd, even to the point of mesmerism, see Winter (1998, 206–343) on "the social body and the invention of consensus."

19. See Susan Layton (1994) on Russian imperial poetry about the Caucasus, and consider studies of U.S. and Soviet science fiction revealing various connections to Cold War geopolitics.

20. Numerous historians and anthropologists have demonstrated how realist forms of representation—novels, ethnographies, documentaries—served colonial rule (British, Dutch, etc.). Strong scholarship has analyzed diorama exhibits reproducing customs and costumes of colonized peoples, such as the carvings and dances of a Malay village. See, for example, Raibmon (2006) and Kruger (2007).

21. I trace these thoughts about learning to see and to unsee to reading the novel *The City and the City,* by China Miéville (2009).

CHAPTER 8

1. See also Tsivian (1991).

2. See Clark (1995) and Golub (1984).

3. In some conditions, certain forms of phatic assault, under which we might include heckling (Zuckerman 2016), disrupt with *excess* contact, even without shifting frames.

4. His late work demonstrated that even the most formally staged performances cannot be reduced to binaries such as onstage/offstage or speaker/audience. He certainly did *begin* from those very pairs and dyads; however, by the time he played out scores of examples, breaking them down into parts that intersect former opposites, the original pairs lost their apical authority, disintegrating the former logic in ways that inspired further thinkers to press the implications of understanding communication as open to multiple lines of participation and to leaks across space, time, and genre. See the corpus of theoretical work by linguistic anthropologists such as Judith Irvine, Elinor Ochs, Jane Hill, Susan Philips, Ofelia Zepeda, and their students for expansion and correction of these concepts.

5. See also Silverstein (2005).

6. On oscillations of wonder and doubt as constitutive for magic, see Levi-Strauss (1963).

7. Bateson, on deuterolearning, or learning the conditions for learning, pointed in this direction, elaborated by many linguistic anthropologists who research language socialization (see Schieffelin 1990 and 2008; Meek 2010).

8. On similar interactional trouble, see Wooffitt (2006).

9. "Modern magic is a paradoxical form of entertainment, seeming at once the performative counterpart to a rational, disenchanted worldview, and a residual or compensatory locus of irrationality and enchantment. Magicians trade on this ambiguity, employing occult iconography at the same time as they pursue projects of demystifying occult practices and beliefs" (During 2002).

10. On colonial entanglements of power with kinship, see Stoler (2010). On tangles across Soviet-era oppositions that clouded distinctions of "us versus them" see Humphrey (1994).

11. See Popkin (1992) on Chekhov's ethnographic observations during his arduous land voyage through Siberia to Sakhalin.

12. Even when Meyerhold fractured and rearranged the scenes in classic plays (such as *Inspector General*), his actors were still in on the arc of the production.

13. "[A]nd even that the Method school in the United States had some affinity with the CIA." Her source, however (she cites the *New York Times*, May 20, 1997) says only that Norman Mailer, an active member since 1958, had said that, "at first it was more a church than a club," "either you were an acolyte or you resisted it," and that even as an outsider and a nonactor he was allowed to speak up, but that over the years the group had become more eclectic and less secretive. With dry amusement, he compared it with the CIA. "They have parallel histories," he said, adding, "We may not have as many scandals as they do." See also Vatulescu (2010) and Cassiday (2000).

14. Some Anglophone readers may sense an echo here with the fictive lighter that appears as a prop in John Le Carré's spy novels, a prop that links the protagonist, a British intelligence office, to his Soviet counterpart and archenemy.

AFTERWORD

1. For accounts of other political and social orders that binary configurations of geopolitical axes can obscure, see Coronil (1996 and 1997) and Ho (2004).

References

Ackerman, Alan, and Martin Puchner. 2006. *Against Theatre: Creative Destructions on the Modernist Stage*. Performance Interventions. Houndmills, Basingstoke, Hampshire, U.K., and New York: Palgrave Macmillan.

Aczél, Tamás, and Tibor Méray. 1959. *The Revolt of the Mind: A Case History of Intellectual Resistance behind the Iron Curtain*. Praeger Publications in Russian History and World Communism, no. 73. New York: Praeger.

Agha, Asif. 2005. "Voice, Footing, Enregisterment." *Journal of Linguistic Anthropology* 15, no. 1: 38–59.

———. 2011. "Meet Mediatization." *Language & Communication* 31, no. 3 (July): 163–70.

Ahearn, Laura M. 2001. *Invitations to Love: Literacy, Love Letters, and Social Change in Nepal*. Ann Arbor: University of Michigan Press.

Air Force Audio Visual Service. 1963. Special Film Project 1236, SAC Command Post. Military Airlift Command, 1365th Photo Squadron.

Air Force Systems Command Foreign Technology Division. 1978. *Paraphysics Research and Development: Warsaw Pact*. Washington, DC: U.S. Department of Defense.

Alpers, Edward A. 2000. "Recollecting Africa: Diasporic Memory in the Indian Ocean World." *African Studies Review* 43, no. 1: 83–99.

Andriopoulos, Stefan 2005. "Psychic Television." *Critical Inquiry* 31, no. 3: 618–37.

Appadurai, Arjun. 1990. "Topographies of the Self." In *Language and the Politics of Emotion*, edited by Catherine Lutz and Lila Abu-Lughod, 92–112. New York: Cambridge University Press.

———. 1996. *Modernity at Large: Cultural Dimensions of Globalization*. Public Worlds, no. 1. Minneapolis: University of Minnesota Press.

Arendt, Hannah. 1958. *The Human Condition*. Chicago: University of Chicago Press.

Army Medical Intelligence and Information Agency. 1972. *Controlled Offensive Behavior—USSR*. Washington, DC: Report submitted to the DIA.

Asad, Talal. 1983. "Notes on Body Pain and Truth." *Economy and Society* 12, no. 3: 287–327.

Ashforth, Adam. 2005. *Witchcraft, Violence, and Democracy in South Africa.* Chicago: University of Chicago Press.

Balina, Marina, Helena Goscilo, and Mark Lipovetsky, eds. 2005. *Politicizing Magic: An Anthology of Russian and Soviet Fairy Tales.* Evanston, IL: Northwestern University Press.

Banerjee, Anindita 2012. *We Modern People: Science Fiction and the Making of Russian Modernity.* Middletown, CT: Wesleyan University Press.

Barchunova, Tatiana. 2007. "Downloading Cosmic Energy: Intersection of Faith-Based and Health-Care Practices (The Novosibirsk Case)." In *Cosmologies of Suffering: Post Communist Transformation, Sacral Communication, and Healing,* edited by Agita Luse and Imre Lazar, 55–68 Newcastle, U.K.: Cambridge Scholars Publishing.

Barish, Jonas A. 1981. *The Antitheatrical Prejudice.* Berkeley: University of California Press.

Barker, Meghanne. 2017. "Framing the Fantastic: Animating Childhood in Contemporary Kazakhstan." PhD diss., University of Michigan.

Barnhisel, Greg. 2015. *Cold War Modernists: Art, Literature, and American Cultural Diplomacy.* New York: Columbia University Press.

Bateson, Gregory. (1936) 1958. *Naven: A Survey of the Problems Suggested by a Composite Picture of the Culture of a New Guinea Tribe Drawn from Three Points of View.* Stanford, CA: Stanford University Press.

———. 1972. *Steps to an Ecology of Mind: Collected Essays in Anthropology, Psychiatry, Evolution, and Epistemology.* New York: Ballantine Books.

Battaglia, Debbora. 2012. "Arresting Hospitality: The Case of the 'Handshake in Space.'" *Journal of the Royal Anthropological Institute* 18, no. s1 (2012): S76–S89.

Bauman, Richard. 1998. *Let Your Words Be Few: Symbolism of Speaking and Silence Among Seventeenth-Century Quakers.* London: Quaker Home Service.

Beard, George M. 1882. *The Study of Trance, Muscle-Reading and Allied Nervous Phenomena.* New York.

Becker, Jonathan A. 1999. *Soviet and Russian Press Coverage of the United States: Press, Politics, and Identity in Transition.* St. Antony's Series. Basingstoke, U.K., and New York: Macmillan; St. Martin's Press in association with St. Antony's College, Oxford.

Behrend, Heike, Anja Dreschke, and Martin Zillinger. 2015. *Trance Mediums and New Media Spirit Possession in the Age of Technical Reproduction.* New York: Fordham University Press.

Bekhterev, Vladimir Mikhaĭlovich, and Lloyd H. Strickland. 1998. *Suggestion and Its Role in Social Life.* Vnushenie I Ego Rol' v Obshchestvennoj zhizni. New Brunswick, NJ: Transaction Publishers.

———. 2014. "Ob opytakh nad myslennym vozdejstviem na povedenie zhivotnykh" [About experiments on mental influence on the behavior of animals]. *Zhurnal Formirujushchihksja Napravlenii Nauki* 2, no. 6: 113–12.

Bekhtereva, N. P., et al. 2002. "On So-Called Alternative Vision or Direct Vision Phenomenon." *Human Physiology* 28, no. 1 (January 1): 16–26.

Bely, Andrey. (1910) 1985. "The Power of Words." In *Selected Essays of Andrey Bely*, trans. Stephen Cassedy, 90–97. Berkeley: University of California Press.

Benedetti, Jean. 1990. *Stanislavski: A Biography*. London: Methuen Drama.

Bennett, Jane. 2001. *The Enchantment of Modern Life: Attachments, Crossings, and Ethics*. Princeton, NJ: Princeton University Press.

Bennetts, Marc. 2012. "Faith Healer Anatoly Kashpirovsky: Russia's New Rasputin." *The Guardian*, June 5, 8.

Bentley, Eric. 1962. "Who Was Ribot? Or: Did Stanislavsky Know Any Psychology?" *The Tulane Drama Review* 7, no. 2: 127–29.

Berlin, Isaiah, and Henry Hardy. (1949) 2004. *The Soviet Mind: Russian Culture under Communism*. Washington, DC: Brookings Institution Press.

Bernstein, Anya. 2011. "The Post-Soviet Treasure Hunt: Time, Space, and Necropolitics in Siberian Buddhism." *Comparative Studies in Society and History* 53, no. 3 (June 30): 623–53.

———. 2013. *Religious Bodies Politic: Rituals of Sovereignty in Buryat Buddhism*. Buddhism and Modernity. Chicago: University of Chicago Press.

———. 2015. "Freeze, Die, Come to Life: The Many Paths to Immortality in Post-Soviet Russia." *American Ethnologist* 42, no. 4: 766–81.

Besant, Annie, and C. W. Leadbetter. 1901. *Thought Forms*. London: The Theosophical Publishing House.

Besnier, Niko. 1993. "Reported Speech and Affect on Nukulaelae Atoll." In *Responsibility and Evidence in Oral Discourse*, edited by Jane H. Hill and Judith T. Irvine, 161–68. Cambridge, U.K.: Cambridge University Press.

Bessire, Lucas, and Faye Ginsburg, eds. 2012. *Radio Fields: Anthropology and Wireless Sound in the 21st Century*. New York: New York University Press.

Beumers, Birgit, and Mark Lipovetsky. 2009. *Performing Violence: Literary and Theatrical Experiments of New Russian Drama*. Chicago: University of Chicago Press.

———. 2010. "The Desire for the Real: Documentary Trends in Contemporary Russian Culture." *The Russian Review* 69, no. 4: 559–62.

Bhabha, Homi. 1984. "Of Mimicry and Man: The Ambivalence of Colonial Discourse." *October* 28: 125–33.

Blackman, Lisa. 2012. "Mental Touch: Media Technologies and the Problem of Telepathy." In *Immaterial Bodies: Affect, Embodiment, Mediation*, 54–76. Theory, Culture & Society. Thousand Oaks, CA: Sage.

Blakely, Allison. 1986. *Russia and the Negro: Blacks in Russian History and Thought*. Washington, DC: Howard University Press.

Bogomolov, N. A. 1999. *Russkaja Literatura Nachala XX Veka I Okkul'tizm: Issledovanija i Materialy* [Russian literature of the beginning of the twentieth century and occultism]. Moscow: Novoe literaturnoe obozrenie.

Bonhomme, Julien. 2012. "The Dangers of Anonymity: Witchcraft, Rumor and Modernity in Africa." *HAU: Journal of Ethnographic Theory* 2, no. 2: 205–33.

Borenstein, Eliot. 2008. *Overkill: Sex and Violence in Contemporary Russian Popular Culture, Sex and Violence in Contemporary Russian Popular Culture.* Ithaca, NY: Cornell University Press.

———. "Plots Against Russia." n.d. Accessed July 22, 2017. http://plots againstrussia.org/.

Bourdieu, Pierre. 1977. *Outline for a Theory of Practice.* Cambridge, U.K.: Cambridge University Press.

Boyer, Dominic. 2005. *Spirit and System: Media, Intellectuals, and the Dialectic in Modern German Culture.* Chicago: University of Chicago Press.

———. 2016. "Revolutionary Infrastructures." In *Infrastructures and Social Complexity: A Companion,* edited by Penelope Harvey, Casper Bruun Jensen, and Atsuro Morita, 174–186. Abingdon, Oxon: Taylor & Francis.

Boym, Svetlana. 1994. *Common Places: Mythologies of Everyday Life in Russia.* Cambridge, MA: Harvard University Press.

———. 2005. "Poetics and Politics of Estrangement: Victor Shklovsky and Hannah Arendt." *Poetics Today* 26, no. 4: 581.

Brenneis, Donald Lawrence. 2013. "Trading Fours: Creativity, Analogy, and Exchange." *American Ethnologist* 40, no. 4: 619–23.

Brenneis, Donald Lawrence, and Fred R. Myers. 1984. *Dangerous Words: Language and Politics in the Pacific.* New York: New York University Press.

Briggs, Charles L. 1986. *Learning How to Ask: A Sociolinguistic Appraisal of the Role of the Interview in Social Science Research.* Studies in the Social and Cultural Foundations of Language, no. 1. Cambridge, U.K., and New York: Cambridge University Press.

———. (1996) 2016. "The Meaning of Nonsense, the Poetics of Embodiment." In *The Performance of Healing,* edited by Carol Laderman and Marina Roseman, 185–232. London: Routledge.

———. 2007. "Anthropology, Interviewing, and Communicability in Contemporary Society." *Current Anthropology* 48, no. 4 (August): 551–80.

Briggs, Charles L., and Richard Bauman. 1992. "Genre, Intertextuality, and Social Power." *Journal of Linguistic Anthropology* 2, no. 2: 131–72.

Brocklebank, Lisa 2006. "Psychic Reading." *Victorian Studies* 48, no. 2: 233–39.

Brown, Kate. 2001. "Gridded Lives: Why Kazakhstan and Montana Are Nearly the Same Place." *The American Historical Review* 106, no. 1 (February): 17–48.

———. 2015. *Plutopia: Nuclear Families, Atomic Cities, and the Great Soviet and American Plutonium Disasters.* New York: Oxford University Press.

Buck-Morss, Susan. 2000a. *Dreamworld and Catastrophe: The Passing of Mass Utopia in East and West.* Cambridge, MA: MIT Press.

———. "Hegel and Haiti." 2000b. *Critical Inquiry* 26, no. 3 (2000): 821–65.

Carlson, Maria. 2000. "Fashionable Occultism: The World of Russian Composer Aleksandr Scriabin." *Journal of the International Institute* 7, no. 3. http:// quod.lib.umich.edu/j/jii/4750978.0007.301?view=text;rgn=main.

Carnicke, Sharon Marie. 1998. *Stanislavsky in Focus.* Russian Theatre Archive, no. 17. Amsterdam: Harwood Academic Publishers.

————. 2010. "Stanislavsky and Politics." In *The Politics of American Actor Training*, edited byargolis, Ellen and Lissa Tyler Renaud, 15–30. Routledge Advances in Theatre and Performance Studies. New York: Routledge.

Carr, E. Summerson, and Michael Lempert, eds. 2016. *Scale: Discourse and Dimensions of Social Life*. Oakland: University of California Press.

Cassiday, Julie A. 2000. *The Enemy on Trial: Early Soviet Courts on Stage and Screen*. DeKalb: Northern Illinois University Press.

Casson, John W. 2000. "Living Newspaper: Theatre and Therapy." *TDR/The Drama Review* 44, no. 2: 107–22.

Caute, David. 2003. "Passports for Paintings: Abstract Expressionism and the CIA." In *The Dancer Defects: The Struggle for Cultural Supremacy during the Cold War*, 539–68.Oxford: Oxford University Press.

Chakrabarty, Dipesh. 1995. "Radical Histories and Question of Enlightenment." *Economic and Political Weekly* 30, no. 14: 751–59.

Chari, Sharad, and Katherine. Verdery. 2009. "Thinking between the Posts: Postcolonialism, Postsocialism, and Ethnography after the Cold War." *Comparative Studies in Society and History* 51, no. 1: 6–34.

Chernetsov, Alexey V., and Liudmila I. Avilova. 2013. "Magical Practices in Russia Today: An Observer's Report." *Russian History* 40, nos. 3–4 (January 1): 559–67.

Chéroux, Clément. 2005. *The Perfect Medium: Photography and the Occult*. New Haven, CT, and London: Yale University Press.

Chudakova, Tatiana. 2015. "The Pulse in the Machine: Automating Tibetan Diagnostic Palpation in Postsocialist Russia." *Comparative Studies in Society and History* 57, no. 2 (April): 407–34.

Chumley, Lily. 2016. *Creativity Class: Art School and Culture Work in Postsocialist China*. Princeton, NJ: Princeton University Press.

Clark, Katerina. 1995. *Petersburg, Crucible of Cultural Revolution*. Cambridge, MA: Harvard University Press.

————. 2011. *Moscow, the Fourth Rome: Stalinism, Cosmopolitanism, and the Evolution of Soviet Culture, 1931–1941*. Cambridge, MA: Harvard University Press.

Cody, Francis. 2011. "Publics and Politics." *Annual Review of Anthropology* 40, no. 1 (October 21): 37–52.

Cohen, Susanne. 2015a. "Humanizing Soviet Communication." *Slavic Review* 74, no. 3: 439–63.

————. 2015b. "The New Communication Order: Management, Language, and Morality in a Multinational Corporation: The New Communication Order." *American Ethnologist* 42, no. 2: 324–39.

Coleman, Steve. 1996. *Sentiment, entelechy and text*. Paper presented in the session "Rethinking the Symbol" (organized by S. Coleman and J. B. Bate) at the Annual Meetings of the American Anthropological Association, San Francisco, November.

Collier, Stephen J. 2011. *Post-Soviet Social: Neoliberalism, Social Modernity, Biopolitics*. Princeton, NJ: Princeton University Press.

Comaroff, Jean, and John L. Comaroff. 1992. *Ethnography and the Historical Imagination*. Boulder: Westview Press.

——. 1999. "Occult Economies and the Violence of Abstraction: Notes from the South African Postcolony." *American Ethnologist* 26, no. 2: 279–303.

Coronil, Fernando. 1996. "Beyond Occidentalism: Toward Nonimperial Geohistorical Categories." *Cultural Anthropology* 11, no. 1: 51–87.

——. 1997. *The Magical State: Nature, Money, and Modernity in Venezuela*. Chicago: University of Chicago Press.

Counts, George S., and Nucia Perlmutter. 1949. *The Country of the Blind: The Soviet System of Mind Control*. Boston: Houghton Mifflin.

Coxhead, Nina. 1976. *MindPower*. London: Morrison & Gibb.

Craig, Edward Gordon. 1908. "The Actor and the Über-Marionette." *The Mask*, April.

Cronin, Paul, and Werner Herzog. 2003. *Herzog on Herzog: Conversations with Paul Cronin*. London and New York: Farrar, Straus and Giroux.

Crowley, David, and Susan E. Reid, eds. 2010. *Pleasures in Socialism: Leisure and Luxury in the Eastern Bloc*. Evanston, IL: Northwestern University Press.

Cruz, Deirdre de la. 2015. *Mother Figured: Marian Apparitions and the Making of a Filipino Universal*. Chicago and London: University of Chicago Press.

Daly, Nicholas. 2003. "Review of Literature, Technology and Magical Thinking, 1880–1920 (Review)." *Victorian Studies* 45, no. 3: 573–75.

Dames, Ed, and Joel Harry Newman. 2011. *Tell Me What You See: Remote Viewing Cases from the World's Premiere Psychic Spy*. Hoboken, NJ: John Wiley & Sons.

Daniel, E. Valentine. 1996. *Charred Lullabies: Chapters in an Anthropography of Violence*. Princeton Studies in Culture/Power/History. Princeton, NJ: Princeton University Press.

Das, Veena. 2007. *Life and Words: Violence and the Descent into the Ordinary*. A Philip E. Lilienthal Book in Asian Studies. Berkeley: University of California Press.

——. 1978. "British Responses to Psycho-Physiology, 1860–1900." *Isis* 69, no. 2: 192–208.

Daston, Lorraine. 1991. "Marvelous Facts and Miraculous Evidence in Early Modern Europe." *Critical Inquiry*, 18, no. 1: 93–124.

——. 2004. *Things That Talk: Object Lessons from Art and Science*. New York and Cambridge, MA: Zone Books and MIT Press [distributor].

Davenport, Lisa E. 2009. *Jazz Diplomacy: Promoting America in the Cold War Era*. American Made Music. Jackson: University Press of Mississippi.

David-Fox, Michael. 2011. *Showcasing the Great Experiment: Cultural Diplomacy and Western Visitors to the Soviet Union, 1921–1941*. New York: Oxford University Press.

Davis, William B. 1960. "How Negros Live in Russia." *Ebony* (January): 65–73.

"Debunking Kulagina." 1968. *Pravda*, June 24.

Douglas, Mary. 1978. *Purity and Danger: An Analysis of Concepts of Pollution and Taboo*. London: Routledge USA and London.

Dunham, Vera. 1976. *In Stalin's Time: Middleclass Values in Soviet Fiction*. Cambridge, U.K., and New York: Cambridge University Press.

Dunn, Elizabeth C. 2004. *Privatizing Poland: Baby Food, Big Business, and the Remaking of Labor*. Ithaca, NY: Cornell University Press.

Duranti, Alessandro. 2008. "Further Reflections on Reading Other Minds." *Anthropological Quarterly* 81, no. 2: 483–94.

During, Simon. 2002. *Modern Enchantments: The Cultural Power of Secular Magic*. Cambridge, MA: Harvard University Press.

Eagle, Herb. 1992. "Socialist Realism and American Genre Film: The Mixing of Codes in Jazzmen." In *The Red Screen: Politics, Society, Art in Soviet Cinema*, edited by Anna Lawton, 249–63. New York: Routledge.

Ebon, Martin. 1983. *Psychic Warfare: Threat or Illusion?* New York: McGraw-Hill.

Egides, A.P. 2002. *Labirinty Obshchenija, ili Kak Nauchitsja Uladit' s Ljud'mi* [Labyrinths of communication, or how to teach yourself to get along with people]. St. Petersburg: AST Press Books.

Eisenlohr, Patrick. 2009. "Technologies of the Spirit: Devotional Islam, Sound Reproduction and the Dialectics of Mediation and Immediacy in Mauritius." *Anthropological Theory* 9, no. 3: 273–96.

Elyachar, Julia. 2010. "Phatic Labor, Infrastructure, and the Question of Empowerment in Cairo: Phatic Labor." *American Ethnologist* 37, no. 3 (July 14): 452–64.

Emerson, Caryl. 1983. "The Outer Word and Inner Speech: Bakhtin, Vygotsky, and the Internalization of Language." *Critical Inquiry* 10, no. 2: 245–64.

Enelow, Shonni. 2015. "Pathological Hypnotism: Hysterical Methods." In *Method Acting and Its Discontents: On American Psycho-Drama*, 31–36. Evanston, IL: Northwestern University Press.

Epstein, Mikhail. 1995. *After the Future: The Paradoxes of Postmodernism and Contemporary Russian Culture*. Critical Perspectives on Modern Culture. Amherst: University of Massachusetts Press.

Etkind, Alexander. 1997. *Eros of the Impossible: The History of Psychoanalysis in Russia by Alexander Etkind*. Boulder, CO: Westview Press.

———. 2008. "Beyond Eugenics: The Forgotten Scandal of Hybridizing Humans and Apes." *Studies in History and Philosophy of Science Part C: Studies in History and Philosophy of Biological and Biomedical Sciences* 39, no. 2 (June): 205–10.

———. 2013. "Post-Soviet Russia: The Land of the Oil Curse, Pussy Riot, and Magical Historicism." *Boundary 2* 41, no. 1: 153–70.

Fabian, Johannes. 1990. *Power and Performance: Ethnographic Explorations through Proverbial Wisdom and Theater in Shaba, Zaire*. New Directions in Anthropological Writing Madison: University of Wisconsin Press.

Faddeev, E.T. 1961. "Tak Chto Zhe Takoe Telepatiia?" [So what is telepathy anyway?]. *Nauka i Zhizn'* 6: 60–63.

Faraday, George. 2000. *Revolt of the Filmmakers: The Struggle for Artistic Autonomy and the Fall of the Soviet Film Industry*. Post-Communist Cultural Studies Series. University Park: Pennsylvania State University Press.

Farber, Vreneli. 2008. *Stanislavsky in Practice: Actor Training in Post-Soviet Russia*. Artists and Issues in the Theatre, vol. 16. New York: Peter Lang.

Farquhar, Judith. 2002. *Appetites: Food and Sex in Post-Socialist China*. Durham, NC: Duke University Press Books.

Favret-Saada, Jeanne. 1980. *Deadly Words: Witchcraft in the Bocage, Les Mots, La Mort, Les Sorts*. Cambridge, U.K., and New York: Cambridge University Press.

Fehérváry, Krisztina. 2002. "American Kitchens, Luxury Bathrooms and the Search for a 'Normal' Life in post-Socialist Hungary." *Ethnos* 67 no. 3: 369–400.

———. 2007. "Hungarian Horoscopes as a Genre of Postsocialist Transformation." *Social Identities* 13, no. 5: 561–76.

———. 2013. *Politics in Color and Concrete: Socialist Materialities and the Middle Class in Hungary*. Bloomington: Indiana University Press.

Fikes, Kesha, and Alaina Lemon. 2002. "African Presence in Former Soviet Spaces." *Annual Review of Anthropology* 31, no. 1 (October): 497–524.

Fitzpatrick, Sheila. 2000. *Everyday Stalinism: Ordinary Life in Extraordinary Times: Soviet Russia in the 1930s*. New York: Oxford University Press.

———. 2005. *Tear Off the Masks! Identity and Imposture in Twentieth-Century Russia*. Princeton, NJ: Princeton University Press.

Fliegelman, Jay. 1993. *Declaring Independence: Jefferson, Natural Language & the Culture of Performance*. Stanford, CA: Stanford University Press.

Forrester, Sibelan. 2013. "Russian Village Magic in the Late Soviet Period: One Woman's Repertoire of Zagovory." *Russian History* 40, nos. 3–4 (January 1): 540–58.

Friedland, Paul. 2002. *Political Actors: Representative Bodies and Theatricality in the Age of the French Revolution*. Ithaca, NY: Cornell University Press.

Friedrich, Paul. 1972. "Russian Pronominal Usage." In *Directions in Sociolinguistics*, edited by Dell Hymes and John Gumperz, 270–300. New York: Holt, Rinehart and Winston.

Frosh, Paul 2011. "Phatic Morality: Television and Proper Distance." *International Journal of Cultural Studies* 14, no. 4 (July 1): 383–400.

Fülöp-Miller, René, F.S. Flint, and D.F. Tait. 1929. *The Mind and Face of Bolshevism: An Examination of Cultural Life in Soviet Russia*. New York: Knopf.

Gaik, Frank. 1992. "Radio Talk Show Therapy and the Pragmatics of Possible Worlds." In *Rethinking Context: Language as an Interactive Phenomenon*, edited by Alessandro Duranti, 271–90. Cambridge, U.K., and New York: Cambridge University Press.

Gal, Susan. 1995. "Language and the 'Arts of Resistance.'" *Cultural Anthropology* 10, no. 3 (August 1): 407–24.

———. 2005. "Language Ideologies Compared." *Journal of Linguistic Anthropology* 15, no. 1: 23–37.

Galison, Peter. 2004. "Image of Self." In *Things That Talk: Object Lessons from Art and Science*, edited by Lorraine Daston, 257–96. New York and Cambridge, MA: Zone Books and MIT Press.

———. 2012. "Blacked-out Spaces: Freud, Censorship and the Re-Territorialization of Mind." *British Journal for the History of Science* 45, no. 2: 235–66.

Galvan, Jill Nicole. 2010. *Sympathetic Medium: Feminine Channeling, the Occult, and Communication Technologies, 1859–1919*. Ithaca, NY: Cornell University Press.

———. 2015. "Occult Networks and the Legacy of the Indian Rebellion in Bram Stoker's Dracula." *History of Religions* 54, no. 4: 434–58.

Gapova, Elena. 2017. *Journal of Soviet and postSoviet Politics and Society*. 3, no.1: 1–31.

Gates, Henry Louis. 1988. *The Signifying Monkey: A Theory of African-American Literary Criticism*. New York: Oxford University Press.

Geertz, Clifford 1980. *Negara: the Theatre State in Nineteenth-Century Bali*. Princeton, NJ: Princeton University Press.

Gell, Alfred, and Eric Hirsch. 1999. "The Technology of Enchantment and the Enchantment of Technology." In *The Art of Anthropology: Essays and Diagrams*, 159–86. New Brunswick, NJ: Athlone Press.

Geltzer, Anna. 2011. "The Rise and Fall of the Extrasense." *Somatosphere*. Accessed July 16, 2017. http://somatosphere.net/2011/12/the-rise-and-fall-of-the-extrasense.html.

Gershon, Ilana. 2010. "Media Ideologies: An Introduction." *Journal of Linguistic Anthropology* 20, no. 2: 283–93.

Geschiere, Peter. 1997. *The Modernity of Witchcraft*. Charlottesville: University of Virginia Press.

———. 2013. *Witchcraft, Intimacy, and Trust: Africa in Comparison*. Chicago: University of Chicago Press.

Gilroy, Paul. 1993. *The Black Atlantic: Modernity and Double-Consciousness*. Cambridge, MA: Harvard University Press.

Ginsburg, Faye. 1994. "Embedded Aesthetics: Creating a Discursive Space for Indigenous Media." *Cultural Anthropology* 9, no. 3: 365–82.

GITIS. 1998. *GITIS/RATI: Rossiskaja Akademija Teatral'nogo Iskusstva* [Informational pamphlet for prospective students]. Moscow: GITIS Press.

Glazov, Yuri. 1985. *The Russian Mind since Stalin's Death*. Sovietica, no. 47. Dordrecht, Boston, and Hingham, MA: D. Reidel; distributed by Kluwer Academic Publishers.

Goffman, Erving. 1974. *Frame Analysis: An Essay on the Organization of Experience*. London: Harper & Row.

———. 1981. "Footing (1979)." In *Forms of Talk*, 124–59. Philadelphia: University of Pennsylvania Press.

Golub, Spencer. 1984. *Evreinov, the Theatre of Paradox and Transformation*. Theater and Dramatic Studies, no. 19. Ann Arbor, MI: UMI Research Press.

Golubev, Alexey. 2016. "Affective Machines or the Inner Self? Drawing the Boundaries of the Female Body in the Socialist Romantic Imagination." *Canadian Slavonic Papers/Revue canadienne des slavistes* 58, no. 2: 141–59.

Gorchakov, N.M. 1954. *Rezhisserskie Uroki K.S. Stanislavskogo* [Lessons with K.S. Stanislavskii, director]. New York: Funk & Wagnalls.

Gordon, Rae Beth. 2001. "From Charcot to Charlot: Unconscious Imitation and Spectatorship in French Cabaret and Early Cinema." *Critical Inquiry* 27, no. 3: 515–49.

Gordon, Robert. 2006. *The Purpose of Playing: Modern Acting Theories in Perspective*. Theater—Theory/Text/Performance. Ann Arbor: University of Michigan Press.

Graan, Andrew. 2010. "On the Politics of 'Imidž': European Integration and the Trials of Recognition in Postconflict Macedonia." *Slavic Review* 69, no. 4 (January 1): 835–58.

Grant, Bruce. 2010. "'Cosmopolitan Baku.'" *Ethnos* 75, no. 2 (June): 123–47.

Group, Army CRV. 2012. *Coordinate Remote Viewing Manual*. n.p.: CreateSpace Independent Publishing Platform.

Gulyeav, P., and M. Airapetiiants. 1961. "Chitateli Sprashivajut Nas: 'Est' li peredacha mysli na rasstojanii?'" [Readers ask us: "Does thought transfer at a distance exist?"] *Tekhnika Molodezhi*, no. 1: 30–33.

Gursel, Zeynep. 2016. *Visualizing World News in the Age of Digital Circulation*. Berkeley: University of California Press.

Gutkin, Irina. 1997. "The Magic of Words: Symbolism, Futurism, Socialist Realism." In *The Occult in Russian and Soviet Culture*, edited by Bernice Glatzer Rosenthal, 225–46. Ithaca, NY: Cornell University Press.

Hacking, Ian. 1988. "Telepathy: Origins of Randomization in Experimental Design." *Isis* 79, no. 3: 427–51.

Hall, Stuart. 1990. "Cultural Identity and Diaspora." In *Identity: Community, Culture, Difference*, edited by Jonathan Rutherford. London: Lawrence & Wishar.

Halpern, Richard. 2011. "Theater and Democratic Thought: Arendt to Rancierre." *Critical Inquiry* 37, no. 3: 545–72.

Hanks, Michele. 2016. "Between Electricity and Spirit: Paranormal Investigation and the Creation of Doubt in England: Between Electricity and Spirit." *American Anthropologist* 118, no. 4 (December): 811–23.

Hastings, Adi, and Paul Manning. 2004. "Introduction: Acts of Alterity." *Language & Communication* 24, no. 4: 291–311.

Hastrup, Kirsten. 1998. "Theatre as a Site of Passage." *Ritual, Performance, Media*, no. 35: 29.

Havel, Vaclav. (1978) 1987 . *The Power of the Powerless: Citizens Against the State in Central Eastern Europe*. Armonk: Routledge,

Haywood, Harry. 1978. *Black Bolshevik: Autobiography of an Afro-American Communist*. Chicago: Liberator Press.

Heifetz, Leonid. 2001. *Prizvanie* [A calling]. Moscow: GITIS Press.

Hellbeck, Jochen. 2009. *Revolution on My Mind: Writing a Diary Under Stalin.* Cambridge, MA: Harvard University Press.

Henderson, Linda Dalrymple. 1983. *The Fourth Dimension and Non-Euclidean Geometry in Modern Art.* London and Cambridge, MA: MIT Press.

Hessler, Julie. 2006. "Death of an African Student in Moscow." *Cahiers Du Monde Russe* 47, no. 1: 33–63.

Hicks, Jeremy. 2012. *First Films of the Holocaust: Soviet Cinema and the Genocide of the Jews, 1938–1946.* Pittsburgh: University of Pittsburgh Press.

Hill, Jane. 1995. "The Voices of Don Gabriel: Responsibility and Self in a Modern Mexicano Narrative." In *The Dialogic Emergence of Culture*, edited by Dennis Tedlock and Bruce Mannheim, 97–147. Urbana: University of Illinois Press.

Hill, Jane, and Judith Irvine. 1993. *Responsibility and Evidence in Oral Discourse.* Cambridge, U.K.: Cambridge University Press.

Hingley, Ronald. 1978. *The Russian Mind.* New York: Scribner.

Hirsch, Francine. 2005. *Empire of Nations: Ethnographic Knowledge and the Making of the Soviet Union.* Culture and Society after Socialism. Ithaca, NY: Cornell University Press.

Hirschkind, Charles. 2006. *The Ethical Soundscape: Cassette Sermons and Islamic Counterpublics.* Cultures of History. New York: Columbia University Press.

Ho, Engseng. 2004. "Empire through Diasporic Eyes: A View from the Other Boat." *Comparative Studies in Society and History* 46, no. 2: 210–46.

Hochschild, Arlie Russell. 1983. *Managed Heart: Commercialization of Human Feeling.* Berkeley: University of California Press.

Hoffmann-Dilloway, Erika. 2011. "Ordering Burgers, Reordering Relations: Gestural Interactions between Hearing and Deaf Nepalis." *Pragmatics* 21 no. 3: 373–91.

Houdini, Harry. 1993. *Miracle Mongers and Their Methods: A Complete Expose.* Skeptic's Bookshelf. Buffalo, NY: Prometheus Books.

Houghton, Norris. 1936. *Moscow Rehearsals: An Account of Methods of Production in the Soviet Theatre.* New York: Harcourt, Brace.

———. 1962. *Return Engagement: A Postscript to "Moscow Rehearsals".* London: Putnam.

Howes, David. 2003. *Sensual Relations: Engaging the Senses in Culture and Social Theory.* Ann Arbor: University of Michigan Press.

———. 2009. *The Sixth Sense Reader.* Oxford: Berg.

Hull, Matthew S. 2008. "Ruled by Records: The Expropriation of Land and the Misappropriation of Lists in Islamabad." *American Ethnologist* 35, no. 4 (November): 501–18.

———. 2012. *Government of Paper: The Materiality of Bureaucracy in Urban Pakistan.* Berkeley: University of California Press.

Humphrey, Caroline. 1994. "Remembering an Enemy: The Bogd Khaan in Twentieth Century Mongolia." In *Memory, History, and Opposition Under*

State Socialism, edited by R. Watson, 21–44. Sante Fe, NM: School of American Research.

———. 2004. "Cosmopolitanism and Kosmopolotizm in the Political Life of Soviet Citizens." *FOCAAL* 44: 138–52.

———. 2005. "Ideology in Infrastructure: Architecture and Soviet Imagination." *Journal of the Royal Anthropological Institute* 11, no. 1: 39–58.

———. 2012. "Favors and Normal Heroes: The Case of Postsocialist Higher Education." *HAU: Journal of Ethnographic Theory* 2, no. 2: 22–41.

Husband, William B. 2002. *Godless Communists: Atheism and Society in Soviet Russia, 1917–1932*. DeKalb: Northern Illinois University Press.

Irvine, Judith T. 1989. "When Talk Isn't Cheap: Language and Political Economy." *American Ethnologist* 16, no. 2: 248–67.

———. 1996. "Shadow Conversations: The Indeterminacy of Participant Roles." In *Natural Histories of Discourse*, edited by M. Silverstein and Greg Urban, 131–59. Chicago: University of Chicago Press.

Irvine, Judith, and Susan Gal. 2000. "Language Ideology and Linguistic Differentiation." In *Regimes of Language: Ideologies, Politics, and Identities*, edited by P. V. Kroskrity, 35–84. Santa Fe, NM: School for Advanced Research Press.

ITAR-TASS. 2011. Psychics Are Said to Help Law Enforcers Investigate Crimes." November 23. Accessed July 20, 2013. http://tass.com/opinions /762719.

Jannarone, Kimberly 2009. "Audience, Mass, Crowd: Theatres of Cruelty in Interwar Europe." *Theatre Journal* 61, no. 2: 191–211.

Jestrovic, Silvija. 2006. *Theatre of Estrangement: Theory, Practice, Ideology*. Toronto: University of Toronto Press.

Johnson, Ann K. 1996. *Urban Ghetto Riots, 1965–1968: A Comparison of Soviet and American Press Coverage*. East European Monographs, no. 437. Boulder, CO, and New York: East European Monographs; distributed by Columbia University Press, 1996.

Johnson, Paul C. 2011. "An Atlantic Genealogy of 'Spirit Possession.'" *Comparative Studies in Society and History* 53, no. 2: 393–425.

Jones, Graham. M. 2009. "Modern Magic and the War on Miracles in French Colonial Culture." *Comparative Studies in Society and History* 52, no. 1: 66–99.

———. 2011. *Trade of the Tricks: Inside the Magician's Craft*. Berkeley: University of California Press.

———. 2014. "Secrecy." *Annual Review of Anthropology* 43, no. 1: 53–69.

Jones, Caroline A., and Peter Galison. 1998. *Picturing Science, Producing Art*. New York: Routledge.

"Kak vidit vas obyknovennaja mukha" [How does an ordinary fly see you?]. 1966. *Znanie-Sila* no. 1: 10–11.

Kaletski, Alexander. 1985. *Metro: a Novel of the Moscow Underground*. London: Methuen.

Kalinin, Ilya. 2015. "Petropoetics." In *Russian Literature Since 1991*, edited by Evgeny Dobrenko and Mark Lipovetsky, 120–44. Cambridge, U.K.: Cambridge University Press,

Kaminer, Jenny. 2006. "Theatrical Motifs and the Drama of Everyday Life in the 1920s Stories of Mikhail Zoshchenko." *The Russian Review* 65, no. 3: 470–90.

Kandinsky, Wassily. (1911) 1946. *On the Spiritual in Art*. Translated by Hilla Rebay. New York: Solomon R. Guggenhim Foundation.

———. (1926) 1979. *Point and Line to Plane*. New York: Dover Publications.

Katznelson, Anna. 2007. "Aesopian Tales: The Visual Culture of the Late Russian Avant-Garde." PhD diss., Harvard University Press.

Kazhinskij, Bernard Bernardovich. (1923) 1962. *Biologicheskaja Radiosvjaz'* [Biological radioconnections]. Kiev: Ukraine Academy of Sciences

Keane, Webb. 1997. "From Fetishism to Sincerity: On Agency, the Speaking Subject, and Their Historicity in the Context of Religious Conversion." *Comparative Studies in Society and History* 39, no. 4: 674–93.

———. 2002. "Sincerity, 'Modernity,' and the Protestants." *Cultural Anthropology* 17, no. 1 (February 1): 65–92.

———. 2008. "Others, Other Minds, and Others' Theories of Other Minds: An Afterword on the Psychology and Politics of Opacity Claims." *Anthropological Quarterly* 81, no. 2: 473–82.

———. 2013. "On Spirit Writing: Materialities of Language and the Religious Work of Transduction." *Journal of the Royal Anthropological Institute* 19, no. 1: 1–17.

Kelly, Catriona. 2001. *Refining Russia: Advice Literature, Polite Culture and Gender from Catherine to Yeltsin*. Oxford: Oxford University Press.

Kelly, John D., and Martha Kaplan. 2001. "Nation and Decolonization: Toward a New Anthropology of Nationalism." *Anthropological Theory* 1, no. 4 (December): 419–37.

Kelly, John. 2012. "Seeking What? Subversion, Situation, and Transvaluation." *Focaal*, no. 64 (November 26): 51–60.

Kennan, George. 1971. *The Marquis de Custine and His Russia in 1839*. Princeton, NJ: Princeton University Press.

Kerans, David. 2001. *Mind and Labor on the Farm in Black-Earth Russia, 1861–1914*. Budapest and New York: Central European University Press.

Kevorkian, Martin. 2006. *Color Monitors: The Black Face of Technology in America*. Ithaca, NY: Cornell University Press.

Khan, Aisha. 2008. "Dark Arts and Diaspora." *Diaspora: A Journal of Transnational Studies* 17, no. 1: 40–63.

Khanga, Yelena, and Susan Jacoby. 1992. *Soul to Soul: A Black Russian American Family, 1865–1992*. New York: W.W. Norton.

Kharkhordin, Oleg. 1999. *The Collective and the Individual in Russia: A Study of Practices*. Berkeley: University of California Press.

Khlebnikov, V. 1986. *O Stikhakh* [On verses]. In *Tvorenija*, 633. Moscow: Sovjetsij Pisatel'.

Khristoforova, O.B. 2010. *Kolduny i Zhertvy: Antropologija Koldovstva v Sovremennoj Rossii* [Sorcerors and victims: The anthropology of sorcery in modern Russia]. Moskva: RGGU: Obedinennoe gumanitarnoe Press.

Kind-Kovács, Friederike. 2013. "Radio Free Europe and Radio Liberty as the 'Echo Chamber' of Tamizdat." In *Samizdat, Tamizdat, and Beyond:*

Transnational Media during and after Socialism, edited by Jessie Labov and Friederike Kind-Kovács, 70–91. Studies in Contemporary European History, no. 13. New York: Berghahn Books.

Kitajgorodsky, A. 1964. "The Fruits of Enlightenment." *Literaturnaja Gazeta* 8: 9.

Kivelson, Valerie A. 2003. "Male Witches and Gendered Categories in Seventeenth-Century Russia." *Comparative Studies in Society and History* 45, no. 3: 606–31.

———. 2013. "Introduction: Bringing the Slavs Back In." *Russian History* 40, nos. 3–4 (January 1): 281–95.

Kivelson, Valerie, and Jonathan Shaheen. 2011. "Prosaic Witchcraft and Semiotic Totalitarianism: Muscovite Magic Reconsidered." *Slavic Review* 70, no. 1: 23–44.

Klassen, Pamela E. 2007. "Radio Mind: Protestant Experimentalists on the Frontiers of Healing." *Journal of the American Academy of Religion* 75, no. 3: 651–83.

Klima, Alan. 2002. *The Funeral Casino: Meditation, Massacre, and Exchange with the Dead in Thailand.* Princeton, NJ: Princeton University Press.

Knebel', M. 1964. *Slovo v Tvorchestve Aktera* [The word in the actor's creative process]. Moscow: Iskra Revolutsij.

———. 1967. *Vsja Zhizn'* [All my life]. Moscow: All-Russian Theatrical Society

Knight, Nathaniel. 1998. "Science, Empire and Nationality: Ethnography in the Russian Geological Society." In *Imperial Russia: New Histories for the Empire,* edited by Jane Burbank and David Ransel, 108–42. Bloomington: Indiana University Press.

Kockelman, Paul. 2010. "Enemies, Parasites, and Noise: How to Take Up Residence in a System Without Becoming a Term in It." *Journal of Linguistic Anthropology* 20, no. 2: 406–21.

Kohn, Hans. 1955. *The Mind of Modern Russia; Historical and Political Thought of Russia's Great Age.* New Brunswick, NJ: Rutgers University Press.

Kolodny, Leon. 1967. "Moscow-Leningrad Experiment." *Moskovskaja Pravda,* April 9.

Komlev, Mikhail. 2013. *Mikhail Vinogradov, Sledstvie Idet: Kak Uberech' Sebja Ot Bed Bol'shikh i Malykh* [Mikhail Vinogradov, the investigation continues: How to defend yourself from tragedies large and small]. Moscow: Ripol Classic.

Kosova, Kristina. 2015. "Communicative Culture and the Role of Phatic Function in Interpersonal Communication." *Vestnik Volgogradskogo Gosudarstvennogo Universiteta. Serija 2. Jazykoznanije,* no. 2 (June): 87–94.

Kotik, Naum. 1907. Emanatsija Psikhofizicheskoj Energii: Eksperimental'noe issledovanie Javlenii Mediumizma, Jasnovidenija i myslennogo Vnushenija v Svjazi s Voprosom o Radioaktivnosti Mozga. [Emanations of psychophysical energy: Experimental research on the appearance of mediumism, clairvoyance and mental hypnosis in connection with the question of the brain's radioactivity]. Moskva: Izd. V.M. Sablina.

———. 1908. *Neposredstvennaja peredacha myslej* [The direct transference of thoughts]. Moscow: Sovremennie Problemy.

"Krik dushi." 1997. Advice section. *Kosmopoliten*, July, 32.

Kruger, Loren. 2007. "'White Cities,' 'Diamond Zulus,' and the 'African Contribution to Human Advancement': African Modernities and the World's Fairs." *TDR/The Drama Review* 51, no. 3: 19–45.

Krugljakov, E.P. 2009. "Why Do We Need to Fight Pseudo-science?" *Nauka I Zhizn'*, no. 12 (December 18). Accessed July 20, 2017. https://www.nkj.ru /interview/16780/.

Kruglova, Anna. 2014. "'Words and Deeds' Dialectic in the (Post?) Post-Soviet Everyday." Paper presented at Association for Slavic, East European and Eurasian Studies annual convention, San Antonio, TX.

Kukulin, Il'ia. 2011. "Alternative Social Blueprinting in Soviet Society of the 1960s and the 1970s, or Why Left-Wing Political Practices Have Not Caught on in Contemporary Russia." *Russian Studies in History* 49, no. 4: 51–92.

Kukulin, S.A., Mark Lipovetsky, and Maria Maiofis. 2008. *Veselye Chelovechki: Kul'turnye Geroi v Sovetskom Detstve* [Merry little fellows: Cultural heroes in Soviet childhood]. Moscow: Novoe literaturnoe obozrenie.

Kulkarni, Dipti. 2014. "Exploring Jakobson's 'phatic Function'in Instant Messaging Interactions." *Discourse & Communication* 8, no. 2: 117–36.

Kunreuther, Laura 2010. "Transparent Media: Radio, Voice, and Ideologies of Directness in Postdemocratic Nepal." *Journal of Linguistic Anthropology* 20, no. 2: 334–51.

Lachapelle, Sofie. 2008. "From the Stage to the Laboratory: Magicians, Psychologists, and the Science of Illusion." *Journal of the History of the Behavioral Sciences* 44, no. 4 (June): 319–34.

Lamont, Peter. 2013. *Extraordinary Beliefs: A Historical Approach to a Psychological Problem*. Cambridge, U.K.: Cambridge University Press.

Lane, Christel. 1981. *The Rites of Rulers: Ritual in Industrial Society—The Soviet Case*. 1st ed. Cambridge, U.K., and New York: Cambridge University Press.

Laplantine, François, and David Howes. 2015. *The Life of the Senses: Introduction to a Modal Anthropology*. Translated by Jamie Furniss. London and New York: Bloomsbury Academic.

Larkin, Brian. 2008. *Signal and Noise: Media, Infrastructure, and Urban Culture in Nigeria*. Durham, NC: Duke University Press.

———. 2013. "The Politics and Poetics of Infrastructure." *Annual Review of Anthropology* 42, no. 1 (October 21): 327–43.

Larson, Jonathan L. 2013. *Critical Thinking in Slovakia after Socialism*. Rochester, NY: University of Rochester Press.

"Last Experiment of Roza Kulesheva." 1978. *Tekhnika Molodezhi*, no. 8: 35–37.

Latour, Bruno. 1993. *We Have Never Been Modern*. Translated by Catherine Porter. Cambridge, MA: Harvard University Press.

Law, Alma H., and Mel Gordon. 1996. *Meyerhold, Eisenstein, and Biomechanics: Actor Training in Revolutionary Russia*. Jefferson, NC: McFarland.

Layton, Susan. 1994. *Russian Literature and Empire: Conquest of the Caucasus from Pushkin to Tolstoy*. Cambridge Studies in Russian Literature. Cambridge, U.K., and New York: Cambridge University Press.

Ledeneva, Alena V. 1998. *Russia's Economy of Favours: Blat, Networking, and Informal Exchange*. Russia's Economy of Favors. Cambridge, U.K., and New York: Cambridge University Press.

LeJeune, Anthony. 1963. "Soviet Pushes Experiments to Get More for Telepathy." *London Sunday Times*, reprinted in *Lawrence Journal World*, July 13, 3.

Lemon, Alaina. 1991. "Mayakovskii and the Language of Lenin." *Chicago Anthropology Exchange* 19: 1–26.

———. 1995. "'What Are They Writing about Us Blacks': Roma and 'Race' in Russia." *Anthropology of East Europe Review* 13, no. 2: 34–40.

———. 1998. "'Your Eyes Are Green Like Dollars': Counterfeit Cash, National Substance, and Currency Apartheid in 1990s' Russia." *Cultural Anthropology* 13, no. 1: 22–55.

———. 2000a. *Between Two Fires: Gypsy Performance and Romani Memory from Pushkin to Post-Socialism*. Durham, NC: Duke University Press.

———. 2000b. "Talking Transit and Spectating Transition: The Moscow Metro," in *Altering States: Anthropology in Transition*, edited by Daphne Berdahl, Matti Bunzl, Martha Lampland, 14–39. Ann Arbor: University of Michigan Press.

———. 2002. "Without a 'Concept'? Race as Discursive Practice." *Slavic Review* 61, no. 1: 54–61.

———. 2004. "'Dealing Emotional Blows': Realism and Verbal 'Terror' at the Russian State Theatrical Academy." *Language and Communication* 24, no. 4: 313–37

———. 2008. "Hermeneutic Algebras: Solving for Love, Time/Space, and Value in Putin-era Personal Ads." *Journal of Linguistic Anthropology* 18, no. 2: 236–67.

———. 2009. "Sympathy for the Weary State?: Cold War Chronotopes and Moscow Others." *Comparative Studies in Society and History* 51 no. 4: 832–64.

———. 2013. "Touching the Gap: Social Qualia and Cold War Contact." *Anthropological Theory* 13, no. 1/2: 67–88.

———. 2015. "MetroDogs: The Heart in the Machine." *Journal of the Royal Anthropological Institute* 21, no. 3: 660–79.

Lempert, Michael. 2007. "How to Make Our Subjects Clear: Denotational Transparency and Subject Formation in the Tibetan Diaspora." *Text & Talk—An Interdisciplinary Journal of Language, Discourse Communication Studies* 27, no. 4: 509–32.

Lempert, Michael, and Michael Silverstein. 2012. *Creatures of Politics: Media, Message, and the American Presidency*. Bloomington: Indiana University Press.

Lende, Daniel H., and Greg Downey. 2012. *The Encultured Brain: An Introduction to Neuroanthropology*. Cambridge, MA: MIT Press.

Lepselter, Susan. 2005. "The License: Poetics, Power, and the Uncanny." In *E.T. Culture: Anthropology in Outerspaces*, edited by Deborra Battaglia, 130–48. Durham, NC: Duke University Press.

Lerner, Julia, and Claudia Zbenovich. 2013. "Adapting the Therapeutic Discourse to Post-Soviet Media Culture: The Case of Modnyi Prigovor." *Slavic Review* 72, no. 4 (December): 828–49.

Levi-Strauss, Claude. 1963. "The Sorcerer and His Magic." In *Structural Anthropology*, 167–85. New York: Basic Books.

Levinas, Emmanuel. 1947. "The Other in Proust." In *The Levinas Reader*, edited by Sean Hand. Oxford: Blackwell.

Lindquist, Galina. 2001. "Transforming Signs: Iconicity and Indexicality in Russian Healing and Magic." *Ethnos* 66, no. 2: 181–206.

———. 2002. "Spirits and Souls of Business: New Russians, Magic and the Esthetics of Kitsch." *Journal of Material Culture* 7, no. 3 (November): 329–43.

———. 2006. *Conjuring Hope: Magic and Healing in Contemporary Russia*. Epistemologies of Healing, no. 1. New York: Berghahn Books.

Lipovetsky, Mark. 2004. "Post-Sots: Transformations of Socialist Realism in the Popular Culture of the Recent Period." *Slavic and East European Journal* 48, no. 3: 356–77.

———. 2010. *Charms of the Cynical Reason: Tricksters in Soviet and Post-Soviet Culture*. Brighton, MA: Academic Studies Press.

———. 2013. "The Poetics of ITR Discourse: In the 1960s and Today." *Ab Imperio*, no. 1: 109–39.

"Lire Dans Les Pensées: La Télépathie." Accessed July 20, 2017. http://lire-dans-les-pensees.blogspot.com/p/la-telepathie.html.

Losev, Lev. 1984. *On the Beneficence of Censorship: Aesopian Language in Modern Russian Literature*. Munich: Verla Otto Sagner in Komission.

Lotman, Jurij Michajlovič. 1985. "The Poetics of Everyday Behavior in 18th Century Russian Culture." In *The Semiotics of Russian Cultural History*, edited by Lidija Jakovlevna Ginzburg, Boris Andreevič Uspenskij, and Alexander D. Nakhimovsky, 67–94. Ithaca, NY, and London: Cornell University Press.

Luckhurst, Roger. 2002. *The Invention of Telepathy, 1870–1901*. Oxford: Oxford University Press.

Luehrmann, Sonja. 2011. *Secularism Soviet Style: Teaching Atheism and Religion in a Volga Republic*. Bloomington: Indiana University Press.

———. 2015. *Religion in Secular Archives: Soviet Atheism and Historical Knowledge*. Oxford and New York: Oxford University Press.

Lungina, Tatjana. 1982. *Vol'f Messing—chelovek-zagadka* [Wolf Messing: The man the riddle]. Ann Arbor, MI: Ėrmitazh.

Lyons, Eugene. 1947. *Mind and Spirit in the Land of Soviets*. Pamphlet Series on Communism, no. 3. New York: Catholic Information Society.

Mack, Raneta Lawson. 2001. *The Digital Divide: Standing at the Intersection of Race & Technology*. Durham, NC: Carolina Academic Press.

Malinowski, Bronislaw. 1923. "The Problem of Meaning in Primitive Languages." In *The Meaning of Meaning*, Supplement I, edited by C.K. Ogden and I.A. Richards, 296–336. Abingdon, U.K.: Kegan Paul.

Mally, Lynn. 2000. *Revolutionary Acts: Amateur Theater and the Soviet State, 1917–1938*. Ithaca, NY: Cornell University Press.

Mandel, Ruth. 2002. "A Marshall Plan of the Mind: The Political Economy of a Kazakh Soap Opera." In *Media Worlds: Anthropology on New Terrain*, edited by Faye Ginsburg, Lila Abu-Lughod, and Brian Larkin, 211–28. Berkeley: University of California Press.

Mandelbaum, W. Adam. 2002. *The Psychic Battlefield: A History of the Military-Occult Complex*. New York: St. Martin's Griffin.

Mangan, Michael. 2007. *Performing Dark Arts: A Cultural History of Conjuring*. Theatre and Consciousness. Bristol, U.K., and Chicago: Intellect.

Manning, Paul. 2009. "City of Balconies: Elite Politics and the Changing Semiotics of the Post-Socialist Cityscape." In *City Culture and City Planning in Tbilisi: Where Europe and Asia Meet*, edited by K. Van Assche, J. Salukvadze, and N. Shavishvili, 71–102. Lewiston: Mellon Press, 2009.

———. 2012. *Strangers in a Strange Land*. Brighton, U.K.: Academic Studies Press.

Manning, Paul, and Ilana Gershon. 2013. "Animating Interaction." *HAU: Journal of Ethnographic Theory* 3, no. 3: 107–37.

Marcus, George E. 1995. "Ethnography in/of the World System: The Emergence of Multi-Sited Ethnography." *Annual Review of Anthropology* 24, no. 1: 95.

Marcus, Greil., and Pietro Ferrua. 1989. *Lipstick Traces: A Secret History of the Twentieth Century*. Cambridge, MA: Harvard University Press.

Marrs, Jim. 2007. *PSI Spies: The True Story of America's Psychic Warfare Program*. Franklin Lakes, NJ: New Page Books.

Martin, Terry. 2001. *The Affirmative Action Empire: Nations and Nationalism in the Soviet Union, 1923–1939*. The Wilder House Series in Politics, History and Culture. Ithaca, NY: Cornell University Press.

Masco, Joseph 2002. "Lie Detectors: On Secrets and Hypersecurity in Los Alamos." *Public Culture* 14, no. 3: 441–467.

———. 2008. " 'Survival Is Your Business': Engineering Ruins and Affect in Nuclear America." *Cultural Anthropology* 23, no. 2: 361–98.

———. 2004. "Nuclear Technoaesthetics: Sensory Politics from Trinity to the Virtual Bomb in Los Alamos." *American Ethnologist* 31, no. 3: 349–73.

Massumi, Brian. 2002. *Parables for the Virtual: Movement, Affect, Sensation*. Durham, NC: Duke University Press Books.

Matusevich, Maxim. 2012. "Expanding the Boundaries of the Black Atlantic: African Students as Soviet Moderns." *Ab Imperio*, no. 2: 325–50.

Matza, Tomas. 2012. "Allan Chumak." *Frequencies: A Collaborative Genealogy of Spirituality*, January 16. Accessed July 22, 2017. http://freq.uenci.es/2012/01/16/allan-chumak.

Maurer, Eva. 2011. *Soviet Space Culture: Cosmic Enthusiasm in Socialist Societies.* Houndmills, Basingstoke, Hampshire, U.K., and New York: Palgrave Macmillan.

McCannon, John. 2002. "By the Shores of White Waters: The Altai and Its Place in the Spiritual Geopolitics of Nicholas Roerich." *Sibirica* 2, no. 2 (January 1): 166–89.

McIntosh, Janet. 2004. "Maxwell's Demons: Disenchantment in the Field." *Anthropology and Humanism* 29, no. 1: 63–77.

———. 2010. "Mobile Phones and Mipoho's Prophecy: The Powers and Dangers of Flying Language." *American Ethnologist* 37, no. 2 (May): 337–53.

McMoneagle, Joseph. 2000. *Remote Viewing Secrets: A Handbook.* Charlottesville, VA: Hampton Roads Publishing.

———. 2006. *Memoirs of a Psychic Spy: The Remarkable Life of U.S. Government Remote Viewer 001.* Charlottesville, VA: Hampton Roads Publishing.

McRae, Ronald M. 1984. *Mind Wars: The True Story of Government Research into the Military Potential of Psychic Weapons.* New York: St. Martin's Press.

Mead, Margaret, et al. 1951. *Soviet Attitudes toward Authority; an Interdisciplinary Approach to Problems of Soviet Character.* New York: McGraw-Hill/Rand Corporation.

Meek, Barbra A. 2010. *We Are Our Language: An Ethnography of Language Revitalization in a Northern Athabascan Community.* First Peoples, New Directions in Indigenous Studies, vol. xxvi. Tucson: University of Arizona Press.

Menzel, Birgit. 2007. "The Occult Revival in Russia Today and Its Impact on Literature." *The Harriman Review* 16, no. 1: 1–14.

Menzel, Birgit, Michael Hagemeister, and Bernice Glatzer Rosenthal, eds. 2012. *The New Age of Russia: Occult and Esoteric Dimensions.* Studies on Language and Culture in Central and Eastern Europe, no. 17. Munich: Otto Sagner.

Merlin, Bella. 2001. *Beyond Stanislavsky: The Psycho-Physical Approach to Actor Training.* New York and London: Routledge/Nick Hern Books.

Messing, Wolf. 1961. Interview. *Tekhnika Molodezhi*, no. 1: 30–33.

———. 1965. "O samom sebe" [About myself]. *Nauka i Religija*, nos. 7–11.

Meyer, Birgit, and Peter Pels, eds. 2003. *Magic and Modernity: Interfaces of Revelation and Concealment.* Stanford, CA: Stanford University Press.

Meyerhold, V.E. 1907. *Kniga o novom teatre* [Book on the new theater]. Petersburg.

———. 1969. "The Fairground Booth." In *Meyerhold on Theatre*, edited and translated by Edward Braun, 119–42. New York: Hill and Wang.

———. 2001. *Lekstii* [Lectures] *1918–1919.* Moscow: OGI Press.

Miéville, China. 2009. *The City and the City.* New York: Del Ray.

Miller, J. Hillis. 2009. *The Medium Is the Maker: Browning, Freud, Derrida and the New Telepathic Ecotechnologies.* Critical Inventions. Brighton, U.K., and Portland, OR: Sussex Academic Press.

Miller, Laura. 2011. "Tantalizing Tarot and Cute Cartomancy in Japan," *Japanese Studies* 31, no. 1: 73–90.

Miłosz, Czesław. 1953. *The Captive Mind*. New York: Knopf.

Mishuris, Kai. 2017. A Study of Mental Abilities: Children, Reason, and Difference in Modern Russian and Soviet History. PhD diss., University of Michigan.

Mogilner, Marina. 2009. "Russian Physical Anthropology of the Nineteenth–Early Twentieth Centuries: Imperial Race, Colonial Other, Degenerate Types, and the Russian Racial Body." In *Empire Speaks Out: Languages of Rationalization and Self-Description in the Russian Empire*, edited by Ilya Gerasimov, 155–89. Leiden: Brill.

Mohr, Gordon. 1982. *Brain-Washing (Mind-Changing): A Synthesis of a Russian Textbook on Mass Mind-Control (Psychopolitics)*. Phoenix, AA: Distributed by Lord's Covenant Church, America's Promise Broadcasts.

Mokhov, Sergei. 2016. "Taking the Spell Off of Death: Media as Mourning Ritual in Russia's Psychic Challenge." *Laboratorium: Russian Review of Social Research*, no. 2: 33–49.

Montesquieu. 1748. *The Spirit of the Laws: Of the Difference of Men in different Climates*.

Morehouse, David. 1996. *Psychic Warrior: Inside the CIA's Stargate Program: The True Story of a Soldier's Espionage and Awakening*. New York: St. Martin's Press.

Morgan, Marcyliena. 2002. *Language, Discourse and Power in African American Culture*. Cambridge, U.K., and New York: Cambridge University Press.

Morris, Rosalind C. 2000. *In the Place of Origins: Modernity and Its Mediums in Northern Thailand*. Body, Commodity, Text. Durham, NC: Duke University Press.

Muehlenbeck, Philip E. 2012. *Race, Ethnicity, and the Cold War: A Global Perspective*. Nashville, TN: Vanderbilt University Press.

Munn, Nancy D. 1986. *The Fame of Gawa: A Symbolic Study of Value Transformation in a Massim (Papua New Guinea) Society*. Lewis Henry Morgan Lectures. Cambridge, U.K., and New York: Cambridge University Press.

Myers, Fred. 2006. "'Primitivism,' Anthropology, and the Category of 'Primitive Art.'." In *Handbook of Material Culture*, 267–84. London: Sage.

Nadkarni, Maya. 2007. "The Master's Voice: Authenticity, Nostalgia, and the Refusal of Irony in Postsocialist Hungary." *Social Identities* 13, no. 5: 611–26.

Nadkarni, Maya, and Olga Shevchenko. 2004. "The Politics of Nostalgia: A Case for Comparative Analysis of Post-Socialist Practices." *Ab Imperio*, no. 2: 487–519.

Nafus, Dawn. 2006. "Postsocialism and Notions of Context." *Journal of the Royal Anthropological Institute* 12, no. 3: 607–24.

Natale, Simone. 2011. "The Medium on the Stage: Trance and Performance in Nineteenth-Century Spiritualism." *Early Popular Visual Culture* 9, no. 3 (August): 239–55.

Natale, Simone, and Gabriele Balbi. 2014. "Media and the Imaginary in History: The Role of the Fantastic in Different Stages of Media Change." *Media History* 20, no. 2: 203–18.

Nelson, Alondra, Thuy Linh N. Tu, and Alicia Headlam Hines. 2001. *Technicolor: Race, Technology, and Everyday Life.* New York: New York University Press.

Nelson, Michael. 1997. *War of the Black Heavens: The Battles of Western Broadcasting in the Cold War.* Syracuse, NY: Syracuse University Press.

Nietzsche, Friedrich. (1886) 1989. *Beyond Good and Evil.* New York: Random House, Vintage Press.

Ngai, Sianne. 2005. *Ugly Feelings.* Cambridge, MA: Harvard University Press.

Noakes, Richard J. 1999. "Telegraphy Is an Occult Art: Cromwell Fleetwood Varley and the Diffusion of Electricity to the Other World." *The British Journal for the History of Science* 32, no. 4: 421–59.

———. 2002. " 'Instruments to Lay Hold of Spirits': Technologizing the Bodies of Victorian Spiritualism." In *Bodies/Machines*, edited by Iwan Rhys Morus, 125–63. Oxford and New York: Berg/Hahn.

Notman, Rolen. 2004. "Chtoby otlichat' lozh' ot pravdy" [In order to discern lie from truth]. *Sovjetskaja Sibir'*, July 22, 8.

Nove, Alec. 1961. *The Soviet Economy.* Routledge Revivals. New York:Routledge,

Novomeisky, A. S. 1963. "Rol' Kozhno-opticheskogo chuvstva v poznanii" [The role of the dermo-optic sense in cognition]. *Voprosy Filosofii*, no. 7.

Nozawa, Shunsuke. 2015. "Phatic Traces: Sociality in Contemporary Japan." *Anthropological Quarterly* 88, no. 2: 373–400.

———. 2016. "Ensoulment and Effacement in Japanese Voice Acting." In *Media Convergence in Japan*, edited by Patrick Galbraith and Jason Karlin, 169–99. n.p.: Kinema Club.

Nun-Ingerflom, Claudio Sergio. 2013. "How Old Magic Does the Trick for Modern Politics," *Russian History* 40, nos. 3–4: 428–50.

Ochs, Elinor, and C. Taylor. 1996. " 'The Father Knows Best' Dynamic in Family Dinner Narratives." In *Gender Articulated: Language and the Socially Constructed Self*, edited by K. Hall, 97–121. New York: Routledge.

Okhlopkov, Nikolai. 1959. "Ob Uslovnosti" [On the conventional/On stylization]. *Teatr* 11: 58–77.

Ong, Aihwa. 1987. *Spirits of Resistance and Capitalist Discipline: Factory Women in Malaysia.* Albany: State University of New York Press.

Ostrander, Sheila, and Lynn Schroeder. 1970. *Psychic Discoveries behind the Iron Curtain.* Englewood Cliffs, NJ: Prentice-Hall.

Oushakine, S.A. 2000. "In the State of Post-Soviet Aphasia." *Europe-Asia Studies* 52, no. 6: 991–106.

———. 2004. "The Flexible and the Pliant: Disturbed Organisms of Soviet Modernity." *Cultural Anthropology* 19, no. 3: 392–428.

———. 2009. *The Patriotism of Despair: Nation, War, and Loss in Russia.* Culture and Society after Socialism. Ithaca, NY: Cornell University Press.

———. 2014. "'Against the Cult of Things': On Soviet Productivism, Storage Economy, and Commodities with No Destination." *Russian Review* 73: 198–236.

Palmié, Stephan. 2002. *Wizards and Scientists: Explorations in Afro-Cuban Modernity and Tradition*. Durham, NC: Duke University Press Books

———. 2011. "From Enchantment by Science to Socialist Sorcery: The Cuban Republic and Its Savage Slot." In *Sorcery in the Black Atlantic*, 121–44. Chicago: University of Chicago Press.

Panasjuk, Aleksandr. 1996. What Is in His Sub conscious? Twelve Lessons in the Psychotechnology of Penetrating the Subconscious of Your Interlocutor [*A chto u nego v podsoznanii? Dvenadtsat' urokov po psikhotekhnologii proniknovenija v podsoznanie sobesednika*].Moscow: Delo.

Pandey, Gyanendra. 1992. "In Defense of the Fragment: Writing about Hindu-Muslim Riots in India Today." *Representations* 37 (January 1): 27–55.

Parry, Jonathon, and Maurice Bloch. 1989. *Money and the Morality of Exchange*. Cambridge, U.K.: Cambridge University Press.

Patico, Jennifer. 2008. *Consumption and Social Change in a Post-Soviet Middle Class*. Washington, DC, and Stanford, CA: Stanford University Press.

Peace, Adrian. 2013. "The Phatic Finger: Public Gesture and Shared Meaning on the Highways of the Australian Outback." *The Australian Journal of Anthropology* 24, no. 1 (April): 99–114.

Pedersen, Morten Axel. 2011. *Not Quite Shamans: Spirit Worlds and Political Lives in Northern Mongolia*. Culture and Society after Socialism. Ithaca, NY: Cornell University Press.

Peers, Eleanor. 2015. "Soviet-Era Discourse and Siberian Shamanic Revivalism: How Area Spirits Speak through Academia." In *Contemporary Pagan and Native Faith Movements in Europe: Colonialist and Nationalist Impulses*, edited by Kathryn Rountree, 110–29. New York: Berghahn Books.

Peirce, C.S., and Joseph Jastrow. 1884. "On Small Differences of Sensation." *Memoirs of the National Academy of Sciences* 3, no. 5 (October 17): 75–83.

———. (1897) 1932. "Division of Signs." In *Collected Papers of Charles Sandes Peirce* Cambridge,U.K.: Belknap Press of Harvard University Press.

Pelevin, Viktor. 1999. *Generation P*. Moscow: Vagrius.

Pels, Peter. 2003. Introduction to *Magic and Modernity: Interfaces of Revelation and Concealment*, edited by Meyer, Birgit, and Peter Pels. Stanford, CA: Stanford University Press.

Peris, Daniel. 1998. *Storming the Heavens: The Soviet League of the Militant Godless*. Ithaca, NY: Cornell University Press.

Pesmen, Dale. 2000. *Russia and Soul: An Exploration*. Ithaca, NY: Cornell University Press.

Peters, Benjamin. 2016. *How Not to Network a Nation: The Uneasy History of the Soviet Internet*. Cambridge, MA: The MIT Press.

Peters, John Durham. 1996. "The Uncanniness of Mass Communication." *Journal of Communication Studies* 46, no. 3: 108–23.

————. 1999. *Speaking into the Air: A History of the Idea of Communication.* Chicago: University of Chicago Press, 1999.

————. 2010. "Broadcasting and Schizophrenia." *Media, Culture, and Society* 32, no. 1: 123–40.

Petrov, Petre, and Lara Ryazanova-Clarke, eds. 2014. *The Vernaculars of Communism: Language, Ideology and Power in the Soviet Union and Eastern Europe.* New York: Routledge.

Philips, Susan. 1972. "Participant Structures and Communicative Competence: Warm Springs Children in Community and Classroom." In *Functions of Language in the Classroom,* edited by V.P. John Cazden and Dell Hymes, 370–94. New York: Columbia Teachers Press.

Pimenova, Ksenia. 2013. "The 'Vertical of Shamanic Power': The Use of Political Discourse in Post-Soviet Tuvan Shamanism." *Laboratorium: Russian Review of Social Research* 5, no. 1 (April 25): 118–40.

Pinch, Adela. 2010. *Thinking about Other People in Nineteenth-Century British Writing.* Cambridge Studies in Nineteenth-Century Literature and Culture, no. 73. Cambridge, U.K., and New York: Cambridge University Press.

Pinchevski, Amit, and Tamar Liebes. 2007. "Eichmann on the Air: Radio and the Making of an Historic Trial." *Historical Journal of Film, Radio and Television* 27, no. 1: 1–25.

Pitches, Jonathan. 2006. *Science and the Stanislavsky Tradition of Acting.* Routledge Advances in Theatre and Performance Studies, no. 3. London; New York: Routledge.

Platt, Kevin M.F. 2016. "Secret Speech: Wounding, Disavowal, and Social Belonging in the USSR." *Critical Inquiry* 42, no. 3: 647–76.

Platz, Stephanie. 1996. "Pasts and Futures: Space, History, and Armenian Identity, 1988–1994." PhD diss., University of Chicago.

Pletsch, Carl E. 1981. "The Three Worlds, or the Division of Social Scientific Labor, circa 1950–1975." *Comparative Studies in Society and History* 23, no. 4: 565–90.

Pomerantsev, Peter. 2014. *Nothing Is True and Everything Is Possible: The Surreal Heart of the New Russia.* New York: Public Affairs.

Popkin, Cathy. 1992. "Chekhov as Ethnographer: Epistemological Crisis on Sakhalin Island." *Slavic Review* 51, no. 1: 36–51.

Popov, Nikolaj Ivanovich. 2006. *Voennaja Psikhotronika—nauka o koldovstve* [Military psychotronics: The science of enchantment]. Tver': n.p.

"Poslednjoe Prorochestvo Vol'fa Messinga/The last Prediction of Wolf Messing." 2012. *Sovershenno Sekretno,* February 1, 3.

Possner, Dassia. 2016. *The Director's Prism: E.T.A. Hoffmann and the Russian Theatrical Avant-Garde.* Evanston: Northwestern University Press.

Potapov, N. 1977. "Seans Chernoj magii" [A séance of black magic]. *Pravda,* May 25, 3.

Pronin, Viktor. 1985. "Sila Slova" [The power of the word]. In *Fantastika,* 57–67. Moscow: Molodaja Gvardija.

"Psychomagnetism." 1961. *Nauka I Zhizn'* 7 (July): 81.

Pursell, Carroll W. 2005. *A Hammer in Their Hands: Documentary History of Technology and the African-American Experience*. Cambridge, MA: MIT Press.

Rafael, Vicente L. 1988. *Contracting Colonialism: Translation and Christian Conversion in Tagalog Society under Early Spanish Rule*. Ithaca, NY: Cornell University Press.

———. 2007. "Translation in Wartime." *Public Culture* 19, no. 2: 239.

———. 2016. *Motherless Tongues the Insurgency of Language amid Wars of Translation*. Durham, NC: Duke University Press.

Raibmon, Paige. 2006. "Theatres of Contact: The Kwakwaka'wakw Meet Colonialismin British Columbia and at the Chicago World's Fair." *Canadian Historical Review* (September): 157–90.

Raikhel, Eugene. 2009. "Post-Soviet Placebos: Epistemology and Authority in Russian Treatments for Alcoholism," *Culture, Medicine, and Psychiatry* 34, no. 1: 132–68.

———. 2013. "Placebos or Prostheses for the Will?" In *Addiction Trajectories*, edited by Eugene Raikhel and William Garriott, 188–212. Durham, NC: Duke University Press.

Raikhel, Eugene, and D. Bemme. 2016. "Postsocialism, the Psy-Ences and Mental Health." *Transcultural Psychiatry* 53, no. 2 (April 1): 151–75.

Ranciere, Jacques. 2011. *The Emancipated Spectator*. Reprint ed. London: Verso.

Randi, James. 1982. *Flim-Flam! Psychics, ESP, Unicorns, and Other Delusions*. Buffalo, NY: Prometheus Books.

Redfern, Nicholas. 2009. *Science Fiction Secrets: From Government Files and the Paranormal*. San Antonio, TX: Anomalist Books.

Reeves, Madeleine. 2013. "Clean Fake: Authenticating Documents and Persons in Migrant Moscow: Documents and Persons in Migrant Moscow." *American Ethnologist* 40, no. 3 (August): 508–24.

Remnick, David. 1989. "The Magic Healer of Soviet TV: Alan Chumak, an Extrasensory Sensation." *Washington Post*, September 4, 1.

Resnick, Elana. 2016. "Nothing Ever Perishes: Waste, Race, and Transformation in an Expanding European Union." PhD diss.,University of Michigan, Ann Arbor.

Reverdy, Pierre. (1918) 1975. "L'image." In *Nord-Sud*, 75. Paris: Flammarion.

Ries, Nancy. 1997. *Russian Talk: Culture and Conversation*. Ithaca, NY: Cornell University Press.

———. 2009. "Potato Ontology: Surviving Postsocialism in Russia." *Cultural Anthropology* 24, no. 2 (May): 181–212.

Rivkin-Fish, Michele. 2009. "Tracing Landscapes of the Past in Class Subjectivity: Practices of Memory and Distinction in Marketizing Russia." *American Ethnologist* 36, no. 1 (February): 79–95.

Roach, Joseph R. 1993. *The Player's Passion: Studies in the Science of Acting*. Theater—Theory—Text—Performance. Ann Arbor: University of Michigan Press.

Robbins, Joel. 2008. "On Not Knowing Other Minds: Confession, Intention, and Linguistic Exchange in a Papua New Guinea Community." *Anthropological Quarterly* 81, no. 2: 421–29.

Robeson, Paul. 1950. *The Negro People and the Soviet Union*. New York: New Century Publishers.

Rogers, Douglas. 2015. *The Depths of Russia: Oil, Power, and Culture after Socialism*. Ithaca, NY, and London: Cornell University Press.

Roosevelt, Priscilla R. 1991. "Emerald Thrones and Living Statues: Theater and Theatricality on the Russian Estate." *Russian Review* 50, no. 1: 1–23.

Rosaldo, Michelle Z. 1982. "The Things We Do with Words: Ilongot Speech Acts and Speech Act Theory in Philosophy." *Language in Society* 11, no. 2: 203–37.

Rose, Nikolas S. 1996. *Inventing Our Selves: Psychology, Power, and Personhood*. Cambridge Studies in the History of Psychology. New York: Cambridge University Press.

Rosenthal, Bernice Glatzer. 1994. *Nietzsche and Soviet Culture: Ally and Adversary*. New York: Cambridge University Press.

———. 1997. *The Occult in Russian and Soviet Culture*. Ithaca, NY: Cornell University Press.

Roth, Christopher, F. 2005. "Ufology as Anthropology: Race, Extraterrestrials and the Occult." In *E.T. Culture: Anthropology in Outerspaces*, edited by Deborra Battaglia, 38–93. Durham, NC: Duke University Press.

Rozinsky, Edward. 2010. *Essential Stage Movement: Psycho-Physical Training for Actors*. Miami, FL: Physical Theater Publishers.

Rutherford, Danilyn. 2012. Commentary: What affect produces. *American Ethnologist*, 39: 688–691.

Rutten, Ellen. 2017. *Sincerity after Communism: A Cultural History*. New Haven, CT: Yale University Press.

Ryan, W.F. 1999. *The Bathhouse at Midnight: An Historical Survey of Magic and Divination in Russia*. Magic in History. Stroud, U.K.: Sutton.

Samuels, David. 2005. "Alien Tongues." In *E.T. Culture: Anthropology in Outerspaces*, edited by Deborra Battaglia, 94–129. Durham, NC: Duke University Press.

Sanders, Todd. 2008. "Buses in Bongoland: Seductive Analytics and the Occult." *Anthropological Theory* 8, no. 2 (June): 107–32.

Saunders, Frances Stonor. 2001. *The Cultural Cold War: The CIA and the World of Arts and Letters*. New York: The New Press.

Scarry, Elaine. 1987. *The Body in Pain: The Making and Unmaking of the World*. New York: Oxford University Press.

Schieffelin, Bambi B. 1990. *The Give and Take of Everyday Life: Language Socialization of Kaluli Children*. Cambridge, U.K.: Cambridge University Press.

———. 2008. "Speaking Only Your Own Mind: Reflections on Talk, Gossip and Intentionality in Bosavi (PNG)." *Anthropological Quarterly* 81, no. 2: 431–41.

Schnabel, Jim. 1997. *Remote Viewers: The Secret History of America's Psychic Spies*. New York: Dell.

Sconce, Jeffrey. 2000. *Haunted Media: Electronic Presence from Telegraphy to Television*. Console-Ing Passions. Durham, NC: Duke University Press.

Segal, Daniel, and Richard Handler. 1989. "Serious Play: Creative Dance and Dramatic Sensibility in Jane Austen, Ethnographer." *Man*, n.s., 24: 322–38.

Seizer, Susan. 1997. "Jokes, Gender, and Discursive Distance on the Tamil Popular Stage," *American Ethnologist* 24, no. 1: 62–90.

Senelick, Laurence. 1991. "The Erotic Bondage of Serf Theatre." *Russian Review* 50, no. 1: 24–34.

Seriot, Patrick. 2002. "Officialese and Straight Talk in Socialist Europe of the 1980s." In *Ideology and System Change in the USSR*, edited by Michael Urban, 202–12. Basingstoke, U.K.: Palgrave.

Sherouse, Perry. 2014. "Hazardous Digits: Telephone Keypads and Russian Numbers in Post-Soviet Georgia." *Language and Communication* 37: 1–11.

———. 2016. "Skill and Masculinity in Olympic Weightlifting: Training Cues and Cultivated Craziness in Georgia." *American Ethnologist* 43, no. 1: 103–15.

Shevchenko, Olga. 2008. *Crisis and the Everyday in Postsocialist Moscow*. Bloomington: Indiana University Press.

Shklovsky, Viktor (1917) 1965. "Art as Technique." In *Russian Formalist Criticism: Four Essays*, translated and edited by Lee T. Lemon and Marion Reis, 5–22. Lincoln: University of Nebraska Press.

Shlapentokh, Vladimir. 1984. *Love, Marriage, and Friendship in the Soviet Union: Ideals and Practices*. New York: Praeger.

Shoaps, Robin. 2002. "Pray Earnestly": The Textual Construction of Personal Involvement In Pentecostal Prayer and Song. *Journal of Linguistic Anthropology* 12, no.1: 34–71.

Siegel, Lee. 2004. "The Method Conspiracy," *New York Times Magazine*, August 1, 17.

Silverberg, Robert. (1972) 2009. *Dying Inside*. 2nd ed. n.p.: Orb Books.

Silverstein, Michael. 1979. "Language Structure and Linguistic Ideology." In *The Elements*, edited by P. Clyne, W. Hanks, and C. Hofbauer, 193–248. Chicago: Chicago Linguistic Society.

———. 2005. "Axes of Evals." *Journal of Linguistic Anthropology* 15, no. 1: 6–22.

Silvio, Teri. 2010. "Animation: The New Performance?" *Journal of Linguistic Anthropology* 20, no. 2: 422–38.

Sinclair, Bruce, ed. 2004. *Technology and the African-American Experience*. Cambridge, MA: MIT Press.

Sinyavsky, Andrei. 1991. *Soviet Civilization: A Cultural History*. New York: Arcade Publishing.

Slezkine, Yuri. 1996. *Arctic Mirrors: Russia and the Small Peoples of the North*. Ithaca, NY: Cornell University Press.

Slotta, James. 2015. "Phatic Rituals of the Liberal Democratic Polity: Hearing Voices in the Hearings of the Royal Commission on Aboriginal Peoples." *Comparative Studies in Society and History* 57, no. 1 (January): 130–60.

Smith, David. A. 2010. "American Nightmare: Images of Brainwashing, Thought Control, and Terror in Soviet Russia." *Journal of American Culture* 33, no. 3: 217–29.

Sneath, David. 2009. "Reading the Signs by Lenin's Light: Development, Divination and Metonymic Fields in Mongolia." *Ethnos* 74, no. 1: 72–90.

Sokolov, Dimitri 2010. *Mistika i Filosofija Spetsluzhb* [Mysticism and philosophy of the special services]. Moscow: Akademija upravlenija.

Solomon, Matthew. 2010. *Disappearing Tricks: Silent Film, Houdini, and the New Magic of the Twentieth Century*. Urbana: University of Illinois Press.

Soloukhin, Vladimir Alekseevich. 1971. *White Grass*. Soviet Short Stories Series. Moscow: Progress Publishers.

Spivak, Gayatri Chakravorty. 1988. "Can the Subaltern Speak?" In *Marxism and the Interpretation of Culture*, edited by Cary Nelson and Lawrence Grossberg, 271–313. Basingstoke, U.K.: Macmillan Education.

Ssorin-Chaikov, Nikolai. 2008. "The Black Box: Notes on the Anthropology of the Enemy." *Inner Asia* 10, no. 1: 37–63.

Stanislavsky, Constantine. (1938) 1970. *Rabota aktera nad soboi v tvorcheskom protsesse perezhivaniia: Dnevnik uchenika* [The work of the actor on the self in the creative process: Diary of a student]. Moscow: Goslitizdat.

———. 2000. *Stanislavsky Repetiruet* [Stanislavsky rehearses: Notes and transcripts]. Curated and edited by I.N. Vinogradskaja. Moscow: Moskovskij Xudozhestvenij teatr.

Stasch, Rupert. 2008. "Knowing Minds Is a Matter of Authority: Political Dimensions of Opacity Statements in Korowai Moral Psychology." *Anthropological Quarterly* 81, no. 2: 443–53.

Steedman, Carolyn Kay. 1987. *Landscape for a Good Woman: A Story of Two Lives*. New Brunswick, NJ: Rutgers University Press.

Steinmetz, George, ed. 2005. *The Politics of Method in the Human Sciences: Positivism and Its Epistemological Others*. Durham, NC: Duke University Press Books.

Stewart, Jacqueline. 2003. "Negroes Laughing at Themselves? Black Spectatorship and the Performance of Urban Modernity." *Critical Inquiry* 29, no. 4: 650–77.

Stites, Richard. 1990. "World Outlook and Inner Fears in Soviet Science Fiction." In *Science and the Soviet Social Order*, edited by Loren R. Graham, 299–324. Cambridge, MA: Harvard University Press.

———. 1991. *Revolutionary Dreams: Utopian Vision and Experimental Life in the Russian Revolution*. Oxford: Oxford University Press.

Stoler, Ann Laura. 2010. *Carnal Knowledge and Imperial Power: Race and the Intimate in Colonial Rule*. With a new preface. Berkeley: University of California Press.

Stoner, Frances. 1995. "Modern Art Was CIA 'Weapon'." *The Independent*, October 22. Accessed July 20, 2017. http://www.independent.co.uk/news/world/modern-art-was-cia-weapon-1578808.html.

Strauss, Leo. 1988. *Persecution and the Art of Writing*. Reprint ed. Chicago: University of Chicago Press.

Strathern, Marilyn. 1988. *The Gender of the Gift: Problems with Women and Problems with Society in Melanesia*. Berkeley: University of California Press.

Strub, Whitney. 2007. "Black and White and Banned All Over: Race, Censorship and Obscenity in Postwar Memphis." *Journal of Social History* 40, no. 3 (March 1): 685–715.

Su, Hua. 2016. "Constant Connection as the Media Condition of Love: Where Bonds Become Bondage." *Media, Culture & Society* 38, no. 2: 232–47.

Suny, Ronald Grigor, and Terry Martin. 2001. *A State of Nations: Empire and Nation-Making in the Age of Lenin and Stalin*. Oxford: Oxford University Press.

Svechenovskaja, Inna, 2011. *Vol'f Messing: Tajny Velikogo Mistifikatora* [Wolf Messing: Secrets of a great mystifier]. Moscow: OLMA Media Gruppa.

Sword, Helen. 2002. *Ghostwriting Modernism*. Ithaca, NY: Cornell University Press.

Tarkhanov, I. R. [1886] 1905. *Gipnotizm, Vnushenie i Chtenie Myslei* [Hypnosis, mental suggestion and mind reading]. St. Petersburg: Izdanie Panteleeva.

Tarkovsky, Andreǰi Arsen'evich. 1986. *Sculpting in Time: Reflections on the Cinema*. Sapetschatljonnoje Wremja. London: Bodley Head.

Taubman, William. 2003. "Did He Bang It? Nikita Khrushchev and the Shoe." *New York Times*, July 26. Accessed July 20, 2017. http://www.nytimes.com/2003/07/26/opinion/did-he-bang-it-nikita-khrushchev-and-the-shoe.html.

Taussig, Michael T. 1980. *The Devil and Commodity Fetishism in South America*. Chapel Hill: University of North Carolina Press.

———. 1984. "Culture of Terror—Space of Death. Roger Casement's Putumayo Report and the Explanation of Torture." *Comparative Studies in Society and History* 26, no. 3: 467–97.

———. 2006. "Viscerality, Faith and Skepticism." In *Walter Benjamin's Grave*, 121–55. Chicago: University of Chicago Press.

———. 2008. "Zoology, Magic, and Surrealism in the War on Terror." *Critical Inquiry* 34, no. 2 (January): 98–116.

Tcherkasski, Sergei. 2009. "Fundamentals of the Stanislavsky System and Yoga Philosophy and Practice." *Stanislavsky Studies* 1. Accessed September 20, 2013. http://stanislavskistudies.org/wp-content/uploads/Sergei_Tcherkasski_Stanislavski_studies_1.pdf.

Teplov, A., and D. Fedotov. 1968. "Zabluzhdenie ili Otkrytie" [Delusion or discovery]. *Literaturnaja Gazeta*, April 25, 3.

Tertz, Abram (aka Andrei Sinyavsky). 1986. *Fantastic Stories*. Translated by Ronald Hingley, Manya Harari, and Max Hayward. Evanston, IL: Northwestern University Press.

"Teatral'noe Iskusstvo v Sluzhbe Bezopasnosti" [Theatrical art in service of security]. 1921. *Zhizn' Iskusstva*, August 2–7, 4.

Thom, Francoise. 1989. *Newspeak: The Language of Soviet Communism*. (*La Langue de bois*). London: The Claridge Press.

Thomas, Nicholas, and Caroline Humphrey. 1994. *Shamanism, History, and the State*. Ann Arbor: University of Michigan Press.

Throop, Jason. 2012. "On the Varieties of Empathic Experience: Tactility, Mental Opacity, and Pain in Yap." *Medical Anthropology Quarterly* 26, no. 3: 408–30.

Thurschwell, Pamela. 2001. *Literature, Technology, and Magical Thinking, 1880–1920*. Cambridge Studies in Nineteenth-Century Literature and Culture. Cambridge, U.K.: Cambridge University Press.

Tolstoy, Lev. 1906. *Tolstoy on Shakespeare: A Critical Essay on Shakespeare*. Translated by Ernest Crosby. Edited by Bernard Shaw. New York: Funk & Wagnalls.

Tolz, Vera. 2014. "Discourse of Race in Imperial Russia (1830–1914)." In *The Invention of Race*, edited by Nicolas Bancel, Thomas David, and Dominic Thomas, 130–44. London: Routledge.

Trouillot, Michel-Rolph. 1991. "Anthropology and the Savage Slot: The Poetics and Politics of Otherness." In *Recapturing Anthropology: Working in the Present*, edited by Richard G. Fox et al., 17–44. Santa Fe, NM: SAR Press.

———. 1995. *Silencing the Past: Power and the Production of History, 20th Anniversary Edition*. Boston: Beacon Press.

Tsing, Anna Lowenhaupt. 1993. *In the Realm of the Diamond Queen: Marginality in an Out-of-the-Way Place*. Princeton, NJ: Princeton University Press.

———. 2005. *Friction: An Ethnography of Global Connection*. Princeton, NJ: Princeton University Press.

Tsivian, Yuri. 1991. *Early Cinema in Russia and Its Cultural Reception*. Chicago: University of Chicago Press.

Tsygankov, V. D., and V. V. Lopatin. 1999. *Psikhotronnoe Oruzhie u Besopasnost' Rossij* [Psychic weaponry and Russian security]. Moscow: Synteg.

Tugarinov, V. 1961. "Eshche Raz O Peredache Myslei'" [Once again on transfer of thought]. *Znanie-Sila* 7: 22.

Turner, Victor. 1982. *From Ritual to Theatre: The Human Seriousness of Play*. New York: Performing Arts Journal Publications.

Uvarova, I. P. 2001. "Mesto Ezopova Iazyka v Sisteme Obshchenija Intelligentsija i Vlasti, 1960–1970—E Gody." [The place of Aesopian language in the system of communication for the intelligentsia and the authorities, 1960–70]. In *Khudozhestvennaia Zhizn' Rossii* [Artistic life in Russia], edited by Nelja Zorkaja, 306–21. St. Petersburg: Aletheja.

Vagin, Igor, and Antonina Gluschaj. 2002. *Osnovnoj Instinkt: psikhologija intimnykh otnoshenij* [Basic instinct: The psychology of intimate relations]. St. Petersburg: Piter Press.

Vasiljev, Leonid Leonidovich. 1962. *Eksperimental'nie Issledovanija Myslennogo Vnushenija* [Experimental research on mental suggestion]. Leningrad: Institute for the Study of Mental Images.

———. 1965. *Mysterious Phenomena of the Human Psyche*. New Hyde Park, NY: University Books.

———. 2002. *Experiments in Mental Suggestion*. Charlottesville, VA: Hampton Roads Publishing.

Vasiljeva, Zinaida. 2013. "The 1960s and the Development of Mass Culture: Notes on the Soviet Variant of Modernity." *Ab Imperio*, no 1:. 159–174.

Vatulescu, Christina. 2010. *Police Aesthetics: Literature, Film, and the Secret Police in Soviet Times*. Stanford, CA: Stanford University Press.

Velminski, Wladimir. 2017. *Homo Sovieticus: Brain Waves, Mind Control, and Telepathic Destiny*. Cambridge, MA: MIT Press.

Verdery, Katherine. 1991. "Theorizing Socialism: A Prologue to the 'Transition.'" *American Ethnologist* 18, no. 3: 419–39.

———. 1996. "The 'Etatization' of Time in Ceau escu's Romania." In *What Was Socialism, and What Comes Next*, 39–57 Princeton, NJ: Princeton University Press.

Vernadsky, V.I. 1926. *Biosfera* [The biosphere]. Leningrad: Nauchnoe khimiko-technicheskoye izdatel'stvo.

Vinitsky, Ilya. 2008. "Amor Hereos; or How One Brother Was Visited by an Invisible Being Lived Spirituality among Russian Freemasons in the 1810s." *Kritika: Explorations in Russian and Eurasian History* 9, no. 2: 291–316.

———. 2009. *Ghostly Paradoxes: Modern Spiritualism and Russian Culture in the Age of Reason*. Toronto: University of Toronto Press.

Vinogradova, Galina. 1996. *Saint Or Satan? The Life and Times of Russia's New Rasputin, Anatoly Kashpirovsky*. Glastonbury, U.K.: Gothic Image Publications.

Voloshinov, V.N. (1929) 1986. *Marxism and the Philosophy of Language*. Translated by Ladislav Matejka and I.R. Titunik. Cambridge, MA: Harvard University Press.

Von Eschen, Penny M. 2004. *Satchmo Blows up the World: Jazz Ambassadors Play the Cold War*. Cambridge, MA: Harvard University Press.

Vorsobin, Vladimir. 1999. "O pervykh opytakh po telepatii rasskazyvaet byvshij sotrudnik 'jaschika nomer 241' vrach Kirill Leontovich" [Doctor Kirill Leontovich, former teamworker for 'box no. 241,' tells about the first experiments on telepathy]. *Komsomol'skaja Pravda*, February 5, 7.

Vygotsky, Lev. (1933) 1986. *Thought and Language—Revised Edition*. Edited by Alex Kozulin. Cambridge, MA: MIT Press.

Wang, Victoria, John Tucker, and Kevin Haines. 2012. "Phatic Technologies in Modern Society." *Technology in Society* 34, no. 1: 84–93.

Warner, Michael. 2002. "Publics and Counterpublics." *Public Culture* 14, no. 1: 49–90.

Washington, Peter. 1993. *Madame Blavatsky's Baboon: Theosophy and the Emergence of the Western Guru*. London: Secker & Warburg.

Weitz, Eric D. 2002. "Racial Politics without the Concept of Race: Reevaluating Soviet Ethnic and National Purges." *Slavic Review* 61, no. 1: 1–29.

West, Harry G. 2007. *Ethnographic Sorcery*. Chicago: University of Chicago Press.

Weygandt, Susanna. 2015. "Embodiment in Post-Somatic Russian New Drama." PhD diss., Princeton University

White, Andrew. 2006. "Stanislavsky and Ramacharaka: The Influence of Yoga and Turn-of-the-Century Occultism on the System." *Theatre Survey* 47, no. 1: 73–92.

Wiener, Margaret J. 2003. "Hidden Forces: Colonialism and the Politics of Magic in the Netherland Indies." In *Magic and Modernity: Interfaces of Revelation and Concealment*, edited by Birgit Meyer and Peter Pels, 129. Stanford, CA: Stanford University Press.

———. 2007. "Dangerous Liaisons and Other Tales from the Twilight Zone: Sex, Race, and Sorcery in Colonial Java." *Comparative Studies in Society and History* 49, no. 3 (June): 495–526.

———. 2013. "Magic, (Colonial) Science and Science Studies." *Social Anthropology* 21, no. 4 (November): 492–509.

Wigzell, Faith. 2013. "Magic in the Russian Marketplace: Creating Trust." *Russian History* 40, nos. 3–4 (January 1): 568–86.

Wilf, Eitan. 2010. "Swinging within the Iron Cage: Modernity, Creativity, and Embodied Practice in American Postsecondary Jazz Education." *American Ethnologist* 37, no. 3 (July): 563–82.

Willerslev, Rane. 2004. "Not Animal, Not Not-Animal: Hunting, Imitation and Empathetic Knowledge Among the Siberian Yukaghirs." *Journal of the Royal Anthropological Institute* 10, no. 3: 629–52.

Williams, Raymond. 1958. *Culture and Society, 1780–1950*. London and New York: Columbia University Press.

———. 1968. *Drama from Ibsen to Eliot*. New York: Oxford University Press.

Winter, Alison. 1998. *Mesmerized: Powers of Mind in Victorian Britain*. Chicago: University of Chicago Press.

Wolf, Eric R. 1982. *Europe and the People without History*. Berkeley: University of California Press.

Wolfson, Boris. 2006. "Fear on Stage: Afinogenov, Stanislavsky and the Making of Stalinist Theater." In *Everyday Life in Early Soviet Russia: Taking the Revolution Inside*, edited by Christina Kiaer and Eric Naiman, 92–118. Bloomington: Indiana University Press.

Wood, Elizabeth A. 2005. *Performing Justice: Agitation Trials in Early Soviet Russia*. Agitation Trials in Early Soviet Russia. Ithaca, NY. Cornell University Press.

Woody, Thomas. 1932. *New Minds, New Men? The Emergence of the Soviet Citizen*. New York: Macmillan.

Wooffitt, Robin. 2006. *The Language of Mediums and Psychics: The Social Organization of Everyday Miracles*. Aldershot, Hampshire, U.K., and Burlington, VT: Ashgate.

Woolard, Kathryn, and Bambi B. Schieffelin. 1994. "Language Ideology." *Annual Review of Anthropology* 23, no. 1: 55–82.

Wortman, Richard. 1991. "Comment: Theatricality, Myth, and Authority." *Russian Review* 50, no. 1: 48–52.

Yamont, Steppa. 1988. "Naiti v Sebe. . . Sebja" [To find inside yourself . . . yourself]. *Vokrug Sveta* 11 (November 1). Accessed July 20, 2017 http://www.vokrugsveta.ru/vs/article/4050/.

Yurchak, Alexei. 2005. *Everything Was Forever, Until It Was No More: The Last Soviet Generation*. In-Formation Series. Princeton, NJ: Princeton University Press,.

————. 2015a. "Bodies of Lenin." *Representations* 129, no. 1: 116–57.

————. 2015b. *Eto bylo navsegda, poka nekonchilos: Poslednee sovetskoe pokolenie* [Everything was forever, until it was no more: The last Soviet generation]. Moscow: Novoe literaturnoe obozrenie press.

Zarrilli, Phillip B. 2007. "An Enactive Approach to Understanding Acting." *Theatre Journal* 59, no. 4: 635–47.

————. 2011. "Psychophysical Approaches and Practices in India: Embodying Processes and States of 'Being-Doing.'" *New Theatre Quarterly* 27, no. 3: 244–71.

Zigon, Jarrett. 2009. "Developing the Moral Person: The Concepts of Human, Godmanhood, and Feelings in Some Russian Articulations of Morality." *Anthropology of Consciousness* 20, no. 1 (March): 1–26.

Zuckerman, Charles H.P. 2016. "Phatic Violence? Gambling and the Arts of Distraction in Laos." *Journal of Linguistic Anthropology* 26, no. 3: 294–314.

Index

Figures are indicated by page numbers followed by *fig.* and notes are indicated by page numbers followed by n.

ω

Made in the USA
Middletown, DE
01 September 2024